ORPHEUS AND GREEK RELIGION

ORPHEUS IN BRITAIN
ROMAN MOSAIC FROM THE ISLE OF WIGHT

ORPHEUS
AND GREEK RELIGION

A STUDY OF THE ORPHIC MOVEMENT

BY

W. K. C. GUTHRIE, M.A.

FELLOW OF PETERHOUSE, CAMBRIDGE

WITH 16 PLATES AND 19 TEXT ILLUSTRATIONS

PRINCETON UNIVERSITY PRESS

PRINCETON, NEW JERSEY

Published by Princeton University Press, 41 William Street,
Princeton, New Jersey 08540
In the United Kingdom: Princeton University Press, Chichester,
West Sussex

Library of Congress Cataloging-in-Publication Data

Guthrie, W.K.C. (William Keith Chambers), 1906–
Orpheus and Greek religion: a study of the Orphic movement / by
W.K.C. Guthrie.
p. cm. —(Mythos)
Originally published: London: Methuen, 1952.
Includes bibliographical references and index.
ISBN 0-691-02499-5
1. Orpheus (Greek mythology) 2. Dionysia. 3. Mysteries,
Religious. 4. Cults—Greece. I. Title. II. Series: Mythos
(Princeton, N.J.)
BL820.O7G8 1993
292.9—dc20 92-41997

First Princeton Paperback printing, 1993
Reprinted by arrangement with Routledge, 11 New Fetter Lane,
London EC4P 4EE, United Kingdom

3   5   7   9   10   8   6   4   2

Οὐκέτι θελγομένας, Ὀρφεῦ, δρύας, οὐκέτι πέτρας
ἄξεις, οὐ θηρῶν αὐτονόμους ἀγέλας ·
Οὐκέτι κοιμάσεις ἀνέμων βρόμον, οὐχὶ χάλαζαν,
οὐ νιφετῶν συρμούς, οὐ παταγεῦσαν ἅλα.
Ὤλεο γάρ · σὲ δὲ πολλὰ κατωδύραντο θύγατρες
Μναμοσύνας, μάτηρ δ᾽ ἔξοχα, Καλλιόπα.
Τί φθιμένοις στοναχεῦμεν ἐφ᾽ υἱάσιν, ἁνίκ᾽ ἀλαλκεῖν
τῶν παίδων Ἀΐδαν οὐδὲ θεοῖς δύναμις;

[Anth. Pal. 7. 8.]

CONTENTS

CHAPTER I

PAGE

FAMOUS ORPHEUS 1

CHAPTER II

WHAT IS MEANT BY ORPHISM?

CHAPTER III

ORPHEUS AND HIS STORY

CHAPTER IV

THE CREATION AND THE GODS AS PRESENTED BY ORPHEUS

CHAPTER V

THE FUTURE LIFE AS SEEN BY ORPHEUS

CHAPTER VI

LIFE AND PRACTICES OF THE FOLLOWER OF ORPHEUS

CONTENTS

ILLUSTRATIONS

FRONTISPIECE

Orpheus in Britain. Roman mosaic from the Isle of Wight
(*Trans. R.I.B.A. 1880–1, pl. IX.*)

PLATES AT END

1. Orpheus. From a wall-painting at Pompeii

2 Orpheus with the Argonauts (Inscr.*ΟΡΦΑΣ*). Sixth century relief at Delphi
   (*Fouilles de Delphes, Sculpture IV 2, pl. 4.*)

3. Orpheus, Eurydice and Hermes. Copy of relief of *c.* 400 B.C.
   (*Nat. Mus., Naples. Brunn-Bruckmann, pl. 341a.*)

4. The death of Orpheus. From a red-figured vase in Boston
   (*Robinson, ' Catalogue of Boston Vases,' frontis.*)

5. Red-figured *hydria*
   (*Formerly in the collection of Professor A. B. Cook; now in the Otago Museum, Dunedin, N.Z.*)

6. Orpheus among the Thracians. Design from a red-figured Attic vase of the middle of the fifth century, found at Gela. Preserved in Berlin
   (*Winckelmannsfest-Programme 50, pl. 2. See A. Furtwängler, ib. pp. 154 ff.*)

7. *a* and *b*, Statue of Orpheus found on the Esquiline Hill and now in the Capitoline Museum, Rome
   c, Monument of a guild of *tibicines* found in the same place and made of the same coarse peperino

8. Gold plate from Petelia
   (*Brit. Mus. Cat. Jewellery no. 3155.*)

9. Gold case and chain for the plate from Petelia

10. Gold plate of Cecilia Secundina
    (*Brit. Mus. Cat. Jewellery no. 3154.*)

11. Relief on a cinerary urn in Rome showing a scene of Eleusinian initiation
    (*Röm. Mitt., vol. xxv [1910], pl. 7.*)

TEXT ILLUSTRATIONS

FOREWORD

THE study of religions customarily exhibits a range of competing theories—or at least contrasting ideas—as a sign that the religion is of interest to scholars as well as its adherents. The history of the study of Orphism, however, displays more than the usual fare of disagreement and conflict. The case of Orphism is as challenging as any, since scholarly debates include disagreement about the nature of the evidence as well as clashes regarding methods of inquiry. Indeed, most scholars question whether Orpheus ever lived and some doubt that any such thing as an Orphic religion ever existed.

Perhaps one should say that Orphism has been the site of productive if intense scholarly conflict. Given the disparities created by sparse and partial data on the one hand, and widely divergent interests and theories on the other, Orphic materials continue to give scholars an opportunity to develop their tools and refine their theories. Scholarly conversation and the testing of hypotheses usually require examining materials and evaluating evidence, but knowledge of the ancient world owes as much to interpretive discussions as it does to the quantity and quality of data. The prospect of inadequate evidence may suggest that silence is the most astute counsel, but scholars inevitably speculate in favor of one hypothesis or another. Continuing to plow old fields may uncover new materials that may serve to determine which construct of Orphism is the more accurate.

Even though substantiating data are important, scholarly debate in itself can develop the tools necessary to generate knowledge. We can refine research tools and develop interpretive hypotheses with or without much evidence, and scholars can work with too few data or too many; theoretical discussions can extend and develop our knowledge as much as evidentiary debates. As we continue to analyze ancient Greek materials, critical readings and appraisals of past scholars can guide and shape our work. Rereading them can demonstrate that their conclusions are debatable rather than fixed, and reappraising them can show how their methods raise questions as well as produce answers. Scholars love to argue with each other, which is well and good, but if we can reappropriate our predecessors as well as argue with and against them, we honor them as well as benefit ourselves. If knowledge derives as much from theoretical discussion as it does from observation, Orphism is a prime case for the study of religion in the ancient world. Moreover, if we can develop our knowledge of the ancient Greeks by rethinking key developments in the scholarship devoted to the Greek world, the work of W. K. C. Guthrie must be put at the top of our list.

Several contentious issues have long been at the heart of the debate about Orphism. One is whether Orpheus was a deity of mythology, a person of history, or a figure of legend. Many scholars would assert that Orpheus was a figure of legend, but the agreement ends when the figure is to be described and interpreted. A second issue is whether an Orphic religion ever existed. If it did, was it a community, a sect, an alternative life style, or the work of Orphic priests who practiced their craft of rituals and initiations to relieve their individual clients of guilt and fear? Did it have characteristic rituals and doctrines? Did it have dogmas? An authoritative sacred text? A third issue revolves around the pressures and influences that gave rise to Orphic materials, including the Homeric and Hesiodic as well as the Babylonian, Egyptian, and Phoenician, dating to the eighth century B.C.E and earlier. A fourth debate concerns the intellectual interests of the people who produced the Orphic literature and their relation to other similar groups such as the Pythagoreans. A fifth issue, perhaps the most sensitive and difficult of all, concerns the sources and their reliability as evidence for "Orphism." Controversy rather than agreement characterizes discussions regarding the sources, even when new materials are found.

Many ancient historians have tried their hand at Orphic studies. As a scholar of ancient religion as well as ancient philosophy, W.K.C. Guthrie stands in the foreground. He wove all the problems I have mentioned and more into the first (1935) and second (1952) editions of *Orpheus and Greek Religion*, while approaching them slightly differently between the two editions in *The Greeks and Their Gods* (Boston: Beacon, 1949). In these books and in several articles devoted to Orphic studies, Guthrie remained consistent in his approach to the materials and steady in his method of explaining them; his interpretation evolved as new studies appeared but he did not depart substantially from his initial study.

Why have Guthrie's inquiries worn so well? Why do we continue to read him? Guthrie's work prevails partly because his method is cautious and even tentative, as several reviewers commented in the early reviews of *Orpheus and Greek Religion*. By "cautious," however, we should not mean that he has "few data, less theory" or even that he is "reluctant to draw conclusions." Guthrie's caution is more than hesitation in the face of fragmentary evidence, much of which is found in authors who lived centuries after the phenomena about which they purport to provide evidence. Were hesitation the virtue appropriate to the materials, conclusions could be reached only when they could not be avoided, as though conclusions were pressed upon scholars rather than drawn by them. Guthrie's caution is rather a matter of being tentative with materials that require reconstruction and that admit more than one interpretation, and hence demand both the willingness to qualify assertions and a preference for probabilities over certainties. The conclusions Guthrie reaches are tentative, and for that reason they are often more stable than those that are bolder and more exciting.

How Guthrie reaches his conclusions is instructive for those reading him more than half a century after he worked out his interpretation. When we read *Orpheus and Greek Reli-*

gion as an "old" book in a "new" context, we reread a text that warrants new discussion and examination because the issues it raises are not settled and the contributions it makes are yet to be realized. Two particular features of Guthrie's scholarly style of reasoning are commendable. The first is his interest in the materials, which demonstrates that he is as devoted to the subject under consideration as he is to his compositional idea of Orphism as a reforming religious movement and Orphic writers as adapters of literature that already lay at hand. Here Guthrie differs from many other Orphic scholars. He has abandoned the search for a single Orphism on the grounds that no Orphism would correspond to our contemporary notions of a religion. Examining the materials to find such a religion, Guthrie concludes, will be either frustrating or condemned to negative results from the beginning by the guiding assumptions. The subject matter—that is, the content and nature of the materials—is defined by Guthrie in such a way as to give direction to his own inquiry without prohibiting alternative interpretations. Indeed, Guthrie's method invites further explorations and different hypotheses. Orphism in Guthrie's terms is an attitude some ancient Greeks displayed towards social life and literature rather than a set of doctrines, thus forming a motif that motivates or organizes the texts they reworked. Interest in a synthetic method means that Guthrie has abandoned a method that permits only one language of explanation and instead draws on multiple explanatory devices—inductive, reconstructive, historical, and social, all of which focus attention on whatever "meaning" may be attributed to the materials.

One of the consequences of Guthrie's conception of the content of the Orphic materials and his method for construing them is that he forswears the quest for an essence of Orphism as the object of investigation. The search for a "master narrative" or a "single Orphism" must, in Guthrie's view, give way to a synthetic picture of Orphism, and a debate about the "correct" Orphism need not be conducted. The positive consequence is that another debate can be opened: how many pictures of Orphism can we compose besides the "reforming" Orphism? An Orphism that overlaps with other religious movements of ancient Greece? An Orphism whose cosmogonic literature can be organized into a genealogy of manuscripts? An Orphism whose beliefs are expressed in the code of food and the rejection of sacrifice? Observing Guthrie's style of investigation will be illuminating and helpful.

Guthrie followed an inductive method. For example, when writing about Orpheus, he interrogated many citations of the name in literature and portrayals in art to reach the fairly modest conclusions that Orpheus may or may not have existed as a Greek person of history, and in any case was not one of the many Greek deities, let alone a deity faded into a hero or a figure of a fairy tale. This is only part of his conclusion, but it is the part that most attracts scholars who restrict their attention to matters of fact and to values such as accuracy and precision. The more interesting conclusion we are offered is that Orpheus was a figure whose character contained features and tensions that made him a legend. As a poet and musician with mystical interests in Apollo, in pre-Homeric times he proclaimed to the Thracians in northern Greece his religious interests in the immortality and divinity of the human soul as well as the need for ritual and moral purity, and thus was adopted by worshippers of Dionysos wanting to reform and spiritualize a wild, ecstatic, religious energy. The reason these conclusions are interesting and durable is that they can be tested and revised or rejected as explanations of the materials Guthrie allowed as evidence for Orphism. His conclusions are convincing because the case for and about Orpheus rests not only on the historical data for a historical figure but also on the interpretive choices Guthrie made in order to shed light on the data we do possess. By working through confusing and disparate data, he drew a picture of a teacher and founder of a religious style whose message, in literature, appealed to diverse interests and groups in ancient Greece. Less like a person of history and more like a character in a narrative, Orpheus's image is that of a teacher and founder of a religious life embodied in texts, thus serving as a model for diverse religious and social interests in ancient Greece. It is thus possible to be agnostic about Orpheus the person but responsibly interpretive about Orpheus the figure. Guthrie gives us a picture of a meaning rather than a person, a meaning whose elements are at once consistent and comprehensive.

Guthrie also followed a reconstructive method. He built his interpretation of Orphism by putting materials together into a sensible shape. For example, his analysis of the Orphic creation accounts, those theogonies and cosmogonies, is a patient and painstaking collation and correlation of themes, motifs, deities, and sources. In the area of Orphic studies which has attracted the most attention and controversy, Guthrie's reconstruction of 1935 has been surpassed only recently, in 1983, when M. L. West published *The Orphic Poems* with a stemma of the Orphic cosmogonic literature. We shall return to this issue, but at this point it is important to appreciate the difficulties the Orphic cosmogonies presented scholars in the 1930s. Part of our problem is that comparisons are difficult to draw, since the Greeks were not generally given to speculation and certainly not to dogmatic statements about the origins of the world or the gods; Hesiod and Orpheus were among the few whose myths dealt with their beginnings. While Hesiod composed a text, Orpheus, unfortunately, like Akusilaos, Epimenides, and Pherekydes, was merely quoted, often by writers living centuries after Orpheus first came into purview. Furthermore, the various parts of the Orphic cosmogonic materials fit so poorly that a coherent picture does not emerge; the various themes and symbols—such as unusual deities, an egg, night, Dionysos, and Zeus—appear thrown together rather than composed. Still another aspect of our difficulty is that Oriental motifs mix rather freely with Greek themes in the Orphic theogonies, adding one confusion to another. Finally, we do not possess the Orphic poems themselves but know them only from fragments and citations. Lost or fragmentary poems can occasion almost as much controversy as those whose first edition is safely ensconced in a library.

When Guthrie developed his interpretation of the Orphic theogonies, the state of the sources was even more confusing than it is today. Christian Augustus Lobeck's work of source criticism, *Aglaophamus sive de theologiae mysticae graecorum causis* (1829), had sobered scholars of the antique world by showing that all that looks Orphic may not be Orphic. Although Lobeck had checked wild speculation about Orphic matters, serious argument about the Orphic creation accounts could continue, with Neoplatonic references as the basis for discussion. In *Die Griechischen Kulte und Mythen* (1887) Otto Gruppe argued that various versions of the accounts can be distinguished: three of them (one by Aristotle's student Eudemos, another by Hieronymos and Hellanikos, and the Rhapsodic Theogony) differ from a fourth in the poem of Apollonios Rhodios and a fifth mentioned by Alexander of Aphrodisias. Although these versions differ significantly, a central theme pervades all of them: everything comes from a primal unity and finally returns to its source, undergoing separation and division only between the beginning and the end. Since this theme was at the center of philosophical discussion in the sixth and fifth centuries B.C.E for the Milesian thinkers as well as for Empedocles and Heracleitus, Gruppe concluded that the Orphic materials are also from that period. Otto Kern, on the other hand, argued in *De Orphei Epimenidis Pherecydis Theogniis Questiones Criticae* (1888) that the Rhapsodic Theogony itself was produced in the sixth century B.C.E.

Guthrie's genius was to begin with Gruppe's modest but stable conclusion that the date of compilation belonged to the Hellenistic era, whereas the date of composition should be located in preclassical Greece. The groundwork for further discussion was thus laid, breaking the impasse that had plagued scholars for as long as they had focused on problems of source criticism. In approximately seventy pages Guthrie focused his interpretive attention on issues of content, congruence of elements in the accounts, the tasks and functions of the deities, and the social and religious meanings the accounts might bear. Above all, he raised issues that continue to interest scholars today, discussing the literature Orphics wrote, the sort of people they were, and the religious attitudes, views, and practices that most aptly characterize them. His conclusions show that in ancient Greece there was little to distinguish Orphism from similar movements that promoted the importance of Oriental influences, Eros as the principle of life, the idea of a creator and his creation, the myth of Zeus and his son, Dionysos, the Titans as the central appeal for worshippers, or the significance of the gold tablets.

The Orphism that emerges in *Orpheus and Greek Religion* is a construct Guthrie built by combining his theoretical interests with the historical evidence. His construct can be compared with others. As I have already mentioned, exploring the materials for religious meaning motivates Guthrie's research. When considering the Orphic eschatological beliefs and the connections between them and the style of life and practices that identified the followers of Orpheus, Guthrie followed a social and historical method. He sought not only to identify strands of belief in Orphic literature, but also to locate them in historical conditions by tracking their social sources and implications. Orphism as a composite religion whose strongest and most striking feature was its eclecticism thus comes into view. Were we to search for a distinct, even unique religion with creeds and dogmas, rituals, and an organization, our phenomenon would never come into focus; indeed, whatever we might want to call Orphic would quickly disappear. Guthrie's depiction of Orphism as a reforming tendency with the energy and intelligence to infuse new meaning into myths already at hand and thus to construct a code of conduct based on a preexistent theory of human nature gives us something to look at. Viewing Orphism as a reform of Dionysiac energy in the direction of Apollonian sanity allow us to focus on the two deities who are polar opposites yet mutually attracting in Orphism.

For an example of his historical and social method, we may turn to Guthrie's discussion of Orphic views of a future life, where he begins by considering two tendencies he finds intertwined in sixth-century Greece. The first is basically Homeric, considering death a negation of all that makes life worthwhile; here, human purposes should be achieved and human goals should be pursued before death. The second tendency is more obviously religious and at home in the mysteries, yearning for an afterlife where unrealized aspirations can be fulfilled; here, life after death may be a reward or a punishment based on actions performed prior to death. On Guthrie's interpretation, Orphic writers sifted through popular religious attitudes to organize their own set of beliefs, at the center of which was the myth of the dismemberment of Dionysos by the Titans, the revenge Zeus took by striking the Titans with lightning, and finally the birth of human beings from the smoldering ashes. Eschatological doctrines could easily be derived from such a myth: human nature, derived from Titanic actions, is evil, but escape from an evil present is possible through proper ritual practices and a strenuous ascetic life. Should an entire lifetime fail to suffice, a theory of reincarnation can allow for multiple opportunities to perform purificatory rites and to subjugate the body.

Closely related to notions of an afterlife is the regimen necessary to attain what Guthrie calls a "blissful communion" with the deity. Because the sources—Aeschylus, Herodotus, Euripides, Plato—do not require and may not suggest the existence of a "unified religious sect," one is tempted to conclude that there were no Orphics, and if there were, that they enjoyed little agreement with each other. Perhaps, as Plato suggests, there were wandering priests who charged fees to enable people to feel relief from their guilt and anxiety, if only momentarily. And perhaps some other Orphic writers formulated a code of conduct designed to express in actions the religious beliefs they held. With such scanty and contradictory evidence before us, we can notice a crucial feature of Guthrie's approach to the materials. The search for items that can confidently be identified as distinctly Orphic turns up precious little, but considering Orphism as a movement which infused new meaning into older, Dionysiac myths and rites changes the focus of investigation. The hypothesis that Orphism was a reforming tendency in ancient Greece invites us to think that Orphics were attempting to transform reverence for Dionysos, however ecstatic it might have been, into a spiritualized Hellenism—that is to say, a calm, sane, and balanced (that is, Apollonian) interest in exuberant yet measured conduct linking life before death to life after death. If Guthrie is right, we should not expect to find a unified religious institution, but rather an ethical and spiritual reform movement that combined diverse interests and tendencies by means of a forthright eclecticism and a willingness to give new meaning to old myths and to put old rituals to new purposes. Rituals of initiation and canons of purity thus mark an "Orphic life." Eliminating meat from the diet and refusing to use wool in temples or for burial express the desire to avoid violence, precisely the value expressed in the myth of the Titans and Dionysos. Refusing to sacrifice to the gods links the religious violence of sacrifice to the ban on killing for food, and thus blends ritual and morality in the desire for goodness.

Exactly what rituals the Orphics actually practiced likely will remain unknown, but Guthrie deploys his central thesis of Orphism as a reform movement to suggest that Orphic writers want to purge from the worship of Dionysos the eating rituals suggesting physical ingestion of the god and to direct energy and attention toward a life of ritual and ethical purity that locates the salvation of individual souls at the core of religious life.

One of Guthrie's fundamental assumptions is that scholars should attempt to specify the nature of Orphism before they question its existence. A dogma of individual salvation hardly requires a formal institution, let alone a corporate organization; since ancient Greeks neither knew dogma nor enjoyed corporate life, the question is moot. At most we would expect a sect, consisting of people aware of their differences from the larger society. But is there evidence for such a group? Perhaps a class of priests did perform rituals, but even here a small group of individuals could gather briefly to receive the priestly ministrations and soon after the ceremonies depart to pursue their other interests; for this purpose, a free-lance priest could serve as well as an organized clergy, as Guthrie suggests. Only this much would be required by Guthrie's thesis of Orphism as a reform movement. What little evidence exists provides little opportunity for positive interpretation.

Two comparisons, however, do invite attention as part of a strategy to portray the contours of a movement that wrought a new mood from old popular beliefs. A first set of comparisons could be drawn between Orphics and other groups: Pythagoreans with their philosophy and way of life; Ionians with their rejection of mythology and interest in natural explanations; a group of thinkers such as Heracleitus, Parmenides, Empedocles, Anaxagoras, Aeschylus, Pindar, Euripides, Plato, and Aristotle. If Orphism is what Guthrie shows it to be, how can we compare it with other religious views or systems of its time? A second set of comparisons can be drawn between Orphics and later Hellenistic times, where warnings about comparisons between Orphism and Christianity are as necessary today as they were nearly sixty years ago. The mistake to avoid is assuming that such religions can ever be but one thing, rather than configurations of items that shift from time to time, with some items falling away as others become incorporated by both external and internal pressures. Despite their differences, both the Orphic literature of sixth-century Greece and that of the later Hellenistic times propounded a theology with a ruling and creating deity and a soteriology with an explanation for the origin and destiny of the human soul.

W. K. C. Guthrie offers his readers an interesting Orphism. It is an Orphism that is both eclectic (because it draws on Oriental as well as traditional Greek sources) and distinct (because it constitutes a religious system somewhat different from other religious movements of its day). Perhaps we should not call it a religion in the modern sense of an organized group with a clergy and sacred text as well as some concept of relations to those outside the group. But it is a religious system in the sense that it develops its elements into a coherent whole: a creator deity who governs the world he made, a myth of human origins explaining the original impurity that infects human nature and that humans inherit from events that transpired before they were born, the hope for escape from punishments after death and for the personal salvation of individual souls that undergo the proper rituals and follow the prescribed ethical and gastronomic guidelines.

Guthrie's Orphism is a religious movement that bears two marks. First, it evolved as elements were added or discarded; the reform did not occur within a brief period of time, and it did not settle itself into strict forms. Second, it held out a hope of individual salvation to Greeks accustomed to the communal traditions and experiences of the city-states. Because the Orphic reform addressed problems of an individualistic age, went off in new directions, and reworked old traditions, it appealed to Greeks, yet it still required a strong foundation. What better foundation than a sacred literature old and traditional in content but new in design and purpose? If that authority was not enough, then an old and revered figure would serve exactly that purpose: the Orpheus of old, but remade into a missionary of Hellenic sanity and beauty, a prophet of Apollonian balance and hope directing Dionysiac energies to replace ritual exercises with spiritual communion, indeed, a teacher of a reforming literary religion. Whoever Orpheus may have been, his followers (or his writers) cast him in the image of a reformer with an ancient authority.

Drawing on a variety of sources and pulling his materials together rather than distinguishing them into separate strands, Guthrie construes Orphism as a reforming religion with a developed theology and a founder and model in the legendary Orpheus. This interpretation of Orphism, which Guthrie proposed in 1935, has worn well. In the preface to the 1952 reprint, he remarked that he found major alterations unnecessary; his confidence in his earlier conclusions enabled him to use a supplement to mention new writings on Orphics and to make minor corrections and additions. Such a book and such authorial confidence invite readers to think about alternative explanations. Although Ulrich von Wilamowitz-Moellendorf adopted a skeptical position regarding the Orphic material in volume two of *Der Glaube der Hellenen* (Berlin: Weidmann, 1931–1932), it was I. M. Linforth's *The Arts of Orpheus* (Berkeley: University of California, 1941) that clearly articulated the position we may describe as the polar opposite of Guthrie's. Although both books are brilliant studies in their own right, they employ radically different methods to reach strikingly different conclusions; Guthrie's asserts that there was such a phenomenon as Orphism and that it can be identified, whereas Linforth denies any historical content to the term. According to Linforth, the literary and archaeological evidence adduced for Orphism is suspect, since the mythological poems associated with the name Orpheus and the ritual activities said to characterize him belong to the general category of mysteries and do not represent specific instances of a religion. Hence, the word "Orphic" is imprecise. At most it means that religious traditions linked to Orpheus can be traced to two sources: the mysteries in general and the legend of Orpheus as a gentle musician, which fused some time before the fifth century to make Orpheus the founder of mystery religions. To delineate the differences between Guthrie's interpretation and Linforth's, the latter's conclusions are worth quoting at length:

> The things associated with the name of Orpheus are so miscellaneous and so disparate that we cannot recognize a comprehensive and unified institution, however loosely organized, with creed, ritual, clergy, and adherents. They form, not a unity, but an aggregation. No idea or practice which is associated with the name of Orpheus by ancient writers can be called Orphic in the sense that it belonged to such an institution; still less can ideas and practices which the ancient writers did not connect with Orpheus be called Orphic in this sense. The unqualified statement that a given idea or practice is Orphic has no meaning if the intention is to assign it to such an institution. The loose use of

the term is to be deprecated as false and misleading. . . . we must renounce the idea of a single, comprehensive Orphic religion, conscious of itself and recognized by the outside world, and . . . we may abandon the attempt to define and describe it. (pp. 291–92)

. . . common human need required a religion in which practice and belief would be united, a religion which would allay the concern which men individually felt for their spiritual welfare, in this life and the next. This need was met by the things that bore the name of Orpheus, the comfortable rites of the mysteries, with the doctrines that were implicit in them, and the poems which gave expression to the doctrines and supplied authority for the rites. This whole manifestation of the religious instinct, in all its breadth and scope, may fairly be called Orphism, if we wish to use the name, because Orpheus was conceived to be its originator and patron. The term may be safely used if it is allowed to be so comprehensive as to include no less than all the activities of men who occupied themselves with the religion of mysteries—their practices, their myths, and their potencies— and with speculation on the implications of this religion as touching the gods and the souls of men. Possessing a unity of spirit and purpose, but no unity of deity, creed, or rites, it shows itself in a multitude of forms and institutions and is modified during the course of time by influences from within the Greek world and from without. (pp. 305–6)

In Linforth's view, the evidence for Orphism has been misread by all those scholars who write about Orphism as though it were a religion or a movement or even as though it existed. He contends that all those phenomena associated with the name Orpheus are so varied that neither belief nor ritual, and neither clergy nor follower, can be identified. As a result, the word "Orphic" lacks referents; at most, "Orphic" is a categorical term to designate any and all Greek mysteries. Orphism for Linforth is a question rather than an hypothesis. The term will not serve to guide historical research since it designates a category rather than a phenomenon. As a consequence, Linforth cannot inductively synthesize Orphic materials to compose a portrait of Orphism, since there are no pieces to put together. Any meaning the word "Orphic" may bear is suspect; lacking significant content or clarity, it is next to useless for historical research. On the one hand, "Orphic" is restrictive because it describes nothing, but on the other hand it is open because it designates ancient mysteries in general.

Finding two scholars whose methods and conclusions are more conflicting than Guthrie's and Linforth's would be difficult. The differences between the two are stark. Linforth cannot make a move toward Guthrie's methods without surrendering his own conclusions. Guthrie can go some distance with Linforth, however, because of his insistence that Orphism is primarily a literature and Orpheus a legendary figure. Thus, Guthrie can agree—indeed, he insisted on precisely the point six years before Linforth published his study—that Orphism was first and foremost a literature. The crux of the difference, however, comes at the point of defining the word "Orphic" in such a way as to be sufficiently broad to include writers who reworked traditional Greek mythology yet sufficiently precise to guide historical research. Guthrie's words regarding the concept of religion are worth quoting at length, for they assume a nonessentialist understanding of religion that allows for historical and cultural variation:

> . . . in speaking of this or that religion of ancient Greece we cannot draw the sharp distinctions which we might between this or that religion of the modern world. It is not a question of tolerance. . . . it is a question of actual unconsciousness in the mind of the worshipper that differences exist which seem plain and obvious to an outsider. . . . Almost all the different shades of belief are to be found which in studying Greek religion we take such pains to separate. . . . representatives of opposing types of religion will invoke the same god in an entirely different spirit . . . [and] gods whom we had thought of as inspiring incompatible beliefs and aspirations are sometimes peacefully united in the same camp. (pp. 7–8)

The next move offers a working definition of Orpheus and Orphism:

> For the present we may notice at least that Orpheus was regarded by the Greeks as the founder of a certain kind of religion, that much has been written on the Orphic religion, sometimes known more simply to-day as Orphism, and that this therefore is a good place to remind ourselves that the term 'religion' is only to be used in the limited sense here described.
>
> Orpheus, whatever may have been his origin, appears in history as a human prophet and teacher, whose doctrine was embodied in a collection of writings. He did not have a new and entirely distinct species of religion to offer, but a particular presentation or modification of religion. Those who found it congenial might take him for their prophet, live the Orphic life and call themselves Orphics. Their rites would be become *Orphica*, and a new spirit would be infused into their religion; but they would not be called upon to worship a different god or to worship their own in a way that was always obviously different. (pp. 8–9)

One of the most vexing problems for all scholars of Orphism is the nature and condition of the evidence. Separating those who think the word "Orphic" has some content and refers to actual literature and people from those who deny any such content and reference is the nature of the materials available for analysis. The alternatives require us to think as much about interpretive commitments and principles as about texts and statues:

> We have reached that great stumbling-block of religious historians, the scantiness of direct evidence for Orphism. This is a misfortune which scholars have never ceased to deplore, but few of them have paused to consider seriously whether it might not in itself constitute some of the evidence for which they are seeking. . . . If Orphism is of the nature I have suggested . . . the comparative rarity of any mention of it or of Orpheus in his capacity as founder of a religion becomes quite natural and is indeed only to be expected. (p. 9)

The trouble is that Orphism always was a literature, first and foremost. The distinction between literature and cult is a useful one in many ways, but it must not blind us to the fact that a genuine living religion may well be founded on a collection of sacred writings, as Orphism undoubtedly was. . . . The influence of Orphic ideas on the mind of Greece was profound, but it is no mitigation of it to say that there may never have existed any body of people to whom it would have occurred to call themselves an Orphic community. (pp. 10–11)

Here we have the two points of methodological conflict that divide students of Orphism: evidence and religion. With regard to the first problem, the paucity of explicit and direct references to Orphism is less the problem than the nature of the evidence. Consequently, the difficulty is not how to read the evidence but how to decide what will be allowed to count as evidence, and thus to formulate a principle to guide historical research. Put most starkly, the problem according to Linforth is that we do not have enough evidence and thus must conclude that "Orphism" is merely the label of a category. He has a rigorous check for every datum he will examine. Guthrie, on the other hand, has fashioned his hypothesis of Orphism as a reform in order to guide his efforts to interpret the materials. He has an interpretive frame within which to locate the data he examines. With regard to the problem of defining religion, it is clear that Linforth's insistence that a religion must include comprehensive and unified institutions with creed, ritual, clergy, and adherents leads him to deny that any such evidence for Orphism has been found—or indeed, could be found. When Guthrie relaxes the term "religion" by allowing it flexibility and variability, he makes room for an "Orphism" that may fit his definition but also may expand or contract it; when he defines Orphism as a reform, he makes room to explain a body of literature by constructing a system of ideas he finds in it, and he allows for the possibility of practices that are consistent with the beliefs woven into the literature. For Guthrie, the problem is that there is too much evidence, and thus he finds it necessary to refine his theoretical equipment in order to present a more sophisticated picture of Orphism.

How can students of Greek religion in general and Orphism in particular work and think between such radically conflicting approaches to the materials? If the problem lay in explicating the materials, scholars could happily contend with one another and their interpretations could blossom in the exchange. But between Guthrie and Linforth we have a conflict over principles of interpretation as well as sharp differences over content. As a consequence, discussion must include issues that we often call "philosophic"—such as the formulation of principles for including, excluding, and defining which materials are allowed to count as evidence for or against a hypothesis, and even the development of social theories that make room for debate about what constitutes various religions and what makes their practices call for attention.

An introduction to a new edition of this book is not the place to answer questions raised by the author of another book. Both books stand on their own, and they can face each other across disputed territory. But this is the place to suggest that rereading Guthrie and Linforth is not quite the same as reading them. We can now read their works not only to consider their compositional ideas and to understand their attitudes to their subject matter, but also to reread their books as moves in and contributions to a debate that is still lively and likely will continue for some time. The options they chose, the proceedings each tried to foreclose, and the space each tried to create for interpretive activity are still before us.

Thus it may be helpful to mention several high points in the discussions that have ensued as it has become clear that the differences that separate Guthrie and Linforth are still open to debate. Interesting exchanges have made for a lively scholarly conversation. The first steps in such an argument were taken by Guthrie himself in *The Greeks and Their Gods*, where he discusses Orphism without engaging in a debate about the evidence, but does develop his notion of religion into a explanatory, conceptual tool for comprehensive use. Religion, he suggests, is best understood as a historical phenomenon to be explained with historical methods and tools; nowhere does he even hint that religion is an effort to explain natural phenomena, and thus he is not tempted to account for deities as forces of nature or prescientific explanations as many scholars did in the 1930s and 1940s. Religion, he suggests, is best understood as a social phenomenon, and thus the contexts in which beliefs and practices occur—in his terms, the lives people lead—offer more satisfying explanations than concepts of races and racial characteristics, as used by the great historians of religions with whom Guthrie was conversant, such as Erwin Rohde and Martin P. Nilsson. Changes in religion, he suggests, are best explained by dialectical tensions within religions and pressures exerted upon religions. For this reason, some of Linforth's efforts to account for religion and religious changes he finds unhelpful, particularly such morally and even aesthetically evaluative notions as "the crude, the fantastic, the tasteless, the indecent in mythology" to interpret the myth of the dismemberment of Dionysus by the Titans, "fondness for the bizarre and the obscene" to describe fragments of the Orphic poems, and "an irresistible attraction in ideas and practices which are repellent to the normal, healthy mind" to characterize the writers of Orphic poems (*Arts of Orpheus*, pp. 363–64). Indeed, "normal" and "healthy," or "elevated" and "defiled" as descriptions of religious beliefs and actions are of apologetic rather than explanatory value.

Empirical discoveries as well as theoretical debates pushed the discussion into new areas by providing new materials for analysis. One is the discovery in 1962 of an "Orphic book" near a tomb at Derveni, near Thessaloniki, which dates to approximately 330 B.C.E. It is a commentary on an Orphic theogonic and cosmogonic poem dating to the early fifth century B.C.E. A provisional text has been published in *Zeitschrift für Papyrologie und Epigraphik* 47 (1982): 1–12; a stemma of it and other Orphic poems is provided in the brilliant work of M. L. West, *The Orphic Poems* (Oxford: Clarendon, 1983). Another is the discovery of gold leaves in addition to those discussed by Guthrie, for which a bibliography and a stemma are given by Richard Jenko, "Forgetfulness in the Golden Tablets of Memory," *Classical Quarterly* 34 (1984): 89–100. For further discussion of the leaves, see also Günther Zuntz,

Persephone: Three Essays on Religion and Thought in Magna Graecia (Oxford: Clarendon, 1971), pp. 277–393; Susan G. Cole, "New Evidence for the Mysteries of Dionysos," *Greek, Roman and Byzantine Studies* 21 (1980): 223–38; Hugh Lloyd-Jones, "Pindar and the After-Life," in *Entretiens sur l'antiquité classique* 31 (1984): 245–83; and Jeffrey S. Rusten, "Interim Notes on the Papyrus from Derveni (Orphic Theogony)," *Harvard Studies in Classical Philology* 89 (1985): 121–40. The discovery—by Soviet archaeologists at Olbia on the northern shore of the Black Sea in 1951—of bone tablets with the name Dionysos carved on them, testifies to the existence of a group of Orphics, again during the fifth century B.C.E.; discussion and bibliography are in West, *The Orphic Poems*, pp. 17–20; West, "The Orphics of Olbia," *Zeitschrift für Papyrologie und Epigraphik* 45 (1982): 17–29; Walter Burkert, "Neue Funde zur Orphik," *Informationen zum Altsprächlichen Unterricht* 2 (1980): 27–42; and Cole, "New Evidence for the Mysteries of Dionysos."

Theoretical discussion has also enhanced our knowledge of Orphism. In *Greek Religion* (Oxford: Basil Blackwell, and Cambridge: Harvard University, 1985) and *Ancient Mystery Cults* (Cambridge: Harvard University, 1987) Walter Burkert focuses on the practices and beliefs of social groups, emphasizing the difficulty of drawing boundaries to distinguish the various mysteries into separate communities. A significantly different focus and emphasis—structural analysis—motivates Marcel Detienne's *Dionysos Slain* (Baltimore: Johns Hopkins, 1979), where the issues of food, sacrifice, and religious beliefs are integral to the social history of the Orphic religious movement.

The possibilities set in motion by the controversial differences between Guthrie and Linforth mark contemporary discussions of Orphism. Scholarly conversation has continued. At the least, the reissue of Guthrie's *Orpheus and Greek Religion* puts in the hands of scholars a monument in the study of Orphism. To repeat, we cannot today read the book the way it was read in 1935. We can read it now as a text in the history of a debate. Some of Guthrie's conclusions will stand and some will fall as new evidence and new interpretations put his work to new analyses. But his method still can be commended to scholars of ancient Greece, particularly its synthetic, inductive, reconstructive, and experimental aspects. Most striking, however, will be his persistent refusal to reduce Orphism to an essence or a single narrative and his insistence on presenting a composite picture of Orphism.

One might be tempted to think that Guthrie's interest in Orphism and religious aspects of ancient history ended when he turned to the history of Greek philosophy to produce what is now one of the standard accounts of ancient Greek thought. One can also incline to a different conclusion—that Guthrie showed that the boundaries between poetry, religion, and philosophy are thin and wavy, blurred and porous, and that neither the study of a religious movement nor the study of a philosophic history gives us a final version or the true essence of an ancient culture. Guthrie opened an extended view of the collection of myths, ideas, and practices which served that culture throughout its history. When we abandon the quest for a "true version" or "the real picture" of Orphism in particular or Greek religion in general, it is possible to move beyond a picture of a singularly miraculous Greek culture to a concept of Greeks as a people whose cultural flowering can be attributed to its imagination, energy, and intellectual, technological, and economic exchanges with its neighbors in the ancient Near Eastern world. Guthrie will remain a steady guide and teacher.

Larry J. Alderink

PREFACE

" Die Modernen reden so entsetzlich viel von Orphikern."—WILAMOWITZ

THERE are two classes of people who will probably regard a book on Orphism with suspicion ; there is a third, small perhaps, but deserving the highest consideration, which may welcome it. To this last class belong those who have learned to read and appreciate classical literature, without ever acquiring a specialist's interest in matters of religion, and who since their sixth-form days have felt an unsatisfied curiosity, not to say exasperation, on reading in their commentaries or hearing from their teachers that this or that passage in one of the great writers, Plato or Pindar or Virgil, is a reflection of Orphic doctrine. ' This passage is Orphic ', runs the simple comment, and the student is left wondering whether or not his understanding of the text has been helped by the vague associations which the note calls up, and if not, whether his own or the commentator's stupidity is to blame.

Of the two other kinds of people, the first is the reader whose interests are purely general, and who has come to look with justifiable suspicion on anything which ends in -ism as savouring of the abstract, vague and dull. The second is the professional scholar, who has more than once been given excellent grounds for believing Orphism to be nothing more than a field of rash speculation on insufficient evidence. The first may in fairness be asked to proceed a little further and find out whether his fears are justified. Both may perhaps be reassured by an explicit recognition of their points of view and of the purpose of the series to which this book belongs. *A Handbook of Orphism* seemed an unfortunate title, and I have avoided it, but the requirements of a handbook have, I hope, been considered. These are in the main two : it should be free from unnecessary technicalities, and it should try to avoid mere theorizing. Aristotle's maxim holds good, that every subject must be given the treatment which its particular nature demands, and in the present inquiry theories not only may but must be discussed. Yet it is worth while trying to make a sharp break between a simple statement of the evidence with the conclusions which may unquestionably be drawn from it, and that which remains no more than speculation, however attractive and plausible it may appear.

The book deals primarily with a special problem. It cannot therefore adequately incorporate the whole background of Greek religion out of which that problem arises. To any who feel that lack, M. P. Nilsson's *History of Greek Religion* (Oxford, 1925) may be particularly recommended. Among the many accounts of Greek religion, I know of none more suitable to serve as an introduction. Again, the study of Orphism leads inevitably, as it has always led, to innumerable questions of comparative religion. These too have been excluded, on the ground that an independent study of the nature of Orphism was a necessary preliminary to them, though this is a fact that does not seem to be generally realized. What I have tried to do therefore is to follow one particular strain as it runs through the literary and other remains of classical and post-classical Greece, and as far as possible to describe it and estimate its influence over the life and thought of the people. It was my ambition to interest in this way those who have felt a desire for a more intimate acquaintance with that people and that age, and also, since it seems inevitable that writers will continue to compare Orphism with other religious systems, to provide future researchers with some sort of material for comparison.

It will be noticed that I have made obvious use of the personal name Orpheus in the title of the book and the headings of its chapters. This is not due to a bias in favour of his historical reality. What it does imply is a desire to keep closely to what was for the Greeks associated with the name of Orpheus, in reaction from the tendency to regard the term Orphic as vaguely synonymous with the whole mystical element in Greek religion. It is no mere frivolity to remind ourselves that in Orpheus we are dealing with someone who has many of the qualities of the Snark and one important point of resemblance to the Cheshire Cat. This comparison seems less absurd if we remember the legend according to which his head, after his death, was found alone, still singing. We can see it so occupied on more than one monument of ancient art, where little more is left to the singer than was in the last stages to be seen of the cat. It may be that our inquiry too will in the end give him no more tangible attributes than a mouth wherewith to sing. If this is so, and he should turn out to be a voice and nothing more, we ought to be glad rather than sorry. That voice was singing for over a thousand years, a difficult feat, perhaps, had its nature been more corporeal, and we shall be better employed in tracing the melodies and the power of its song among the people than in pursuing the search for something which, when we think we have found it, may prove to be a Boojum after all.

Any personal help which I have had in the work has come from Professor A. B. Cook. My debt to him is manifold. It includes free and informal access to a vast store of learning, practical help to a beginner in the tiresome but necessary business of preparing illustrations (as well as the provision of actual material for many of them), and last but not least, contact with a personality whose influence never failed to dispel the occasional moods of despair to which a writer is subject in the less inspiring stages of his first book. The complete proofs have been read by my friend Mr. W. Hamilton, Fellow of Trinity College, to whom I owe the removal of a number of blemishes. It is also fitting that I should remember here the benefactors to whom in one way or another I owe the continuancè of my studies, of which this book is the first concrete result. Their names are too numerous to mention, but I should not like to omit the Managers of the Craven Fund, who first made it possible for me to contemplate an academic life, nor the Governing Body of Peterhouse, who have allowed me to continue it in ideal surroundings.

Acknowledgments are due to the Trustees of the British Museum for permission to reproduce the photographs of plates 8, 9 and 10, and to the Cambridge University Press for providing the blocks for several of my text-illustrations. A more personal debt is that to Commendatore Settimo Bocconi of the Capitoline Museum, who allowed me to take a camera into the Museum and photograph the monuments reproduced on plate 7, on the understanding that my photographs were not for publication, and afterwards with great courtesy relaxed that restriction at my request.

The necessary examination of Greek literature has been made inestimably easier, one might almost say that to carry it out efficiently has been made for the first time possible, by Otto Kern's collection of the fragments relating to Orphism, which appeared in 1922. This book is divided into two parts, *testimonia* and *fragmenta*. I have referred to the first part by the abbreviation ' Kern, *test.*', and to the second by the abbreviation ' *O.F.*' Translation, from both ancient and modern authors, I have usually preferred to do for myself, even when an English translation is published, and I must therefore take responsibility for it except in the few instances where I have made explicit reference to a published translation. My bibliographical index includes only those works which I have had occasion to refer to. It is thus neither a complete list of works on the Orphics nor exclusively confined to them. For a bibliography of that sort readers may look at Kern's *Fragmenta*, pp. 345 ff. A number of relevant works published since 1922 will, however, be found in my own list. Notes have, after much misgiving, been collected at the end of each chapter. The printing of the chapter-number at the head of every page may facilitate reference to this arrangement. Finally I would express a hope that my somewhat erratic spelling of Greek names may be received with toleration, and offer an apology to any whom it may offend.

W. K. C. GUTHRIE

PETERHOUSE,
    CAMBRIDGE,
        November, 1934

PREFACE TO SECOND EDITION

THE author of a book of this nature whose publishers offer to reprint it under present conditions must count himself particularly fortunate, and I am very ready to agree with the suggestion that no major alterations should be made in the text, but any additions or modifications confined to a new preface. It would no doubt have been a good thing to undertake a thorough revision, incorporating the many helpful suggestions of reviewers and other friends as well as the contributions of subsequently published writings. On the other hand, no striking new evidence has appeared on the subject or is likely to appear. It is a question of arguing to different conclusions from the same material, and the views here put forward may perhaps be allowed to stand alongside those of others, which anyone seriously interested must read and compare. I have summed up my position, with some reference to later discussions, in ch. xi of my book *The Greeks and their Gods* (Methuen, 1950), which there is no need to repeat. It will perhaps be helpful in the present edition (*a*) to mention the more important writings dealing with the Orphics which have appeared since completion of work on the first edition or were overlooked in it, and (*b*) to add some notes on points of detail, mainly by way of reference to relevant passages in books or articles, though admittedly it has not been easy to select passages for annotation. This has been done in a supplement. An asterisk in the margin of the text indicates reference to a note in the supplement.

W. K. C. GUTHRIE

PETERHOUSE,
  CAMBRIDGE,
    April, 1952

CHAPTER I

FAMOUS ORPHEUS

' For those who wish to find answers, it is a real step forward even to ask the right questions.'—ARISTOTLE.

'Ονομακλυτὸν 'Ορφήν—famous Orpheus. In these words, torn from their context like so many fragments of ancient literature and imbedded in the writings of a later author, Orpheus makes for us his earliest appearance in history. They are the words of the poet Ibykos who lived in the sixth century B.C. Famous he was at the first date at which we hear of him, and famous he has been ever since. So far is it from being true that the person who gives his name to this book is recondite, obscure or little known. Comparatively few Englishmen, it is true, may know very much about a thing called Orphism (and small blame to them, for the word, besides being ugly, is of modern coinage and far from being contemporaneous with that which it tries to describe), but few, on the other hand, are ignorant of the singer who with his lute made trees and the mountain tops that freeze bow themselves when he did sing. A man may take no pleasure in the romantic poets of the last century ; he may even believe with Robert Browning (though let us hope with more regard for accuracy in his naming of the ancient deities) that the eye of faith has no need

> To puzzle out who Orpheus was,
> Or Dionysius Zagreas.

Even so, he is probably not so unversed in the literature of his own country as not to have heard of the Muse herself, that Orpheus bore. Everyone, in short, has heard of Orpheus.

It is when we try to be a little less poetic and a little more historical that we find our difficulties beginning. As we try to trace him back through the ages he becomes more shadowy, more elusive, more Protean in his aptitude for slipping away from any-one who tries to lay actual hands on him and make him tell just what he is and what he stands for. In a way that is a misleading statement. If we take it, as I think we fairly may, that most educated people know and think of Orpheus simply as the great musician, then they will not be disappointed. That character is delineated with equal clearness whether we turn to Shakespeare with his lute or to Pindar with his ' Orpheus of the golden lyre, father of lays .

It is only when we have once looked at the ancient world and found how much more it promises to tell us of Orpheus that we can begin to feel the longing for a little more express and definite information than at a superficial view it is prepared to give. We find ourselves among men to whom he meant much more than a kind of superior snake-charmer, who understood the power of melody to sway the creatures of animate or inanimate nature to his will. That in itself would mean more to the Greeks than it does to us, for they understood better than most of us do the intimate connexion between music and the human mind ; but they saw more in it than that. What I am speaking of now is something which must appear to every student of the Hellenic mind as one of the most striking problems which his study raises, as well as one of the most interesting and at times the most baffling. I mean the contrast which is presented by the scantiness of the definite evidence in our possession for Orpheus and his influence in the classical age of Greece, and the un-doubted truth, which we all feel to a greater or less degree, that a distinctive spirit did invade Greek literature, Greek philosophy, and above all Greek religion, which in some way was associated with the name. Through the Greeks it naturally affected the Romans, and Christianity itself has known its appeal. Art as well as literature bears witness to its influence, and in one way or another, by a black-figured vase or the words of Ibykos or Pindar, by the art of the Catacombs or the poetry of those anonymous writers who round about the birth of Christianity were still composing verses in the name of their ancient prophet, we are made aware of its workings from the sixth century B.C. down to and beyond the beginning of our own era. Few scholars would deny the reality of this distinctive spirit, or their own faith that it must have been considerably more widespread than the actual references to Orpheus and his followers would seem to indicate. It is one way of stating the purpose of this book to say that it aims at finding out how far this faith is justified by the actual evidence at our disposal.

There is one question which springs to the mind the moment it begins to think about this subject at all. Was Orpheus a real man, a historic character who at some period in the past was born, lived and died like the rest of us, or was he simply an imaginary creation of the Greek mythological genius ?   This is a natural question, and human curiosity prompts us to make it the first that we ask.   Nevertheless, we may be too hasty in assuming either its primary importance or the possibility of answering it before we have given consideration to a great many other questions concerning his religion and his influence.   More urgent, as well as being likely to yield its solution earlier, than the question ' Was Orpheus a real man ? ' is the question ' Did the Greeks believe he was ? '   Was he to them a man or a god or a god-man or demi-god ?   And if the last, in what sense ? It is this which is going to affect the quality of his religion, and not his historical or mythological existence established as a question of fact by a consensus of historians.   This is not to deny a connexion between the two questions of fact and of belief.   When we know something of the Greek beliefs about him, and the way in which his personality and his teaching worked upon their minds, we shall be more entitled to make up our minds on the other matter too.   In fact, the best evidence for the historical existence of Orpheus will be found if his religion seems to be such as could only be set in motion by a real personal founder.   If there were no other evidence for the real existence of the founder of Christianity, a strong case might still be made out based on the difficulty a man might feel in accounting for the rise of Christianity without the impulse of a historic Jesus behind it.   This should make it clear that to raise the question of the historical existence of Orpheus before we have examined from as many aspects as we can his influence over the minds of Greece is to put the cart before the horse and to neglect our most valuable source of evidence.   Other evidence there is, and we shall do our best to examine it ; but the final answer to the question must lie in the book as a whole, and perhaps must be left there for each reader to extract according to the dictates of his own temperament and predilections.

The discussion of the other evidence which I mentioned belongs to another chapter.   It may be remarked here that any direct testimony which we possess to the real humanity of Orpheus is of very late date compared with the fact to which it would testify.   The bearing which this obvious and insufficiently precise remark may have on the question cannot yet be decided.   We may notice, however, that the evidence is vague enough to have called forth the most widely differing opinions from serious scholars in this and the last century.

Jane Harrison was one who possessed to a remarkable degree the faith in the humanity of Orpheus, as well as that faith, which I have remarked on already, in the breadth and depth of the influence that lies behind our few classical references to Orpheus and the Orphics. When she comes to argue the case for his humanity, it is this faith which is her strongest weapon. It may well be true that it is as good a weapon as anyone could desire, when it is founded on the knowledge of ancient religion which Jane Harrison possessed. The interesting fact remains that when she turns to discuss the direct evidence which the ancient sources provide, she relies chiefly on the opinions of Konon, Strabo and Pausanias. Of these the first two lived at the beginning of the Roman Empire, and the third a century or more after them. Yet they are her witnesses for a man who lived, as she herself believed, ' before the dawn of history '.

Jane Harrison held that to disbelieve in the humanity of Orpheus was to misunderstand his nature completely. In support of her belief she cites as direct evidence the opinions of writers who lived under the Roman Empire. Yet this evidence is of such a kind that a learned German of the last century (Bernhardy) could write of Orpheus as ' that religious symbol which even before the time of Alexander did not pass for the name of any poet who had ever lived '. This is the sort of contrast which we are likely to meet, and it may serve as a hint that famous Orpheus is not going to yield up his secrets without a struggle. Herodotus does not mention him in person, but only ' the *Orphica* ', that neuter plural which cannot be translated into English until one has decided what is the noun to be supplied, and made it into Orphic rites or Orphic literature or whatever the context may seem to demand. Of the other writers of the classical age in Greece none was very much interested in the historical question of Orpheus' earthly existence. Euripides certainly was not, neither was Plato. Aristotle is reported to have said that there never was such a person.* Yet if we say that the lack of early evidence to the contrary points to Aristotle's statement being true, an interesting question remains. Who wrote the body of writing current in the fifth and fourth centuries which Plato could quote unhesitatingly and cheerfully as the poems of Orpheus ? Did he believe in the attribution which he himself was making? Were they really from the workshop of Onomakritos, the pious forger whom Peisistratos kept at his court, or of some South

---

* See below, pp. 58 f.

Italian devotee who hid his identity under the revered and
ancient name ?   No less an authority than Aristotle lent his
weight to the theory that Onomakritos was the author.   It is
when we bend our mind to problems of this sort that those two
words of Ibykos, if they recur to us, may seem to have been
flung across the abyss of two and a half millenniums simply as
an ironic comment on the voracity of time and the secrets which
have become lost to us in its passage.   It is our task to see
whether, in this matter of famous Orpheus, long and unnum-
bered time, as it hides what is apparent, may be persuaded
to complete the circle of birth and bring things forth from
their obscurity in due course.

CHAPTER II

WHAT IS MEANT BY ORPHISM?

THE NATURE OF THE EVIDENCE

' Now all these events arose from the same cause, and a multitude of others besides, more wonderful even than these, but through length of time some of them have been suppressed altogether, and others have been told to us scattered, each one apart from the other.'—PLATO, *Politicus*, 269b (*referring to the stories of the age of Kronos*).

GREEK religion was a many-sided thing. To the mind of a studious age it appears rather to be a medley of religions, and as investigators we try to separate the threads and trace each one back to its own beginning. It is right and proper that we should. In the Greece of historic times, the most obvious division to make is that between Olympian and chthonian religions, the cults of the pure air about the tops of the sacred mountain with their accompanying characteristics of sanity, light-heartedness, frankness, and the cults of the earth and the regions beneath it, often marked by a darkness and impressiveness and mystical yearnings after a union between man and god. When we have noted this we can draw further distinctions of increasing complexity and subtlety, to which no limit is set save by the industry and perspicacity of the scholar himself.

The perception of these distinctions is a necessity for anyone who wants to understand the Greeks and their religion. Yet it may lead to error if certain precautions are not taken. It is inevitable that in discussion of the different varieties of religious belief and experience with which the Greek world presents us, the term ' religion ' should frequently be applied to each one separately. We speak naturally of Olympian religion, chthonian religion, Dionysiac religion, and so forth. This usage by its familiarity may cause us to lose sight of a fact worth remembering, which is this. The detached observer speaks also of Christian religion and Moslem religion ; but here he is not alone. The people of whom he is speaking are equally conscious that they belong to different religious worlds. This consciousness is an important part of their religion itself, and they are ready to kill and be killed in the avowal of it. Both may claim Judaism as one of the ancestors of their faith, and the Mohammedan may grant Jesus a place among the prophets. They remain mutually exclusive, in the sense that it is impossible to imagine a Christian calling himself at the same time a Mohammedan, or a Mohammedan a Christian. It would be possible to write a good book about the nature, origin and diffusion of Islam with little or no reference to the Christians save as the enemies whose militant opposition retarded the progress of the faith. We are apt to imagine that we are dealing with differences as clearly marked as this whenever we distinguish between religion and religion, and at the same time to use those terms in describing phenomena about which the assumption would be quite unjustifiable. It would be unjustifiable in discussing the religions of classical Greek or Graeco-Roman paganism. Hence my appeal for caution. The term ' religions ' I retain, for it is a useful one, and innocuous once we have made up our minds what we mean by it.

To us the differences between the worship of Olympian Zeus and the mysteries of Demeter may seem as great as those between any two religions of more modern times. Yet not only did they never lead to wars or persecutions, but it was perfectly possible for the same man to be a devout participant in both. More than this, Kore daughter of Demeter, in whose honour as well as her mother's the mysteries were held, had Zeus himself for father, and Zeus could be addressed as Chthonios as well as Olympios. A totally different god in reality, you may say. Fortunately there is no need to go into such troubled questions just now. Totally different he could not have been for the fifth-century Athenian, and the instance is only one out of many which might have served to illustrate the point that in speaking of this or that religion of ancient Greece we cannot draw the sharp distinctions which we might between this or that religion of the modern world. It is not a question of tolerance. A state of tolerance prevails over a large part of the civilized world to-day, but it has not obliterated the definite line which can be drawn between Christian, Moslem and Hindu. It is a question of actual unconsciousness in the mind of the worshipper that differences exist which seem plain and obvious to an outsider. A parallel can easily be seen within the Christian world itself. Its differences have not all been unconscious, as the long history of persecutions bears witness. But there exist to-day, worshipping side by side in the same church and with apparent unanimity, people of very varying degrees of spirituality, mental powers and education, according to which they believe, this one in a kindly father-god, another in a righteous but despotic Jehovah, another in a being whose nature is simply man's own perfected and with whom complete spiritual union is the not impossible aim ; immortality is conceived now as an expedient of divine justice, with the torments of hell for the condemned, now with the torments rejected as unworthy of divinity, now as a realistic extension of the individual personality, now as an almost Neoplatonic state of union with the supreme spirit in which the survival of personality may be but dimly apprehended. Almost all the different shades of belief are to be found which in studying Greek religion we take such pains to separate, and the conception of God's relation to men may vary from one as external as Homer's to the purest forms of mysticism. Religion in the last resort is of the individual, and no two men's religions are exactly alike. Those of similar temperament will prefer to group themselves together, and in classical Greece there were many kinds of religion to reflect this tendency. Some of them were devoted to particular gods, making it easy to suppose at first sight that each god or set of gods stood for a different type of religion, here the Olympians, there Dionysos, and there Demeter and Kore. In fact, however, we find that representatives of opposing types of religion will invoke the same god in an entirely different spirit (the change may be marked by a change of epithet), and also that gods whom we had thought of as inspiring incompatible beliefs and aspirations are sometimes peacefully united in the same camp. Much confusion has been caused by attempts to discover a non-existent order and reason in matters whose explanation is simply the calm unconsciousness of incongruity which can be seen within the limits of any one denomination to-day.

What has all this to do with Orpheus ? For the present we may notice at least that Orpheus was regarded by the Greeks as the founder of a certain kind of religion, that much has been written on the Orphic religion, sometimes known more simply to-day as Orphism, and that this therefore is a good place to remind ourselves that the term ' religion ' is only to be used in the limited sense here described

Orpheus, whatever may have been his origin, appears in history as a human prophet and teacher, whose doctrine was embodied in a collection of writings. He did not have a new and entirely distinct species of religion to offer, but a particular presentation or modification of religion. Those who found it congenial might take him for their prophet, live the Orphic life and call themselves Orphics. Their rites would become *Orphica*, and a new spirit would be infused into their religion ; but they would not be called upon to worship a different god or to worship their own in a way that was always obviously different. Hence the ever-present difficulty of deciding whether this or that belief or practice can properly be called Orphic or not. We have reached that great stumbling-block of religious historians, the scantiness of direct evidence for Orphism. This is a misfortune which scholars have never ceased to deplore, but few of them have paused to consider seriously whether it might not in itself constitute some of the evidence for which they are seeking. Yet it is a remarkable phenomenon if Orphism is to be given the important position as a separate religion which is sometimes assigned to it.[1] If Orphism is of the nature I have suggested (a fact which admittedly awaits demonstration), the comparative rarity of any mention of it or of Orpheus in his capacity as founder of a religion becomes quite natural and is indeed only to be expected. Professor Boulanger, commenting on the complete absence of epigraphical testimony, has remarked (*Orphée*, p. 51) that although the worshippers of Kybele, of Attis, of Adonis, of Sabazios, of Dionysos, of the Eleusinian divinities had carved on their tombs an expression of their faith, nothing of the sort exists for Orphism. This need not surprise us. In the absence of any other evidence we cannot say that the dead worshippers of any of the deities he mentions had Orpheus for their prophet, but it is quite possible that some of them did. To assume that every worshipper of Dionysos was an Orphic is manifestly wrong, but it is equally untrue to say that none was. Only, when it comes to an inscription on a tomb, a man will be content to avow his faith in the deity he worships. He will not think it necessary to mention the name of the prophet from whose books he drew his faith and his code. One is tempted to remark, without claiming completeness for the parallel, that, however zealous a reader of the Old Testament a man may be, at his death he will prefer to commend himself to God ; his debt to Moses or to Isaiah will probably go unacknowledged, at least on his tomb-stone. It can scarcely be objected that this is being too literal,

1

and that what is meant is not an explicit reference to Orpheus or *Orphici* but an undefined expression of the sort of beliefs the Orphics are known to have held, since for those beliefs we are certainly not *privés de tout document épigraphique ;* the inscribed gold plates from Italy and Crete are epigraphical testimony of the highest interest and importance.

It seems worth while dwelling a little on this point, for it affects our attitude towards one or two of the most important of our problems.   There is for example the question in what form Orphism survived into Roman times.   Diodoros, at the beginning of the Roman Empire, says, after explaining a myth, ' In agreement with this, it is pointed out, are the expositions in the Orphic poems and the things which are introduced in the mysteries, the details of which it is not lawful to recount to the uninitiated ' (Diod. 3. 62. 8 = *O.F.* 301).   Pausanias, writing of the antiquities of Greece 150 years later, has this remark : ' Whoever has seen an initiation at Eleusis, or read the writings called Orphic, knows what I mean ' (Paus. 1. 37. 4 = Kern, *test.* 219).   Both passages have been taken as pointing a contrast between Orphism as a literary tradition and nothing else, and the mysteries as living religion, and it is supposed that this contrast is one which could not have been made in an earlier age.   Thus the passages become evidence for a decline in the vitality of the Orphic religion in the Roman period.   The trouble is that Orphism always was a literature, first and foremost.   The distinction between literature and cult is a useful one in many ways, but it must not blind us to the fact that a genuine living religion may well be founded on a collection of sacred writings, as Orphism undoubtedly was.   This, in fact, rather than anything else is what the quotation from Pausanias brings out, for he is referring to beans, with which in the mind of the Orphic, as of the Pythagorean, certain prohibitions were connected.   He is quoting the poems as an authority for ritual, and the contrast in these passages is not necessarily between a literary tradition, without influence on religious life, and the living religions of the time as something separate.   All that is said is that you will find more of these matters whether you look at what people do in the mysteries or at the writings which for some of them serve as the authorities ᶠ ˷ their behaviour. Franz Cumont wrote : ' No-one has furnished the least bit of certain proof that there existed in Italy at the end of the Republic or under the Empire a single Orphic community '. He again is arguing for the decline of Orphism as a vital force, yet it would be far from easy to produce certain proof of anything calling itself an Orphic community in fifth or fourth century Greece. The influence of Orphic ideas on the mind of Greece was profound, but it is no mitigation of it to say that there may never have existed any body of people to whom it would have occurred to call themselves an Orphic community. The question of course demands further consideration, which will be more in place later on. The present paragraph may simply serve to illustrate a view of the general nature of Orphism which it seemed better to state at the outset, although it may depend for its complete justification on much of what follows later.

It remains for this chapter to give some sort of summary of the materials available for our study. In order to make quite sure that we are starting with our feet planted on firm ground, it will be good, if only as discipline, to confine ourselves for the moment to explicit information about Orpheus, the *Orphici* or the *Orphica*, resisting the temptation to mention anything else, however certainly Orphic its character may appear. Since we are leaving until later the task of unravelling the tales which the evidence tells, we shall not pause yet to consider whether the picture of Orpheus which we are getting is a consistent one, but only try to collect the most important sources of information in order to gain some idea of their nature and extent. It will be convenient, and should not now be misleading, to make a division for this purpose between the evidence for the purely literary side of Orphism, neglecting the question of its influence on the popular religious mind, and the evidence for its validity as a living religious force.

It is generally agreed that there was considerable activity, whether nascent or renascent, in the sphere of Orphic and kindred religion, in the sixth century B.C. ; but as the arguments for it depend either upon inference or upon the statements of authors living from 800 to 1800 years later, the consideration of them must be left for the present.

To pass to the first of our two divisions, the existence of a sacred literature ascribed to Orpheus, evidence is not lacking to show that this was in being in the fifth and fourth centuries B.C., and moreover that it was believed in those centuries to be of great antiquity. Orpheus heads the list when Alexis, a fourth-century comic poet, describes a representative pile of books : ' Come and choose any book you like from here. . . . There is Orpheus, Hesiod, tragedies, Choirilos, Homer, Epicharmos ' (*Athen.* 4. 164). In the *Hippolytos* of Euripides Theseus, taunting his son with the ascetic life he leads through having taken Orpheus for his lord, ascribes it to his 'paying honour to the vapourings of wordy volumes'. Plato mentions the poet several times and quotes from his writings. Some examples are : from the *Cratylus* (402*b*), 'Orpheus says somewhere' followed by two hexameter lines; from the *Philebos* (66*c*), 'As Orpheus says' followed by a single hexameter; from the *Laws* (2. 669*d*), 'Those whom Orpheus speaks of as having reached the years of pleasure', and the famous passage in the *Republic* (2. 364*e*) where the itinerant priests are spoken of as producing 'a mass of books of Orpheus and Musaios'. In the *Laws* again (8. 829*d*) the Hymns of Orpheus are mentioned, and in the *Ion* (536*b*) he is spoken of as one of the models of later hexameter poets.[2]

Eudemos, the pupil of Aristotle, is quoted by one of the Neoplatonists as having described a theology 'which he called that of Orpheus', and further testimony comes from the master himself. Aristotle indeed, introducing a spirit of scientific criticism which showed him to be before his time, ventured to doubt not only the authenticity of the poems but the existence of Orpheus himself. He attests none the less the existence of the literature and its common ascription in the fourth century. He twice refers a belief to the Orphic poems, but both times with the reservation 'so-called'. On one of these passages his Greek commentator Philoponos (sixth century A.D.) remarks : 'He says *so-called* because it is unlikely that the verses are by Orpheus, as he himself says in the *de Philosophia*' (a work now lost). Besides these two explicit references we shall find when the time comes that some of his more vague remarks about early writers on the gods must include Orpheus in their scope. It is only natural that when he himself felt doubtful about the authenticity of the poems he should avoid as far as possible committing himself by mentioning the reputed author by name more often than was necessary. It is part of Aristotle's method to gather in the opinions of all sorts of men as the raw material of his philosophy, and consequently θεολόγοι, the old religious poets, appear more than once in his works. In the *Metaphysics*, for example (A3, 983*b*27), he speaks of 'those who first in far off times, long before our own generation, wrote about the nature of the gods', and in passing we may note that the doctrine which he there ascribes to them is identical with that attributed by name to Orpheus in Plato's *Cratylus* (402*b*). It is worth giving serious consideration to anything which Aristotle has to say on our subject. The combination of fourth-century date with an acute critical mind and a lively interest in the matter in question lends a peculiar value to any relevant pronouncement he may make. On the last of these qualifications, his interest and his appreciation of the importance to a philosopher which these ancient religious poems possess, there are clear indications in his work, and the point has been well brought out by Professor Jaeger in his book on Aristotle (English ed., Oxford, 1934, pp. 128 ff.). Other examples of their mention in the *Metaphysics* are 1000*a*9, 1071*b*27, 1091*a*34 and *b*8.[3]

Interesting are the glimpses which are to be seen of a tradition as old as the fifth century that there existed among the mountains of Thrace certain tablets(*sanides*) bearing writings of Orpheus, just as the Jews received their sacred law on tables of stone from Sinai. In the *Alcestis* of Euripides the chorus lament that they have found no remedy for the blows of Fate ; nothing avails, ' no charm on Thracian tablets which tuneful Orpheus carved out '. On this passage the scholiast quotes ' the natural philosopher Herakleides ' (Herakleides of Pontus, a contemporary of Plato) as stating that according to report there actually exist on mount Haimos certain writings of Orpheus on tablets.[4] This must surely recur to us when we read in the dialogue *Axiochos*, once attributed to Plato, that the lot of the soul in Hades was the subject of the writing on certain bronze tablets which two seers had brought to Delos from the land of the Hyperboreans (*Axiochos*, 371*a*).

Before we turn to glance at later testimony, an exception should be made to the exclusion of the sixth century from the present brief review, and room be given to a mention of Onomakritos. We first hear of this remarkable person in a passage of Herodotus (7. 6 = Kern, *test.* 182). Hipparchos, son of Peisistratos, had banished him from Athens on account of an insertion which he had thought fit to make with his own hand in an oracular saying of Musaios, who usually appears in tradition as the son or the pupil of Orpheus (ch. v, n. 2 below). Onomakritos had been entrusted with the redaction of his poems, but his manner of carrying out the task had caused a breach in what had been a very close association with the tyrant and his family. Finding, however, that during their exile at the Persian court he could be of considerable use to them owing to the very qualities which they had formerly deplored, the Peisistratids decided to forgive him, and we find him now with them at Susa helping to persuade the Great King to lead an expedition against Greece by the simple expedient of reciting to him all in the oracles that was favourable to such an enterprise and suppressing anything that boded failure.

For further information about Onomakritos we have to look
to the writers of a later age, but there is the good authority of
Philoponos for supposing that Aristotle himself believed the
Orphic poems, in the form in which he knew them at least,
to be the work of Onomakritos. Among writers of the first
few centuries A.D., both Christian and pagan, the theory was
well known. (Examples—Tatian, Eusebios, Suidas' Lexikon,
Pausanias—are to be found in Kern, *testt.* 183 ff.) According
to one of the accounts mentioned by Tzetzes (twelfth century),
he was one of a commission of four appointed by Peisistratos
for his recension of the Homeric poems, and there are stories
that in this work too he was at his old game of interpolating
lines of his own invention. (Kern, *testt.* 189, 190.) We shall
meet him again.

The Alexandrian age is not rich in examples for our present
purpose, but Apollonios in his epic of the Argonauts keeps up
the tradition that Orpheus is not only a singer but a religious
one, and that when he sings his subject is the gods and their
relationships, and the origin of all things (*Arg.* i. 494 = *O.F.*
29). For a real outburst of interest in the content of the
Orphic writings and quotations from their text we must wait
until the beginning of the Christian era. It was a fashion
among the Neoplatonist philosophers, who were active from
the third century A.D. onwards, to quote copiously from the
poems of Orpheus and thus lend to their doctrines the dignity
which derives from a hoary antiquity. The Christian apologists
too, who made it their business to denounce the beliefs of the
pagans and show their religious practices to be either immoral
or ridiculous, found in the same body of writings a target for
their abuse. Examples from the works of these two schools
are too numerous to make it desirable to quote for the sake of
illustration, and they can be left until their proper place in the
discussion.

No doubt Onomakritos was not the only person to be attracted by the idea of inserting new lines under an old name,
and the poems used by the Neoplatonists can hardly be the
same as those which Plato knew. To what extent they had
been transformed is a problem by no means easy to decide.
The possibilities of transformation in six or seven centuries are
obvious : let us look for a moment to see whether there is any
evidence on the side of conservatism. First of all there is the
question, what's in a name ? There are two names in particular
whose survival is relevant, that of Orpheus as the author of the

poems and the term *hieros logos* as the title of the chief of them.
Both are of respectable antiquity. Of Orpheus we already
know something. The term *hieros logos*, sacred story, is a
common one which must have called up quite definite associations in a reader's mind. We meet it in Herodotus (2. 81 =
Kern, *test*. 216) in conjunction with Orphic ritual, where,
having commented on a certain practice as being in agreement
with the Orphic, he adds, ' there is a *hieros logos* which is told
about it '. Plato makes frequent use of the term and expresses ✱
great reverence for that which it describes. Moreover, the
teachings which he takes from this storehouse correspond with
what we know from other sources to be Orphic and are certainly
nothing to do with, say, Homer or Hesiod. As an example out
of many the 7th Letter will serve (335*a* = *O.F.* 10) : ' We
must ever maintain a real belief in the ancient and sacred
stories, which reveal that our soul is immortal, and has judges,
and pays the utmost penalties whenever a man is rid of the
body '. The possibility of new lines or whole poems being
inserted under these venerable names depends on the view
which was taken of such conduct at the time, as well as on the
strength of the tradition and consequently of the old associations
which the names called up. These are things which it is not
time to measure yet, but it is a line of inquiry which may well
bear fruit.

As more immediately convincing evidence that the Neoplatonic versions of the writings contain a large amount of older
material we have one or two striking coincidences with quotations in Plato, which show beyond a doubt that both authors
were excerpting from the same poems at the time.[5] Moreover,
as has already been mentioned, Damaskios, a Neoplatonic
philosopher of the sixth century, gives Eudemos as the authority
for one of his quotations.

Finally we have to mention the existence of certain complete
writings which have come down to us with the name of Orpheus
attached to them. Of these the most important are an account
of the voyage of the Argonauts, in which the singer himself
plays the central part, and a collection of 87 hymns to various
deities. The exact date of these writings is difficult to decide,
but they cannot well have been put together in their present
form before the beginning of the Christian era, and their date is
probably to be set between the limits of the second and fourth
centuries A.D.

We turn now to the second of the heads under which we are
considering the material, and look to see what evidence there is

that the teachings of Orpheus affected the life of the people,
how far he gave them a religious ritual, set tabus in their way,
or otherwise determined their conduct.   I would once more
emphasize the fact that much of what has already been mentioned as Orphic literature may well be the visible basis of a
genuine religion with its roots in the hearts of the people,
although we have not yet considered it from that point of
view : there are no *a priori* grounds for believing that a clearly
marked division between literature and cult ever existed.   To
those new to the study of these subjects, this may seem a
superfluous insistence on an obvious truth, but such a division
has nevertheless been frequently taken for granted.   Of course
if it can be proved that in a certain instance a written work,
religious in form, has actually no more than a purely literary
significance, there is no more to be said ; and I am not trying
to deny that such instances occur.   I only say that it is not an
assumption which can be made offhand without an inquiry
into the merits of the individual case.

The most ancient surviving testimony to Orphic practice is
in Herodotus, and takes us back therefore to the fifth century
B.C.   It is a reference to the prejudice against introducing
articles of wool into the temples or being buried in them.   This
is an Egyptian custom, says Herodotus, and ' in this they
agree with the practices which are called Orphic and Bacchic,
but are really Egyptian and Pythagorean '.   He adds that there
is a sacred story, or precept (*hieros logos*), on the subject.
This prohibition is probably closely connected with the next
that we hear of, to take the surviving evidence in its chrono-
logical order, that against the eating of animal flesh.   Our
earliest witnesses for this are first Euripides (*Hipp.* 952 f.,
quoted n. 2), and second Plato.   In an important fragment of
Euripides we have another mention of this form of abstention.
It is not there attributed by name to the Orphics, but the
parallel as well as other indications make it clear that the
passage describes many traits of the Orphic religion (pp. 199 f.
below).   It is here that we find one of our earliest references to
the god Zagreus, whom many have thought to deserve above
all others the name of the Orphic god.

Orphism was a way of life, and an ascetic one.   When Plato
mentions as Orphic the custom of abstaining from animal flesh,
he does so in the following words : (He is dividing the men of
the past into two classes, those who both ate animals and
sacrificed them, and those who held that to do either of these
things was impious : of the latter) ' They abstained from

flesh under the impression that it was impious either to eat it or to pollute the altars of the gods with blood ; and so there was appearing among our ancestors the kind of life which is called Orphic, and which keeps to everything that has no life in it and abstains from all living things '. Aristophanes is probably referring to the same thing when he says it was Orpheus who taught us to abstain (the same Greek verb) from bloodshed. He may be thinking of cannibalism, a feature which Orpheus was said, at least by later writers, to have eradicated from primitive life (see n. 5). The two were probably thought of together ; Plato, immediately before the words just quoted, speaks, in the same breath and with reference to the same practices, of animal and human sacrifice, and the ancient sacrifice was generally a meal as well.[6]

As founder of mystery-religions, Orpheus was the first to reveal to men the meaning of rites of initiation (*teletai*). We read of this in both Plato and Aristophanes. (Arist. *Frogs* 1032, Plato, *Rep.* 364e, a passage which suggests that literary authority was made to take the responsibility for the rites.) It is little enough, but quite definite and valuable testimony. In the same passage of Plato we read of a class of priests who went about preaching the way of salvation in the name of Orpheus. To hear these people mentioned by a special name of their own we have to wait until a little later, although we are still in the fourth century B.C. when Theophrastos gives a picture of the Orphic initiators (*Orpheotelestai*), who have the superstitious at their mercy (Theophr. *Char.* 16 = Kern, *test.* 207). Yet Plutarch * tells a story of the encounter of one of them with Leotychidas, son of Ariston, who was king of Sparta in the first quarter of the fifth century (*Apophth. Lacon.* 224e = Kern, *test.* 203). They seem to have been a kind of false prophets such as almost every religion knows, who made a living by painting vivid pictures of the rewards and punishments of the future life and representing their own ritual (to be performed for a consideration) as the only way of securing the former and avoiding the latter.

This less worthy but certainly popular side of Orphism is represented for us again by the charms or incantations (φαρμακά, ἐπῳδαι) of Orpheus, which we may also read of as early as the fifth century. Our authority is Euripides. We have already noticed the ' charm on Thracian tablets ' in the *Alcestis*, and in the *Cyclops* one of the lazy and frightened Satyrs, unwilling

---

* Or his imitator. There is good reason for supposing the *Apophthegmata* to be spurious.

to help Odysseus in the task of driving the burning stake into
the single eye of the giant, exclaims : ' But I know a spell of
Orpheus, a fine one, which will make the brand step up of its
own accord to burn this one-eyed son of Earth ' (Eur. *Cycl.*
646 = Kern, *test.* 83).

This brief summary has included a mention of all the
important places in classical Greek literature where direct
allusion is made to the influence of Orpheus on the popular
mind. It does not represent all the evidence which we shall
take into consideration when we are trying to estimate the
extent of that influence and determine its nature, but it is
well to remember that it is a not unfair representation of the
amount of express contemporary testimony to which, in the
last resort, all our investigations of this period must go back.
As examples from the wider field of evidence, whose value we
shall try to determine later on, may be mentioned a number
of other passages in Plato, certain extracts, eschatological and
otherwise, from the poets, and the inscribed gold plates from
the South Italian graves. The possibility that Orpheus may
at some time have made his presence felt at the Eleusinian
mysteries also is one that can scarcely be dismissed without
discussion ; and with due caution it may be noted that where
a writer like Plato has mentioned a belief or a rite without
adding the information that it is Orphic, the fact is frequently
suggested to us by one of his assiduous commentators in the
first few centuries of the Christian era.

This brings us conveniently to the mention of the writers
of the Graeco-Roman period, among whom allusions to Orphic
rites are frequent. Again much of our information comes from
the Neoplatonists and their opponents, the Christian apologists.
When a Neoplatonist quoted the Orphic writings, it was often
to impart an aroma of antiquity to his doctrines. When we
find ritual referred to it seems most often to be due to one of
two intellectual features of the age. They may be briefly
mentioned here. I am excepting the zeal of the Christian
writer to find material for destructive criticism. The first was
the spirit of study. Writers of the Roman Empire were by no
means pioneers in the field of learning and scholarship. They
had the traditions of the Alexandrian period behind them, and
it is likely that, had not so many of the writers of that period
perished, we should know a great deal more about Greek
religion than we do. The real pioneer of scientific study for its
own sake was Aristotle, but the ideal was pursued with almost
excessive enthusiasm in the libraries of Alexandria, where the

term *grammaticus*, man of letters and learning, first gained a meaning. This ideal, foreign to the spirit of classical Greece, was inherited by men of all nationalities under the Roman Empire, along with so much of the Hellenistic world, and the study of religion had its place among the rest. It is an ideal not usually sought in a period remarkable at the same time for its creative originality, and in this the Alexandrian and Roman ages were not exceptional. In the sphere of religion this lack of originality had effects which do not at first sight seem consistent. In popular life it led to an artificial striving after new religions, not prompted by a true spiritual revival or inspired by a new religious genius, but often imported from other countries simply in a weary search for novelty. On the other hand, the need for a living religion, as well as reaction from the futility of those which were being popularly put forward as substitutes, drove some of the better spirits to an attitude of religious conservatism. This is the second of the intellectual features of the age that I have thought worth mentioning. As the best example of both I would cite the name of Plutarch.

Now it is true that Orphism does not seem to have escaped contamination from the waters of the ubiquitous Orontes. So little hope was there of this that one would be fairly safe in assuming, on the circumstantial evidence alone, that contamination had taken place. Yet the name persisted, and that could not have been without significance. It meant that certain beliefs and ceremonies, as well as certain poems, were being associated in some minds with what was believed to be one of the oldest religious traditions of Hellenism. Evidence for the extinction of the Orphic religion by the time of the Roman Empire is of the sort I have already mentioned (p. 10). Evidence for its continuance is not lacking. Cicero speaks of Orphic rites in the present tense (' a fourth Dionysos . . . in whose honour the Orphic rites are believed to be performed '), a fact which is brought home to us in a significant way by the arrangement of Kern, who prints side by side with the passage a quotation from Johannes Lydos (early sixth century) containing the same comment in exactly the same words, except that Lydos ends his sentence ' in whose honour the Orphic mysteries *used to be* performed '. There was still a trade in the charms and spells of Orpheus in the time of the patriarch Athanasios (early fourth century), who waxes indignant over the old women who ' for twenty obols or a glass of wine will disgorge a spell of Orpheus at you '. This is the sort of thing, he thunders, for which you spurn the Cross of salvation. It is curiously parallel to Plato's denunciation of the wandering priests of his own day.[7]

With the spirit of study was born naturally the desire to travel as a means of acquiring education, and it was this which produced the work of Pausanias on the antiquities of Greece as they appeared to the curious traveller in his own day. His interest was by no means limited to the ancient buildings which he saw, and although sometimes inclined to be credulous he is a mine of information on subjects related to religious, and especially local, cult and ritual, both of his own and of previous ages. Orpheus, *Orphici* and *Orphica* all find scattered mention in his descriptions.

Finally, this outline summary would be inadequate without a reference to the possibility (I shall not call it more at present) that in the collection of hymns in hexameter verse which have come down to us under the name of Orpheus we have documents of genuine popular religion. The evidence for this, as well as the evidence for connecting them with any form of Orphism, belongs to a later stage of the inquiry.

FIG. I.—FROM A BLACK-FIGURED VASE. LYRE-PLAYER AND INSCRIPTION Χαῖρε 'Ορφεῦ.

The foregoing summary has included no mention of the artistic tradition. This is because it is less prominent than the literary in a discussion of either the writings or the religion of Orpheus. In art the emphasis is rather on his own legend and character, although there are one or two monuments whose possible religious significance has been the subject of much discussion. A brief description of our knowledge of Orpheus in art seemed therefore to form most naturally a separate division of the evidence.

He appears on a number of vase-paintings, of which the earliest is black-figure (fig. 1). We see him enchanting by his music, pursued by the enraged Maenads or prophesying in the form of a trunkless head after his death. Most famous are a series of vases from Italy, which show Orpheus playing his lyre in the world of the dead and the presence of the underworld deities. These have provoked much discussion, as possibly throwing light on the eschatological beliefs of the Orphics.   ✱

In sculpture he appears on a metope of the Treasury of ✱ the Sicyonians at Delphi, a work of the sixth century. He is

FIG. 2.

(a) Reverse of a Thracian coin of the beginning of the third century A.D.
(b) Reverse of a coin of Alexandria, time of Antoninus Pius.
(c) Reverse of a Thracian coin of the time of Gordianus Pius (238-244 A.D.).
The relief of pl. 3 may be compared.

standing with his lyre beside the ship *Argo*, on whose expedition legend says that he sailed. At his head his name is written in the form *Orphas*. There exist also copies of a relief of about 400 B.C. showing Orpheus taking farewell of Eurydice, whose right hand is held by Hermes, the guide of souls to the underworld. A statue of the first century B.C. found in Rome gives an early example in art of the animals gathered round Orpheus listening to his song (but cp. ch. iii, n. 14 below). Another example is to be found in our own country, on a Roman mosaic from the Isle of Wight (see frontispiece). According to R. Eisler (*Orpheus*, 1925, p. 97), the mirror reproduced in fig. 9, p. 66 is of the fifth century B.C. Numismatics has a contribution to make, for several cities in regions with which he was associated by legend chose his portrait as a device for their coins (fig. 2).

FIG. 3.—ORPHEUS PLAYING TO THE MUSES AND HERAKLES
From a wall-painting at Pompeii

Other extant artistic monuments to him are of much later date. He is to be found for example on wall-paintings at Pompeii (pl. 1 and fig. 3), and was a favourite subject of early Christian art. The common representation of him sitting playing his lyre surrounded by beasts wild and tame who are lulled into amity by his music suggests naturally the picture of the lion and the lamb lying down together, and he was also taken as the symbol of the Good Shepherd. This was for various reasons, some of which may interest us later. He is therefore a familiar figure in the paintings of the Catacombs. In speaking of Christian art one may mention the enigmatic seal in the Berlin Museum which has carved on it a human figure nailed to a cross (fig. 19). Above the cross are seven stars and a crescent moon, and around and beneath it the words *Orpheos Bakkikos*.

Besides the representations which we can still look at for ourselves, we are allowed to form an idea of others now perished, from the words of those who saw them. Pausanias is our most fruitful source of information. The extant examples of Greek painting, except vase-painting, are necessarily few, but an idea of the content of some of the better-known pictures is to be gained from descriptions in literature. Pausanias gives a detailed account of the most famous of all, the great fresco which Polygnotos in the fifth century painted on the walls of the *lesche* at Delphi. Here was the underworld depicted, and there was Orpheus. His attitude and surroundings are described by Pausanias with great precision of detail. From Pausanias we also hear of statues and images of Orpheus in various parts of Greece. Some were of the primitive form called *xoanon*. Plutarch also speaks of a *xoanon* of Orpheus in Macedonia which was made of cypress-wood.[8]

NOTES TO CHAPTER II

[1] The interesting line of thought suggested by the comment of E. Maass (*Orpheus*, pp. 69-71) on Eur. *Rhes.* 972, that the name of Orpheus is suppressed out of reverence (*übereifrige Ehrfurcht und Scheu*), could hardly be made to explain the rarity of *Orphica*, which are certainly not more frequently met with in ancient literature than Orpheus himself. Possible, but less likely than the explanation offered in the text, is the assumption of intentional secrecy due to persecution or ridicule (which are just arguable from such a passage as Eur. *Hipp.* 953 ff., quoted *infra*, n. 2) or to the esoteric (ἀπόρρητον) character of mystery-religions.

[2] Eur. *Hipp.* 952 ff. = Kern, *test.* 213: ἤδη νυν αὔχει, καὶ δι' ἀψύχων βορᾶς σῖτ' ἐκκαπήλευ, 'Ορφέα τ' ἄνακτ' ἔχων βάκχευε, πολλῶν γραμμάτων τιμῶν καπνούς.

Plato, *Crat.* 402b = O.F. 15 : λέγει δέ που καὶ 'Ο. ὅτι 'Ωκέανος πρῶτος καλλίρροος ἦρξε γάμοιο, 'Ος ῥα κασιγνήτην ὁμομήτορα Τηθὺν ὄπυιεν.

Phil. 66c = O.F. 14 : *Ἑκτη δ' ἐν γενεᾷ, φησὶν 'Ο., καταπαύσατε κόσμον ἀοιδῆς.

Laws 2. 669d = O.F. 11 : ὅσους φησὶν 'Ο. λαχεῖν ὥραν τῆς τέρψιος.

Rep. 2. 364e = *O.F.* 3 : βίβλων δὲ ὅμαδον παρέχονται Μουσαίου καὶ Ὀρφέως.
Laws 8. 829e = *O.F.* 12.
Ion 536b = Kern, *test.* 244 : ἄλλοι ἐξ ἄλλων (*sc.* τῶν ποιητῶν) αὖ ἠρτημένοι εἰσὶ
καὶ ἐνθουσιάζουσιν, οἱ μὲν ἐξ Ὀρφέως κ.τ.λ.
    ³ Eudem. *ap.* Damask., *de prim. princip.* 124 = *O.F.* 28.   Arist. *de. an.* A5
410b28 = *O.F.* 27, where also is the note of Philoponos. For a fuller discussion
of the significance of this note in its context; see below, pp. 58 f.
    ⁴ Eur. *Alc.* 965 ff., to be found with the scholiast in Kern, *test.* 82.
    ⁵ Cp. Plato, *Symp.* 218b = *O.F.* 13 : . . . εἰ τις ἄλλος ἐστὶ βέβηλός τε καὶ
ἄγροικος, πύλας πάνυ μεγάλας τοῖς ὠσὶν ἐπίθεσθε, with the opening of a poem of
Orpheus quoted by Christian writers (*O.F.* 245 f.) : φθέγξομαι οἷς θέμις ἐστί ·
θύρας δ᾽ ἐπίθεσθε βέβηλοι. It is also instructive as an example to trace the
Orphic saying that Zeus is or holds the beginning, the middle and the end of
all, from the time of Plato down to that of the Neoplatonists, *O.F.* 21.
Cp. Kern, *de theogg.* 35, Gruppe, *Suppl.* 703 f. Again, the lines on the subject
of cannibalism quoted by Sextus Empiricus from a poem of Orpheus (and
perhaps referred to by Horace, *A.P.* 391 f.) can be traced back on good
grounds into the fifth century. See the parallels in *O.F.* 292, and *cf.* Maass,
Orph. p. 77, n. 104. The discussion of this question belongs to chapter iv.
    ⁶ Herod. 2. 81 = Kern, *test.* 216 : οὐ μέντοι ἔς γε τὰ ἱρὰ (Aegyptiorum) ἐσφέρεται
εἰρίνεα οὐδὲ συγκαταθάπτεταί σφι · οὐ γὰρ ὅσιον. ὁμολογέουσι δὲ ταῦτα τοῖς Ὀρφικοῖσι
καλεομένοισι καὶ Βακχικοῖσι, ἐοῦσι δὲ Αἰγυπτίοισι καὶ Πυθαγορείοισι · οὐδὲ γὰρ τούτων
τῶν ὀργίων μετέχοντα ὅσιον ἐστι ἐν εἰρινίοισι εἵμασι ταφθῆναι. ἔστι δὲ περὶ αὐτῶν ἱρὸς
λόγος λεγόμενος. Abstention from meat, Eur. *ap.* Porphyr. *de abstin.* 4, p. 261 ;
Nauck = fr. 472 Nauck ; Plato, *Laws* 6. 782c = Kern, *test.* 212 ; Arist. *Frogs*
1032 = Kern, *test.* 90.
    ⁷ Cic. *de nat. deor.* 3, Ch. xxiii, and Joh. Lyd. *de mens.* 4. 51 = Kern,
test. 94. Athanas. *cod. Reg.* 1993, f. 317 = Migne PG 26. 1320 = Kern, *test.*
154. Cf. also Achilles Tatius (end of third century A.D., Schmidt-Stählin,
*Gesch. Gr. Litt.*⁶ 2. 1047) in Arat. *Phaen.* = *O.F.* p. 150 : ἧς δόξης ἔχονται οἱ τὰ Ὀρφικὰ
μυστήρια τελοῦντες.
    ⁸ Individual references will be given later, but most of those that are
required for the representations of Orpheus in art which I have mentioned
will be found in Kern on pages 43 and 44.
    It is possible that the *xoana* might have a bearing on future research into
the origin of Orpheus, and the hint is perhaps worth throwing out. The question
of the nature of *xoana* is interesting, and Stanley Casson (*Technique of Early
Greek Sculpture*, Oxford 1933, pp. 50 ff.) suggests the possibility that they are
Minoan or Mycenean cult-figures which have survived the influx of invading
races. They often existed, as he points out, in very inaccessible places, in
particular the more remote and hidden parts of the Peloponnese. Anyone
thinking on these lines would of course have to satisfy himself that images
believed to represent Orpheus were in fact intended to do so by their maker.
The unrealistic shape of *xoana* probably precluded the presence of attributes,
which when they occurred are likely to have been later additions (Casson,
p. 57). Account would also be taken of the general evidence for the survival
of Minoan-Mycenean cults themselves, as it is set forth by M. P. Nilsson in
The Minoan-Mycenean Religion and its Survival in Greek Religion (Lund 1927).

CHAPTER III

ORPHEUS AND HIS STORY

WE must not expect to find the legend of Orpheus told as a simple and single story, without variations and without inconsistencies. That would be surprising, if we consider the different people who have told it, the variety of the motives which prompted them, the remoteness of the times to which they believed their stories to refer, and the ever-present doubt whether even the basis of those stories, the one-time existence of their hero, is a historical fact or not. Even persons whose existence is incontestable, but whose fortune it has been to fire in some way, religious or otherwise, the imagination of their generation, have frequently in the course of time had a string of quite legendary stories associated with their name. With varying degrees of certainty these can be detached and the historical kernel at their centre laid bare. Here we have not only the remoteness and elusiveness of the hero to contend with. There is another consideration which makes it inevitable that the web of his character and his story should be well tangled by the time it reaches us. Many have become the subject of legend because, like Mahomet, they were the founders of a great religion ; others because, like Alexander or our own King Arthur, they have appealed to the imagination of poets and artists. The appeal of Orpheus, on the other hand, has always been much more universal than that of most other great figures of legend. Some revered him as a religious founder. Others, at all times, have seen in the magic of his playing, in his gentleness and his tragic death a rich material for the exercise of their artistic skill. Considered as such, his story can be severed from all connexion with religion, and moreover the artist is thinking in every case of his own composition, his poem or his vase, not of the preservation of a consistent tradition or the aching head of a twentieth-century mythologist. Thus besides the inconsistencies caused by the existence of two kinds of tradition, distinguished by their motives (religious or

artistic), there are more to be expected within the limits of each
division. It is not only the artist who adapts a tale to suit his
own purposes. I have said that religion is of the individual,
and each man will see in his prophet that which his own temperament leads him to expect from religion. Orpheus has
played many parts in his time, according to the religious outlook of the author who was writing about him and according to
whether that author happened to be his admirer or (like so many
of the Christian apologists) his bitter enemy.

Besides the poets like Ovid, and besides the true believers,
there is a third class of those who, like Strabo or Pausanias,
were actuated by a spirit of honest inquiry. They must be
given the credit that is due to good intentions at least.

We may say that Thrace was the home of Orpheus with the
knowledge that we are speaking of him as he was conceived to
be by every normal Greek or Roman from the fifth century B.C.
onwards. One or two of our informants leave some doubt
whether they thought his true origin was Thracian or Macedonian, for they speak of him as having been born or as living
in the neighbourhood of Olympos ; but this, though an interesting detail, is a matter of little consequence to history. We may
be content with the words of Karl Robert (*Heldensage*, i. p. 398) :
' Even if it is doubtful whether Thrace was his home, in any
case he was localized there very early, and after that passed
for a Thracian throughout the whole of antiquity '.[1]

His date was generally supposed in antiquity to lie in the
heroic age, several generations before Homer ; and considering
his reputation as the Father of Lays, it is not surprising that
we find him represented by some of the Greek historians to be
Homer's direct ancestor (Kern, *testt.* 7-9). Thus if we are
asking ourselves what kind of knowledge the ancients themselves were likely to possess about his history, we should consider him, in respect of time, on a par with a figure like
Herakles. This was an antiquity sufficiently remote to allow
plenty of room for speculation. Herodotus even gives it as
his opinion that Hesiod and Homer, living about 400 years
before his own time, were the first to give the Greeks a theogony ;
' and the poets who are said to have lived before them are in
my opinion later ' (Hdt. 2. 53 = Kern, *test.* 10). The reason
for this opinion is probably to be found in the observation of
a scholiast that no poem of the age of Homer's heroes has
been preserved, ' and that too though Homer himself introduces
poets, Phemios and Demodokos, and though Orpheus, Musaios
and Linos are said to have lived before him. In spite of this

it is true that nothing earlier than Homer's poetry has been preserved to subsequent ages save a name. We have no poem earlier than the *Iliad* and the *Odyssey*'. (Kern, *test.* 11.) It may well have been a feeling that the poems current in his time under the name of Orpheus must be later than Homer, which gave Herodotus his belief that Orpheus himself was later, without leading him to the even more critical conclusion that the ancient Thracian had nothing to do with them at all.

Orpheus was the son of a Muse, Kalliope being the one most often mentioned as his mother. His father is sometimes said to be Apollo, more often Oiagros, a Thracian river-god.[2] (Authorities in Kern, *testt.* 22-26.) Of his birth there are no stories, except for a passing reference at the end of the Orphic *Argonautika* to the marriage of his mother with Oiagros having taken place in a cave in Thrace : ' Thence I made all speed to snowy Thrace, to the land of the Leibethrians, my own fatherland ; and I entered the far-famed cave, where my mother conceived me on the bed of great-hearted Oiagros '.

We are told much about his character and influence, but little of the incidents of his life. The only stories of this kind are the death of Eurydice, and his journey to the shades to fetch her, the slender tradition of a sojourn in Egypt, the voyage of the Argonauts, and the various accounts of the events which led to his death and the miraculous events which followed it.

References to the expedition of Jason and the Argonauts in search of the Golden Fleece are frequent in Greek literature from Homer and Hesiod onwards.[3] Yet they remain isolated and unsatisfying references until the time of Pindar, who gives us the first attempt at a connected story and incidentally the first mention of Orpheus as a participant. A little earlier than Pindar (sixth century) is the sculptured representation of Orpheus with the Argo which is at Delphi (pl. 2). Apart ✱ from Pindar's lyrical account, which simply forms an episode in the body of a poem whose object is the glorification of a winner in the Pythian games, we have to rely largely on epic poems of a later date, the *Argonautika* of Apollonios Rhodios (*c.* 240 B.C.), Valerius Flaccus (*c.* A.D. 80) and Orpheus, the anonymous poem, perhaps as late as the fourth century A.D., which tells in the first person of the adventures of Orpheus with the heroes. These with occasional references in some of the later prose authors make up the sum of our authorities for his activities on the voyage.

We may ask ourselves briefly here of what sort these activities were, and in what ways he made himself of use to the expedition. This was something that exercised the minds of antiquity too. 'It is a question', says the scholiast, commenting on the introduction of Orpheus in Apollonios (Kern, *test.* 5), 'why a weakling like Orpheus sailed with the heroes. It was because Cheiron with his gift of prophecy told them that if they took Orpheus they would be able to pass the Sirens.' This passage gives an indication which side of his character comes to the fore in the narratives of the expedition. It is by the magic power of his song that he earns his place among the heroes. The uses of this gift are many and various. At the outset he is called on to assist in settling a quarrel by making the participants forget their wrath in listening to his singing (Ap. 1. 492 ff.). This story of Apollonios is left out by the Orphic *Argonautika*, which makes up for the omission by telling how Argo at first resisted all the efforts of the heroes to drag her into the water, until Jason signed to Orpheus to take up his lyre, and how she then slid into the sea of her own accord (*O.A.* 245 ff.). His actual office was that of *Keleustes*, singer of the chanties which gave the rowers their time ; but his music, as we have seen, could do much more than that. There is one story that he calmed a stormy sea by its power (Philostratos, *Im.* 2. 15), and according to the Orphic account he successfully charmed the Clashing Rocks while the Argo passed through (*O.A.* 680 ff.). By the same power, when Kolchis was reached, he called down sleep upon the eyes of the dragon which guarded the Fleece (*O.A.* 991 ff.).

We find also that he was not only a musician, who could work magic by his music, but in all religious matters the leading spirit of the expedition. This is naturally most obvious in the Orphic version of the story. There we find him performing the inaugural sacrifice before the start, persuading the Argonauts to become initiated at Samothrace into the mysteries for which the island was famous, sacrificing after the accidental killing of King Kyzikos, performing purificatory rites at Malea on the return journey to free the heroes from the curse which King Aietes had laid upon them, and finally, his last act before returning to his home in Thrace, staying behind alone to offer sacrifice at Tainaron (believed to be one of the entrances to Hades) to the rulers of the world below. These are incidents of the Orphic version, but he is prominent in the other stories too. It is from others that we learn how he saved the company in a storm by praying to the Dioskuroi, gods of mariners, because he was the only one who had been initiated in their mysteries (Diodoros, 4. 43. 1), how at lake Tritonis he bade them take the tripod of Apollo and offer it to the gods of the place if they wanted a safe return (Ap. Rhod. 4. 1547), and how when Jason dedicated the Argo at Corinth, it was Orpheus who composed the dedication-hymn (Dio. Chrys. 37. 15 = *O.F.* 290). Worth noticing too is the subject of the song which he sings in Apollonios to calm the spirits of the quarrellers, and that which in the Orphic *Argonautika* he sings in the home of the Centaur Cheiron. In both his song is of the origin of all things, of the birth of the world and the gods.

The story of the wife of Orpheus is bound up with his descent to the world of the dead, and so lets us see him in one of his most interesting and important aspects. The secrets of Hades were in his possession. He could tell his followers what the fate of their souls would be, and how they should behave to make it the best possible. He had shown himself capable of melting the hearts of the powers below, and might be expected to intercede again on their own behalf if they lived the pure life according to his precepts. That was the important thing. The reason which once took him there was secondary.

It is not so easy to decide whether it is secondary in time also. Our evidence for the beliefs about Orpheus before the sixth century is so scanty that it is difficult to judge with certainty whether he was originally an underworld spirit, to whom was later attached the romantic story of the descent in search of a lost wife, or a follower and imitator of Apollo, who took a nymph for wife and for whom the journey to Hades to fetch her was an adventure into unfamiliar surroundings, though he later became the patron of a religion which laid great stress on the life after death and so had this purely personal errand magnified into a reason for knowing all about the realms of the dead and possessing peculiar powers as adviser and intercessor. The latter view suggests a further possibility, that the whole story of the descent may have been attached to one who was originally a follower of Apollo only when he had been appropriated as founder by the aforementioned mystical sects. I hope to show later that this is the most reasonable supposition. There certainly seems to have been, in every age, enough of the Apolline in Orpheus to support the opinion that he belonged at first to the sunny, open-air religion of the Hellenes, a priest of Apollo bearing in himself many of the attributes of the god he served ; it was later that he met

Dionysos and became the expounder of a sacramental religion
and of the life hereafter.   For the present we had better
continue the legend.

In the description which Pausanias gives of the underworld
scenes painted by Polygnotos, there is no mention of Eurydice
being present to explain the situation (Paus. 10. 30. 6 = Kern,
test. 69).   It may be that in the eyes of some, his followers,
Orpheus had an established position there, as it were in his
own right.   No particular errand had to be supposed to account
for his presence, for by the time of Polygnotos he was certainly
the patron of a religion in which all the emphasis was laid on
eschatological dogma.   If Pausanias is to be trusted (and there
is no reason to doubt that, in describing things he had seen
himself, he was a careful, as he was a detailed, recorder), this
is our earliest piece of evidence for the presence of Orpheus
among the dead.   Yet it is of course late enough to make it
certain that the conjugal motive, even if it were a later addition
to the story, must have been added long before then.   Its
omission in the painting at Delphi cannot be due to its not
having yet been invented.   The famous relief of Orpheus and
Eurydice (pl. 3) belongs at latest to the beginning of the fourth
century.   Both Euripides in the fifth century and Plato in the
next speak of the descent of Orpheus to fetch his wife.   Neither
of them mentions her by name, and our next witness, the
Alexandrian poet Hermesianax, calls her Agriope, a name (' wild-
eyed ' or   wild-voiced ') which suits well the Thracian nymph or
Dryad whom he might naturally be supposed to have married
(Kern, *test.* 61).   Eurydice (' wide-ruling ') we first hear of in
literature in the lament for Bion (first century B.C., Kern, *test.*
62), though one or two of the South Italian vases, which furnish
after Hermesianax the next evidence of Orpheus in the underworld, put her in the picture with her name written beside her.
Most of them, however, like Polygnotos, show an Orpheus who
might well be supposed to be at home in the underworld, without the necessity of any conjugal errand to account for his
presence.

After the Alexandrians the Romans, and it is only in them,
in poets like Virgil and Ovid, that we get the theme elaborated
into a complete and circumstantial story.   So suddenly does
this seem to happen, and so many are the Alexandrian models
of later poets which are lost to us, that Gruppe (in Roscher's
Lexicon, 3. 1159) supposes a particular poem of late Alexandrian
date, now lost, to have fixed the legend in the form in which
it burgeoned in Roman times.[4]

The wife of Orpheus, whatever her name, was probably a Thracian nymph-or Dryad whose love he won by the sweetness of his music.[5] She was killed by the bite of a snake, which according to Virgil's account she trod on while trying to escape the attentions of an unwanted lover, Aristaeus. Orpheus, after wandering disconsolate and turning vainly to his lyre for solace, descended at last through the gate at Tainaron to the realm of Pluto. There he began to play, and the shades crowded round him as birds to a leafy tree at evening or in time of storm. The Eumenides and Kerberos himself were softened, and Ixion's wheel stood still. Thus he obtained his prayer to lead Eurydice ✱ back to the upper air once more. It is possible that in one version of the story he was successful in this. The reference in the *Alcestis* (357 = Kern, *test.* 59) suggests success rather than failure, and Hermesianax definitely affirms it. Plato, in a dialogue full of fancies which it would be absurd to regard as simply taken over from existing mythology, speaks of his failure, but not in the familiar form. He says that the gods sent Orpheus back empty-handed from Hades, showing him only a phantom of his wife, not giving him the woman herself, for the reason that he was only a poor-spirited musician trying to get down to Hades alive instead of having the courage to join his beloved in the proper way, by dying (*Symp.* 179d = Kern, *test.* 60). That at least has the merit of being a reason, and not simply a tabu like the prohibition against looking back which is familiar to all. The element of tabu might seem at first to argue a primitive origin for this part of the story, but not only did the belief in injunctions of this sort never die out ; it had a vigorous recrudescence in the superstitious Hellenistic and Graeco-Roman ages. The story of failure through looking back, therefore, may well be an addition by no means universally adopted until Alexandrian times, if not invented by the Alexandrians. It was at all events a story well suited for exploitation in the romantic and pathetic spirit which they were the first to bring into literary favour, as has been amply proved by its treatment in subsequent ages. A variation on it is that the tabu was one against speech (*Culex,* 291).[6] In Ovid's story Orpheus made an attempt to return, but found the way barred by Charon.

After the loss of his wife, and the period of mourning which Virgil and Ovid describe him as passing by the banks of the Strymon, Orpheus shunned entirely the company of women, and so did not avoid the report which so often attaches to those who live celibate lives, of having another outlet for his passions.   He became for some the originator of homosexual love.   Mention of this occurs in an Alexandrian poet (Phanokles = Kern, *test.* 77), and though Virgil does not repeat it, Ovid characteristically inserts three pretty lines on the subject.

About the cause of his death there are various accounts, though about the manner of it there is no doubt what was the most popular belief.   Pausanias, indeed, trying to give, in addition to his own opinion, some account of the ' many untrue things ' which the Greeks believe, mentions a story of suicide after the loss of his wife.⁷   Another story is referred to in the epitaph on the tomb of Orpheus which was shown at the town of Dion in Macedonia.   According to this he was a victim of the thunderbolt of Zeus (n. 11 below).   Pausanias mentions this story too, and adds a statement of the offence.   Orpheus gave trouble in much the same way as Prometheus, for ' in his mysteries he taught men things unknown to them before'.   Strabo accounts for the tragedy by a conspiracy among those of his countrymen who did not accept his teachings.   (Quoted at end of chapter, p. 61.)

Strabo, for all we know, may have been historically correct with his picture of a religious reformer who got a little above himself and whose excessive zeal or ambition met with the common fate ;   but nevertheless his version was not the one most commonly believed.   In the established tradition it is the women of Thrace who make him their victim.   On the reason for this there is some divergence of opinion.   The dramatic version of Aeschylus, which is the earliest that we know of, told how Orpheus was a devoted worshipper of Apollo the Sun-god (Kern, *test.* 113).   It was his custom to go up to Mount Pangaion first thing every morning in order to greet the sun.   In this he incurred the anger of Dionysos, who was winning Thrace to his own wild religion, and Dionysos sent against him his savage women converts, the Maenads.   These tore him in pieces, as in their orgies they were accustomed to dismember animals, and as in the *Bacchæ* of Euripides they tear Pentheus (Kern, *test.* 113).   Virgil seems to follow Aeschylus in describing the murder as an act of Bacchic frenzy :

> Inter sacra deum nocturnique orgia Bacchi
> Discerptum latos iuvenem sparsere per agros,

but he prefers to account for their fury in another way.   It was caused by the disdain with which he treated them after the death of Eurydice.   Konon mentions that he refused to initiate them into his mysteries (*test.* 115, p. 61 below), and

Pausanias that he enticed their husbands away from them. Phanokles gives jealousy as the reason, and Ovid, as we noticed, follows him.

Among our earliest evidence for the legend of Orpheus' death are the representations of it on vase-paintings, which go back to the fifth century B.C.[8] On these Orpheus is never depicted as torn to pieces (it has been suggested (Robert, *Heldens.* I, p. 404, n. 3) that this may have been for artistic reasons), but the infuriated women are provided with a large assortment of weapons for the deed. Sometimes only one attacker is shown, sometimes more. Some are armed with spears, some with axes, some with stones ; others have snatched up in haste more homely implements, sickles, pestles, even spits. This seems to imply the story of natural feminine wrath rather than of divine command, which is better suited by making him the victim in a Bacchic orgy. Virgil can combine the two with the freedom of a great poet, but Phanokles, who tells the first story, makes the women accomplish their vengeance with swords, not with the frenzied hands of Maenads. That the vase-painters had in mind, as motive for the

Fig. 4.—THE DEATH OF ORPHEUS.
Red-figured vase.

murder, the enticement of the men and indifference to the feelings of their women is also shown by several examples where the theme of the murder is combined with another, that of Orpheus charming Thracian warriors with his lyre [9] (see figs. 4 and 5 and pl. 4).

The late mythographical writer to whom we owe the reference to Aeschylus' play about the death of Orpheus, adds that he was buried by the Muses, his mother and her sisters. Killed as he was in Thrace, they may have buried him near the spot or taken the remains to the neighbourhood of Mount

Olympos (see n. 1). Pausanias says that the tomb was near the town of Leibethra on Olympos. An oracle of Dionysos told the Leibethrians that if they allowed the bones of Orpheus to see the sun, the city would be destroyed ὑπὸ συός. Not

FIG. 5.—DESIGN ON A RED-FIGURED VASE IN NAPLES.
(*Upper half*) Women preparing to attack him.
(*Lower half*) Orpheus playing to Thracian men.

unnaturally, they made light of the idea, and one day it happened that the tomb was overturned and broken ; whereupon the Σύς, one of the torrents of Olympos, flooded and washed away their city. After this the inhabitants of the neighbouring city of Dion gathered the bones and gave them fresh burial.

At Dion the tomb was shown as late as the time of Pausanias himself : ' If you leave Dion by the road towards the mountain, when you have gone twenty stades you see on your right a column with a stone urn set upon it. According to the local story, the urn contains the bones of Orpheus.' Pausanias, though he knows of the story that Orpheus was struck down by a thunderbolt, says that the tale told locally around Dion is that of the murderous women, whom the inhabitants believe to have carried out their crime in their own neighbourhood.[10] Pausanias was a traveller who visited the places he wrote about, so it is unlikely that the inscription on the tomb was in reality that quoted by Diogenes Laertios, which contains a reference to the thunderbolt of Zeus.[11] According to the account of Konon (first cent. B:C. ; Kern, *test.* 115, and cp. Harrison, *Prol.*[3] 467 ff.), Orpheus was buried by the Thracians.

More firmly established was the claim of the Lesbians to possess at least the most important parts of Orpheus and to have erected a shrine to him on their island. The form of the legend with which Milton shows himself familiar in *Lycidas* was also the most widely spread in antiquity. The head and ✱ the lyre of Orpheus were thrown into the river Hebros, whence they floated across to Lesbos off the Asiatic coast, the head singing as it went. The Lesbians buried the head, as Phanokles says in his poem and also a third century writer of *paradoxa*, quoting the work of a local historian. Lucian tells us that the temple of Bakchos on the island in his time was said to have been built over the spot where the head was buried. The lyre, tradition said, had been dedicated in the temple of Apollo, ' where it was preserved for a long time '. Philostratos (third cent. A.D.) tells how the head attained wide fame as a giver of oracles. This in his time was only a tradition of the past. His story is that the prophesying was suppressed by Apollo himself. Finding that his privilege was being infringed, the god stood over the head as it spoke, and said, ' Cease from the things that are mine, for I have borne enough with thy singing ' (Phanokles = Kern, *test.* 77 ; Antigonos of Karystos Paradoxographos = *test.* 130 ; Lucian, *adv. indoct.* 109 ff. = *test.* 118 ; Philostratos, life of Apollonios, 4. 14 = *test.* 134 *fin.*). According to the account of Konon (p. 62 below), the head was found at the mouth of the river Meles, by Smyrna. This is interesting when we consider, as we shall later on, how many indications there are to direct the mind to Anatolia when thinking of things Orphic.

Ancient art provides a number of interesting illustrations of this myth. An Etruscan bronze mirror from a tomb at Chiusi

(Clusium), whose style points to its having been made at the end of the fourth century B.C., shows the head of Orpheus looking up from the ground with parted lips (fig. 6, and see the discussion in *Mon. d. Linc.* 30, 1925, 542 ff.). I mention this first because it is the only example with an inscription. Beside the head is written (to be read upside-down, and from right to left) ΥΡΦΕ. A number of people stand around listening, of whom the seated youth on the right is taking down the oracles on tablets. (The Etruscan inscription on the tablets has unfortunately still to be deciphered.) With this is to be compared the design on a red-figured *Kylix* of the fifth century (fig. 7, from G. Minervini in *Bull. Arch. Nap.* 6 (1858), pl. 4). Again we have the head prophesying with parted lips, and a seated youth busily writing down its responses on tablets. On the right stands Apollo, and although his attitude has been variously interpreted, it is most naturally taken as referring to the story of his disapproval. Throwing out his hand with a commanding gesture, he is saying, ' Cease from the things that are mine ! ' The reverse of the vase shows the finding of Orpheus' lyre by two Lesbian women. Through the kindness of Professor Cook I am able to publish for the first time a vase in his possession which shows a similar scene (pl. 5). This is a red-figured *hydria*, noted by Professor Cook as Attic work of the last quarter of the fifth century. We see here the head in the same attitude of prophecy, with Apollo standing over it, his head wreathed with bay, and a lyre and a long bay-branch in his hands. The identification of the women on this vase is more difficult. She on the right is probably the Pythia, who by the delicate gesture of her right hand seems to sympathize with the hero and to deprecate the stern measures which Apollo intends to take. The woman on the left stands closely wrapped from head to foot in *chiton* and *himation*. Her hair falls about her shoulders and she wears a look of great distress. She might be the mother of Orpheus were it not that she does not correspond in type to any of the Muses. Perhaps Professor Cook is right in wanting to identify her as the ghost of Eurydice. There is no mythological point in her presence by the oracle on Lesbos, but another female figure was needed to complete the painter's pattern, and while he was thinking of Orpheus, Eurydice is the one who would most naturally come into his mind.

The oracle of the head of Orpheus is also the subject of the carvings on a number of ancient gems, which are discussed by A. Furtwängler in *Antike Gemmen*, vol. 3, 245 ff. That

FIG. 6.—BRONZE MIRROR
FROM CHIUSI

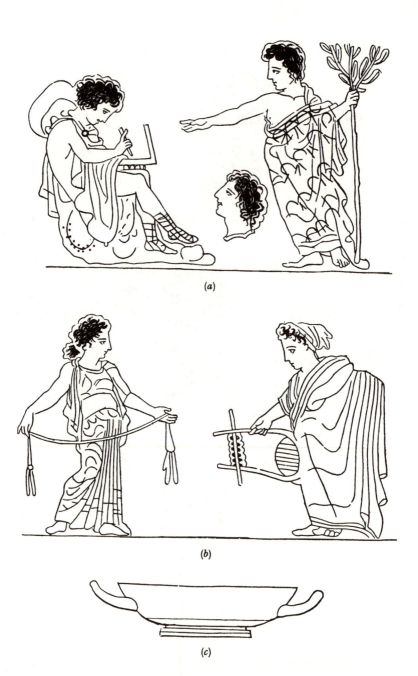

(a)

(b)

(c)

Fig. 7.—Designs from a Red-figured *Kylix*

reproduced in fig. 8 is again from Professor Cook's collection. It is a carving in sliced chalcedony, of Hellenistic date, and resembles those illustrated on pl. 20. 53 = pl. 22. 5 in vol. 1 of Furtwängler's book.[12]

The individuality of Orpheus refuses to be submerged. That is one certain conclusion from a study of the complex character with which the ancient evidence presents us. There are times when he seems on the point of becoming merged with the lyre-playing god Apollo, and others when, thinking of his death perhaps, we wonder whether he is only an incarnation of the Thracian Dionysos. Always he emerges as something different, not quite like either of the gods, and definitely more than a mere abstraction of certain of their qualities. The complexity of his character, indeed, has sometimes caused scholars, both ancient and modern, to suppose that he is not a single personality but two or more. The first thing to do is to try to describe the character itself.

FIG. 8.
HELLENISTIC GEM
IN THE COLLEC-
TION OF PROF.
A. B. COOK.
(Scale 2 : 1.)

Some sides of this character we have already become acquainted with in describing the sources of our knowledge and in telling the story of Orpheus. One at least is so well known that little need be said about it. Orpheus is first and foremost the musician, with magic in his notes. Aeschylus knew him as the man who charmed all nature with his singing (*Agam.* 1629 f.). In this he was not alone among the heroes of legend, which contained also figures like Linos (sometimes represented as master of Orpheus, Diod. 3. 67. 2 = Kern, *test.* 43), Musaios (usually his pupil, see Kern, *testt.* 166 ff.), Thamyris of Thrace and Amphion of Thebes; but just as Apollo had no serious rival among the gods, though Hermes might have invented the lyre, so Orpheus among the heroes was supreme in his art. (Cp. Athenaios 14, p. 632c = Kern, *test.* 46. In *testt.* 46 ff. are collected passages which testify to the musical powers of Orpheus.)

Closely allied with music in the Greek mind was magic, and for some the name of Orpheus was associated with charms, spells and incantations. For at least a thousand years it was a name to conjure with. (Cp. pp. 17 f., 19, above.)

Orpheus was the prophet of a particular type of mystery-religion, a modification of the mysteries of Dionysos. His teachings were embodied in sacred writings. Such was the belief in his antiquity that, coupled with his reputation as a poet, it made some regard him as the inventor of writing, while others thought of him as so old that they could not believe he wrote down his own poems (Kern, *testt.* 123 [Alkidamas], 32 [Aelian]). So strong was the religious purpose of these writings that to a mind like Plato's it sometimes seemed wrong to class them with poetry at all. The passage where he draws this distinction is interesting. It is *Protagoras* 316d = Kern, *test.* 92 : ' In my opinion the didactic art is an ancient one, but those among the old writers who practised it were afraid of the odium of the name and so took refuge in a disguise. For this purpose some, like Homer, Hesiod and Simonides, used poetry, others religious rites and prophecies, I mean the school of Orpheus and Musaios.'

The influence of Orpheus was always on the side of civilisation and the arts of peace. In personal character he is never a hero in the modern sense. His outstanding quality is a gentleness amounting at times to softness. (Cp. pp. 28, 31, above.) From warlike attributes he is entirely free, differing in this from the archer-god whom in some other ways he so closely resembles. The atmosphere of calm which surrounds him differs strangely too from the normal habits of the wild mountain-god whose religion he adopted. Music may excite as well as soothe, but the cymbals and tympana of a Thracian or Phrygian orgy seem at first to have little to do with the sweet tones of Orpheus' lyre. The power of the lyre was to soften the hearts of warriors and turn their thoughts to peace, just as it could tame the wildest of the beasts. Not only animals but men gathered round to listen to the song. In the vase-paintings which show this scene, the expressions on the faces of the listeners leave no doubt of the effect which the music is having (pl. 6). This is reflected in the statement of a later author that Orpheus ' by his playing and singing won over the Greeks, changed the hearts of barbarians and tamed wild beasts ' (Ps.-Kallisth. I. 42, 6. 7 = Kern, *test.* 144). He made men give up cannibalistic feasts, an achievement which in Graeco-Roman times was attributed to many gods without much discrimination ; but for Orpheus it can be traced back to the fifth century. (See ch. ii, n. 5.) He taught men also the arts of agriculture and in this way inclined their natures towards peace and gentleness. Themistios, who lived in the first century of the Byzantine Empire, but was a zealous reader of Plato and Aristotle, writes : ' Even the initiations and rites of Orpheus were not unconnected with the art of husbandry. That is in fact the explanation of the myth when it describes him as charming and softening the hearts of all. The cultivated fruits which husbandry offers us have a civilising effect on human nature in general and on the habits of beasts ; and the animal passions in our hearts it excises and renders harmless ' (Them. *Or.* 30, 349*b* = Kern, *test.* 112).

Orpheus was not regarded as a god, but as a hero, in the sense of some one who could claim close kinship with the gods, in virtue of which he had certain superhuman powers, but who had to live the ordinary span of life and die like any other mortal. The tomb would be regarded as a sacred spot (there would in all probability be more than one), and a cult of the dead hero be found there. In general such a cult is quite clearly distinguished from the cult of a god. The cult of saints forms a serviceable parallel. Orpheus was probably never, certainly scarcely ever worshipped as a god.[13] He was, however, essentially a prophet and high priest of religion. This makes the question of his relations to the gods a particularly interesting one. Moreover, these relations appear a little strange if looked at in detail.

We can be quite clear on what I should say was the most important point to one who wants to know the facts about classical Greek religion. To the question ' who was the god of the Orphic religion ? ' there can be but one answer—Dionysos. Orpheus was a religious founder, and the religion he founded was a species of the Bacchic. This remains a fair answer in spite of the qualifications with which it is at once necessary to safeguard it. First of all the remarks at the beginning of the last chapter must not be forgotten. Other gods not only existed (and the writings of Orpheus included a theogony), but were owed their due of prayer and sacrifice ; but Dionysos was the centre. Secondly, Dionysos, like many other deities, was *Polyonymos*, worshipped under many names, and also with many different epithets before his name. The names and epithets of a god, though sometimes obscure, may reveal many things, *e.g.* the aspects of life that are his particular province, or the fact that among some people he has usurped the cult once paid to another deity in the same place. In the course of time he can accumulate a mass of these titles which leave no doubt of his composite origin, without necessarily losing unity in the eyes of his worshippers.

Certainly from the time of Herodotus the Orphic religion was Bacchic. Yet we have seen that Orpheus himself is far from being a Bacchic figure. If he preached the religion of

3

Dionysos he at the same time reformed it. Tradition puts his home in the country from which Dionysos-worship spread through Greece, but there are stories which suggest that the relations between the two were not always peaceful. The only legend which shows a striking parallel between the two is the story that Orpheus was killed by being torn in pieces just as Dionysos was said to have been torn by the Titans and as his symbol was torn by his worshippers during the orgies of his religion, and this was connected in the minds of the Greeks with the idea of bitter enmity between the two ; for tradition said that the dismemberment of Orpheus was executed at the commands of Dionysos. This incident reminds us that Orpheus was not only unlike Dionysos but in many respects similar to and closely connected with another god, Apollo. In the legend it was jealousy at being neglected in favour of Apollo that drove Dionysos to the murder. In himself Orpheus has many Apolline characteristics, his music, his calm and civilised air. A Roman statue of late Republican date found on the Esquiline Hill (probably but not certainly from the monument of a guild of flute-players) shows him for once as a completely Apolline type, a nude youth crowned with bay playing the lyre (pl. 7). The statue might well be taken for Apollo were it not for the animals and birds which in the well-known way crowd around him and even perch on his knee.[14] It is worthy of mention that Apollo's music too was said to gather wild beasts around him. See the choral ode to Apollo in Euripides, *Alc.* 578 ff. This brings the two figures into very close connexion indeed. Besides the Apolline side of his nature must be mentioned his frequent connexion with Apollo in myth. Other instances are easily found besides the legend used by Aeschylus of his incurring the anger of Dionysos by assiduous worship of Helios-Apollo. The tradition that Apollo was his father was not the prevailing one in the classical age, but in Pindar he is ' sent by Apollo '.[15] The story of Apollo, jealous of his rights, putting a stop to the successful career of the head of Orpheus as giver of oracles in Lesbos, argues the sort of rivalry which is evidence of very closely related functions. The gifts of poet and seer were near allies, as the history of the Latin word *vates* shows, and Orpheus too was a prophet, a talent which always belonged *par excellence* to Apollo. As ' companion of Apollo ' ('Απόλλωνος ἑταῖρον) he appears on the metrical inscription copied from a basis seen in Thrace.[16]

It is well to bear in mind, before we leave the question, that these two gods, in spite of the persistent antagonism of their characters and of the religious spirit which each represented, were not always separated in the minds of the Greek people, nor their cults kept strictly apart. This is seen best at the most famous of all seats of Greek cult, at Delphi. Among the gods whom Apollo was supposed to have superseded at the shrine Dionysos is mentioned, and the Delphic Oracle was instrumental in spreading the worship of Dionysos. This alliance meant a modification for both types of worship, though they were too radically different ever to become merged.[17] This did not prevent the flexible mind of the Greek from associating the two in cult and so, by a step easier for them than for us, addressing the two at the moment as one. A late (A.D.) oratorical writer says, addressing Apollo : ' at Delphi they honour thee with double title, calling thee Apollo and Dionysos'; but we are not compelled to go beyond the classical age to find an example. A fragment of Euripides contains the invocation : ' Lord Bakchos to whom the bay is dear, Paian Apollo, sweet musician'.[18] This union was the work of Delphi. The Orphics never had the power to bring it about, but it was their purpose to foster it, and in their syncretistic literature they identified the two gods by giving out that both alike were Helios, the Sun. Helios = supreme god = Dionysos = Apollo (cp. Kern, Orpheus, 7). So at least the later writers say. Olympiodoros (O.F. 212) speaks of ' Helios, who according to Orpheus has much in common with Dionysos through the medium of Apollo ', and according to Proklos (O.F. 172) ' Orpheus makes Helios very much the same as Apollo, and worships the fellowship of these gods '.. Helios and Dionysos are identified in Orphic lines (O.F. 236, 239).

In view of the interest in life after death which is such a prominent feature of Orphic religion, and the legend of the descent of Orpheus to the shades, one would expect to find a close connexion between him and the underworld gods, Pluto and Persephone. In fact, however, his relations with them seem to have been purely external. He intercedes and has influence with them, but there is no evidence for a belief that he was their priest or representative, nor are there traits in his character which might make us suspect that he was at one time identical with Pluto. Nothing, that is to say, suggests the intimate relations, difficult to disentangle and appraise, which unite him with Dionysos and Apollo. Gruppe (Roscher 3. 1108) can mention only one or two instances of a cult connexion at places like Tainaron, which might even be the result of the legend of the descent. Apart from this there are only the

theories that his name might be connected with ὄρφνη, ' darkness ' (one of many suggested etymologies), and that Eurydice,
the wide-ruling, might be a title of Persephone. Both are
doubtful.[19]

What were the original religious connexions of Orpheus
in prehistoric Thrace, it may well be thought impossible to
decide. Most probable is the theory which makes him a figure
of the Apolline religion, priest or in some other way satellite
of the god. Later he, or those who followed or believed in
him, embraced the established cult of Thrace, that of Dionysos.
In doing so they modified and civilised it considerably by the
addition of some Apolline features and some which were original and can only be called Orphic. There will be more to say
about this sequence of events before we close the chapter.

The character of Apollo in historical times gives him the
right before all others to be called the typical god of the Greeks.
We may say that his history too gives him additional claim to
the title, since whenever and wherever the Greeks may have
found him, he was in all probability with them when, some
time in the second millennium B.C., they came from the North
to overrun the original stock of the Peninsula.[20] Compared
with his cult, that of Dionysos, in its pan-Hellenic form, was
a later intrusion. I say in its pan-Hellenic form, for it is
difficult to penetrate far enough into the mists of antiquity to
say how long it was known in Greek lands or to what people
it originally belonged. Whether or not the theory is right
which sees its origin in East Boiotia and Euboia, from which it
was carried to Thrace by early colonists,[21] it was in Thrace
that it first began to gain more than local importance and from
Thrace that it started to make its conquest of Greece in historical
times, so that in the eyes of the historical Greeks Thrace was
its place of origin. If therefore it were a question of the religion
of Greece proper, the view that the Orphic religion resulted
from a toning-down of Dionysiac cult by its contact with that
of Apollo would seem all the more probable ; it would fit in
with the picture of a wild and barbarous religion capturing the
fancy of a more civilized people but being inevitably remodelled
to suit their more advanced, and in many ways different
culture. Arguments of this sort fall to the ground if we follow
Orpheus back, as a religious founder, to his original home in
Thrace. There, as the Greeks saw it, Dionysos too was at
home, and it is at least possible that he was established there
early enough to exclude such a sequence of events as took place
in historical Greece. Thus the question whether Dionysos or

Apollo is the younger god cannot, so far as our knowledge goes, either support or disprove the theory of an Apolline origin for Orpheus. It yet remains a likely view that, as stated by E. Gerhard,[22] Orpheus was originally a figure in a purely Apolline cult which kept itself free from contamination in spite of the orgiastic Bacchic religion of neighbouring Thracian tribes. The later identification of Orphic with Dionysiac religion Gerhard regards as the natural result of the original *Tiefsinn* of the Orphic and the ever-increasing supremacy of the Dionysiac. The religion which was gaining such a general hold on the Greek mind would naturally ally itself with the best and highest elements in older teaching.

If one thinks of Orpheus as having been originally a Hellene, and transformed into a Thracian by a tradition which was only gaining ground in the fifth century B.C., it becomes yet easier and more natural to believe in his primary connexion with Apollo. Those who do so think of him bring forward as evidence the vases of the fifth century which show him in Greek dress, and which emphasize that dress, as Kern (*Orph.* p. 15) points out, by showing it in contrast to the Thracian costume of the men who stand around him [23] (pl. 6). Let us draw our own conclusions from the same facts. Orpheus is in Greek dress but with Thracians surrounding him. Where then is Orpheus ? In Thrace. The vases, it is rightly pointed out to us, are valuable as illustrations of an earlier belief about Orpheus than that reflected in the paintings and literature which depict him as a Thracian ; but we must make use of all they tell us. Orpheus is neither a Thracian himself nor a Hellene living quietly at home. He is a Hellene living in Thrace. How he got there the vases do not tell us, but the fact of his presence is much, especially when we consider how good a parallel it forms to the story in the tragedy of Aeschylus. On the vases we see him surrounded by foreign men, tc whom his appearance affords the sharpest contrast, though his music is successful in transforming their possibly hostile intentions. In the play we saw him coming into conflict with the god of these people, the Thracian Dionysos, whose religion, though it may have cost him his life, he succeeded, as subsequent history shows, in taming as he tamed the spirits of his worshippers in the paintings. It is difficult to rid the mind of this picture of Orpheus as in origin the missionary of the Hellenic spirit in a land whose religion, like the rest of its civilization, was barbarous and untamed. His activity lay in Thrace, and the religion whose possibilities for reform he seized on and exploited was

Thracian. Is it now surprising if later tradition made him
into a Thracian himself ? To go further back than I have here
tried to do is to enter the realm of pure conjecture. Orpheus,
or (to remind ourselves that we are not committed to a belief
in his existence) the spirit which that name represents, may
have come northwards with colonists from Thessaly or Boiotia ;
or perhaps he was an invader who, coming down from the
original country of the Hellenes, stayed in Thrace to propagate
the religious ideas which fired his brain as in his northern
home he worshipped the god of a people from yet further north,
the Hyperborean Apollo. There can be little profit in further
speculation on this subject.

Little though it is, we must not ignore the evidence that the
alliance between Dionysiac and Apolline cult existed from an
early date. In the *Odyssey*, the honey-sweet wine with which
Odysseus drugged the Cyclops had been given to him as a
present by one Maron, at Ismaros in Thrace, the later Maroneia.
This Maron is called priest of Apollo by Homer, and described
as living in Apollo's grove (*Od.* 9. 197 ff.). Yet even here he is
the dispenser of godlike wine, and he whom Homer names as
his father, Euanthes, is said by the scholiast on the passage
to have been son of Dionysos. Elsewhere, *e.g.* in Euripides
(*Cyclops*, 141 ff.), Maron himself is son of Dionysos and nursling
of Silenos. Macrobius, in a chapter full of interesting quotations designed to prove the identity of the two gods (1. 18),
mentions that they were worshipped as one in Thrace.

So far we have been proceeding on the tacit assumption
that because Orpheus himself came originally from Thrace,
and in prehistoric times, the same is true of the phenomenon
known as the Orphic religion. This is not necessarily correct.
The Orphic religion, whose features are to be described in the
following chapters, does not seem to have existed before the
sixth century, and makes its first appearance in South Italy or
Athens. This makes very attractive the view, so well set forth
by Professor Boulanger, that Orpheus existed long before
Orphism. In Italy in the sixth century there were sects
practising a form of mystery-religion which had much in
common with Pythagorean beliefs. ' One can easily see the
reasons which led the pre-Orphic *thiasoi* of Southern Italy to
seek the patronage of Orpheus. Instead of deifying the founder
of the sect as the Pythagoreans did, they wanted to give their
doctrine the appearance of centuries-old antiquity. And they
could not have chosen a more venerable authority than that of
the inspired theologian, who was believed to be much older

than Homer and happened to possess at that.time, by a singular combination, the double authority of antiquity and of living presence ' (A. Boulanger, *Orphée*, 1925, pp. 30 f.). We shall perhaps find more definite reasons for his adoption as well. (Cp. pp. 219 f. below.)

No one would suggest that a figure like Orpheus had originally no connexion with religion of any sort, and this opinion of Professor Boulanger accords well with the theory of an Apolline origin for him. If then we sum up what we have been saying, we get something which is consistent in itself and does not come into violent conflict with the ancient evidence. Orpheus was a Thracian hero closely associated with the cult of Apollo, and was therefore in his early days in conflict with the pre-eminently Thracian worship of Dionysos, an essentially different type of religion. He was thought of as a figure of peace and calm, the maker of a music with magically soothing properties.[24] As a singer he was also a *theologos*, that is to say, his song was of things divine, the gods and the universe. He was adopted as founder and teacher by mystical sects probably early in the sixth century. The leaders of these sects sometimes did not hesitate to take the ancient name themselves and compose religious poems in it, openly and with no intention of deceiving. Sometimes the sacred writings were believed to have been really the work of the adopted founder of the sect. The gods worshipped by these Italian devotees were chthonian, and the religion in Greece at that time became identified with the worship of the chthonian Dionysos. There is plenty of evidence for the interaction of Apolline and Dionysiac religion before then, and some of the work of reconciliation may well have been attributed already to one who was so well-suited to act as mediator, one who, though priest and prophet of Apollo, had in the first place always had a streak of mysticism in him (such as would be better satisfied by a purified Dionysiac religion than by Apollo), and secondly was thought to be familiar with Dionysos because a dweller in his country. The relations of Athens with South Italy were close, and it is scarcely possible to give an opinion on a point of detail like whether the first Orphic religion arose in the one or the other (see pp. 216 f. below). We may say then, with Aristotle in one of his rare fits of modesty, that to make this our hypothesis is in accordance with good reason, though the words ' necessarily true ' may be left for mightier brains to pronounce. Of course if we believe the Orphic religion to have arisen far from Thrace and much later in time than Orpheus himself, we are not thereby denying the admixture of Thracian elements in Orphic beliefs.   Even if those who adopted him had at the time no connexion with the land of his origin, they could not first of all have taken Orpheus for their patron and Dionysos for their god had their religion been antagonistic to the Thracian, nor could they, having done so, have prevented the infiltration of more and more Thracian elements into their religion in succeeding centuries.

Some may think that this picture has too much an air of cold-blooded deliberation, of committee-work in fact, to be historically probable ; I mean the picture of certain chthonian sects adopting Dionysos as their god but purifying and exalting his orgiastic religion by the introduction of Orpheus as high priest and mediator.   They may be reminded of the practice in the early Church of taking over pagan festivals and legalising them by attaching them to saints, and of the motives which led to this procedure.   In an age when the worship of Dionysos was spreading like wildfire through Greece, it would naturally have particular attractions for the adherents of already existing chthonian cults.   The similarities were obvious, but at the same time the excesses of a Dionysiac orgy may well have been repellent to some sensitive spirits among the older sects.   Seeing the impossibility of making their followers give up the new god, they would then have sought to turn this devotion into better channels by accepting it and making the calm and civilized Orpheus into the prophet of Dionysos himself.   Supposing the events to be as I have imagined, this is the sort of motive which must have led to his adoption.

We can scarcely reflect on the evidence for the story and character of Orpheus which has been set down, without having somewhere lurking in our minds the question of his possible historical existence.   This is a question which will always be decided by the temperament of the individual reader rather than by strict deduction from unmistakable ancient information.   The sources of our knowledge of his age and country are too dark and troubled : but a decision had better take account of what information there is, and we may try to state the case impartially so far as it emerges from evidence already considered.   In favour of his historical existence is his individuality. I hope I have shown what I feel sure is true, that he refuses to be merged in the nature of any of the known gods, Apollo, Dionysos, or even, I should dare to add, the gods of the underworld, in such a way as to suggest that he was merely a projection into humanity of any one of them. It might be said indeed that this complexity of character, which makes it impossible to pin him down and identify him with any one god although he seems to share in the attributes of many, goes so far as to deserve the name, not simply of complexity, but, to put it bluntly, of scrappiness. No human being could have had this character, and he was perhaps, instead of being a weaker reflection of one god, a hypostasis of qualities taken from several. We should of course admit at once that the character of Orpheus grew like a snowball with the passage of the centuries. Much had been added to it by the classical age, when he was the recognized founder of a highly developed religion.[25] When in the course of time that religion was subjected to all the influences of a wider Hellenism, Orpheus adapted himself to the change. Even in the earliest form of his character which we know, the magical element is prominent. This, however, should not deter us from believing in his humanity if we want to. If the attribution of magical gifts were really a deterrent, we should have to disbelieve in the real existence of Pythagoras, and not only of him but also of Plato and Virgil.

In the story of Orpheus which I have outlined there is one element which has not received much attention from commentators. Little has ever been said on the subject of Orpheus' relations with women. One might call it the misogynistic element in the Orpheus-legend. That active misogynism was a part of Orpheus' character, and that he was not simply a passive and innocent victim of the mad frenzy of Maenads, is emphasized in many ways by legends attested for us from the Alexandrian age. There are strong suggestions in the vase-paintings that the same legends were current in the fifth century. I have referred to them above: the choice of men only to form his audience, and the homely assortment of weapons with which the women attack him, making it clear that he is not taking the part of victim in a Bacchic orgy. The simple story demanded of Aeschylus by the requirements of tragedy may not have been the only one at his disposal. It does not of course exclude the other, since a refusal to worship the Thracian Dionysos, with the rites which that worship demanded, is a very natural corollary of anti-feminism; and one can then understand all the better the willingness of the women to become the instruments of divine vengeance.

This personal antagonism of Orpheus to women, and their resentment of it leading to his violent death, were represented as the ground for practices current in historical times. In

Konon's version of the legend, Orpheus showed his dislike by his refusal to allow them to participate in the rites he taught, and at the end Konon mentions that entry into the sacred precinct round the shrine of Orpheus is still strictly forbidden ✱ to women (p. 62 below). Similarly the practice of tattooing among Thracian women was said to be the punishment inflicted on them by their husbands for the murder of Orpheus. To Plutarch indeed it does occur that to protract the punishment thus far shows a certain lack of proportion : ' We can find no praise for the Thracians, that they brand their wives to this day to avenge Orpheus '.[26]

We may compare this with other examples of respect shown to a hero's prejudices in later years. Rohde (*Psyche*, Eng. trans., p. 134, and n. 107 on p. 153) mentions several, *e.g.* no woman was allowed to approach the sacred grove or the grave of the hero Eunostos at Tanagra. Rohde rightly stresses the fact that heroes are most frequently historical persons, and this evidence of characteristics shared with other heroes might be used as an argument in favour of the real humanity of Orpheus.

As such, however, it would be difficult to defend. Not only does the example of the tattooing show how easily stories of this sort may be purely aetiological, but the institution of exclusive rites for one sex only, and the division of the sexes into two hostile camps, is a well-known fact of primitive life, of which the misogynism of Orpheus is no doubt a later reflection. Nevertheless, the tradition does present peculiar features (absent for instance from the myth of Pentheus), which to some extent weaken its aetiological character. This character would be much stronger if women had been actually excluded from Orphic rites in historical times, but, if we may trust Plutarch (*Alexander*, ch. ii), they took a keen part in these rites as in all types of Dionysiac religion.

The survey of Orpheus' character in isolation, as we have so far made it, is not the only evidence to be taken into account in deciding this question, which may be given some further discussion before we close the chapter. There are two classes of testimony, first our own deductions from what is known of his story and character, and secondly the opinions of ancient authors on the point. With regard to the first, the classificatory methods of mythologists seem to have limited the possibilities between which we have to choose when trying to determine the nature of a figure of legend. It will probably be wisest to limit ourselves to the divisions they have discovered. Not that way lies the danger that the hard and fast methods of the classifier may lead to error, but in ignoring the possibility that the same figure may at a certain date belong to several classes at once. If we say that it is not the character of *x* at a certain date that we are seeking, but the *origin* of *x*, the answer may be that, if we go back to his origin, there just is no such person as the *x* whom we know, say, from a fifth-century tragedy and later testimony. Follow up that part of the story which says that he slew a dragon and afterwards married the princess whose life he saved by the feat, and you cry triumphantly that he is the invention of popular imagination, a creature of pure *Märchen*. But perhaps there is some action attributed to the hero, say a realistic stroke of policy, which has no parallel in such tales. Ah, then he is after all a historical prince of olden times ; or this fact may be pointed to in some other way, for instance by archaeological evidence. There was then a historical person called *x*. True enough, we say convinced, but this is nevertheless not a complete answer to the question, into what class of legendary figure falls the *x* we know, the hero of Sophocles' play, the person of whom Plato tells a story. We must be more explicit about the threads which are there interwoven.

This may prove in the present case to have been a digression, but even a brief and tentative trespass into these dangerous regions is the better for some statement of policy. For the present we need only note that a Greek hero will probably fall into one or more of three classes. He may have arisen from the imagination of simple minds, making up stories for their children or each other, a creation of fairy tale, usually known to mythologists by its more general German name of *Märchen*. Secondly, he may have been a god whom time has degraded to the heroic plane, or thirdly he may be a historical character. The stories told of him may be similarly divided each into one or more of several classes. They may be fragments of otherwise lost history, fairy tales, or aetiological myths. This last term is used in at least two senses not always made distinct. The fact to be explained may be a rite or custom, practised from time immemorial for long forgotten reasons and so accounted for in historical times by a subsequently invented myth ; or the myth may be the result of man's early curiosity about the universe. Some phenomenon of weather or season has to be explained, and this is done in an unscientific and imaginative age by the invention of a story with personifications of the forces involved. Again a hero or a story may be invented because some family or city, or perhaps religious sect, having attained a position of influence, wishes to attach to itself the nobility of an ancient ancestry. The hero may be created, and his name forged out of their own, or he may be borrowed from elsewhere, and a myth be invented to establish the connexion.

In recent centuries, theories about the original character of Greek legendary figures have followed each other like waves, and each wave when at its height tended to swallow every hero and every myth without sufficient discrimination, though there were many which did not deserve to be included simply because the theory was the favourite one at the time. If we look at the present state of these studies, it is probably fair to say that the days of the indiscriminate application of sweeping theories are over. The present age has seen too many waves disintegrate on the firm shore of common sense, and proceeds—the only reasonable way—to judge each case on its merits, not by neglecting previous theories but by treating each one as a possibility to be considered, not a certainty.

This brief mention of the possibilities which exist on general grounds is enough to make it clear that some are much more prominent than others in the present case. There is little element of *Märchen* in the legends of Orpheus, nor would one expect an origin in *Märchen* for, nor an accumulation of *Märchen* motifs around, a figure possessing the close and influential connexion with religion which he always, to our knowledge, had. If Professor Rose is right in regarding the loss of Eurydice by looking back as 'a very old tale', we would have in that a folk story based on the primitive belief in tabu ; but that is for one thing an unimportant detail, not generally agreed on, in the story of Orpheus, and for another, I have shown reasons for believing, with others, that it is a late addition. These reasons at least make it uncertain that it is early. (See p. 31 above and n. 6.) As for the journey to Hades itself, that, if it is old (and similar journeys are well attested from primitive peoples), is an instance not of *Märchen* but of sincerely held belief. In a primitive society, those who told, or had told of them, that they had visited the realm of the dead, firmly believed in the reality of their journey, which was in their eyes one to another part of the physical globe. But these descents (καταβάσεις) were fashionable at every period, and the ascription of one to a hero when he had become the patron of a religion whose appeal lay in its eschatology makes one at least suspicious of the antiquity of that part of his story.

The conjugal motive for the exploit may make us think of old tales, but these tales were available also to the seventh or sixth century story-teller who wanted a model, and the fact itself is one ascribed to Pythagoras.

If anyone chooses to believe that the story of Eurydice contains an element of *Märchen* (and though I have shown myself inclined to believe that it does not, I cannot see that the word ' prove ' has any place in this discussion), he has not of course shown thereby that the origin of famous Orpheus is to be sought in that quarter. There are many more characteristic stories of him than that, and none of them, so far as I can see, resembles folk-tale. Is Orpheus then a faded god ? If so, he will probably be one of the spirits of the life-giving vegetation which springs from the earth. The two possibilities may be discussed as one, since all the evidence for his having been a god at all is at the same time evidence for his having been a god of vegetation. In discussing the faded-god hypothesis, we are fortunate in having, amid the many border-line cases which always haunt these fields of investigation, one certain instance which may be used for purposes of comparison. No one would deny that Hyakinthos was the deity of vegetation belonging to a certain locality in pre-Greek times. It is needless to go over the evidence for this again, but one or two relevant points may be mentioned. His death was the most prominent feature in his legend, as the death of a vegetation-deity must always be. His tomb was shown as being beneath the altar of Apollo at Amyklai, and since his cult as a god had been superseded on the coming of the Greeks by that of Apollo, his legend was adapted to fit this by a later myth which made Apollo responsible for his death. The death of Orpheus, too, is a highly important, perhaps the most important, part of his story, and moreover according to a widely spread version it was caused by Dionysos, god of the vine and frequently of the fruits of the earth in general. In the same version too (the version of Aeschylus) this death took the form of a ritual act, suggesting that the story is aetiological, in which case Orpheus would be the god himself, torn to pieces in his own rites according to the savage form of communion to which the name *omophagia* bears witness. Orpheus would then be a form of Dionysos himself, or (to use our comparison with Hyakinthos) a pre-Greek deity of similar function whose place Dionysos usurped, this piece of history being represented in the myth by the attribution of his death (the original and essential part of the story) to the instigation of the usurping god.

On the other side we may say, first, that the comparison with Hyakinthos does not take us very far. Both died, and it is necessary for every vegetation-god to die. What we should have to prove, though, is not this but its converse, that every one who dies is a vegetation-god, and death is rather too common a phenomenon for that. Also, it must be admitted that the obviously non-Greek name of Hyakinthos was one of the first things to attract the attention of scholars, and has always been given first place among the evidence for his origin ; and the name of Orpheus is not obviously non-Greek. Many experimenters in etymology might be quoted as having proved to their own satisfaction that it is Greek.[27] I need scarcely return here to what I have emphasised all along, that Orpheus is a much fuller, more many-sided character than Hyakinthos. More important is the point that Hyakinthos was attached in classical times to one god only. His cult was replaced by that of Apollo, and being thus degraded to the rank of hero he became the companion of Apollo, killed by him in error. Orpheus too was the companion or worshipper of Apollo, from the time of Aeschylus at least to that of an inscription of perhaps the second century A.D. I have expressed my opinion that this connexion is an essential and original one, an opinion based on his thoroughly Apolline nature. There is indeed nothing Dionysiac about him, save his connexion with a particular (not the ordinary Dionysiac) type of mystery religion, and this suggests that he took over the religion of Dionysos from outside, because he saw possibilities of modelling it on new lines. Yet it was to Dionysos and not to Apollo that (I repeat, according to one version) he owed his death.

Thus the simple sequence of one-time god replaced by an invader's cult, and sinking to the position of hero in attendance on the newcomer, while his death, originally one of his essential myths as vegetation-deity, becomes attributed to his successor, is pretty thoroughly broken by the presence of a different god putting in a strong claim to even closer kinship with the hero. It was in fact jealousy at being neglected for Apollo that drove Dionysos to the deed. While we are meditating on this, it naturally recurs to the mind that there is another version of his death besides the one which attributes it to the agency of Dionysos. There is the story, which I have related, of the women of Thrace acting on their own account, angered by the indifference, or active hostility, which Orpheus showed towards them, and his success in enticing their men away from them. This is the version of Phanokles the Alexandrian, Konon,

Virgil and Ovid, and one of those recorded by the antiquarian Pausanias. I have given my grounds for believing that it is also the one which the fifth-century vase-painters depicted. Even the killing at Dionysos' instigation showed Orpheus as the apostle of a hostile religion (not killed in error, as Hyakinthos by Apollo), and this other tale of feminine wrath bears less obviously the marks of an aetiological story, if we except the method of killing by tearing to pieces, which appears in Konon and Virgil's poem, but not in Phanokles or on the vase-paintings. At a time when both versions existed, this *sparagmos* might well have been taken from the other, which gave Dionysos as the author of the murder, or from the common equation of Thracian women and Maenads. There are many stories of women being driven mad by Dionysos from the same motive of resistance to his cult. Thus for example he drove Agave to murder unwittingly her own son Pentheus, maddened the daughters of Minyas, and the women of Argos who were cured by the seer Melampous. We may notice one thing about these stories : it is generally agreed that they are comparatively late among the myths of Dionysos, reflecting indeed the historical fact of the resistance offered to his cult as it spread through Greece. This gives further encouragement to believe, if there are already other grounds for doing so, that the myth which makes Dionysos cause the death of Orpheus through the agency of frenzied women may be later than that which makes the women act on their own initiative.

It will perhaps be expected that at this point something more will be said about the chthonian aspect of Orpheus. When I said that all the evidence for regarding him as a god pointed at the same time to his having been a god of vegetation, I implied the identification of vegetable and chthonian deities. The primitive mind, having postulated a spirit of the fruits of the earth, was quick to see a connexion between that spirit and the underworld kingdom to which not only fruits but also men when their time comes are taken by death. The corn spirit dies each year and is reborn with the new shoots in spring. He comes up from the earth into the sunlight, and it is natural therefore to suppose that having died in the autumn he returns to spend the winter in the subterranean regions whence he sprang and will spring again. This then is the common if not the universal belief. (He may be thought of as not dead, even temporarily, but lying bound in a distant wintry land.) The phenomena of birth, death and rebirth take place before our eyes in the flowering and withering of plants in their seasons, and so when man feels a desire to know more about these mysteries, and derive therefrom some hope and comfort for himself, the gods of the cornfield and the vine become also the patrons of those religions which seek to probe the secrets of the after-life. In this way Kore-Persephone, Dionysos, Pluto, Adonis, Osiris get their double rôles, and it is ever so. When therefore I spoke of the possibility of Orpheus being a god of vegetation, I meant a spirit of the earth and the regions beneath it, with all that that implies, but have so far only spoken of one of the two aspects which this character would give him. About the other aspect I have not much to say at this point. That I do not think Orpheus likely to have been an underworld god must have emerged clearly from the picture I have given of him. One or two isolated points have already been mentioned, the connexion of his name with ὀρφνη, which is, to say the least of it, not without a rival among etymologies, the Apolline cast of his character, and the impression (perhaps too personal) that his relations with the underworld gods have always been markedly external. I would add the probability that his close connexion with the underworld did not exist before he became the patron of sixth-century mystics. This is a view which can only be justified by the evidence distributed through this and other chapters.

It remains to refer again to the remaining hypothesis, that there once existed, in prehistoric Thrace, a person called Orpheus. What evidence for this we may draw from his own character as painted in the legends, has already been pointed out. It is permissible to add that any reasons we may have succeeded in producing against the supposition that he is in origin a faded god have a certain value as negative evidence for believing in the only likely alternative. To me it seems probable that it is the true one, but what we may say about this shadowy figure beyond the fact of his existence is even more doubtful than that fact itself. Probabilities are that he was a Greek, that he was a bard and musician, that he was officially a servant of Apollo but distinguished from other worshippers of the god, as indeed from most of his fellow-men, by a type of quiet mysticism rare in any age. In this form of religion he tried to interest the men, and the men only, of Thrace. Judgment on this view I am content to leave to others. I have tried to give a likely account in a consistent form, mainly in order to give anyone who may wish to form his own opinion something definite with which to compare it. But the important thing is this. Apart from the uncertainty of the results, let no one think that, even if they are infallibly correct, we have discovered ' the origin of Orpheus'. The question we

have been discussing may have an interest of its own,_ but the
Orpheus whom we know and are interested in is, among other
things, the man who wrote this or that cosmogonical poem
which Plato and many a one after him could quote line for line,
or again the man who went down to Hades and charmed Persephone by his playing ; and whatever else may be uncertain in
this subject, I am ready to assert with confidence that no living
inhabitant of prehistoric Thrace ever did either of these things.*

In one of the remoter parts of Asia Minor, near what was once
the southern boundary of the Phrygians, there is a warm spring
flanked by a Hittite monument, and known to the Turks as
Plato's Spring. The reason for the name is that it was at this
spot, according to Arab legend, that Plato succeeded in stopping
the Flood by making the waters run underground. Perhaps the
relations between the Athenian philosopher and the magician
of the Arabs are comparable to those between the historical
musician and priest (whose existence, alas ! unlike that of the
philosopher, must possibly remain an undemonstrable postulate
of our own) and the magical player in Hades. Perhaps they are
closer, perhaps more distant. Speculation on this point is a
pleasant and possibly fruitful occupation.

We turn to our second class of testimony, the opinions of
ancient authors. There was little scientific study of mythology
before the Alexandrian age. Of the researches of later antiquity
a great many are lost, and some of those which have survived
are marred by obvious bias, some by a conspicuous lack of
the scientific spirit. Too many of the later authors had their
own axe to grind, and others were hampered by their own
lack of discriminating powers. There was one notable exception
to the lack of scientific students of the subject in pre-Alexandrian
times. The mind which founded scientific logic and biology did
not fail to include even mythology in its illimitable range.
Amid the many treatises on the subject which time has
swallowed up, few, surely, are so much to be regretted as
the first book of Aristotle's *de philosophia*. The *de philosophia* was a general and systematic exposition of philosophical
questions, and the first book contained a history of philosophy and pre-philosophical speculation, taking the subject as

---

* The moral which I am trying to apply is essentially that which has been
put by Professor Cornford in these words : ' That the content of every divine,
semi-divine, or heroic figure is, either wholly or in part, a projection from the mind
of the group which carries on the cult appears to me an obvious fact. The only
question in any particular case is whether there was, or was not, a single important
historic person to serve as a core round which the projection could crystallize.'

4

far as Plato. It was Aristotle's habit to introduce a subject
by a survey of the achievements of previous thinkers. Thus at
the beginning of the *Metaphysics* we find him reviewing his predecessors in Greek philosophy from Thales downwards. The
difference in the *de philosophia* was that he did not stop at the
beginnings of scientific Greek thought, with just a passing reference
to the older tribe of *theologoi*, or at the most a mention of the
Egyptians as the inventors of mathematics. The few quotations
that we have show that he discussed in some detail the ancient
forerunners of philosophy, both Greek and Oriental. He was not
here content with a vague expression like ' those who first, in
far off times, long before our own generation . . .' (cp. p. 12
above). The scientist in him wished to decide which were the
oldest of Egyptian priests and Persian Magi, and when he comes
to the ancient theological poets of Greece itself, there is something
quite reminiscent of modern criticism in his note on the authenticity of the Orphic poems. In view of the interest which must
attach to Aristotle's opinion on the historical existence of Orpheus,
no excuse is needed for appending a short discussion of the two
passages which promise to let us know what it was. These are :
Cicero, *de natura deorum*, 1. 38. 108, and the note of Philoponos
to Aristotle's *de anima*, 1. 5. 410*b*28, printed by Kern as *test*. 13
and fr. 27 = *test*. 188.

The passage in Cicero is simple and its sense is plain. *Orpheum
poetam docet Aristoteles nunquam fuisse*—' Aristotle says that the
poet Orpheus never existed '. I cannot understand how some
have taken the passage to mean ' Aristotle says that Orpheus
never was a poet ', since to do this involves complete neglect of the
context. The speaker is contesting the Epicurean theory that
both perception and thought take place as a result of the effluence
from objects of their images, these images being themselves
material, composed of fine atoms thrown off by the actual objects.
How then, he asks among other questions, can I form a mental
picture of some one who never existed ? Yet Orpheus, or as you
would have it, his image, often enters my mind.

I believe, though the evidence is only circumstantial, that
Cicero is using the same portion of the *de philosophia* which
Philoponos expressly says that he is quoting. This makes it even
more important than it would otherwise be that there should be
no discrepancy between the two passages. The words of Philoponos are these :

λεγομένοις (sc. Ὀρφικοῖς ἔπεσι) εἶπεν, ἐπεὶ μὴ δοκεῖ Ὀρφέως εἶναι
τὰ ἔπη, ὡς καὶ αὐτὸς ἐν τοῖς περὶ φιλοσοφίας λέγει · αὐτοῦ μὲν γάρ
εἰσι τὰ δόγματα, ταῦτα δέ φησιν Ὀνομάκριτον ἐν ἔπεσι κατατεῖναι.

I read for the moment φησιν with Rose (Arist. fr. 7). If these
words are translated as if the whole sentence αὐτοῦ—κατατεῖναι
were to be taken as coming from the *de philosophia*, I do not see
how it could possibly be reconciled with the statement in Cicero.
Yet this is how they are usually taken, and E. Gerhard (*über
Orpheus*, n. 2) says that it is ' no contradiction of the denial of
Orpheus' existence as a historical person if he has laid stress on
his legendary personality in order to draw attention to his teaching
as distinguished from the revival of it '. This does not reassure
me, but I see no reason why we should take the words as Aristotle's.
To do so is to translate the sentence as if it ran αὐτοῦ μὲν γάρ
φησιν εἶναι τὰ δόγματα, ταῦτα δὲ 'Ονομάκριτον ἐν ἔπεσι κατατεῖναι.
It is part of the duty of a commentator to add words of his own
in amplification of the meaning of his author. Philoponos as
good as tells us that that is what he has done here, and we are
not bound to believe that he and Aristotle were in agreement
about the existence of Orpheus. He mentions it as a fact which
is generally believed, as in Neoplatonist circles it was. We may
then translate : ' He says so-called, because it is unlikely that the
verses are by Orpheus, as he himself says in the *de philosophia*.
The doctrines are his, of course, but it was Onomakritos, said
Aristotle, who put them into verse.' If we read φασιν in the
last clause with Kern, the question becomes even easier, since we
need not suppose that any of the sentence αὐτοῦ—κατατεῖναι is to
be attributed to Aristotle.

I should like to close this chapter by setting down, without
further comment, some of the accounts of Orpheus given by the
scholars of the ancient world. These are they whom I mentioned
at the beginning as a third class of writer, neither poets nor
religious devotees, but men actuated by a spirit of honest inquiry,
whose intention was to attain objective truth :—
    1. Paus. 9. 30. 4 ff., in Kern, *testt.* 142, 93, 116, 123, 120.
The passage comes at the end of a description of the statuary
in the sanctuary of the Muses on Helikon.
    ' Orpheus is represented with Telete standing at his side, and
around him are carved stone and bronze animals listening to his
song. Among many wrong beliefs which the Greeks hold, is
the one that Orpheus was the son of Kalliope the Muse, not of
the daughter of Pieros, that the animals were drawn entranced
towards his music, and that he went down alive into Hades and
begged for his wife from the gods below. Now in my opinion
Orpheus was one who surpassed those who went before him in the
composition of verses, and reached a position of great 'power

owing to the belief that he had discovered how to initiate into communion with the gods, how to purify from sin, to cure diseases and to avert divine vengeance. They say that the wives of the Thracians plotted his death, because he persuaded their husbands to follow him in his roamings, but that they refrained from fear of the men until they had filled themselves with wine, when they carried out the impious deed. Others say that it was through being struck by a thunderbolt of the god that Orpheus met his death, and the reason for this was the doctrine which he taught to men in the mysteries, things which they had not heard before. Yet others declare that after the death of his wife he went for her sake to Aornon in Thesprotis, where there was of old an oracle of the dead. Thinking that Eurydice's soul was following him, and then turning back and losing her, he took his own life in his grief.'

2. (a) Before translating the first short passage from Diodoros (first cent. B.C.), I cannot resist quoting what he says two chapters before as he first approaches the subject of Dionysos. It is interesting to see how ancient are the difficulties with which we are wrestling, and the passage lets us know the treatment he proposed to give his subject.

Diod. 3. 62 (in Kern, O.F. 301). ' The ancient mythographers and poets in writing about Dionysos contradict one another frequently, and have left us many portentous stories. This makes it difficult to give a clear account of his birth and his acts. Some say there was one Dionysos, others that there were three, others demonstrate that he never was born in human form nor existed at all, but consider that Dionysos is just the gift of wine. For ourselves, we shall try to run briefly over the chief points of each account.'

In relating the myths of Dionysos, he comes to Orpheus in this way (3. 65). The story he is telling is one which he introduces with the words ' mythology tells that . . .' Dionysos, who is treated as a human being, is invading Europe from Asia by the Hellespont. Lykurgos, king of Thrace, plots against him and the plot is revealed to him by ' one of the natives, whose name was Charops.[28] . . . After this, in return for the service rendered him by Charops, Dionysos is said to have given him the kingdom of Thrace and taught him the ceremonies and rites of initiation.' (What follows is in Kern, test. 23.) ' The myth goes on that Oiagros, the son of Charops, inherited the kingdom and had with it the mystic initiation ceremonies handed down to him, which later Orpheus the son of Oiagros learned from his father. Orpheus, being by training and natural gifts a quite exceptional character, made many changes in the rites, and for this reason the initiations which owed their origin to Dionysos came to be called Orphic.'

(b) Diod. 4. 25. The name of Orpheus has occurred in connexion with a story of Herakles, that he became an initiate at Eleusis at the time when Musaios, son of Orpheus, was presiding over the ceremonies. From there I translate, noting that whereas the last passage was in indirect speech, as being only the relation of a myth, this one is in direct speech.

'Since I have mentioned Orpheus, it will not be inappropriate to make a digression and say a little about him. He was the son of Oiagros, a Thracian by race, in culture, music and poetry easily the first of those whose memory has been preserved; he composed poetry of a merit which astonishes, distinguished by its exceptionally melodious quality. His reputation grew so great that he was believed to move both the beasts and the trees by his song. When he had spent much time in study, and found out the myths which are concerned with theology, he went to live in Egypt, where he added greatly to his knowledge and became the foremost of the Greeks in theology, cult ceremonies, poetry and music. He was a member of the expedition of the Argonauts, and out of love for his wife was led to perform the incredible feat of descending into Hades, where he charmed Persephone with his music and prevailed on her to further his desires and allow him to bring up his dead wife from Hades like another Dionysos; for the myth says that Dionysos raised his mother Semele from Hades and gave her a portion of immortality, changing her name to Thyone. Now that we have told of Orpheus, we shall return again to Herakles.'

3. Strabo, 7. 330, fr. 18 = Kern, test. 40. 'Beneath Olympos is a city Dion. Near it is a village called Pimpleia. It was there, they say, that Orpheus the Kikonian lived, a magician who at first was a wandering musician and soothsayer and peddler of the rites of initiation. As time went on he began to think more of himself and aim at getting power and an unruly following. Some received him willingly, but others, more suspicious, used both guile and force against him and destroyed him.'

4. Konon, fab. 45 = Kern, testt. 39 and 115. 'Orpheus, the son of Oiagros, and of Kalliope, one of the Muses, was king of the Macedonians and of the country of the Odrysai. He was skilled in music and particularly in the lyre; and, since the Thracians and Macedonians are a music-loving race, he won great favour with the people thereby. The manner of his death was this: he was torn in pieces by the women of Thrace and Macedonia because

he would not allow them to take part in his religious rites, or it may be on other pretexts too ; for they do say that after the misfortune that he had with his own wife he became the foe of the whole sex. Now on appointed days a throng of armed Thracians and Macedonians used to gather at Leibethra, and come together in a certain building which was large and well adapted for the performance of initiatory rites ; and when they entered to take part in the rites, they laid down their arms before the door. The women watched for this, and, filled with anger at the slight put upon them, seized the arms, slew those who attempted to over-power them, and rending Orpheus limb from limb, cast the scattered remains into the sea. No requital was exacted from the women, and a plague afflicted the land. Seeking relief from their troubles, the inhabitants received an oracle, saying that if they should find the head of Orpheus and bury it, then they should have rest. After much difficulty they found it through a fisherman at the mouth of the river Meles. It was still singing, and in no way harmed by the sea, nor had it suffered any of the other dreadful changes which the fates of man bring upon dead bodies. Even after so long a time it was fresh, and blooming with the blood of life. So they took it and buried it under a great mound, and fenced off a precinct around it, which at first was a hero-shrine but later grew to be a temple. That is, it is honoured with sacrifices and all the other tributes which are paid to gods. No woman may ever set foot within it.'

NOTES TO CHAPTER III

The authorities for the story and character of Orpheus are set forth most completely (apart from the passages in Kern's *testimonia*) by O. Gruppe in Roscher's *Lexikon der Klass. Myth.* 3. 1058 ff., and the legends are outlined and briefly discussed by K. Robert, *die griechische Heldensage* (Berlin, 1920), 1. 402 ff. Cp. Harrison, *Prolegomena,*[3] chap. ix.

[1] The traces of belief in a possible Macedonian origin in the neighbourhood of Olympos seem to be these. Apollonios (*Arg.* 1. 23) says that he was born at Pimpleia, a village near the town of Dion on the north side of the mountain, and Strabo (7. 330, fr. 18 = Kern, *test.* 40) says that he lived there, though he calls him a member of the Thracian tribe of the Kikones. Konon (*fab.* 45 = Kern, *test.* 39) says that he was a king ruling over both the Macedonians and the Thracian Odrysai, which is not very helpful and reminds us how close together were the people who are disputing ownership of the singer. Euripides (*Bacchae* 560 = Kern, *test.* 38) describes him as exercising the spell of his music in the shady grottoes of Olympos. Besides the indifference of some writers whether he was Thracian or Macedonian must be reckoned the fact that the district by Olympos to which he was assigned, Pieria, was originally inhabited by a Thracian tribe, the Pieres, who according to Thucydides (ii. 99) took to Thrace on being driven from their home by the Macedonians and settled in the country about Mount Pangaion. Even Apollonios in the above-mentioned story of his birth gives him the Thracian Oiagros as his father, and the Scholiast on Apollonios 1. 31 speaks of Pieria itself as a Thracian mountain (Kern, *test.* 5).

Another complication, similar to that caused by the migration of the Pierians, is the existence both of a town Leibethra in Macedonian Pieria and a tribe of Leibethrii in the neighbourhood of Pangaion (v. Maass, *Orph.* p. 135, with the quot. from Himerios in n. 18). This makes it difficult to judge of the statement attributed to Aeschylus in the *Bassarides* (Ps.-Eratosth., Kern, *test.* 113) that he met his death while worshipping Apollo on Pangaion and the Muses took his body and buried it 'in the place called Leibethra'. That he lived and was buried in the Olympian Leibethra is the story of Pausanias (9. 30. 9 = Kern, *test.* 129). See on this point Maass, *Orph.* pp. 134 ff., who wishes to make the whole scene Thracian, in the neighbourhood of Pangaion.

K. Robert (*Heldensage*, 1. 410 ff.) argues the probability that Olympos is the original home of Orpheus, for (i) the tradition that he had a Muse for mother is almost universal and that which gives him Apollo, another Olympian figure, for father is probably older than that which gives him the Thracian Oiagros ; though he sensibly adds that in the earliest times it is improbable that anyone inquired at all who his parents were : (ii) the vase-paintings which show him in Greek dress are earlier, those which give him Thracian dress are later. Against this has been quoted the principle that all early vase-painters were reluctant to depict barbaric costume, even where it was appropriate, but that later this reluctance disappeared. This principle is enunciated *e.g.* by W. Helbig (*Unters. üb. die Campan. Wandmal.* 176 f.), who mentions examples of obviously Asiatic figures so treated : ' Whereas the Amazons on r.f. vases of severe style are armed like Greek hoplites, they usually appear on later type types with Asiatic clothing and armour. With Priam, Paris, Memnon, Medea and other heroes and heroines of Asiatic origin, the earlier vase-painting gives no expression to their Oriental character, or at most hints at it.' Nevertheless, some of the vases which show Orpheus as a Greek show him also in the company of Thracians whose native dress has been by no means shirked by the painter. These vases may have more to tell us about the original character (if not the actual native spot) of Orpheus. Cp. p. 45 above.

Considering then the confused nature of the evidence, and more especially the close relationship of the places and peoples which come into the question, I think the conclusion to be drawn is that the matter is of comparatively little importance. Granted that one or other of the two traditions represented the true and ultimate provenance of Orpheus, it would not even then settle with finality the important question whether he is in origin barbarian or Hellene ; for the claim of the Macedonians to be genuine Hellenes was look ed on doubtfully by a Greek of Attica, and the Thracians themselves, in spite of their backwardness in civilisation, were bound to the Greeks by many ties of tradition and spoke a kindred language. For further details of the modern controversial literature, see Gruppe in Roscher's Lexicon, 3. 1078 ff. Maass (*Orph.* esp. pp. 157 ff.) argues that Orpheus was in the very first place a god of the Minyai in Boiotia. His religion went to Thrace, where it first opposed the native Dionysiac religion and later allied itself with it. Against this course of events is the opinion of Gruppe that the Dionysiac religion itself came from East Boiotia to Macedon and Thrace, districts colonised by Boeotian and Euboean settlers. Gruppe's evidence is a mass of instances of the same cults and the same places in both parts. There was *e.g.* yet a third Leibethra in Boiotia, the cult of the Muses is found on Helikon as well as on Olympos and Pangaion, etc., etc. (Gruppe, *Gr. Myth.* pp. 211 ff.)

² Oiagros, a river in Thrace. See authorities in Robert, *Heldens.* 1. 410, n. 5, esp. Servius *ad* Virg. *Georg.* 4. 524 : *Oeagrus fluvius est, pater Orphei, de quo Hebrus nascitur.* The name looks temptingly Greek, but there is little agreement in the etymologies proposed. He is the lone hunter according to Maass (*Orph.* p. 154). Fick (*ap.* Kern, *Orph.* 16) makes him the lone dweller in the fields, and Kern remarks (*ib.*) that owner of sheep and lands is also possible. Cp. n. 28 below.

³ The Orphic Argonautica has recently been edited with translation by G. Dottin (Budé, 1930). References for the expedition of the Argonauts

in literary tradition are conveniently collected by him in the preface, pp. i-viii. See further André Boulanger, *l'Orphisme dans les Argonautiques d'Orphée, Bulletin Budé*, Jan., 1929, 30-46, which I read after writing the description in the text. We await an edition by Miss J. R. Bacon.

⁴ The *locus classicus* is of course the beautiful passage in Virgil, *Georg.* 4. 453-527. The story is told by Ovid in *Met.* 10. 1-85. Gruppe gives a full list of references to it in the Roman age.

⁵ Cp. E. Maass, *Orph.* p. 150, n. 40 (on the wall-painting at Pompeii, Helbig, *Wandg. Camp.* no. 893, pl. 10).

⁶ Maass (*Orph.* p. 151, n. 43 *fin.*) regards the prohibition not as primitive tabu but as 'dogmatischer Glaubensmoral' as *opposed* to 'primitiver Mythus'. He thus reaches on quite other grounds the conclusion I have suggested in the text. To Rose (*Handbook of Greek Mythology*, Methuen, 1930, p. 255) it is 'a very old tale . . . of the man who went to the other world to fetch his wife and (usually) lost her after all his efforts because he broke some tabu'. These quotations are chiefly interesting as illustrations of how far mythology is from being an objective study. For an example of the tabu against looking in an American story, see Frazer's *Pausanias*, vol. 5, p. 155. That the failure of the mission is an Alexandrine addition to the story is the opinion of Kern, *Orph.* pp. 13, 24 f.

⁷ Robert (*Heldens.* 1. p. 403, n. 6) suggests that this rationalistic account may have arisen out of the passage in Plato's *Symposium* referred to on the previous page.

⁸ The following is a list and brief description of the most important vases showing the death of Orpheus. It will, I hope, make them easier to find than they have been hitherto. Each has been published so many times that when two writers give a different reference it is not easy to find out at once whether they are referring to a different vase or not. Enough time may be wasted in the search even without the additional difficulty caused by inaccuracies. This makes it justifiable to note at once a confusion in so well-used a work of reference as Roscher's Lexicon.. The vase *Mus. Greg.* 2. 60. 1 (no. ii below) is identical with the *amphora* from Vulci reproduced by Gerhard, *Trinksch. und Gefässe*, 2, pl. 1, and illustrated in Roscher, 3. 1183, 4, no. 8. In Roscher it is identified with the *stamnos* from Chiusi (no. iii below) reproduced and described in *Ann. del Inst.* 1871, *tav. d'agg.* K, and pp. 128 ff., and also shown by Gerhard, *ib.* pl. J. 3. See the identification in the text of Roscher, 3. 1184 (D)₁ and the illustration, *ib.* 1187, no. 12. The mistake continues in Harrison, *Prol.*³ 462, n. 4.

Besides the illustrated list in Roscher, H. Heydemann in a note to his article in *Arch. Zeit.* 1868, pp. 3 ff., gave a list with full reff. of the vases known at the time. A later list is in Robert, *Heldens.* 1. p. 404, n. 1. These lists often give fuller reff. than I shall. Those in Heydemann's list I mark with H., those in Robert's with R. Where I have not attributed the description to anyone else it is my own, from the vase itself or a reproduction. The descriptions are only intended to facilitate identification :—

i. The subject of Heydemann's article in *Arch. Zeit.* 1868, pp. 3 ff. He gives a drawing. Also reproduced in Harrison, *Prol.*³ 460. R.f. *hydria* from Nola. O. sits on a rock playing, in a Greek *chlamys*, naked from the waist up, crowned with bay. A satyr listens behind him, a man in Thracian dress in front. One woman hurries up with a large pestle, another stands with a spear.

ii. *Museo Gregoriano*, 2. 60. 1 (the ref. 2. 80 in Heyd. is a mistake); Gerhard, *Trinksch. u. Gef.* 2, pl. J. 1; sketch in Roscher, 3. 1183, 4, no. 8. H. R.f. *amphora* from Vulci. O. in girdled *chiton* with *chlamys* across arms, long hair wreathed with bay, stands shrinking back. The lyre is in his lowered r. hand, his l. is raised to ward off the blow. A woman is attacking him, brandishing a double axe over her head. Behind her a tree.

iii. *Ann. del Inst.* 1871, pp. 128 ff., *tav. d'agg.* K; Gerhard, *Tr. u. Gef.* 2, pl. J. 3; sketches in Roscher, 3. 1185 ff., figs. 11 and 12; and Harrison, *Prol.*³ 463, fig. 142. R. (= my fig. 4).

R.f. *stamnos* from Chiusi. O. is in the attitude most familiar in these vase-paintings, of which that in no. 2 was a variation. He sinks back with his l. hand on the ground behind him for support, while his r. holds the lyre aloft to ward off the impending blow. He wears only a *chlamys* which leaves him naked in front. He is attacked by two women on foot to l., armed with stones, and one on horseback to r., armed with a spear.

iv. In Nat. Mus. at Naples. Heydemann in *Neapl. Vasens. Mus. Naz.* (1872), no. 2889 (description only), sketch by F. Hauser in *Arch. Jahrb.* 1914, p. 28, fig. 2, reproduced from *Mus. Borb.* 9. 12. R., H. (= my fig. 5).
R.f. *krater.* Upper strip: O. sits playing on a rock, a fillet on his hair, wrapped in cloak which leaves one shoulder bare. On either side of him two men in Thracian dress listening. All stand leaning on spears except one, who sits, hands clasping knees.

Lower strip : six figures, four women and two youths, running, and all armed in various ways (spears, axe, staff and the implement usually taken to be a pestle).

v. In Nat. Mus. at Naples. Heyd. *N.V.M.N.* no. 3114 (description only). R., H.
(Short description from my own notes made in Naples revised with Heyd.)
R.f. Nolan vase. O. with long hair bound by a fillet, *chlamys* over l. shoulder, sinks back in the familiar attitude. He is attacked by a woman with an axe.

vi. Gerhard, *Auserl. Vasenb.* 3. pl. 156. R., H.
R.f. *stamnos.* O. in Greek clothing, his long hair escaping from under a fillet, sinks to the ground in the familiar attitude. He is attacked by seven women. The nearest has stuck her spear into his breast. Arms of women : spears, axe, stone, sickle with toothed edge, and something which looks rather like a rolling pin but is perhaps intended for a species of knife (? pestle half concealed behind another figure).

vii. Robinson, Cat. of the Vases of Boston, no. 432, reproduced by F. Hauser in *Arch. Jahrb.* 1914, p. 27, fig. 1. R. (= my pl. 4).
R.f. *hydria.* O. with long curls escaping from under fillet, wearing *chiton* with girdle and *chlamys*, is attacked by five women variously armed (spears, dagger, sickle). He sinks down in the familiar attitude in front of a tree. At each end stands a youth with spear in short tunic and cloak. One of them wears a Thracian cap.

viii. In Munich. O. Jahn's cat. (1854), no. 383. H.
(From Jahn's description.) A r.f. vase. O. in *chlamys*, looking back and falling in the familiar attitude, is attacked by a woman with drawn sword. Her arm is tattooed.

ix. Some fragments reproduced and described by Harrison in *J.H.S.* 1888, pp. 143 ff. with pl. 6. R.
Kylix, with painting on white ground. O. is sinking back in the familiar ✱ attitude. Facing him is a woman, her r. hand (lowered) holding a partly-preserved weapon which looks like a double axe. Her right arm is tattooed with a stag, her l. with a pattern resembling a ladder.

x. Gruppe in Roscher (3. 1184(C), 1185, 6, fig. 10) shows a drawing of a vase for which he gives the single ref. *Mon. Ined.* 8. 30. It should be 9. 30.
R.f. Nolan vase, showing O., his long curls bound by a fillet, wearing only *chlamys* which leaves him naked in front, being attacked by a woman who steps on to him and drives her spear into his breast. He sinks down in the familiar attitude. On each side a woman comes up with a stone.

[9] Cp. nos. 1, 4, 7 in the above list.
[10] The stories of Pausanias referred to in this paragraph are in book 9, ch. 30 ; some printed in Kern, *testt.* 129, 123, 120.
[11] Diog. L. 1. 5 (Kern, *test.* 125) :

Θρῆικα χρυσολύρην τῇδ' 'Ορφέα Μοῦσαι ἔθαψαν,
ὃν κτάνεν ὑψιμέδων Ζεὺς ψολόεντι βέλει.

An epigram with the same second line is quoted by Alkidamas (fourth cent. B.C. ; or his imitator) as being on the tomb of Orpheus, though which tomb he does not mention, and there must have been more than one. Again in the *Peplos* (a work once ascribed to Aristotle), two lines are quoted as being from the tomb of Orpheus among the Kikones in Thrace, and of these the first is a variant of Diogenes'. Diog. has simply, it would seem, confused these two epigrams. See Kern, *testt.* 123-125 for texts and reff., and cp. Maass, *Orph.* p. 140, n. 24.

[12] On the oracle-shrine of Orpheus at Lesbos, see Harrison, *Proleg.*[3] 465 ff., and Kern, *Orph.* 1920, pp. 9 f. Kern, following K. Robert, contests the view that the vase illustrated in my fig. 7 has anything to do with the Lesbian oracle mentioned by Philostratos.

[13] The sentence in Konon (Kern, *test.* 115 *fin.*, remarked on by Harrison, *Prol.*[3] 468 f.) is interesting as showing how a cult may develop : ' So they took it (*sc.* the head of O.) and buried it under a great monument, which they surrounded with a sacred precinct. The place was at first a hero-shrine, but later came to rank as a temple, for it is celebrated with sacrifices and all the other honours which are appropriate to gods ' : τέμενος αὐτῷ περι-είρξαντες ὃ τέως μὲν ἡρῷον ἦν, ὕστερον δ' ἐξενίκησεν ἱερὸν εἶναι. θυσίαις τε γὰρ καὶ ὅσοις ἄλλοις θεοὶ τιμῶνται γεραίρεται.

θύειν is to sacrifice to a god. The corresponding word in hero-cult is, strictly speaking, ἐναγίζειν, with the nouns ἐνάγισμα, ἐναγισμός. See Rohde's *Psyche*, Eng. trans. ch. 4, § 2 and n. 15.

[14] The statue is described in Helbig-Amelung, *Führer durch die Samml. Klass. Ant. in Rom*, 1913, no. 1039. So far as I know, no reproduction of it has ever been published. At the

FIG. 9.—BRONZE MIRROR OF THE FIFTH CENTURY B.C.

time I supposed it to be the earliest represen-tation in art of the beasts listening to O. Frazer, at least (*Paus.* 5. p. 155), referring to a list of the works of art depicting this subject given by Stephani in the *Compte Rendu* (St. Petersburg) for 1881, says ' None of these works of art seems to date from before the beginning of our era '. R. Eisler, however (*Orpheus*, Teubner, 1925, p. 95, *Abb.* 34), illustrates a bronze mirror depicting the subject whose style suggests that it is to be dated in the fifth century B.C. (fig. 9).

[15] This passage in the 4th Pythian (177) has often been taken as meaning that Apollo was his father, but Kern (*Orpheus*, 6) has pointed out that the words do not bear that sense.

[16] Published in *Bull. Corr. Hell.* 2, p. 401 ; copied by an American missionary and now apparently lost. Roman Imperial date.

[17] See Rohde's *Psyche*, Eng. trans. 287-289. In A. W. Pickard-Cambridge's *Dithyramb, Tragedy and Comedy* (Oxford, 1927), figs. 1 and 2, may be seen

reproductions of two vases illustrating the presence of Dionysos at Delphi. Rohde (*ib.* 290 f.) makes a well-drawn distinction between two types of prophecy. One is prophecy as an art, the knowledge of how to interpret signs and omens, telling the will of the gods from the flight of birds or the entrails of a sacrificial victim. The seer remains perfectly human and self-possessed, but, because instructed, claims to be able to read what the god has to say. The second is the prophecy of inspiration. When the prophet speaks he is not himself ; the god has entered into him and possessed him, and he is only a mouthpiece through which the god himself is speaking. I should add that the distinction is clearly made by Plato, *Phaedrus* 244 a-d. (Latin expresses it well, even though it was in another connexion that Tacitus wrote this sentence : *se enim ministros deorum, illos conscios putant.*) Of these two kinds, the first is the original gift of Apollo. The second (the type of prophecy which was made famous by his priestess at Delphi) is an innovation in his cult, but is exactly the type of prophecy which had always been associated with Dionysos. With this distinction in mind we might ask ourselves which type of prophecy seems properly to belong to Orpheus, if we want to decide whether he was originally an Apolline figure. I should reply emphatically in favour of the former, because to me the idea of a frenzied or possessed Orpheus seems utterly foreign to all that we know of him. (Macchioro's view may be contrasted : see below, n. 24.) There is little direct evidence on the subject. One might quote the opinion of Pliny, *N.H.* 7. 203 = Kern, *test.* 89 : *Auguria ex avibus Car . . . adiecit ex ceteris animalibus Orpheus.* The taking of auguries from birds and animals is the most usual form of the first kind of prophecy.

[18] Menander Rhetor, p. 446, 5 Sp.
   Eur. *ap.* Macrobius 1. 18, δεσπότα φιλόδαφνε Βάκχε, Παιὰν Ἀπόλλον εὔλυρε. Macrobius also quotes Aeschylus as writing *ad eandem sententiam,* ὁ κισσεὺς Ἀπόλλων ὁ Βακχεῖος ὁ μάντις.

[19] That O. is in origin an underworld god, consort of Eurydice the ✱ underworld queen, is one of the main theses of E. Maass' learned work *Orpheus* (Munich, 1895). Gruppe (Roscher, 3. 1108) also thought probable the identification of Eurydice with the underworld goddess, and it was the opinion of Jane Harrison. See her note in *Arch. für Religionsw.* 1909, p. 411, where, however, she admits that Dieterich thought the view *unwahrscheinlich.* Incidentally, the name is not confined to the wife of O. The *Kypria* (Oxford text, fr. 22) speaks of Eurydice as the wife of Aeneas. (If Eurydice were the goddess of the underworld, it would not necessarily follow that O. is an underworld god. He would still in all probability be the human hero, who marries this infernal queen. I learn from Professor Cook that this motif is common in Celtic folklore, and it is noticeable that O. is a Northern figure, as also is Odysseus, who plays the same part with regard to Circe and Calypso.)

[20] To say this is to take sides in a vexed question. Wilamowitz held that the origin of Apollo was in Asia Minor. M. P. Nilsson, a follower of this view, has epitomized his own arguments in a note to *Minoan-Mycenean Religion etc.* (1927), p. 443, n. 1. He gives some references for the controversy. The opposite view has been clearly stated by H. J. Rose, *Hdbk. Gr. Myth.* pp. 135 f. ; see also the references in his n. 2, p. 158. The tradition which supports him most convincingly is that which connects Apollo with the Hyperboreans. Rose points out that worship in Asia Minor may mean no more than that the Greeks brought Apollo there in the age of colonization. Is it fanciful, in the present state of our knowledge of early Greek infiltrations, to suggest that the same people coming from the North, and worshipping Apollo, may have split and descended some into Greece and some into Asia Minor, so that the introduction of Apollo into both countries may have been simultaneous, and in both cases from the North ?

[21] Maintained by O. Gruppe in *Griech. Myth.* (1906), pp. 211 ff. See n. 1 *fin.* above.

[22] *Über O. und die Orphiker* (Berlin, 1861), p. 11. In n. 25 of the same monograph will be found summarized earlier statements of the opposite view (*e.g.* those of O. Müller, Preller, etc.) that O. was from the beginning closely connected with Dionysos-worship.

[23] I may mention here the view which Kern is defending when he makes these observations about the vases. It is that the name and whole personality of Orpheus are a creation of sectarians of the sixth century. If I cannot agree that he has proved his case, I hope I may recall with gratitude many of the keen observations which he has made in its support, the more so as I hold that agreement on the character of Orpheus as it was imagined in the sixth and fifth centuries is of far greater importance than any question of his origin.

[24] It is difficult not to think of these qualities, and those I mentioned on p. 40, as essential and original elements in the character of O. That is why I cannot agree with V. Macchioro, who bases his conclusion about O. on ' the tradition regarding O. as a musician, who by means of music and divination brought about the orgiastic frenzy of initiations '. I doubt whether this applies necessarily and originally to Orphic initiations, though by Plutarch's time the rites may have deserved the name he gave them of κατάκοροι καὶ περίεργοι ἱερουργίαι. Macchioro concludes that Orpheus is a similar figure to the primitive Jewish prophets, the Nebi'im, in describing whom he says : ' From time to time . . . they fell into a sort of frenzy ; they undressed ; they lay on the ground unconscious ; they looked like madmen '. I cannot imagine Orpheus behaving like this. (Macchioro, From Orpheus to Paul, 1930, pp. 133, 135.)

[25] Kern (Orph. 31 f.) takes the various traits in the character of Orpheus and sets them side by side with writings on similar subjects which were composed at various dates and attributed to him. There were for instance a collection of oracles, works on medicine, magical poems, works on agriculture. This juxtaposition affords him proof that the characteristics gathered round Orpheus as a result of the existence of the writings. It seems to me more likely that a writer on, say, medicine, wishing to attach to his treatise a name of authority, would choose the name of one known as a healer than that he should choose a name just because it was held in general reverence, and the name, revered before, owe its reputation for medicine to the existence of this treatise. The assumption is moreover unnecessary to explain the character of Orpheus. What more natural than that the great singer (a side of him which not even Kern can trace to an origin in Orphic writings) should have magical powers, or that the hero-priest of Paian Apollo should be versed in prophecy and healing ? (As regards the latter, the belief in the healing power of music itself must not be forgotten.) I have mentioned some ways in which their functions were alike, and the chorus of the Alcestis recurs to the mind (965 f.) : κρεῖσσον οὐδὲν Ἀνάγκας ηὗρον, οὐδέ τι φάρμακον Θρήσσαις ἐν σάνισιν, ἃς Ὀρφεία κατέγραψεν γῆρυς, οὐδ' ὅσα Φοῖβος Ἀσκληπιάδαις ἔδωκε φάρμακα.

[26] Plut. Ser. num. vind. 557d = Kern, test. 77 fin. ; the custom also mentioned by Phanokles, Kern, ib., and on vases the attacking women are sometimes shown tattooed. Cp. n. 8, nos. viii. and (esp.) ix.

[27] Mention must in fairness be made of the well-founded view that the termination -eus belongs to pre-Greek names, and the obvious possibility that the name of a pre-Greek hero may have had its stem Graecised and provided in later antiquity with a Greek derivation. (See M. P. Nilsson, Homer and Mycenae, Methuen 1933, pp. 81, 65.) Although I have not much faith in the power of etymology to give certain results, I think that it is here if anywhere that a solution lies to the problem of the origin of the name Orpheus.

[28] Of etymologies there is no end. Charops means gleaming-eyed. Gruppe (in Roscher, 3. 1112) says that he must therefore be the dog of the lone hunter (Oiagros), and hence apparently his father! Maass (Orph. 153, n. 46) connects the name with Charon and so with Hades. (It occurs in Homer as the name of a Trojan, Il. 11. 426, and was also an epithet of Herakles.)

CHAPTER IV

THE CREATION AND THE GODS AS PRESENTED BY ORPHEUS

'*Omnis sermo apud Graecos, qui de antiquitatis origine conscribitur, cum alios multos, tum duos praecipue auctores habet, Orpheum et Hesiodum. Horum ergo scripta in duas partes intelligentiae dividuntur, id est, secundum litteram et secundum allegoriam, et ad ea quidem quae secundum litteram sunt, ignobilis vulgi turba confluxit. Ea vero quae secundum allegoriam constant, omnis philosophorum et eruditorum loquacitas admirata est.*'

'*The whole sum of the writing which has arisen among the Greeks on the subject of the far-off origins of the world is attributed to many authors, but two names stand out, Orpheus and Hesiod. Now the writings of these fall into two parts, divided according to the way they are interpreted, literally or allegorically. The parts that are taken literally have attracted the low minds of the vulgar, but those whose value lies in their allegory have ever called forth the admiring comments of philosophy and scholarship.*'—RUFINUS (O.F. p. 133).

'*Among the lowest tribes we usually find, just as in ancient Greece, the belief in a deathless " Father," " Master," " Maker," and also the crowds of humorous, obscene, fanciful myths which are in flagrant contradiction with the religious character of that belief. . . . For the present, we can only say that the religious conception uprises from the human intellect in one mood, that of earnest contemplation and submission : while the mythical ideas uprise from another mood, that of playful and erratic fancy. These two moods are conspicuous even in Christianity. The former, that of earnest and submissive contemplation, declares itself in prayers, hymns and the dim religious light of cathedrals. The second mood, that of playful and erratic fancy, is conspicuous in the buffoonery of miracle plays, in Märchen, these burlesque popular tales about our Lord and Apostles, and in the hideous and grotesque sculptures on sacred edifices. The two moods are present, and in conflict, through the whole religious history of the human race. They stand as near each other, and as far apart, as Love and Lust.*'—ANDREW LANG.

WE have seen that Orpheus was known to everyone as the author of a religion based on the written word. The most important part of this Orphic Bible was that which told of the Creation. Orpheus was famous for many things, but best of all, perhaps, he was known as the *theologos*, one of the most famous, if not the most famous of all that tribe. It is only what everyone would expect that when Apollonios in his epic makes him raise his voice in song, the theme of his lay is cosmogonical. Yet the writings on these subjects which are attributed to him have been the subject of endless comment and controversy. This has not been primarily concerned with the independent question of the content and meaning of the poems, though they have had their due of exegesis too. The differences of opinion have arisen mainly out of this, that after speaking of Orpheus as the author of a quotation from a cosmogonical poem one has to put the name mentally between inverted commas and admit that there is a great deal more to be said before he knows who really wrote the lines or even at what approximate date they were composed. Of all the problems that beset the student of Greek literature, none, surely, is more vexed than the question of the dates and contents of the various theogonies. Many points which we should like cleared up must remain in doubt for ever. That is an admission which the scantiness of the remains renders necessary at once. It will be well to say something of the nature of the difficulties with which we are faced.

Curiosity about the origins of the world was a never-failing characteristic of the Greek mind. This found expression in two ways, the mythological and the philosophical. Mythology came first, naturally, and then in the sixth century B.C. arose the first school of philosophers, who in their own eyes at least were enlightened, having freed their minds from the unreasoning acceptance of myth. In later years the attitude of philosophy to mythology varied, and the two main views it adopted are seen at their best in Plato and Aristotle respectively. Plato spoke of the theological poets as ' divine men ', or ' the sons of gods, who may be expected to know the truth about their own parents ', that is to say, as men inspired, to whom a more than human insight had been granted (p. 240 below). If they did not use reason, that was because to them had been granted a faculty which transcended reason. The truth implied by this might easily be that the philosopher read into the theological poems a philosophical meaning which could never have been in the mind of the writer. If we see this process at its best in Plato, we see it at its worst in the Neoplatonists, his commentators. An obvious example of it in Plato is the passage in the *Phaedo* where he draws the comparison between the true philosopher and the man who has been initiated in the mysteries. When they say that the uninitiated will have an unpleasant lot in the next world, the religious teachers are speaking in riddles. In truth they are not such worthless teachers as men believe who try to force a literal meaning on their doctrines. ' For the initiated are in my opinion none other than those who have been true philosophers.' Unfortunately the gentle irony of Plato is entirely lacking in his would-be followers (cp. p. 243 below).

The other point of view is represented by the saying of Aristotle: ' But what is given us in the form of mythical sophistry is not worth the attention of a serious thinker '. Myth is unnecessary to the philosopher, and can do nothing but confuse the issue.

The reason it has seemed worth while to mention the philosophical attitudes to myth is that the source of our knowledge of a myth is so often the writing of a philosopher, and the nature of his reference to the myth may well be affected by the view which he holds himself. It is time to return to the theogonies, by which I mean mythological accounts of the origins of the world, what there was in the beginning, how the gods arose, what were their relations with each other in those far-off times, and how the world we know came to be created. Of these theogonies there were many, but only one, that of Hesiod, exists to-day. Ancient authors speak of others, and occasionally quote small fragments of their writings. Thus we know of theogonies by Akusilaos of Argos, Epimenides of Crete, Pherekydes of Syros. That these men lived and wrote may be taken as certain, though legends gathered about their names, and we need not assume that the quotations from them in writers of the Christian era are genuine. Epimenides and Pherekydes are well authenticated figures of the sixth century B.C., and the latter wins a word of praise from Aristotle for having had a more philosophical conception of his subject than most writers of his class (*Met.* 1091b9).

Some of the difficulties of research into the ancient *theologoi* (to give them their Greek title) are beginning to appear. With the exception of Hesiod, we rely for our knowledge of them on information which is at least second-hand, or on short quotations whose genuineness cannot be lightly accepted. For the information and quotations we have often to go to writers whose subject was the same but their conception of the truth about it quite different. The objectiveness of their report is therefore under suspicion. To this we must add that Plato and Aristotle, whose authority would be invaluable, speak with maddening frequency in vague terms. When quoting a mythological account, they prefer to refer it generally to ' the *theologoi* ' than to mention any one writer by name.

Among the many names to which theogonical and cosmogonical writings were attached, two, as is rightly remarked by the Christian apologist, stand out, Orpheus and Hesiod. The other writers whose names I have quoted were always known to be later than Hesiod, who was sometimes regarded as the father of this kind of composition. Herodotus thought him so, and there were others too who doubted the authenticity of the theogony of Orpheus. The weight of that ancient name, however, was not taken away from it, and this must have suggested to many of the ancient world that, if not the poems, at least the stories which they told belonged to a time before Hesiod and Homer himself. That was one reason why it stood out. Another was that it undoubtedly had peculiar features. In Plato we find one or two quotations from a poem of theogonical content which is said to be by Orpheus (ch. ii, n. 2), but the bulk of the direct evidence for the Orphic theogony comes to us from writers of a much later date. In the later Neoplatonists we find numerous references to, and actual quotations from, a poem or poems on the origin of the world, the gods and mortal creatures, referred to as either ' of Orpheus ' or ' the Orphic '. These references and quotations are incomparably more numerous than those in any earlier writers. More than one consideration helps to account for this lavishness. There was no doubt that Plato, the hero if not the master of the school, did make use of the Orphic writings. He found his ideas concerning the relationship between man and God at many points in sympathy with the mystical doctrines of the *theologos*, which therefore he did not hesitate to introduce at certain points into his work. It was the natural tendency of the Neoplatonists to stress (if I may use for the present so mild a word) the mystical side of their master's philosophy, since their own was so entirely mystical and they wished to suppose it a legitimate development from pure Platonism. In their commentaries therefore they made a point of illustrating a sentence of Plato, whenever they could, by a quotation from the Orphic poems.

There was another, with some an even stronger reason for the practice. The later Neoplatonists found themselves among the last defenders of pagan Hellenic culture against the rapidly advancing power of Christianity. It was too late to use the cruder method of simply attacking Christianity itself and calling it all that was bad. The best hope now lay in questioning its originality, in saying, ' What you believe does represent a profound and valuable truth, but it is a truth that has been known to us Greeks ever since the dawn of our history '. In their attempt to make this good, they had no better material for propaganda than the Orphic poems. Here was expressed no mere external relationship between man and God, but one capable of a highly mystical interpretation, a real spiritual kinship as opposed to a relation as of master and servant or, as in Homeric genealogies, of physical son and physical father. The resemblance went further than this. The Orphic doctrines included a belief in original sin, based on a legend about the origin of mankind, in the emphatic separation of soul from body, and in a life hereafter which for the pure-living would be very much better than this life on earth. The myths themselves in which these doctrines found expression were often crude and ungainly, but the zest for allegorizing among the Neoplatonists was not easily daunted.

The bulk of the quotations in the Neoplatonists are by reason of their subject-matter most naturally to be ascribed to a single series of writings. This would give accounts of the origin of the universe, of gods and of men, and perhaps go on to describe the religious life and the rewards and punishments which are to be ours according as we do or do not cultivate and nourish the divine element in our being ; since all this is the direct outcome of the dogmas concerning our origin and our place in the cosmological scheme. If Orphism were a philosophy, one would say it was a philosophy whose ethic was made duly dependent on its metaphysic. We find one or two references by name (if it can be called a name) to a series of poems of this sort, and this is in all probability the one habitually used by the Neoplatonists. Damaskios (O.F. 60) says he will describe ' the theology in the so-called Orphic *rhapsodiai* ', and having done so concludes, ' This then is the usual Orphic theology '. Suidas (Kern, *test.* 223), in a list of the writings of Orpheus, gives ' sacred discourses in twenty-four *rhapsodiai* (parts or lays) ' (ἱεροὶ λόγοι ἐν ῥαψῳδίαις κδ'). It is usually referred to by modern scholars as the Rhapsodic Theogony.[1] Another version, differing in some points from this, is described (O.F. 54-59) as ' the Orphic theogony according to Hieronymos and Hellanikos '.

The Neoplatonists believed that the Orpheus whose poems they studied was the Orpheus of Greek legend, the singer who lived in the Heroic age. To them therefore he was, of course, the same whom Plato knew, occasionally quoted expressly, and according to their interpretation of him made use of continually. The question then in its simplest and crudest form is, was the Rhapsodic Theogony, of which the Neoplatonists have preserved many fragments for us, a work of the sixth century B.C. or earlier, and identical with that read by Plato, or was it put together at some later date, and if so when ?   Other authors come into consideration, when they show by a turn of phrase or by a thought an acquaintance with Orphic literature in the sixth to the fourth

5

centuries B.C. Among these are Aeschylus, Aristophanes and the philosophers Empedokles and Herakleitos. The relations of these thinkers to Orphic doctrine deserve special consideration in a later chapter, and only so much as is necessary to the argument will be mentioned here.

To expect a complete and definite answer to the problem of dating the Orphic theogonies would be to show unwarrantable optimism ; but it is equally true that to attempt a discussion of their content without first making clear our attitude to the problem would be to invite confusion of thought. So much has been written about it that whatever is said here must be largely a summary and appraisal of previous controversy, in which the protagonists, after Lobeck, have been O. Gruppe and O. Kern.[2] I have chosen to start from Gruppe's arguments for the reason that, whatever may be said about his conclusions, he more than any other scholar has a well-defined method of approach to offer, and thus, besides making it easier to follow his thoughts, holds out the best hope of coming to a conclusion on reasonable lines. I am further tempted to do this because later writers (Rohde, Gomperz), while recognizing the importance of his work, have carried single arguments of his to conclusions which he never intended.

Gruppe begins by mentioning the versions of the Orphic theogony which are known to us from different sources. The Neoplatonist Damaskios tells of three, one which he calls ' the Orphic theogony which is in Eudemos ' (fourth cent. B.C., the pupil of Aristotle), another ' according to Hieronymos and Hellanikos ', and thirdly the Rhapsodic, of which he says that it is the usual or customary Orphic theogony. One would therefore expect it to be the version from which the other Neoplatonists in general quote, and this expectation is confirmed by the fragments themselves. Differing more or less from these three are the theogony put into the mouth of Orpheus in the poem of Apollonios Rhodios, and the Orphic theogony quoted by Alexander of Aphrodisias. Finally Gruppe mentions a theogony in Clemens Romanus not named as Orphic but belonging to the same circle of thought, which again shows points of difference from the rest. Putting in the obvious but necessary word of caution that one cannot trust the accuracy of a single recorder, he sensibly concludes th .. there is a group of closely related Orphic theogonies which must be treated as a class, since it is impossible to separate them.

In this group Gruppe sees one central doctrine, which may best be summed up in the words in which it is ascribed to Orpheus' pupil Musaios (Diog. L., *prooem.* 3) : ἐξ ἑνὸς τὰ πάντα γίνεσθαι,

καὶ εἰς ταὐτὸν ἀναλύεσθαι—' Everything comes to be out of One
and is resolved into One '. At one time Phanes, at another Zeus
contained the seeds of all being within his own body, and from
this state of mixture in the One has emerged the whole of our
manifold world, and all nature animate and inanimate. This
central thought, that everything existed at first together in a
confused mass, and that the process of creation was one of
separation and division, with the corollary that the end of our
era will be a return to the primitive confusion, has been repeated
with varying degrees of mythological colouring in many religions
and religious philosophies. The best-known example is our own
Bible. ' The earth was without form . . . and God *divided*
the light from the darkness . . . and God made the firmament,
and *divided* the waters which were under the firmament from the
waters which were above the firmament. . . . And God said, let
the waters under the heaven be gathered together unto one place,
and let the dry land appear : and it was so.' The next point is
to notice that as far as Greek thought is concerned, this fundamental idea appears in two different ages. It is first of all the
keynote of the philosophies of the sixth and fifth centuries B.C.
The purely physical systems of the Milesians are based on it, as
well as the more mystical cosmologies of Empedokles and Herakleitos. This statement calls forth the caution that, since the Stoics
borrowed the physical side of their system from Herakleitos, the
earlier form did reappear in the later age. The second appearance
of the idea is in the Christian era, in mystical religious movements
like Neopythagoreanism and Gnosticism, culminating in Neo-
platonism. In this later form the idea is bound up with highly
abstract notions about the effluence of the sensible world from
the Intelligible, which of course are entirely absent from the
early cosmologies. The argument then continues its admirably
methodical course by inquiring whether the fragments on examination seem to belong to the earlier or the later world of thought.
Of course if we took the Neoplatonists' statements about them at
their face value, there could be no question of assigning them to
the earlier phase, since the Neoplatonists profess to find in them
all that they themselves believed. Few people, however, would
dispute the assertion that they only achieve their end by forcing
into the actual words of the fragments a quite distorted meaning.
Having made this justifiable criticism, Gruppe expresses his belief
that the actual theogonical fragments are quite in keeping with
the earlier stage of thought. These speak of a primitive world-
order, of which the creator is Phanes, and which is swallowed
with its creator by Zeus, out of whom is created the second

world-order, in which we live. According to the Neoplatonic interpretation, the age of Phanes is the intelligible world of the Platonic Ideas, and the age of Zeus the world of matter and sense. In truth, however, there is nothing in the fragments to suggest the Platonic antithesis of intelligible and sensible, and plenty to indicate that the world of Phanes is intended to be every bit as material as our own, only previous to it in time. Going further into detail (where we may follow him in a different connexion), Gruppe sees striking resemblances to the thought of Herakleitos and Empedokles.

Granted that the Orphic theogonies show a close relationship in ideas to the philosophies of the sixth and fifth centuries B.C., the next step is to answer the question, did the philosophers take their ideas from the Orphic poet, or was it the other way round? If the latter, then the poems probably arose in Stoic circles, in which a revival of Heracliteanism was the fashion. Gruppe sees no reason to doubt that the content of the poems belongs to the earlier of his two periods of thought, the beginning of the fifth century or earlier. Ideas in them which have been called Stoic he finds in the fifth century, e.g. the four elements, which are in Aristotle and ascribed by him to Empedokles. On the contrary, he finds contradictions between the Orphic writings and the Stoic beliefs, for example the Orphic statement that the primitive world-stuff was created in time. The case is strengthened by the citation of parallels between the two Orphic versions of Apollonios and ' Hieronymos and Hellanikos ' and the theogony of Phere-kydes, and the conclusion is that the later Orphic theology has its origin in pre-Heraclitean times. Against the argument ex silentio (absence of reference to this theology in classical times), which of course is never a conclusive one, Gruppe urges the crudity of the Orphic myths, which ' gave offence to the refined taste of the contemporaries of Perikles and Plato ', and suggests that the secret (ἀπόρρητον) character of much of their content may also have contributed to the same result. (Another reason is suggested below, p. 201.) Finally the presence of Oriental elements in the myths is invoked as additional confirmation of their early date, since these, in Gruppe's view, are due to early and not Hellenistic influences. The same fact has of course been used to prove the opposite view by supporters of the late date of the myths.

That in brief summary is Gruppe's line of argument. I have omitted the thesis that the theogony in Homer (Iliad 14) is Orphic, as well as the other thesis that the theogony used by Plato was identical with it and that neither is the same as the version customarily used by the Neoplatonists, since these arguments are not relevant to the question of the origin of the later versions. Gruppe's argument that the Rhapsodic Theogony was not used by Plato has been taken by later writers as proof that it was not in existence in his time, and that makes it worth while to repeat here the definite statement of the author of the argument (*Suppl.* 742) that ' Plato's lack of acquaintance with our Rhapsodies is no clear disproof of their antiquity '.

Gruppe's conclusion then about the Orphic poems quoted by the Neoplatonists is that the date at which they were put together cannot be decided, but there is nothing against supposing that the main doctrines which they contain belong to the sixth century. He calls our attention to two things, first that Orphic literature continued to be written from the time of its origin in the sixth century or earlier down to the Christian era, secondly that within this literature there existed such a strong tradition, as far as the content was concerned, that it always retained the climate of thought of the period in which it originated—the sixth century B.C. If it seems to show Stoic elements, for example, they will be found to be those elements which Stoicism borrowed from earlier philosophy. The Rhapsodic Theogony itself is nothing more than an attempt to put together all earlier strata of Orphic tradition, reconciled as far as possible. It is not concerned to make its thought consistent, *e.g.* to present a single system of pantheistic philosophy, and the reconciliation attempted is purely external. It contains no demonstrable traces of late doctrines, and the date of its compilation must remain obscure. (The studies of language and metre, he notes, have so far not helped in deciding that.) Plato shows familiarity with a different form, but that is no proof of its later date.

' The power of myth-*making* was practically extinct in the Hellenistic age.' The words are those of Gomperz, but the idea, with very little difference even of expression, is the background of the argument here.

I have quoted Gruppe's conclusions because they seem the most reasonable, and his arguments because they seem the most helpful. Kern's work on this subject has been directed towards proving that the bulk of the Rhapsodic Theogony is an actual work of the sixth century. If I have not quoted his arguments, it is not so much because statements like ' simpliciorem fabulam antiquiorem esse per se patet ' or ' inter omnes viros doctos constat Hieronymi theogoniam aetatis Alexandrinae signa prae se ferre ' are unconvincing in themselves, as because they are unhelpful in that they close the way to further discussion. Kern is supported by Gomperz, who in defending the antiquity of the Rhapsodies exclaims

indignantly, ' Gruppe's would-be proof that Plato was not acquainted with the Rhapsodist Theogony I regard as wholly
unsuccessful '—as if Gruppe had tried to use that proof to attack
the antiquity of the Rhapsodies. Rohde puts the date of the
Rhapsodies later, maintaining in opposition to both Gruppe and
Kern that ' in the very few passages in which a real coincidence
exists between the Rhapsodies and Pherekydes, Herakleitos,
Parmenides or Empedokles, the poet of the Rhapsodies is the
borrower not the creditor '. He praises Gruppe for supporting his
view by the proof that Plato was unacquainted with the
Rhapsodies ! [3]

Having taken the plunge into this dark and tortuous labyrinth,
what thread are we going to catch hold of in order to make our
way back to where there is at least a patch of daylight on which we
can fix our eyes amid the surrounding gloom ? In the first place,
the real differences between the views here quoted can easily be
exaggerated, and are in fact, for the student of Orphic lore in
general, very small indeed. ' Viewed in full light,' says Gomperz
generously, ' the difference between Rohde and myself shrinks to
a minimum.' Kern argues that the poems themselves are old : [4]
Gruppe says that we cannot tell at what date they were composed,
but that they consist in the main of a medley of older tradition,
a tradition, be it noted, in which conservatism was the dominant
note. Rohde quotes this view with full approval.*

The important lesson to be learned from the controversy
is this of Gruppe's, that the date of The Theogony, or even of
This Theogony, is bound to be a date of compilation rather than
composition, and surely this is something which reduces considerably the importance of the question. What is important
is to consider each single feature or element in the theogony
(the same one will probably be repeated in several versions),
and, if we can, say something about its affinities and perhaps
the probable date of its introduction. A glance at the history
of the winged monster Chronos-Herakles, at the story of Phanes
springing from the egg or being swallowed by Zeus, or the place
of principles like Time and Night in the Orphic theogonies, is far
more likely to lead to interesting results than an attempt to
settle the actual date at which the unpoetical verses were written
down in which some of these stories are now enshrined.

The first thing to do will be to give a short account of the
theogony in outline. The version mentioned by Damaskios as

---

* Neither Kern's view nor Gruppe's, of course, would exclude the possibility of isolated interpolations being inserted in the *hieroi logoi*. *O.F.* 226
(p. 141 below) may be cited as an example.

being that of Eudemos (*O.F.* 28) would have especial interest since Eudemos lived in the fourth century B.C. Unfortunately Damaskios tells us nothing about it beyond the bare fact that it made Night the first principle. In this it certainly differs from the 'customary Orphic theology' of the Neoplatonists, according to which Night had several generations of forbears, but agrees, according to Damaskios, with the theogony alluded to by Homer (in *Iliad* 14), though he has to admit that Eudemos himself denied this agreement. The omission of the higher principles of the Rhapsodic Theogony Damaskios accounts for in Neoplatonic fashion by the argument that, belonging to the intelligible world, they are passed over by Eudemos as altogether ineffable and unknowable.

Of the theogony according to Hieronymos and Hellanikos it must be said, with Gruppe (*Culte und Mythen*, 633), that Damaskios does not expressly call it Orphic. He has promised to describe the Greek theogonies, not the Orphic in particular, and although he begins with 'that in the so-called Orphic Rhapsodies', there is no necessity to suppose that when he goes on with 'that of Hieronymos and Hellanikos' he thinks of it as Orphic also. That it belongs to the Orphic circle we infer from another source, the Christian apologist Athenagoras, who attributes an almost identical account to Orpheus. According to these accounts, there was first water and (presumably) some solid matter, from which was formed a slime or mud that finally was to harden into earth.[5] As it is impossible for a Neoplatonist to conceive of the Universe as going back ultimately to two principles instead of an undivided One, Damaskios adds that 'the one principle before the two is omitted by the account as being altogether unutterable'. Out of water and earth was born a monstrous figure, a serpent having the heads of a bull and a lion, and the face of a god between ; and the name of the figure was Chronos (Time) and Herakles. Together with him, relates Damaskios, was Necessity, the same nature as Adrasteia, who broods over the whole universe, reaching even to its confines. It is with Time that the theogony of the Rhapsodies begins, and to account for the absence of any remoter principle Damaskios gives the same Neoplatonic reason as when he was speaking of Eudemos : the Rhapsodies omit the two earlier principles (and the one before them which has been passed over in silence), and start with the third 'as first containing anything which may be spoken of and is commensurate with human hearing'. (*O.F.* 54-59.)

We have now entered the limits of the Rhapsodies, and, so long as the version of Hieronymos lasts, there is not much difference between them.* Out of Chronos are born Aither with Chaos and Erebos, or as the Rhapsodies have it, Aither and a great yawning gulf, and darkness over all. Next, Chronos fashions in Aither an egg. The egg splits in two and Phanes, the first-born of the gods (Protogonos), springs forth. ' And at the birth of Phanes the misty gulf below and the windless *aither* were rent ' (*O.F.* 72). In the version of Athenagoras the two halves of the egg form the heaven and the earth, but in the Rhapsodies these do not appear until a later stage. Phanes is the creator of all, from whom the world has its first origin. (The seemingly redundant expression is necessary because in the Orphic tale there is, as we shall see, a second beginning of all things in the age of Zeus.) He is imagined as marvellously beautiful, a figure of shining light, with golden wings on his shoulders, four eyes, and the heads of various animals. He is of both sexes, since he is to create the race of gods unaided, ' bearing within himself the honoured seed of the gods ' (*O.F.* 85). As in its description of Chronos, the Hieronymian version is more garbled and picturesque. In addition to the golden wings, it gives him bulls' heads growing on his sides and on his head ' a monstrous serpent, appearing in all manner of forms of beasts '. He has many names, Phanes, Protogonos, Erikepaios, Metis, Dionysos, Eros.

The fragments do not allow us to form a coherent picture of the creation accomplished by Phanes. He made an eternal home for the gods and was their first king. The lines describing the making of the sun and the moon (which is a world in the heavens, containing ' many mountains, many cities, many mansions ' (*O.F.* 91)) must be referred to him. There are men too in the age of Phanes (*O.F.* 94), but they are not of our race. As we shall see, all this belongs to a vanished era, and the men of Phanes' time, we are told, were the men of the Golden Age.

Phanes bore a daughter, Night, whom he took as his partner and to whom he gave great power. She assisted him in the work of creation, and he finally handed over his sceptre to her, so that she became the next in order of the rulers of the universe. As a mark of the pre-eminent position which she was afterwards to hold unchallenged, he gave her the gift of prophecy. She gave her oracles from a cave, at the entrance to which was the dim and abstract Orphic goddess Adrasteia (the same as Ananke, Necessity) whose solemn business it was to make laws for the gods.

Night bore to Phanes Gaia and Ouranos (Earth and Heaven), who in their turn were the parents of the Titans, Kronos, Rhea,

* The fragments (in the strict sense) of the Rhapsodies are translated in Appendix 3, pp. 137 ff.

Okeanos, Tethys and the rest. To Ouranos Night handed over
the supreme power. There follow the common Greek stories
about the Titans, the supremacy of Kronos, his mutilation of his
father Ouranos (with the birth of Aphrodite), his marriage with
Rhea, his swallowing of his children and the trick by which Rhea
saved the life of Zeus and restored the others to the light of day.
The Kuretes appear as the guardians of Zeus. In the Orphic
version the unique position of Night is continually emphasized.
Each god who is destined to succeed to the supreme power in the
Universe seems to owe something to her care. In this generation
'above them all she tended Kronos, and cherished him' (*O.F.* 129).

We are now approaching our own era. Of our world Zeus is
not simply supreme ruler, but creator. How can this be, since all
was created before he was born ? There is no subtlety about the
answer. Zeus swallows Phanes, and with Phanes, who is the
first-born and the origin of all, he may be regarded as taking into
himself all things that exist : ' Thus then engulfing the might of
Erikepaios, the First-born, he held the body of all things in the
hollow of his own belly ; and he mingled with his own limbs the
power and strength of the god. Therefore together with him all
things within Zeus were created anew, the shining height of the
broad *aither* and the sky, the seat of the unharvested sea and the
noble earth, great Ocean and the lowest depths beneath the earth,
and rivers and the boundless sea and all else, all immortal and
blessed gods and goddesses, all that was then in being and all
that was to come to pass, all was there, and mingled like streams
in the belly of Zeus' (*O.F.* 167).

In the work that he has to do, Zeus seeks the advice of Night,
who has lost none of her dignity as the being of supreme wisdom
and prophetic powers, to whose opinion even the highest of the
other gods must show deference. It was Night who unfolded a
plan for the subduing of Kronos, whose place Zeus was to usurp,
and Night he addresses, in the most respectful terms, when he is
in need of help for the creation of the new world. ' Mother,' he
says (a term of respect, not one implying kinship), ' highest of
the gods, immortal Night, how am I to establish my proud rule
among the Immortals ?' (*O.F.* 164). Again he puts to her what
for a Greek was the one eternal problem involved in the making
of a universe : 'How may I have all things one and each one
separate ? ' And Night answers : ' Surround all things with the
ineffable *aither*, and in the midst of that set the heaven, and in
the midst the boundless earth, in the midst the sea, and in the
midst all the constellations with which the heaven is crowned '
(*O.F.* 165).

Having created all things anew, Zeus becomes, in the famous line, ' beginning, middle and end of all ' (*O.F.* 21, 168).* As in the mythology common to Greece, Athena springs from his head ' Gleaming with arms, a brazen glory to behold ' (174), and becomes the ' accomplisher of his will ' (176). The Kyklopes, first of all craftsmen, fashion for him the thunder and the thunderbolt. By Rhea (identified in the Orphic poem with Demeter : ' Aforetime was she Rhea, but when she came to be called mother of Zeus she became Demeter ' (145)) he has a daughter Kore-Persephone, the maiden who was destined to be ravished by Zeus and carried off by Pluto. To Pluto she bore the Furies, to Zeus she bore Dionysos, the last to rule over the gods. (See App. 2, pp. 133 ff. below.) To him Zeus handed over the power, ' for all he was young and but a greedy infant ' (207). He set him on his throne and put his own sceptre in his hand, and said to the new generation of gods : ' Give ear ye gods ; this one have I made your king ' (208). But the Titans, who of course had also found life again in the new order created by Zeus (210), were jealous of the child, and plotted against him. According to some authorities they were incited by Hera, the lawful wife of Zeus, to attack the son of another mother. With a mirror and other playthings they distracted his infant mind, and while he played slew him and tore his body in pieces. His limbs were collected by Apollo at Zeus's orders and taken to Delphi (210, 211). The heart was saved by Athena, who brought it to Zeus that out of it Zeus might cause Dionysos to be reborn. Alive again, he remains for the Orphics the supreme object of worship. We remember too that Phanes himself was also called Dionysos, so that in reality he has existed from the beginning of all, one god thrice-born, Dionysos-Phanes, Dionysos-Zagreus (as the Titans' victim is sometimes called, though not frequently in the extant authorities), and Dionysos the resurrected.

Thus in the divine dynasty of the Orphic theogony six generations are represented as having held in turn the supreme government of the Universe : Phanes, Night, Ouranos, Kronos, Zeus, Dionysos, and the command of the poet is fulfilled, that command which is expressed in one of the few precious lines attributed to Orpheus by Plato himself : ' And in the sixth generation bring to a close the order of your song ' (*Philebos* 66c).[6]

Yet the story is not quite finished, and in what follows we have the link between all these warrings in heaven, these seemingly domestic affairs of the Immortals, and our own religious life. The most heinous part of the Titans' crime has still to be told. When

---

* Compare Milton, *P. L.* 5, 165 : ' Him first, Him last, Him midst and without end '.

they had slain the infant Dionysos, they tasted of his flesh. In wrath at the outrage Zeus launched a thunderbolt at them and burned them up, and from the smoking remnants of the Titans there arose a race which this age had not yet known, the race of mortal men. Our nature therefore is twofold. We are born from the Titans, the wicked sons of Earth, but there is in us something of a heavenly nature too, since there went to our making fragments of the body of Dionysos, son of Olympian Zeus, on whom the Titans had made their impious feast. So now to Dionysos we make prayer and sacrifice ' in all the seasons of the year ' as the sacred writings say, ' yearning to be set free from our lawless ancestry ' (232, p. 214 below). Dionysos can free us, wherefore we call him ' Liberator ', Dionysos the immortal, the resurrected, of whose nature there is yet a small part in each and every one of us. Knowing all this, what other aim can we have in life but to purge away as far as possible the Titanic element in us and exalt and cherish the Dionysiac ? At this point we must stop for the present. The story of the Creation is finished, and the rest will find its proper place later, the questions of how this purification is to be accomplished, and what reward there is for the pure, and punishment for the neglectful, now or in the life to come. Our present task is to take the story which has been barely and uncritically related, and see if the picture can be filled out by further description or comment on the various figures and elements which have appeared.

The account just given has been put together solely and directly from the fragments of the *hieroi logoi* and the Hieronymian version as they have been collected by Kern. Any sidelights obtainable from other sources have been deliberately avoided in order to give nothing but the bare outline of the story. The obvious question to ask before going further is how far this theogony may be called Orphic in the sense that it was peculiar and differed from the ordinary background of mythology which was the heritage of every Greek. A comparison with Hesiod and Homer shows that much of the mythological background is the same, but that the differences are in matter many and striking, in spirit so vast that it is scarcely possible to exaggerate them. The poet was imbued with Greek mythology and wished to write in its terms, but only to transform its significance. The same gods appear, but are given new functions and new duties ; actual lines and half-lines of Hesiod and Homer are inserted, but put to entirely new uses. A glance at the beginning of Hesiod's account may serve to bring out these points. First of all there was Chaos, then Earth ($\Gamma\tilde{\eta}$) and Tartaros in the depths of the earth ($\chi\theta\acute{\omega}\nu\iota$), and Eros. By

what means these came into existence is not related. From Chaos
are born Erebos and Night, and from Night Aither and Day.
Earth bears Heaven, who is afterwards her partner. All these are
early principles in the Orphic theogonies as well, and although
their mutual relationships may not be quite the same, that is not
a matter of great importance. Again in the stories of Kronos,
how he attacked his father Ouranos only to be paid back in his
own coin and treated in the same unfilial way by his own son
Zeus, whom he had vainly tried to destroy at birth, we have
further examples of stories which are related by the Orphic poet
because they are part of the common stock of Greek tales about
the heavenly dynasties. The differences appear rather in what
is present in the Orphic versions but lacking in Hesiod. In
Hesiod there is no world-egg, and although Night finds her place
in the genealogy there is no hint of the unique position which she
holds in the Orphic theogony as protector and adviser of successive
rulers of the Universe. Eros is mentioned as one of the earliest
principles, and the Orphic Phanes is identical with Eros, but with
Hesiod the bare mention of his name, and the words ' fairest
among the immortal gods ', are made to suffice. He is not the
flashing, golden-winged apparition of the Orphic poem, nor, what
is more important, is he the First-born and source of all life to
come, and the one supreme object of worship to those who know.
There is no Chronos in Hesiod, none of the curious second beginning
of all things within the body of Zeus, above all none of the story of
Dionysos and the Titans. From this it follows that the human
interest with which the Orphic poem ends is entirely lacking in
Hesiod, and his theogony is divorced from ideas of good and evil.
Hesiod's narration keeps us in an atmosphere of clear, cold daylight : it is a straightforward account of plain, if miraculous,
facts. The Orphic poems are pervaded with a sense of the mystery
and paradox of life, from their preoccupation with the eternal
question—how shall all be one yet each thing apart ?—to their
culmination in the revealing of our own half-divine, half-earthly
nature, with the complete change of outlook, the new obligations
and the undreamed-of yearnings which that revelation imparts.
In short, the fundamental difference between the two systems lies
here : the one could never be made the doctrinal basis of a
religious life ; the other both could be and in fact was.

It is in the early stages of the Orphic theogony that we have
for comparison the two versions of (a) the Rhapsodies and (b) the
Orpheus of Athenagoras and the Hieronymos and Hellanikos of
Damaskios, and it is therefore the differences between these two

versions which may be expected to arouse first of all the curiosity of a systematic reader. It is customary nowadays to regard the two latter, which I have grouped together, as identical, though Lobeck (*Agl.* 493) described the passage in Athenagoras as more dependent on the Rhapsodies. There are indeed points of difference between them, notably the way in which, in the Orpheus of Athenagoras, the two halves of the egg from which Phanes sprang go to make Heaven and Earth. In Damaskios nothing is said of this, and Earth had already been formed at an unusually early stage for any cosmogony.[7] Their great point of resemblance, and joint difference from the Rhapsodies, is the description of Chronos. In view of this description, which constitutes its distinctive feature, the question of the possible date of this version has a certain general interest, since it opens the discussion of whether the Greeks were accustomed at an early date (in the classical periods of the sixth and fifth centuries B.C.) to think of their gods, and in particular of so abstract a principle as Time, in the form of monsters which suggest at first sight rather the extravagance of the Oriental imagination than the traditional calm and sanity of the Hellenic mind. What far-reaching effects the answer to this question may have, no one will doubt who has read Robert Eisler's chain of reasoning in *Weltenmantel und Himmelszelt*, which is as follows : Time was never thought of as a god by the Greeks except in the Orphic tradition ; therefore if a Greek poet ventures so far into metaphor as to speak, like Sophocles, of χρόνος εὐμαρὴς θεός, of time as a kindly god, to indicate that sorrows are healed by time, or like Pindar of time as ' father of all ', he must be supposed on every occasion (*ausschliesslich*) to have the Orphic deity in his mind. But our authority for this deity is the theogony of Hieronymos and Hellanikos. Consequently Sophocles and Pindar are conjuring up in their minds as they write the picture of a winged serpent with the heads of animals. That there is another authority for the Orphic Chronos, that it is this other which is described by Damaskios as the ' customary ' Orphic theogony, and that as far as we know it gives the god no more exotic epithets than ' ageless,' ' great,' ' whose counsels never perish,' is nowhere mentioned by Eisler.[8]

We cannot learn much about the date of the Hieronymian version from the mention of its authors or narrators. Hieronymos is otherwise unknown. If he is the same as the Hieronymos mentioned by Josephus as having written the ancient history of Phoenicia, that would only explain *obscurum per nihilominus obscurum*. With Hellanikos we are little better off.[9] In any case, Damaskios' way of referring to it is a little discouraging.

' According to H. and H.' does not mean that he has himself found
it in the writings of these two authorities. What he says is :
' The theogony spoken of as that of Hieronymos and Hellanikos,
if indeed he be not the same man . . .'

Let us make quite sure that we have one thing clear. In
contrasting the two Orphic versions we are not at the moment
discussing the *presence* of Time as a deity in the Orphic theogony, since he occurs in both, but simply his description. This
in Damaskios' account of H. and H. is as follows : ' He is a
serpent having heads growing upon him of a bull and a lion,
and in the middle the face of a god ; and he has also wings
upon his shoulders, and is called ageless Time, and Herakles the
same'. The discussion of date is usually made to centre round
the Oriental tone of this description. On this there is little disagreement. For a die-hard defender of the origin on Greek soil
(Hellenic or pre-Hellenic) of Hellenic myths, something might
prehaps be said. Evidence is not lacking for the presence in
Greek mythology from an early age both of monsters and of
winged creatures, for which it is not necessary to seek an Oriental
origin. Without becoming recondite we may remind ourselves
of the winged as well as wingless Nike, of the winged horses of
Pelops, seen by Pausanias carved on the chest of Kypselos at
Olympia, and described by Pindar, and of the strange creature who
was put on the Acropolis in an age before the Parthenon, and may
still be seen there, a coiling serpent with three human heads.
Some, though imported, were imported at an early date. The
Lycian Chimaira is in Homer. For the wings, an attractively
succinct example occurs to the mind. In the *Birds* of Aristophanes, Peisthetairos is trying to persuade the birds that they
themselves are the real gods, and that they ought to persuade
mortals to honour them as such. The birds object : ' And how
are men going to believe that we are gods, and not jackdaws,
when we flutter about and wear wings ? ' ' Nonsense,' says
Peisthetairos. ' Why, Hermes flies and has wings, though he is a
god, and a whole host of other gods too. Then there's Nike, who
flies with golden wings, yes, and by Zeus, Eros too. And Hera,
or so Homer said, resembled a wild dove.' Yet when this has
been said, and a great many more creatures of more or less doubtful
origin quoted in support of the same theory, the depicting of
ageless Time himself in this form shows correspondences with
Oriental, and in particular with Persian religion, which are too
detailed and exact to be passed over. This is ground which has
been thoroughly gone over by more competent authorities, and
need not be reworked here.[10] It would take us far afield. Still

less need we re-open discussion on the general *a priori* possibility of contact between Greek and Oriental minds at an early date. This too has often been dwelt on, perhaps most picturesquely by Gomperz (*Greek Thinkers*, i, p. 95). Professor Cornford (*From Religion to Philosophy*, p. 176) sums up thus, as far as relates to Orphic thought : ' Whether or not we accept the hypothesis of direct influence from Persia on the Ionian Greeks in the sixth century, any student of Orphic and Pythagorean thought cannot fail to see that the similarities between it and Persian religion are so close as to warrant our regarding them as expressions of the same view of life, and using the one system to interpret the other '. When the fact we are faced with is the resemblance of the Orphic χρόνος ἀγήραος (Ageless Time) in its mythological representation to the Persian Zrvān Akarana (Endless Time), a resemblance not ✷ merely general but extending to detail, then even the ' hypothesis of direct influence ' becomes difficult to escape. Yet so it is.

That, very briefly, is the position with regard to Oriental influence. What effect is it to have on our view of the date of Chronos the monstrous serpent as a figure in Greek mythology ? If we read the opinion of one scholar we feel enlightened. As we compare the inferences of others from the same set of facts, the fog descends again. Gruppe says that the Oriental elements in the Hieronymian version cannot be explained as borrowings of the Hellenistic age, and that the most important of them were already known to the pre-Socratic philosophers. Kern notes that the description of Chronos in the Rhapsodies is much simpler than that in the Hieronymian version, and concludes that the simpler story is obviously the older. The Hieronymian version, he says, bears unmistakably the marks of the Alexandrian age, a sentiment which he contentedly but vaguely ascribes to ' omnes viri docti '. On a more general line of thought, one is inclined to respect and give wider application to Jane Harrison's observation that it was only natural for Greek art to be more susceptible to outside influences when in its infancy ; as it grew to its own strong and individual maturity it cast them off. Surely if this applies to art it applies to the Hellenic mind in general ? Toying with this idea we are met by Gomperz : ' As his (the Greek's) ancient native traditions failed more and more to satisfy his increasing curiosity and thirst for knowledge, foreign sources would be drawn on more freely in an age of acute intellectual vigour and progress '. To make any fresh suggestion seems like putting only one more on an already massive pile of theories fatal to each other and discouraging to the observer. Yet if the subject is worth discussing at all, the very multitude of theories is an indication that it is time to step back, to recapture if possible a little of that insight into the general features of Hellenic culture which ought to be the product of a classical education, and with that for a background to mediate as far as possible between opposing views and try to form a synthesis in which their soundest points may be embodied.

My own solution would be somewhat on the lines of Gruppe's, and form in some ways a parallel to Jane Harrison's remarks on the progress of Greek art. The Hellenic mind at its most vigorous must be distinguished both from the receptive state of its childhood and the indiscriminate search for novelty which marked its decline. In this period of its maturity, covering roughly the late sixth to the fourth centuries B.C., it was less susceptible to new influences from outside, and was concerned to modify those which had already entered its world, and to make them conform more nearly to its own standards. It did not care for monstrosities either in its thought or in its art. This was the age which saw the birth of rationalism in philosophy on the one hand, advocating the rejection of the myths as not conformable to reason. On the other hand, among those who remained loyal to the religious traditions, it saw a purifying of the myths from much of their ancient crudity. Idealist representations of the gods in art went hand in hand with the high moral tone and enhanced beauty of the myths in the literature of a Pindar or a Sophocles. A comparison of the sculptured monuments of the seventh century, which form what archaeologists call the Orientalising period of Greek art, with those of the classical age, soon makes clear the development of the Hellenic mind from a slavish imitation of Eastern types to a realization of its own peculiar contribution to the art and culture of the world. The difference between the two has been well summed up by a German writer. Ancient Asiatic art, wrote Julius Langbehn, is marked by its abstract (*begrifflich*) character, finding its expression in symbolism, which again, to speak more concretely, shows itself in the production of mixed animal and human types, and all sorts of winged creatures. It is in short completely opposed to realism. Some winged creatures, as we have noticed, are indigenous to Greece, and the difference between these two has been put with such un-Teutonic brevity by Langbehn that I must quote it as it stands : *diese fliegen, jene nicht.*[11] Greek art on the other hand was founded on poetry, defined for this purpose as meaning sensibility to natural experiences (*Empfindung*), though, be it added, to the highest and most nearly perfect in natural experience. In opposition to the lifeless symbolism of Asiatic art, classical Greece offers an idealism based on realism, that is, the representation of all the finest features in nature. For an illustration of the state of Greek culture in the eighth and seventh centuries, the field of art had to be chosen because in the history of Greek literature that period is almost a blank page. Of their art we have specimens, chiefly in bronze, and they show that it was not lacking in creatures like sphinxes and griffins who had wings but could never have flown. For example, a glance at the chapter on 'The Early Archaic (Orientalising) Period' in Miss Lamb's *Greek and Roman Bronzes* (Methuen, 1929) gives us at once instances of winged, and of mixed animal and human, types. A small figure from Sparta (seventh century) represents a lion with a serpent's tail; the Tyszkiewicz plate (seventh century, Lamb, pl. 18*b*) shows figures with human head, lion's body and wings, and other examples include sphinxes and griffins. Crete was an important centre of Greek art at this time, and a fruitful transmitter of Oriental types. More important still, its religious art must have directly affected the Orphics, since they took up Cretan elements into the very centre of their creed (pp. 108 ff. below, and for the Kuretes, pp. 160 f.). This makes it particularly relevant for our purpose to notice the bronze tympanum from the Idaean Cave, birthplace of the Cretan Zeus (Cook, *Zeus*, 1, p. 644 and Pl. XXXV), which shows the Cretan god with his attendant Kuretes, but shows him as a purely Assyrian type.

We return now to the subject immediately under discussion. We are presented with two versions of a myth, in one of which Time is represented as a winged and multiform creature whom one sees quite naturally, if he makes the picture in his mind's eye, in the form of an Assyrian or Persian relief, certainly not in any form in which he would have been modelled by any Hellenic sculptor of classical times. In the other version, shorn of his monstrous attributes, he appears almost in the form in which a Greek rationalistic philosopher of the sixth century might have cast him, if he were putting his system into poetic shape—ageless, great, whose counsels fail not. That time always was, that time has great power for good or evil, that by time all things may be accomplished—these surely are sentiments to which the most philosophic mind might own. 'The simplest tale must be the oldest', said Kern. But simple is an ambiguous word. Who has the simpler mind, the man who conceives of time as a creature of grotesque mythological shape, or the man who has learned to think of it without these picturesque and concrete attributes? I suggest that the latter shows the higher stage of civilization, and that therefore, on Kern's own argument, that the simpler version must be the earlier, we should put the grotesque one first and regard the other as a refinement on it produced by a more cultured age.

It is right to take into account the fact that Orphism was somewhat removed from the main stream of Greek culture, and that a crudity which had been purged away from the upper levels might have survived in the undercurrent. If the only Orphic description of Time were the Oriental, this consideration might weigh with us. When, however, we are presented with the two versions, it is at least a reasonable supposition that the development was in the direction I have suggested and not in the other. To suppose that everyone imbued with Orphic traditions cut himself off entirely from the current of thought around him would be absurd. Again we might be disposed to doubt if there were no evidence at all for the presence of Time in Greek cosmogony before the Hellenistic age. Against this is its prominent position in the cosmogony of Pherekydes as well as in that attributed to Orpheus. It is, however, to this fact, the comparative seclusion of Orphic ideas from the main flow of Greek thought, that I am tempted to attribute something else, namely the survival of Phanes in his barbaric form into the Rhapsodies, which on this supposition we are regarding as a product of at least the beginning of the age of enlightenment, say the age of Peisistratos.[12] Philosophy was being born, and therefore a principle like time, which to the rational thinker is merely an abstraction, could not retain its fully mythological dress. But Phanes is not the projection into mythology of a well-known phenomenon of the external world. He is a god and nothing else, and if his devotee is not to give up belief in his actual existence, there is not the same necessity, or indeed opportunity, for modifying his original mythological character.

We have been led to make one or two general remarks on the intellectual and religious climate of classical Greece, and these may help us when we turn to ask, as the arguments of Eisler demand that we should, what are likely to have been the feelings of the poets. How would Sophocles, for instance, have regarded this kind of religious lore when he was composing his own lines ? One must be careful not to exaggerate. The first impulse of an enthusiast is to say that he looked on the world with the eyes not of a religious teacher, nor of a philosopher, but of a poet. Yet this would not be true. It would be true if modified to this extent, that he looked on the world with the eyes first of a poet and then with those of a religious teacher or a philosopher, and that in itself means much. It means, in my opinion, that he did not believe Time, the kindly god, to be a monstrous serpent. But the poets of Greece were none the less more than poets. The plays of Sophocles were performed at the great religious festivals, before an audience of the whole city assembled to do honour to Dionysos, and they had a message to deliver ; so that it would be wrong to dismiss *a priori* the possibility of religious influences, including that of Orphism, on his thought and his work. We shall find good evidence that Orphism made a strong appeal to the supple, and hence both receptive and independent mind of Pindar. Yet Pindar remains the classical example of a great mind anxious to purge away the grosser elements of his country's religious traditions, solely out of the love which he bears towards those traditions themselves. The argument of the preceding pages has been directed towards showing that in crediting Sophocles with the rejection from his own religious thought of the more fantastic Oriental conceptions we are not attributing to him a lofty poetic isolation from the religion of his contemporaries. He was one of the leaders of classical Hellenism, to which the fantastic was repugnant. It may be that Pindar's poetic description of time as ' lord of the gods ' betrays an acquaintance with the Orphic theogony, even, if you like, with the cruder Orphic theogony which the authors of the Rhapsodies themselves rejected. It is nevertheless a much more important observation that he left all the crude parts out.[13]

The comparison of the two descriptions of Time in the varying versions of the Orphic theogony has left little to be said at present on the general subject of his presence there. The position of time at the beginning of the world might suggest a more philosophical origin for the myths, were it not for the probability that it is only a transplantation of Persian religious ideas modified in due course by the transforming genius of the classical Hellenic mind. That this was the course of events I suggest only as a theory, but the arguments of the Orientalists on the point (which I can only judge on the evidence they themselves set before us) seem difficult to escape.[14] Again, even granted the theory of borrowing from Persia, we cannot take it as finally proved that this borrowing took place in early and not in Hellenistic times. Nothing better can be done than to state what seems the likelier view and indicate the evidence on which it rests. That evidence is by no means all included here, because I have not thought it proper that the question of date should be allowed to dominate the arrangement of the book. I shall, for instance, say in a later chapter what I can about the relation of Orphism to the philosophies of Greece.

I can only suggest that, should there be any who wish to make this sketch the starting-point of their own researches, they should read the whole before proceeding to form conclusions.

The egg from which sprang Eros-Phanes has the distinction, rare indeed for an Orphic dogma, of being mentioned in a famous passage of classical literature. The race of birds, in Aristophanes' comedy *The Birds*, having wrested from the gods the supreme power in heaven, are anxious to prove, as many have been since, that the power which they now hold by force is really theirs by ancient right. They therefore recite, to a submissive audience of mere human beings, a new version of the origins of the world, designed to show that the race of birds is of more ancient lineage than the gods. This not unnaturally involves some perversion of the usual tales, and even the scholiast on the passage recognised that it was not necessary to refer the birds' cosmogony to any single one of the known *theologoi*. Except, however, for the line which speaks of the birth of the birds themselves, the account is fairly obviously put together out of the stock materials. It runs as follows (*Birds*, 693 ff. = Kern, *O.F.* 1) :—

' Chaos was and Night and black Erebos at first and broad Tartaros, but there was no earth nor yet air nor sky. Then in the infinite bosom of Erebos first of all black-winged Night bore a wind-sown egg, from which in the circling seasons came Eros the much desired, his back gleaming with twin golden wings, swift as the whirling winds. He mingling in broad Tartaros with winged and gloomy Chaos hatched out our race, and brought us first to see the light. Before that there was no race of the Immortals, until Eros mingled all things together. Then from their mingling with each other was born Heaven and Ocean and Earth and the deathless race of the blessed gods. Thus are we far the oldest of the gods. . , .'

In the study of Orphic dogma, it is in many ways fortunate that we have beneath our feet several strata of modern literature on the subject. The labours of others have saved us much misguided search. The case of the Egg is typical. The first step was to cast about for a theory of its origin based on the discovery of parallel conceptions in the mythology of other lands. The Egg as the symbol of creation—who was the first to think of this profound allegory ? The hunt was up and examples multiplied themselves surprisingly. The Egg was run to earth in India, in Persia, in Assyria, in Egypt, brought in fact ' from the farthest East and even from the icy regions of Siberia and Kamtschatka '. It is not left for us to follow it there. It is not even left for us to take what is logically the next step, though great minds saw it many years ago, and with some it has not even yet superseded the idea of a chain of borrowers. This step is to reflect that in taking the Egg as the symbol of the beginning of life, the makers of myths were after all doing a very simple and natural thing, and if it is common to the stories which many different peoples have made up about the origins of the world, that is really not surprising, and there is no need at all to suppose that they handed on the great thought from one to the other.[15]

If we may trust the Neoplatonists, the World-egg was a prominent feature of the theogonies ascribed to Orpheus, and it is usually referred to to-day, without more ado, as the Orphic Egg. There is every reason for thinking that the name is justified. According to a sentence in Damaskios whose meaning is only partly clear (the Neoplatonic preoccupation with triads and the intelligible world renders some of it obscure), this World-egg was also a feature in the cosmogony of Epimenides the Cretan. If that is so (and Damaskios is quoting Eudemos), it was probably because he found it in Orphic tradition, which in all likelihood was older than he. It is, however, a matter on which one can hardly dogmatize. In this early part of his cosmogony, Aristophanes may well have had Epimenides in mind, since according to them both Night existed before the Egg, and appears to have produced it.[16] In the Orpheus of the Neoplatonists the Egg was produced by Chronos, whom neither Aristophanes nor (so far as we know) Epimenides mentioned, and Night is the daughter of the god who emerged from it. A case has, however, been made for supposing an earlier version of the Orphic theogony itself in which she occupied this earlier stage. This will come up for consideration when we are speaking of Night. In view of the development of the ' question of the date of the Rhapsodies ' into one of the bogeys of modern scholarship, I am going to ask pardon for repeating the few facts about the Egg in a laborious way designed to make clear yet once more the policy which is being pursued here. After that we may perhaps be a little less meticulous in expression. The World-egg, which is a feature in the cosmogonies of the Neoplatonic Orpheus, appears in the fifth century in a cosmogony quoted by Aristophanes, and is attributed to Epimenides who lived at the end of the seventh century. It can therefore be traced back to a pre-classical stage of Greek

FIG. 10.—
THE ORPHIC EGG.
This little cornelian shows Eros seated in an egg, which has split in half.

thought. We are therefore entitled to say 'this bit of the Rhapsodies goes back to pre-classical times', since if we say instead, 'in speaking of a world-egg, the author of the Rhapsodies, at whatever period he—or they—may have lived, was drawing on a tradition which went back to pre-classical times', I do not see that we gain anything by the refinement.

Before we leave the Egg, an interesting path of thought is opened up by the epithet which Aristophanes applies to it. He ✱ calls it ὑπηνέμιον, a word whose first meaning is 'borne or wafted on the wind'. ᾠον ὑπηνέμιον could also mean a wind-egg, one which is sterile and produces no chicken. No doubt Aristophanes knew of this, and the incongruous juxtaposition of sense and nonsense which the association suggests is quite in keeping with his sense of humour. But it is another meaning which would be uppermost. According to Aristotle, wind-eggs are those that are produced by the hen alone, without impregnation, and Lucian speaks of Hera as having borne in Hephaistos 'a wind-child (ὑπηνέμιον παῖδα), without resort to her husband' (Arist. *Hist. Anim.* 6. 2. 559b20, Luc. *de sacrif.* 6). The Egg, then, from which Eros, creator of gods and men, was to be born, was laid by Night unaided by any male partner, and this Aristophanes expresses by saying that it was brought on the winds. The idea behind this is that the soul, the life-principle, either is itself air or being of similar substance is blown about with the winds and is drawn into the body at birth. The breath is the life. The Latin word for soul, *anima*, means also breath, and the history of the Greek word *psyche* is the same. The word ὑπηνέμιον was becoming a common-place, as the above quotations show, and examples from ancient philosophers and poets might be multiplied to illustrate both the belief that our soul is air breathed in from outside and also the complementary notion of the impregnation of a female by the winds.[17] The ramifications of these ideas are fascinating, and sometimes (as when treated by a Virgil) beautiful, but what interests us particularly here is that they were taken up into (though doubtless not originating in) the doctrines of Orpheus. Whether they originated there or not, they became established as Orphic doctrine quite early, since it is as such that they are quoted by Aristotle. More definitely, the theory which he ascribes to the 'so-called Orphic poems' is that the soul 'comes into us from space as we breathe, borne by the winds' (*de an.* 1. 5. 410b28). The same theory is credited to those near allies of the Orphics, the Pythagoreans, by Cicero (*de nat. deor.* 1. 11. 27). The theory of wind-impregnation was accepted by Aristotle in all seriousness, and was probably dissociated in his mind from the

other (*Hist. Anim.* 6. 2. 560*a*6).   The Attic Tritopatores, who ✱
had certainly been wind-spirits (Rohde, *Psyche*, Eng. tr. ch. 5,
n. 124), found a place in an Orphic poem as ' doorkeepers and
guardians of the winds ' (Suidas, *s.v.* Tritopatores, Harrison,
Proleg.[3] 179, n. 2).

From the egg laid by Night, say the birds, came Eros.   Is this
the same as the Phanes of the Rhapsodies, who was also called
Eros ?   Did Aristophanes know that he was called Phanes too,
and call him Eros simply from that strange shyness which seems
to have worked upon all the writers of the classical age to make
them refer to anything Orphic in its least specifically Orphic form ?
We shall probably never know for certain, but let us do our best,
since if it is Phanes whom we have here, it is easily his earliest
appearance.   What is there to make us think that he might be
the Orphic god ?   He is one of those who came at the very
beginning of things, not the youthful son of Aphrodite that he
became in classical times.   But that might come straight from
Hesiod.   He is golden-winged, as he is in the Rhapsodies, and as
he is addressed in his Orphic hymn.   The wings themselves prove
nothing, since the figure of Eros as a winged youth was already a
commonplace of art and literature.   In all probability Eros always
had been winged.   It will be noticed that in this cosmogony Chaos
is winged too, a circumstance for which I know of no parallel, and
can suggest no better motive than the natural eagerness of the
birds to set as many winged creatures as possible among the
highest principles.   As for the epithet ' golden ', was not that a
common tag, and very naturally so ?   If your winged creature is
a god, it is almost inevitable that you should imagine his wings
as formed of the precious, shining stuff.   Only a little way back
in this same play, as it happens, one of Aristophanes' characters
has been speaking of the winged Nike, and she too is given ' twin
golden wings ' in exactly the same words, down to the dual number,
as Eros.   (They were useful in any case for the anapaestic tetra-
meters in which the characters were speaking.)   The description
becomes a little more significant when we notice in conjunction
with the golden wings the epithet ' gleaming ' (στίλβων).   We
recall involuntarily the lines from the Rhapsodies : ' And all the
others marvelled when they saw the unlooked-for light in the
aither ; so richly gleamed (ἀπέστιλβε) the body of immortal
Phanes '.   Doubting still, we add in our minds the rest of what
Aristophanes has to say about his Eros.   He was born from an egg,
and he is the creator of the world and the gods.   It becomes
increasingly difficult to withhold belief, and I for one am ready to

give up the struggle and affirm that in describing Eros as he did, Aristophanes must have been playing with the phrases of a poem in the Orphic tradition. I cannot see any opportunity here to apply the ingenious argument of turning the tables, whereby, if a correspondence is noticed between the Rhapsodies and a classical author, the arguer turns round and answers, 'Yes, but the writer of the Orphic poems which the Neoplatonists quote had obviously borrowed this from the classic '.

Extant classical literature offers no other description of Eros similar to this of Aristophanes, and no single mention of the name Phanes, which we would conclude from the Neoplatonists' authority to have been the characteristically Orphic title of the god. Fortunately we are just saved from entire dependence on the Neoplatonists or their contemporaries for this name. Diodoros, who lived in the reign of Augustus and so some three centuries before Proklos (see also n. 30 below), quotes a line of Orpheus which says that the Egyptian god Osiris is called ' Phanes and Dionysos '. This is the earliest known mention of the name, unless indeed it is included in the jumble of deities invoked on the weird and unintelligible inscription of the gold tablet unearthed in South Italy and known as the Timpone Grande tablet (b) (O.F. 47). This would give us a foothold three or four centuries further back, but it must remain doubtful. I can do nothing better than refer to Professor Murray's clear and reasonable discussion of it in the appendix to Jane Harrison's *Prolegomena* [3] (p. 664).

The derivation of the name from φαίνω is universal in ancient authorities. He is called Phanes because he first shone forth—appeared in a blaze of light—or alternatively because he makes visible, gives light to, the rest of creation. He is sometimes called light itself, or by a slight and very natural transference is identified with the sun, though this fusion was probably not made in the Rhapsodic account of the Creation, which seems to have been remarkably consistent, and according to which, of course, Phanes existed before the sun, which was first created by him. If the name is old, then in all probability, as has been suggested, the popular etymology is not the true one ; but until we can propose another, that suggestion does not take us very far, and anyway the popular etymology of a religious name is invariably more important than the true one.

Sometimes coupled with Phanes as an epithet, sometimes appearing independently, is the name Protogonos, First-born. We find this word first in a mutilated fragment of Euripides, who was certainly not a stranger to the wordy writings of Orpheus

(*O.F.* 2). It is surrounded by bits of words, all tantalizingly incomplete. ' A dazzling light . . . *aither* . . . Eros . . . Night.' They may be these, but the words are just sufficiently broken to make other restorations possible, at least of the last three. Chance has been ungenerous here, and we can do no more. Again, the recently mentioned tablet from South Italy begins ' To Protogonos Ge the Mother . . .' It can scarcely be maintained that we have here a separate mention of a god Protogonos. The word is much more naturally taken as an epithet of Ge, ' Earth the first-born '. This reminds us that Protogeneia was the name of a sister of Pandora and daughter of Erechtheus, the chthonian hero of Attica. Protogonos as an epithet was also applied to the chthonian goddess Kore-Persephone. The application of the epithet to Phanes, coupled with his creative powers, appealed to the Christian writer Lactantius. This theologian's thesis was that many of the pagan writers, if they had only held fast to what they felt when they let nature and reason be their guides, would have found themselves possessed of the same true doctrine as the Christians. He finds a signal example in Orpheus, who taught of ' that first-born god, to whom he ascribes the first place ', and who was ' the supreme power and the maker of heaven and earth ' (*O.F.* 88, 89).

A third name for Phanes is Metis—Wisdom or Counsel. That Phanes, being what he is, should appropriate this title calls for no comment. In Hesiod, the first of the many wives of Zeus is called Metis, and it was her fate, as it was that of Phanes, to be swallowed by him. She was about to bear Athena at the time, and Zeus took this course because it had been prophesied that after Athena she would bear a son destined to usurp the power of his father. The bringing of Athena into the world was made by Zeus his own care, and the result was the famous phenomenon of cephalogony. There is little resemblance indeed between the Hesiodic goddess and the Orphic Phanes, though a confusion of the two in the mind of one man may have been responsible for the second, distorted version of a certain line in an Orphic address to Zeus. In describing all that is mingled in the body of Zeus the creator, this hymn enumerates fire and water and earth and *aither*, night and day, and ' Metis, the first father and Eros of many delights ' (*O.F.* 168). This line was repeated by Syrianos in the form (*O.F.* 169) : ' And Metis, first mother, and Eros of many delights '.

Yet a fourth title of Phanes in the *Orphica* of the Neoplatonists is Erikepaios, a non-Greek name for which no certain interpretation has been found.[18] It is not once mentioned in the whole of older literature, and our evidence for it would belong entirely to the Christian era were it not for the recent discovery of a papyrus which is dated by the experts in the third century B.C. On this fragment it has been claimed with good ground that the name appears, in the form Irikepaigos. There is an Orphic flavour about the whole fragment, with its mentions of One Dionysos, and of the playthings (tops, knuckle-bones, mirror), with which the young god is beguiled. (Compare below, pp. 120 ff.) The whole seems to have been a leaf of instructions for an initiation ceremony, with directions for the sacrifice, formulas to be repeated and so forth (*O.F.* 31. First published in 1921).

The three names, Phanes, Metis and Erikepaios, were used by Gruppe to support a theory of the place of origin of the Phanes-myth. It will be interesting to mention it here, in so far as it concerns these three names, on account of the remarkable piece of confirmatory evidence which followed it. We need not at the moment stop to consider the main thesis, which is that the class of myths which tell of death, or absorption, and renewal of life (and symbolize, in Gruppe's view, the periodical renewal of the universe), to which class the Phanes-myth belongs, appeared in its original form in Babylonia. Thence it spread over the Near East, and took root particularly in Syria and Asia Minor. The gods of Babylon themselves were not imported, but the myth was attached to the local deities of the districts to which it spread. In this way would arise, for example, the myths of Attis and Adonis. Asia Minor, with the prominence of Kybele and Attis worship, became the centre and rallying-point of these myths, and it is to this centre that Gruppe would assign the origin of the Phanes-myth. We now return to our three names. In a passage of Johannes Malalas (an Antiochene historian of the sixth century A.D.) occur these words : ' And he made known that the Light, cleaving the *aither*, lightened the earth and all creation . . . and the name of the Light the same Orpheus, having heard it by his gift of prophecy, declared to be Metis, Phanes, Erikepaios ; which being interpreted in the common tongue is Counsel, Light, Lifegiver '.[19] Now why, Gruppe argues ingeniously, should Malalas think it incumbent on him to translate the word Metis ? We think of it as a good, well-known Greek word, a little poetical perhaps, yet surely familiar to all who spoke the common tongue. He seems to think that all three are on a par, and yet one of them, Erikepaios, does not suggest to us a Greek word at all. Perhaps then to one of his age they were on a par, having their origin alike in one of those lost languages, of varying degrees of kinship with the Greek, which were spoken in places like Thrace and the countries of Asia Minor.

In these languages it was possible to find, side by side, word-forms identical with the Greek and others widely different.[20] To one who knew the languages (as they would certainly still have been known in the sixth century), all alike would be foreign words. Probably, then, all three, those that sound like Greek and those that do not, come alike from Asia Minor. Phanes occurs in Herodotus (3. 4) as the name of a native of Halikarnassos, and on an Anatolian coin struck probably at Ephesos (Head, *Hist. Num.*[2] 571, C. T. Seltman, *Greek Coins*, 1933, p. 27, and pl. I, fig. 19. Head remarks that it is the oldest known inscribed coin). ' As for Erikepaios ', says Gruppe, ' it must be admitted that up to now no traces of his cult in Asia Minor have been forthcoming.' These words were published in 1909, and Gruppe must have been ignorant of what was then a very recent discovery made in Lydia by the Austrians Keil and von Premerstein. This was an altar, with the dedicatory inscription ' To Dionysos Erikepaios '. The occurrence in Anatolia of deities known other- ✱ wise from the Orphic cycle alone is an interesting and promising line of research, and to those whose interest lies mainly in the direction of origins may well prove a profitable field.[21]

The only thing one would wish otherwise in this interesting line of argument is Gruppe's choice for a starting-point of the fact that Malalas thought all the words alike in need of translation. Anyone who has dipped into the works of that foolish man knows that he possessed an unfailing zeal for explaining things that were in no need of explanation. The reader of the *Orphic Fragments* has an example ready to his hand. Fr. 62 is another quotation from Malalas in which he takes five lines of Greek hexameters and translates them all, substituting δύνατε for κραταιέ, βασιλεύων for ἀνάσσων, and εἰς τὸν ἀέρα ὑψούμενε for ἀειρόμενε.[22] The argument itself, however, remains undamaged, and the glib translation of Erikepaios, meaningless to modern readers of Greek, is in itself interesting. On the rendering given by Malalas, ' eri ' would contain the root of ' life ', and ' kep ' or ' kap ' of ' giving '. (The name of the god occurs both as Erikepaios and Erikapaios. See Gruppe, *Suppl.* 740.) For the latter, Gruppe pertinently compares the town of Pantikapaion in the Tauric Chersonese, and there was a river Pantikapes in European Sarmatia (' All-giving '). For the first part of the name we have no such convincing parallels, and Gruppe can only suggest as a possibility the Er of the myth in Plato's *Republic*. A. B. Cook, however, compares the mythical river Eridanos, which on this analogy he tentatively translates ' River of Life ' (*Zeus*, 2, ii. 1025). If we want another instance besides Malalas of the search for an interpretation of Metis, it might just be worth while comparing the allegorical-etymological passage of a Christian writer in *O.F.* 56 (p. 135). Zeus θεῖον ἀνιμᾶται πνεῦμα, ὅπερ Μῆτιν ἐκάλεσαν. This is so bad that some one may suspect that no attempt at etymology can have been intended, but the context leaves little room for doubt, since whenever the name of a god is mentioned some similar effort is made. Here we see some one offering his own interpretation of a perfectly well-known Greek word, and considering himself at liberty to propose a meaning quite different from the usual one.[23]

So far we have spoken of those names of Phanes which were peculiar, or almost peculiar to him. They show on the surface little trace of syncretism. This syncretism (a word, unfortunately, too convenient to dispense with) is the religious phenomenon whereby the personalities of divinities once held to be distinct become blended and indistinguishable from each other. It has been succinctly defined as the identification of deities of related function (H. J. Rose, *Hdbk. Gr. Myth.* p. 149). This phenomenon was not entirely absent from classical Greece, but its predominance dates from Hellenistic times. On the causes of this there will be more to say later, but we may briefly mention now that it is the natural concomitant of a tendency towards monotheism. The many gods of Olympos become the one god with many names. After what we know already of the Orphic writings, it will come as no surprise to learn that they were marked by syncretism, so far as we can judge, right from the outset. Here was a system which, on the side of doctrine, taught of the absorption of everything, gods included, into one god, and their rebirth from him again, and on the side of active religion taught the complementary idea of the worship of one god above all others.

This preliminary mention of syncretism is simply intended as a very brief preparation for some of the other names which we find accumulating around Phanes—Eros, Zeus, Dionysos. There is little further to be said about them, since in the light of the theogony they explain themselves. He is Eros, because the usual Greek mythological substitute for evolution was not simply creation but procreation. Life springs from Love, and so Love has to be there before life in order to provide the vital force which will mingle or marry two beings that further beings may be produced. Obviously he is continuing this same work to-day, so that the simultaneous existence of the twin conceptions of him—primeval cosmic figure, the first creator, and handsome youth or mischievous boy going about among human beings with his bow and arrows—is a simple thing containing no real contradiction.

Phanes again is Zeus, or rather Zeus became Phanes by the
process of swallowing him, and finally Phanes is Dionysos because
in that form he was reborn from Zeus. Probably the Rhapsodic
Theogony gave him no other names, thus showing itself to be
strictly consistent, and this fact may well give us a general prejudice in favour of its early date. In later literature the Orphic
god shared the fate of others and was overwhelmed by the spirit
of the times in a flood of indiscriminately applied appellations.

Phanes was imagined as uniting in himself the characteristics
of both sexes. Bisexual beings were in particular favour in
Oriental mythology, but were certainly known to classical Greece.
The reasonable Hellenic mind did not like to have them among
its own myths without accounting for their presence. If they
had crept in by natural, popular channels, then a story was either
discovered or invented to account for their form, and frequently
they were introduced deliberately to convey a certain idea or add
force to an argument.[24]   It was different in the later days of the
decay of polytheism. On all sides attempts were being made to
describe the one supreme god, who was really exalted so far above
the rest of creation as to be indescribable. This inarticulate
striving after expression showed itself in many ways, one of which,
the piling on to the one supreme deity of the names and powers
of all the ancient pantheon, has already been mentioned. Another
was to show that in him all contradictions were reconciled, and
the result is a superficially nonsensical description in which the
most contradictory epithets are applied simply because they are
contradictory. The tendency was the same, whether you were a
Neoplatonist philosopher wrestling with the ineffability of the One
which is above being and thought or a devout Christian trying to
express the infinite power of God to a pagan world. It robs of
significance such descriptions as that of Synesios (*Hymn.* 2. 63 =
O.F. p. 206) : ' Thou art Father, thou art Mother, thou art Male
and thou art Female, thou art Voice and thou art Silence. . . .'

To return to Phanes, he was composite because he had alone
to start the process of creation, and this he could not do, in the
way in which creation was mythically portrayed, unless he made
up in his own person for the lack of a partner. Not ' female and
male ' but ' female and father ' says the line quoted by Proklos
(*O.F.* 81). He was described as male and female, said Lactantius
(*O.F. ib.*) ' quod aliter generare non quiverit '. Similarly, in the
Hieronymian version the goddess Adrasteia, who existed from the
first with Chronos, is represented as male and female ' as a sign
that she was the cause of bringing all things to birth ' (*O.F.* 54).
The line ' With four eyes looking this way and that ' (*O.F.* 76)

may be connected with this characteristic of Phanes. He was in all ways two-formed.[25] To a similar impulse, the impulse to unite in the creator, who at the beginning of things necessarily stood alone, the various powers of the creatures, is most naturally to be attributed the collection of animals' heads with which Phanes was credited. According to Proklos (*O.F.* 81, cp. fr. 82), the *theologos* ' modelled ' him with the heads of a ram, a bull, a lion and a snake. He was indeed, to translate literally the adjective which Proklos applies to him, ' a very whole animal '. From giving your god the strength of a lion and the wisdom of a serpent it is but a step to imagining him as actually compounded of these animals. Whether you take that step or not depends on your mentality. There are those who like to treat a simile as a simile, and there are others who prefer to see it expressed in a way which appeals more immediately to the eye, the way of symbolism. We have already noted that the latter is in particular the way of the Oriental, and the prophet Ezekiel in his first chapter provides a well-known example.

The position of Night in the Rhapsodic Theogony is remarkable. Phanes is the creator and first ruler of the gods. In due course he hands over his sceptre to his daughter Night, who rules in his place. He himself goes into retirement, and all we hear of him is the arrangement described in *O.F.* 105, according to which he sits in the recesses of the cave of Night. In the middle is Night, prophesying to the gods, and at the entrance Adrasteia who makes their laws. Phanes sits still and takes no further part in things. Night in her turn hands over the power to her son Ouranos, but unlike Phanes she does not sit back as if her work was done. She continues to exercise great influence, giving oracular advice to her successors, who come to her for help and regard her with awe. This active part she plays right through the reigns of Ouranos, Kronos and Zeus, during which Phanes is as if he had never been. This seems to me the strongest argument for a theory which has been put forward on other grounds, and which accords with Gruppe's view of the Rhapsodies as a compilation of different strata of tradition, the theory namely that there was an earlier version of the Orphic theogony in which Phanes was lacking and Night had supreme place. Phanes is never mentioned before the Hellenistic age, and the cosmic Egg only once in Aristophanes, but the fourteenth book of the *Iliad* knows that Night is an awful power superior to the gods, just as she is in the Rhapsodies. Hypnos relates how once he incurred the displeasure of Zeus, who wished to cast him down from heaven into the sea, ' had not

Night saved me, the subduer of gods and men. Her I reached in
my flight, and Zeus stayed his hand for all his anger. Yea he
dreaded to do what was displeasing to swift Night.' Used to
support a theory of an earlier Orphic theogony, in which Night had
first place and there was no Phanes, this passage is of course
a weak ally. In the first place it is not explicitly ascribed to
Orpheus, and in the second it simply provides an argument *ex
silentio*. The striking thing about it is the *resemblance* which it
shows to the position of Night in the Rhapsodies, and the absence
of Phanes might in this case be best explained by the obvious
fact that he had nothing to do with the story. It is thus an
argument that could not stand alone, but becomes interesting in
the light of the strong suspicion raised in our minds by the composition of the Rhapsodies themselves that they contain two
different strata of myth. The same thing may be said about
Aristotle's reference to the *theologoi* who derive everything from
Night (*Metaphysics* 1071b27). Whether he was thinking of Orpheus
among them or not we cannot help wondering, but we cannot say.
There is another passage in which Aristotle is making the same
point against the *theologoi*. When he speaks of those who derive
the world from Night, he is using them to typify the class of
writers who in contradiction of his own philosophy make the
potential prior in time to the actual, that is to say, the imperfect
and confused prior to the finished and complete. About these
same people he speaks again at 1091b4, and here his commentator
Alexander of Aphrodisias understands him to be referring to
Orpheus.[26] Alexander illustrates the point by a partial summary
of the genealogy of the gods in Orpheus which is a little confusing.
He gives two lists, the first of generations in order of their birth,
and the second of rulers in order of their succession, and the two
do not tally. Speaking of the generations he says, ' First according
to Orpheus Chaos came into being, then Okeanos, third Night,
fourth Ouranos, then Zeus the king of the immortal gods '. The
succession of rulers is, first Erikepaios, then Night, then Ouranos.
One had thought that the generations mentioned in a theogony,
where only one name is mentioned in each, stood for the succession
of supreme gods, so that the two lists should be the same. Yet
the first has no mention of Erikepaios, and the second none of
Okeanos. The second is like the theogony of the Rhapsodies,
the one usually quoted by the Neoplatonists, and the first is not.
At this point another fact begins to assume significance. The
first list is given by Alexander in brief, dry prose ; for the second
he quotes hexameter verses. This may be accidental, but on the
other hand it may mean that Alexander took the second list from

the poems current in his own day, whereas the first was a matter of tradition which the commentators, convinced of the unity of Orpheus, fondly imagined to contain-nothing essentially inconsistent with the poems they knew.   (The passage of Alexander is quoted in *O.F.* 107.)

I must risk anticipating here in order to mention a theory which finds exceptional support in this passage of Alexander, although the evidence here supplied has not hitherto been used in its defence.   It was Gruppe's belief that the Orphic theogony used by Plato was not the Rhapsodic, but one quite different in which Okeanos is father of the gods and there is no Phanes.   The details of the argument are difficult, because for one thing it is not easy to determine exactly what theogonical passages in Plato have an Orphic poem as their source.   They are also, however, unimportant, because whatever the order of the generations within the theogony, the fact that it made Okeanos the father of gods and men, and did not know of Phanes, would be sufficient to show that it was of a fundamentally different kind from the Rhapsodic.   It is obvious without any further argument that the existence at least of these two types of Orphic theogony is strongly attested by the passage of Alexander which we have been discussing.

The theogony of the *Birds* is of great value as testimony for the currency of a creator born from an egg and with the name of Eros as early as the fifth century.   Further than that it would be unwise to press it.   It shows Night as existing previously to the egg-born god, not his child as in the Rhapsodies, and this might be taken to represent an intermediate stage.   But in the fragmentary state of our knowledge of the ancient theogonies, it is just as likely that Aristophanes used a comic poet's rightful prerogative to make a hotch-potch of the accounts which he was parodying, and even perhaps invent a new order of his own.

We have noted that the stories of the Titans, and of how Zeus was saved from his father Kronos, whose throne he was to usurp, are retailed in the Rhapsodic Theogony much as they had been in Hesiod.   The next thing to attract our attention is the swallowing of Phanes by Zeus, with all that it signified.   Why this strange fancy of a fresh beginning of things ?   Why, when a creator had been portrayed, carrying in him the seeds of all things that were to be, and had safely brought all these things to birth, should there arise another god who should engulf creator and creation in his own body simply to bring them forth again as they were before ?

I said a moment ago that if Gruppe was right in supposing an Orphic theogony in which Okeanos held highest place and there was no Eros or Phanes, then whatever else there might be to say about it, it must be of a fundamentally different kind from the Rhapsodic. It is here that that fundamental difference would lie, in the representation of creation simply as a genealogical tree and the absence of any trace of the idea of the absorption of all things into one and their emergence from one into plurality again. How shall all be one yet each thing apart ? The poet of the Rhapsodies had this question in his mind, but it did not trouble the author of a theogony whose first god was Okeanos. He is more likely to have been akin to Homer and Hesiod, neither of whom thought of raising the problem of creation in the form which afterwards became the typically Greek expression of it. Homer of course did not trouble himself with the problem of creation at all. Who then did raise it in that form ? Two very different classes of people, or at least two classes of people who thought themselves very different. It was raised by the first philosophers in Ionia, who were convinced that the manifold world must have evolved from a single primitive matter, and thought that the only problem to be settled was what that primitive material could have been. It was raised secondly by those religious spirits whose thoughts took a mystical turn and who felt a dim consciousness that they were of one nature with the life-giving god whom they worshipped. They raised it in the form, ' How can I, separate and isolated in a distinct material body, become one with him ? ' The philosophers began to ask their questions in the sixth century B.C. The others have probably been asking theirs, though sometimes vaguely and scarcely consciously, since man first had a mind, but we know that side by side with the speculation of Ionia this spirit also was emerging into consciousness and taking a firmer hold on the religious life of a large proportion of the people.

What significance we may attach to this kinship between the Orphic myths and these two trends of thought, the one disinterestedly observing the macrocosm, the other absorbed in the more intimate problems of the microcosm, is something which may be left to a later chapter. At the moment we have another consideration to weigh, namely, that although this kinship of ideas may betray the world of thought in which the Orphic poem had its origin, and from which it took its colour, the motive which gave it its first impulse along those lines may yet have been something different.

More than one person has claimed to put his finger on the one idea in the Orphic poems which may be called original. It is a

7

rash procedure, but I am going to make one more attempt and say that the conception which seems to me to have the best right to be called an Orphic idea is that of a creator.[27]   The supreme ruler of the universe is to be at the same time its creator, one whose way of working resembles that of the God of Genesis rather than those of the gods of Hesiod.   Granted a wish to express in this way the nature of the deity (a wish, surely, which may have arisen at some time among the Hellenes as naturally as it arose among the Hebrews), what was to be done ?   The Hellene was an incurable conservative, at least as far as form was concerned.   He might introduce the most revolutionary theories, but if it were in any way possible he would squeeze them into the old framework with an air of having done nothing really new at all.   There must be no wholesale uprooting of the traditional gods and setting up of strange gods in their place.   The gods of Homer and Hesiod must be respected, and also, perhaps, the gods of the already existing theogony of Orpheus.   These *theologoi* unanimously declared that the ruler of our world was Zeus, and every citizen of Athens was ready to vouch for the truth of it.   A religious man could not ignore this.   He would show himself to be as bad as the atheist philosophers at whom Aristophanes mocked, if he were to say ' Zeus is no longer, but in his place—Phanes now is king '.   There would be natural sectarians who would acknowledge in their hearts the supremacy of Phanes-Dionysos over all gods, but a way must be found whereby Zeus could remain formally supreme, not only to escape condemnation from the outer world who had not taken Orpheus for their lord, but also because there would be many who longed for the mystical belief in Phanes-Dionysos, but were just as pleased if they could tell themselves all the time that they were committing no disloyalty to the national gods, since no belittlement of Zeus was involved in the new belief. The trouble now was that the ancient poets in whose writings the character of Zeus had taken shape and hardened into tradition never intended him to figure as creator.   Consequently he was quite unfitted to play the part.   Phanes then must do the hard work of creation, but when all things are ready we make Zeus take them to himself and produce them again.   By assimilating to himself the nature of Phanes, that is, of Eros the principle of life, Zeus acquires creative power in addition to his kingship.[28]   Faced with the problem of using it, he has not a plan in his head, but has to be helped at every stage.   Having accomplished the necessary preliminary step, he runs to Night, the unfailing stand-by of the younger gods, and says in effect, ' What am I to do next ? ' (*O.F.* 164, 165).   Even Proklos is afraid there may be something shocking in this idea : ' The Maker of all is said to have gone into the oracle of Night before the whole creation, and from there to have been filled with the divine plans and to have learned the principles of creation and to have found a way out of all his difficulties, *if it be not blasphemous to say so* ' (*O.F.* 164).

The episode of the swallowing, which for the poet of the Rhapsodies serves as the device whereby this remarkable transformation is accomplished, was not of course the invention of his own imagination. That would not have accorded at all with the conservative spirit of the Greek. Not only was Kronos known to have swallowed all his children save Zeus, who was saved by a trick, but Zeus himself in Hesiod had swallowed Metis (p. 97 above), a personality whose name was actually shared by Phanes. The more we observe the ingenuity of the Greek mind in completely changing the significance of a story, the less we feel surprised that for all the progress made by their thought, there was so little change in the mythical material from which it drew its expression.[29]

We come now to what must have been for a worshipper the central point of Orphic story, the tales of Dionysos son of Zeus and his sufferings. We find these established and widely quoted as part of the Orphic corpus by the Neoplatonists, and attributed to a poem of Orpheus by Clement of Alexandria. Pausanias the student, who must have been alive at the same time as Clement and about a hundred and fifty years before our Neoplatonist authorities, makes the following interesting observation : ' The Titans were first introduced into poetry by Homer, who said that they were gods occupying a place under what is called Tartaros. Onomakritos took over the name of the Titans from Homer and founded rites in honour of Dionysos, making the Titans to be for Dionysos the author of his sufferings ' (Paus. 8. 37. 5 = Kern, *test.* 194). This is one of the most striking pieces of external evidence which we possess for the origin in the sixth century of much of Orphism as we know it. (For Onomakritos see p. 13 above.) The careful statement of Pausanias rings true, and we need not doubt it on the ground that our other authorities, contemporary with or later than Pausanias, refer the story of Dionysos and the Titans to Orpheus simply. This need not even argue ignorance on the part of the others of the activities of Onomakritos. It would be known that he edited the poems of Orpheus, just as in the same age the poems of Homer were also edited at Athens. No doubt interpolations were made in the Homeric epics as well, but the corpus as a whole remained Homer for the vast majority

of Greeks.   Certainly the interpolations in Orpheus, to judge by
this statement of Pausanias, were by no means slight, but
the credulity of the very pious must be taken into account.
Onomakritos was to them a θεῖος ἀνήρ, one inspired, and the
certainty that what he added was in accordance with the spirit
of prophecy and truth would induce a state of indifference in
which the line of demarcation between original and reformed
theology would soon become blurred.   The result is well illustrated in a sentence of Sextus Empiricus, who sees no objection to
quoting as an authority ' Onomakritos in the *Orphica* ' (*test.* 191).
     Besides the Neoplatonic references, let us note this of Diodoros
(p. 96 above) : [30] ' This god (*i.e.* Dionysos) they say was born of
Zeus and Persephone in Crete, and Orpheus in his religious writings
represents him as being torn in pieces by the Titans' (*O.F.*
p. 231).   Plutarch also refers to the story (*de esu carn.* 1. 996c =
O.F. ib.), and before we go on to discuss its significance it is worth
while translating in full the long account of Firmicus Maternus
(time of Constantine and his successor) in his work *On the Errors
of Pagan Religions*.   It will be better to have his story as a whole,
and any parts which do not come directly into the present discussion form an example of Euhemerism too good to miss (ch. 6,
p. 15, Ziegler = *O.F.* p. 234).   The gods are given their Roman
names, so that Dionysos becomes Liber.
     ' Liber was the son of Jove, a king of Crete.   Considering that
he was born out of wedlock, his father's attentions to him were
excessive.   The wife of Jove, whose name was Juno, was filled
with a stepmother's anger and sought in every way by guile to
bring about the death of the child.   Now the father was setting
out on a journey, and because he knew of the concealed displeasure
of his wife, and in order to prevent her from acting treacherously
in her fury, he entrusted the care of his son to guards who in his
opinion were to be trusted.   Juno, being thus given an opportune
moment for her crime, and with fuel added to her rage through
the circumstance that the father had on his departure handed
over to the boy his throne and his sceptre, first of all corrupted
the guardians with royal payment and gifts, then stationed
her followers, called Titans, in the inner part of the palace, and
with the aid of rattles and a mirror of ingenious workmanship so
distracted his childish mind that he left his royal seat and was
brought to the place of ambush, led there by the irrational
impulse of childhood.   Arrived there he was caught and killed,
and that no trace of the murder might be found, the band of
her followers cut the limbs in pieces and divided them among
themselves.   After that, adding crime to crime, on account of

the extreme fear in which they held their master they cooked the child's limbs in various ways and consumed them, feeding on human flesh, a banquet unheard of up to that day. The heart, which had fallen to her share, was saved by his sister— whose name was Minerva—who had herself assisted in the crime, with the double purpose of using it as unmistakable evidence in laying information against the others and of having something with which to soften the brunt of her father's anger. On Jove's return his daughter unfolded the tale of the crime. The father, on hearing of the fatal disaster of the murder, was overcome by the keenness of his bitter grief. As for the Titans, he procured their execution after various forms of torture. In vengeance for his son he left no form of torment or punishment untried, but exhausted the whole range of chastisement in his fury, uniting to the feelings of a father the unchecked power of a despot. Then because he could no longer endure the torments of his sorrowing heart, and no solace availed to assuage the grief occasioned by his bereavement, he made a statue of the boy out of gypsum by the modeller's art, and the heart (the instrument whereby, when it was brought by his sister, the crime was laid bare) was placed by the sculptor in that part of the statue where the linea-ments of the breast were represented. This done, he built a temple in place of a tomb, and appointed the boy's tutor (whose name was Silenos) to be priest. To soften the transports of their tyrant's rage, the Cretans made the day of the death into a religious festival, and founded a yearly rite with a triennial dedication, performing in order all that the child in his death both did and suffered. They tore a live bull with their teeth, recalling the cruel feast in their annual commemoration, and by uttering dissonant cries through the depths of the forest they imitated the ravings of an unbalanced mind, in order that it might be believed that the awful crime was committed not by guile but in madness. Before them was borne the chest in which the sister secretly stole away the heart, and with the sound of flutes and the clashing of cymbals they imitated the rattles with which the boy was deceived. Thus to do honour to a tyrant an obsequious rabble has made a god out of one who was not able to find burial.' [31]

We have already had occasion to remark on something which finds further confirmation here, and which throughout our inquiry cannot be over-emphasized. To begin an examination of Greek literature with the object of detecting and isolating Orphic elements, and to find, as the investigation proceeds, the traces of anything that can be called Orphism dissolving one after the other into thin air, has been the experience of many scholars. It will continue to be the experience of all who confine their search to such concrete phenomena as ' Orphic myths ' or ' Orphic rites '. A small residue will be left, certainly, but its scantiness will be a disappointment to the researcher and moreover will by no means truly represent the contribution of Orphic thought to the development of Greek religion. Few who had a message to preach in Greece would think of doing so by inventing new myths or new rites, and thus alienating at the outset the conservative minds of those whom they wished to influence. The change was accomplished by the infusion of new meaning into the myths and rites that were ready to hand. It is not therefore on the myth of Phanes that our attention must primarily be concentrated, nor on the sufferings of Dionysos, but on the theories of a creator and of the divine kinship of mankind. We have now to say something of a certain Cretan ritual, because it was absorbed by the Orphics like other religious elements which were suitable to their purposes. If it was practised at Athens, then no doubt Orpheus was the name under whose patronage it was brought there. But it was not an Orphic ritual in the sense that it was invented by the priests of Orpheus or in its original form had anything to do with them at all. We can have no sure basis of profitable inquiry until we have clear in our heads the conception of the Orphic religion as contentedly eclectic in its matter, single and original in the thought that lay behind it.

The statement of Diodoros establishes the fact that the Dionysos whose story and whose rites were given such a prominent place in Orphic belief and practice was the Dionysos of Crete. We need scarcely remark that Dionysos was worshipped in other places besides Crete, or that his origin, though obscure, lies more probably in the North of Greece than in the South ; and we may say with almost equal assurance that the god of the Cretans was not originally called Dionysos. There were many Dionysi. A speaker in Cicero's dialogue De natura deorum (3. 23) enumerates five in support of his argument. The god ' in whose honour the Orphic rites are supposed to be performed ' finds fourth place in the list with the others. The Cretans indeed, in later days at least, could point to the borrowing of their rites by the Greeks of the mainland and base on it a claim to the origin among themselves of all ritual ceremonies. To this extravagant claim Diodoros gives serious consideration in an interesting passage (5. 77) : ' I have related the tales which the Cretans tell about the gods who are said to have been born among them. Now in saying that homage to the gods and sacrifices and mystic initiations have been introduced from Crete to the rest of mankind, this in their opinion is

the weightiest testimony which they bring : the initiatory ceremony of the Athenians at Eleusis, which is, I suppose, the most
magnificent of all, and that in Samothrace, and that in Thrace
among the Kikones (the country of Orpheus the initiator), all
these, they say, are divulged in the form of mysteries, but at
Knossos in Crete it is the custom, and has been since ancient times,
to let all partake openly of these rites.   What in other countries
is divulged under pledge of secrecy, no one in their country conceals
from anyone who may be desirous of learning about such things.'

No doubt the Cretan rite had existed from very ancient times,
and although its elements must have been common to many other
peoples as well, there is no more reason to doubt that it was in
its Cretan form that it was adopted by the Orphics.   So much
truth we may for the present allow to have lain in the boast of
the Cretans.   We must try to determine more closely what
this Cretan rite was and what religious beliefs must have been
behind it.

The rite has been fully described and commented on by Jane
Harrison (*Proleg.* ch. 10), so that a short outline will be sufficient
here.   Firmicus remains our chief witness.   The very unsuit-
ability of parts of the ritual which he describes to fulfil the purpose
which his previous narrative assigns to it, forms a good guarantee
of the genuineness of the ritual itself.   A live bull (*i.e.* raw, *Prol.*[3]
485, 486) is torn in pieces and eaten by the worshippers, and they
take to the woods in wild and noisy procession.   The orgiastic
music of flutes and cymbals adds to the din, and certain sacred
objects are carried about with them which Firmicus at least
supposes to be relics.

The classical age provides a striking illustration of this descrip-
tion in the fragment of Euripides' *Cretans* quoted by Porphyrios
(*De abstin.* 4. 19), which runs as follows.[32]   The chorus, says
Porphyrios, are addressing Minos :

' Son of the Phoenician princess, child of Tyrian Europa and
great Zeus,[33] ruler over hundred-fortressed Crete—here am I, come
from the sanctity of temples roofed with cut beam of our native
wood, its true joints of cypress welded together with Chalybean
axe and cement from the bull.   Pure has my life been since the
day when I became an initiate of Idaean Zeus and herdsman [34] of
night-wandering Zagreus, and having accomplished the raw feasts
and held torches aloft to the Mountain Mother, yea torches of
the Kuretes, was raised to the holy estate and called Bakchos.'

The first conclusion which may be drawn from this passage is
that Idaean Zeus (from Mount Ida in Crete) and Zagreus are one
and the same, and that this god was no Olympian.   He belongs

to the other of the two broad divisions of Greek gods. His worshippers stand in no purely external relationship to him, in which sacrifices are performed in a bargaining spirit, as to a ruler from whom good gifts may be expected if his claim to obedience is recognized. These are the ceremonies of the mystic, whose aim is nothing less than to assimilate himself to the object of his worship, as the last words make clear. These last words also tell us that this same god of Crete, Zeus-Zagreus, was also called, in the fifth century, Bakchos or Dionysos. We have then a chthonian ritual to secure communion with the god, apparently in its most primitive form. Communion was attained by the eating of raw flesh, and we may trust Firmicus sufficiently to add that the flesh was that of a bull. The *cista* carried in procession, which the myth made into the receptacle of the heart, is most naturally to be explained as an instance of the universal mystic chest of chthonian Dionysos. The serpent who lives in holes in the earth was sacred as symbolizing the spirit of the earth and fertility, and in this form the god could be carried, a living image, in the procession of his worshippers. Pick up any coin of Asia Minor dating from the end of the third century B.C. onwards, and the chances are that you will find on it the sacred *cista* with the serpent issuing from it. *Cistophori* became a generally current type throughout the peninsula, and, as it happened, in Crete itself (Head, *Hist. Num.* 534, 479). Finally we have the fact that the central act of a communion ceremony, allegorized more or less according to the degree of civilization attained by the participants, is the absorption of the god himself in some visible, physical form or symbol, simultaneously with which the worshipper believes that he acquires the spirit of the god, his strength or his holiness or whatever of his characteristics he may most desire.[35]

We may now try to picture a little more clearly the nature of this Cretan mystery-god. He was Zeus Chthonios, that is to say, he was an example of the great god who lived in the earth. These deities of the soil are as old as agriculture, and the god-in-the-earth of Crete must have been worshipped before ever the gods of Homer, with their human outlook and contrasting personalities, set up house upon Olympos. Then Zeus became inevitably connected in the minds of Greeks and their neighbours with the idea of supreme god, and so simple people in speaking of the god of the earth found it quite natural to say ' the Zeus of the earth '. Etymologically, the uses of the word Zeus no doubt came in the order, general—particular—general. Historically, if the supreme chthonian deity of Crete is called Zeus in the fifth century, it is most likely that he is called by this name because he has borrowed it from the supreme god of the Hellenes. What his name was in the days of King Minos we cannot say for certain, but it is most likely to have been the name which was Hellenized into Zagreus. This is a name at whose origin we can only guess, and which whenever we meet it clearly signifies a purely chthonian deity. In what is supposed to be the oldest extant reference he is invoked by the side of Ge, in a fragment of Aeschylus by the side of ' the Hospitable ' (Hades. The authority for this quotation says that Aeschylus called him brother of Hades), and Kallimachos calls him son of Persephone.[36] As for the name itself, the most convincing theory of its origin (more convincing, perhaps, than most etymologies) is that which makes it an ethnic from Mount ✱ Zagron between Assyria and Media (Miss G. Davis, quoted in *Zeus*, 1, 651). It was an Oriental name which travelled to Crete *via* Phoenicia. The etymology of the Greeks made the name mean ' Great Hunter ' (*Etym. Magn. s.v.*). All that is to our purpose is to note that it was Cretan before it was Greek, a fact with which Miss Davis's idea accords. The scanty references in themselves give no clue, and we may cling rather to what they do put beyond doubt, the entirely chthonian character of the god to whom the name belonged. That Zagreus was the original name of the local chthonian deity of Crete, to whose name and ritual later circumstances brought a more widespread fame, may remain no more than an attractive theory, although we may add that the original title of the Cretan god is certainly not represented by any of the other names by which, in his mingling with a wider civilization, he came to be called. The suggestion may also be considered as a protest against the practice of concealing our ignorance with the formula : ' It was his Orphic name '—by which is meant the Orphic name of Dionysos. Any references to the Orphic story of the sufferings of the god, either in the Neoplatonists themselves or earlier, speak of him as Dionysos or Bakchos. For the name Zagreus in this connexion we have to look to Nonnos or pseudo-Nonnos. (Literary references to Zagreus will be found in *O.F.* p. 230.)

From the time of Homer onwards the orgiastic worship of Dionysos, a Thracian god, had been making headway through Greece against the calm and reasonable religion of the Olympians. To give a detailed account of that worship here could only be to make an inferior reproduction of the eighth chapter of Rohde's *Psyche* (Eng. tr.). The character of a Bacchante is in any case familiar enough to us all to bring up at once some of the right associations in the mind. A few points may be mentioned to serve the purpose of comparison. The worshippers trail dancing over the mountains, using various means to induce in themselves the condition desired, namely ' madness ' or ecstasy.   They utter loud cries, they make music with flutes and cymbals.   Arrived at the culminating pitch of frenzy, they tear and eat raw an animal victim.   Dionysos appeared to them in the form of a bull.   The ultimate aim was union with the god, by the attainment of ecstasy and the sacred meal to become oneself a Bakchos.[37]   Is it surprising, that in an age marked for the Greeks by colonization and expansion no less than by a lively interest in religion, the Cretan god should have become Dionysos, and the Cretans be supposed to be worshipping the same divinity as the Thracians and, by now, a great many of the Greeks themselves ?   I am not seeking to overlook or deny the racial kinship of Thracians and Phrygians, the similar character of Thracian Dionysiac and Asiatic cults, the possibility that the Cretans were originally of Southern Anatolian stock, with the final conclusion that the Thracian and Cretan rituals may be in their prehistoric origin one and the same thing born in the same place.   These inquiries are alien to the history of Orphism, for which the important fact is that in the mind of the historical Greek the two were separated, one to the North of him and the other to the South, and that he had to notice similarities and draw his own conclusions.

The accounts of Euripides and Firmicus both come from ages when the unity of Cretan with ordinary Dionysiac worship was considered as established.   The *mystes* of Idaean Zeus became a Bakchos.   Euripides himself makes no secret of the fact that he is fascinated by the thrilling service of the Thracian god, so much so that his play the *Bacchae* is our richest source of information on the cult.   These accounts may therefore be considered suspect as a source from which to extract the original Cretan form of the rite.   But in meeting the impact of Hellas, or of Thrace through the medium of Hellas, was it the Cretan religion which was forced to adapt itself and conform, or did it simply absorb into its own age-old practices the names of the alien gods ?   There is strong *a priori* evidence for the latter alternative.   The great and ancient civilization of Crete was the teacher rather than the pupil of its young successor on the mainland.   If the orgiastic worship of the Thracians was received with opposition, as in many parts of Greece it was, this opposition was largely fed by feelings of contempt for the Thracians themselves, who to Greek eyes were barbarians and beyond the pale.   It was with far other feelings that the Greek looked on Crete.   It was the home and birthplace of his own Zeus.   The incongruity of supposing the Olympian to have been born there never once tempted him into the heresy that the

Cretan-born was another, the god of a different people who had taken the name of his own. The sanctity and universality of the supreme god of Crete were too firmly rooted in his mind, and as Zeus he reigned unquestioned from the time of Hesiod. It was left to post-classical writers, like Kallimachos, to play with the idea of different birthplaces of Zeus, and the subject of his Cretan origin caused grave misgivings among those of the ancients who first attempted the science of mythology. It is likely then that the ritual of the Cretan *mystes* did not suffer much alteration by becoming one with the mysteries of the continental Dionysos, but that the union was made easy by an initial similarity. This is confirmed in one noteworthy point. The Thracian Dionysos was imagined in the form of a bull. The worship of a bull-formed god seems clearly indicated by the Cretan rites. Did the Cretans borrow the picture from Dionysos ? The stories of Pasiphae, of the Minotaur, of Europa provide the answer.

It is time to step back from this medley of Thracian and Cretan religion, in which we are in danger of losing sight of our subject, which is the Orphics. I am supposing that Orphic religion took shape in the sixth century. This is an impression which forms and hardens in the mind as it broods over Orphic thought and practice. It is difficult to bring together a mass of concrete evidence for it, since it is largely a matter of the climate of thought to which it seems most naturally to belong, although the probability that Onomakritos was one of the founders of the movement lends distinct colour to the view, and other testimony will come to light as we go on (cp. *e.g.* p. 126 and App. 2, p. 134 below). I may add in parenthesis that it is a view which in no way excludes the possibility that in previous centuries poems were already current under the name of Orpheus. If they were not, it is not so easy to see why the reformers of the sixth century like Onomakritos chose to put themselves and their writings under the patronage of his name. The important thing to remember is that these earlier poems of Orpheus were not Orphic, using that term in the sense which will have become clear by the time the end of this chapter is reached. In the sixth century then, let us say, a new spirit was being introduced into religion by men who took Orpheus for their prophet and the cult of Dionysos as the centre of their worship. From the activities of Onomakritos we may assume that Athens was a centre of the movement. Now at Athens in the time of Onomakritos the orgiastic worship of Dionysos was as well known as in his own home in Thrace. Two passages in Aristophanes (*Frogs*, 357, *Clouds*, 985) make it clear that the rite of eating the bull was itself familiar to his audience, though one of them implies that it was not the sort of thing that was still done.[38] In fact the cult of Dionysos was already universal in Greece, there were already ' many Dionysi,' and the Cretan god himself, we may be sure, had already become Dionysos through contact with the Hellenized form of the Thracian.

To the Orphic, then, who wished to put his new wine into the old bottles, to set his new thoughts in the framework of existing cult and myth, there presented itself the phenomenon of Dionysos-worship going on all around him, with variations no doubt both of cult and myth according to the locality, and the nature of the gods whose worship in different places he was usurping or sharing. We can only inquire which form in particular he chose to make the interpreter of his thoughts, always with the proviso that the religious enthusiast does not differentiate with academic nicety between variations which the cult and myths of his god may have assumed in their transitions through time and space.

Ritual has had an incidental mention in this chapter, but its object is to elucidate the mythology of the Orphics. We have seen evidence that the myth under discussion, that of the sufferings of Dionysos, was based on Cretan sources. The question which we must face is, what did Onomakritos (who will serve as well as any other name to represent the sixth century reformer) find to his hand in the way of mythological material in Crete ? Briefly and broadly, he must have found a blend of the Cretan Zeus with Dionysos. The ancient chthonian cult was being carried on as it ever had been, but the mythology of Crete must have suffered a shake-up from the invasion of foreign deities with similar functions but different names. When Onomakritos turned his eyes to Crete and wrote his poem on the sufferings of Dionysos, there would already be in Crete the state of affairs described later by Euripides, in which the *mystes* of Idaean Zeus is initiated at the same time to Zagreus and his longing is to become one with Bakchos.

So much we may assert, that at the time when the Orphics were introducing their new ideas there was going on in Crete an absorption of Dionysiac by the ancient Cretan religion, with a consequent identification of the ancient Cretan god with Dionysos. If I go on to suggest in more detail a possible order of events, up to and including the adoption of these elements by the Orphics, it must only be after a warning that no more than a possible account is intended. We are dealing with a topic where no certain knowledge of detail is available. Yet we have the authority of Plato for supposing that to think out an account which is possible and reasonable is never waste of time. In this case it will clear our minds, and may even help towards understanding the complicated interactions of the two elements of religion, cult and myth. Here then is the account.

There were three prominent features of ancient Cretan ritual, the procession carrying the serpent-emblem of the chthonian god, the slaying and eating of the bull, and a warlike dance performed by the young warriors in which they clashed their arms together. Evidence for this last is not direct, but rests on the supposition that the story of the Kuretes is an aetiological myth. It is one of the most transparent cases, and no one, so far as I know, has doubted the validity of the inference. The dance itself has been variously explained as rain magic, apotropaic magic, initiation ceremony, greeting to the morning sun, and sheer joy in bodily movement and noise. The worship of these early Cretans may be said to be directed towards one god, the ubiquitous and supreme earth-spirit.

The imaginative Hellenes now enter with their own gods into the scene of this ancient civilization whose ruins they have inherited. The supreme god of Crete they identify with their own Zeus. From this contact comes the story of the birth of Zeus which we have in Hesiod and elsewhere. These general terms, unsatisfactory as they are, are all that we can use in speaking of causes, since who shall speak exactly on the how, the where and the who of these myths? The story is this. Rhea had borne several children to Kronos, which he, having heard that a child of his own should one day usurp his kingdom, promptly swallowed. Rhea in grief went to her mother Earth for advice, and when she was about to bear another child her mother sent her to Crete. Here she bore Zeus and hid him in a cave on Ida. The Cretan daemons called the Kuretes danced around the infant clashing their shields in order that his cries might not be heard. This tale, so unsuitable to the Olympian Zeus of Homer, obtains universal assent as part of the canon of Greek mythology. The armed dance of the Cretan warriors is now regarded as a rite commemorative of the saving of Zeus. His religion remained chthonian. He who had performed it became himself a ' new Kures,' and the god was addressed as Kuros. The latter means simply ' youth ', and it was from the dance of the Kuroi of Knossos that the story of the Kuretes had its rise.[39]

In the meanwhile the orgiastic worship of Dionysos has descended upon Greece, with its frenzied processions of night-wandering, torch-bearing, intoxicated worshippers, and its animal-tearing, flesh-eating consummation. Opposed at first, it has worked itself into the life of the people by its appeal to the feelings, its satisfaction of the instinct to let oneself go and in the process to be exalted out of one's own nature and caught up in the nature of a higher, more universal being.   It reaches Crete, where it finds that a similar religion has been carried on for centuries, and the Idaean Zeus becomes Dionysos.   Henceforth they are one.   But if Dionysos to his Cretan worshippers was one with Idaean Zeus, then it was in his honour too that the armed dance was performed. He too, therefore, must have been saved at his birth by a circle of friendly daemons.   Otherwise why should the commemorative dance be performed in his honour ?   Another circumstance helped this transference.   There was another class of attendant daemons closely resembling the Kuretes, called Korybantes.   These figures were probably North Anatolian,* and were allied at first to the

FIG. 11.—INFANT DIONYSOS SURROUNDED BY ARMED FIGURES LEAPING AND CLASHING SWORDS ON SHIELDS. COIN OF MAG-NESIA IN IONIA.

Great Mother of Phrygia.   Her cult was of the same ecstatic type as that of Dionysos.   To ' korybant ' served as a verb in Greek, meaning to be in a state of ecstasy or divine madness in which hallucinations were possible.   Naturally, then, these attendants of the Phrygian goddess attached themselves at an early date to Dionysos, seeing that men of Thracian race moved over with their religion into Phrygia at some time in the second millennium B.C.   Dionysos then had attendant daemons already, and it was easy to suppose, if you were a Cretan, that these were no others than the Kuretes.   That is theory, plausible enough.   This is fact, that as soon as Greek literature emerges for us from the dark ages, that is to say by the sixth century at latest, we find that Kuretes and Korybantes have become identified.   They are identical to Sophocles and Euripides.   Orgiastic Korybantic elements are introduced into the cult of the Kuretes, whose simple, primitive mystery was probably in the first place free from them.   More important for us, the attendants of Dionysos, be they called Kuretes or Korybantes, are now represented as surrounding the god, who is seen as an infant, clashing their shields with their swords.[40]   (Cp. fig. 11.)

All that we have so far taken into account has happened without the assistance of the Orphics.   The typical orgies of

* Northern on account of the β, if the etymology from κορυφή holds good. Wilamowitz has recently denied it, solely on the ground that the name Korybant is not Greek (*Der Glaube der Hellenen*, i. 129).   But surely it is from a closely allied language ?

Dionysos had nothing to do with Orphic influences, which form in many important respects a contrast to them, as we shall discover when we turn from the myths to the practices of the Orphic. Of Dionysiac religion in, as it might be called, its raw form we have no better memorial than the *Bacchae* of Euripides. The mysteries of the Orphic, secret, that must not be spoken of, which are hinted at in some of his other plays (p. 237 below), are banished here in favour of the freedom and wildness of the untouched Thracian cult. Yet in the *Bacchae* are united all the elements of which we have spoken. One doubt remains. If Dionysos was now imagined as being encircled in his infancy by protective daemons, did his Cretan worshippers know from what he was being protected? It is scarcely probable that the religious mind, although accepting in general the single nature of Idaean Zeus and Bakchos and making the attendants of the one wait also, and in the same way, upon the other, transferred the well-known myth of the birth of Zeus in its entirety to Dionysos. Hellas itself had made Dionysos son of Zeus, and that rendered easy the assimilation of their natures and their servants. But the imagination boggled at making Dionysos son of Kronos, or even at crediting Zeus, for the sake of consistency, with the deplorable attitude towards his children which his father had shown towards him. Of that we never hear a hint. There were other stories too of the birth of Dionysos, which certainly made it out to be eventful, but none of them rendered necessary, or even possible, the presence of an armed guard. Now it is highly improbable that the inconsistency thus involved in uniting as if to one god the service paid to Idaean Zeus and Dionysos appeared to the devout follower in the intellectual way in which it suggests itself to the cold-blooded scholar in his study. If we ask the question, what did a Cretan at the beginning of the sixth century imagine to be the reason why the infant Bakchos needed this protection, the most probable answer is that he neither knew nor cared. It is not beyond a doubt the right answer. We do not know. There must have been some myth of the dismemberment of Dionysos aetiologically connected with the dismemberment of the animal by his worshippers, and this myth may have been no more than embellished by Onomakritos in the way which is represented for us of a later age by the bald statement of Pausanias that he ' made the Titans the authors of the god's sufferings '. At any rate we have brought our tale down to about the point where the Orphics must have stepped in. They stepped in because they had a new religion to preach, a code of conduct based on a theory of the origin of mankind, and they wanted a mythical framework in which to propound it. In the study of Greek religion, scholars frequently protest, with complete justification, against those who describe the origin of a myth or a rite in a way which suggests that it was the production of a committee or a single man appointed for the purpose of inventing it. That is not the way in which myths or rites arise. But the rise of the phenomenon known as Orphism presents an entirely different problem from that of any individual myth or rite, whether it be one used by the Orphics or not. All the evidence points to its having been in its origin the product of a few individual minds active over a limited period of time. We need not therefore hesitate to speak in this way of the Orphics, and may conclude that they meditated on the religious elements which I have described as existing before their time, and either invented, to suit their own purposes, a story explanatory of the picture of the infant Bakchos surrounded by leaping, noisy daemons, or at least remodelled an existing one. It was they who said that the child was attacked by the Titans, that his guard proved insufficient, and that the Titans killed him and tasted his flesh. If there were already in existence an aetiological tale of the slaying of the god, the eating of the flesh no doubt formed a part of it, since it was a part of the actions of the bacchants. (See Appendix 1, pp. 130 ff. below.) The essential thing is that the Orphics added the Titans. When Zeus made war on the Titans, as every one knew from Hesiod, his weapons were his thunderbolts and lightnings. With these he burned up the earth around them, and the hot smoke scorched and defeated them. To have as many familiar elements as possible in their story was very naturally the aim of the Orphics, and here was one which suited their purpose admirably. Zeus attacks the Titans, fresh from their crime, with his well-known weapons. They are burned up, and from their ashes springs the race of men. The climax is original, is Orphic (and in this all our evidence concurs), because it enshrines the peculiarly Orphic thought of our own mixed earthy and heavenly nature. Here then we may end our reasonable account, like Timaeus with a prayer to all the gods and goddesses that it may be found to them not unpleasing and to ourselves not inconsistent.

Before we leave the story of the Titans' crime, a word should be said about the playthings by means of which, according to the myth, they distracted the infant god and achieved their purpose. Clement of Alexandria gives the following account of the deed (*Protr.* 2. 17. 2—18. 1 = *O.F.* 34) : ' The mysteries of Dionysos are simply barbarous. While he was but a child the Kuretes danced and leaped about him in arms, but the Titans insinuated them-

selves by fraud, beguiled him with childish playthings, and tore
him limb from limb, helpless infant though he was, as the poet of
the mysteries, Orpheus the Thracian, says :

> Tops of different sorts, and jointed dolls, and fair golden
> apples from the clear-voiced Hesperides.*

The symbols in this mystery are purposeless objects, but it may be
of some purpose to bring them to your notice—a knuckle-bone, a
ball, tops, apples, a mirror, a lump of wool.'

Over a century ago Lobeck, in a passage of astonishing learning
(*Agl.* 699 ff.), was prepared to show that in spite of the attempts to
attach an original mystical significance to these objects, every one
of them was in origin nothing but what the story made them out to
be—children's toys.   The strongest support to a contrary theory
was furnished by the words *konos* and *rhombos* in the Orphic
lines.   The former means, in the first place, a pine cone, and pine
cones were carried by the worshippers in Dionysiac processions
on the tips of their wands, the *thyrsoi*.   The latter means a bull-
roarer, an instrument which when whirled around the head produces a noise, and is or has been used in the religious ceremonies
of primitive peoples in many lands.   It happens, however, that
both words also mean spinning-top,[41] and Lobeck went so far as
to discover a passage in a Greek writer which explained exactly
the difference between the two, for every small boy, it seemed,
knew that a *konos* was not the same as a *rhombos*.   One was the
kind you whipped, and the other was not.   We shall soon come
to some evidence, unknown to Lobeck, that in the story of the
divine child it was spinning-tops that were in question.   The
knuckle-bones, the ball and the jointed dolls speak for themselves.
The last named are literally ' toys that bend their legs '—a nice
touch, almost suggesting that the writer, for all his dusty tags
from Hesiod, had not forgotten his own childhood.   The last
article in Clement's list, a tuft of raw wool, has in Lobeck's
opinion crept into the text by some corruption, though he has no
emendation to offer.   His argument is that all the articles quoted
by Clement as ' symbols in the mystery ' are simply reminders of
the toys offered to the child.   He dismisses the wool therefore
with the words *quid enim puer ludibundus lana succida facere possit ?*
This is surely question-begging as part of an argument that the
things mentioned are all toys and not objects of original religious
significance.   When Lobeck himself quotes for us passages from
the *Etymologika* showing that religious significance was attached to

---

* κῶνος καὶ ῥόμβος καὶ παίγνια καμπεσίγυια,
  μῆλά τε χρύσεα καλὰ παρ' Ἑσπερίδων λιγυφώνων.

wool (it was used, say Photios and the *Etym. Magn.*, in mystic ceremonies and in spells, and specifically at Athens), we are led by his own learning to doubt his original assumption that all the objects mentioned are without exception examples of children's toys. The doubt grows when we find that in all the special section which he devotes to the discussion of these objects there is no mention of either the mirror or the golden apples of the Hesperides, neither of which falls very easily into line with the ball, dolls, tops and knuckle-bones as part of the ordinary stock-in-trade of the toyshop. Clement goes on, immediately after the passage quoted, to reveal the contents of the sacred caskets used in the mysteries of Bakchos. The list consists partly of different kinds of sacrificial cakes, partly of the sacred plants, ivy, narthex, pomegranate, and a serpent is also mentioned. No doubt this is, as Lobeck took it to be, simply an extension of the previous list, that of the toys of Dionysos, and Clement means us to understand that they also were kept and displayed in the *cistae mysticae*. ' These then ', concludes Lobeck, ' were the famous mysteries of the *cistae*, partly models and memorials of the toys with which Bakchos played in his early infancy, partly various kinds of sacred cake.' He keeps up to the end the distinction between the two, but surely the one thing that we can learn with certainty from Clement's description is that the two classes of sacred object, those that were originally simply toys introduced for the purpose of the story, and those that were originally religious symbols, were not kept distinct at all, but were confused. He mentions the toys and immediately calls them the symbols of the mystery, and then goes on to imply that they and certain other things which were not toys were kept alike in the mystic caskets. In these circumstances there is no reason against supposing that of the actual list of playthings in the story of the infant Dionysos some were simply toys, which afterwards attained religious significance owing to their mention in the story, and others were sacred objects included in the story because of their already established sanctity. There is no need, in fact, to lump them all together. We must remind ourselves yet again that the story in this elaborate form, with child-god reigning supreme, malicious Titans and list of playthings, is no product of the myth-making imagination of primitive folk, but far more probably the artificial production of a few reforming spirits in a civilized state. Nothing could be more in keeping with the methods of these people than the insertion among the toys which their tale demanded of one or two objects to which they attached a deeper significance. The mirror may be an example of this. Certainly the Neoplatonists saw in it an allegory of the nature of mankind, and one so good that Plotinus himself deigned to notice it, although elsewhere, unlike his followers in the school, he preserves an unbroken silence on the subject of the Orphic theogony (O.F. 209). Proklos of course, when he sees in the picture of Dionysos looking at his reflection in the mirror an image of the opposition between the eternal intelligible world and the unreal world of birth and decay, is introducing Platonic notions which could not have been in the minds of the creators of the story (O.F. ib). Nevertheless they too had a religious doctrine to propound, and it may well be that in that same picture we are meant to see a foreshadowing of the double nature of mankind, his heavenly nature which is his real self, and his earthly or Titanic which is no better than a shadow. So much we may conjecture, while admitting freely that a mirror would have served better than most objects even its ostensible purpose of simply distracting a child's attention. If it could not do that in the first place, the story would be marred. The same thoughts arise over the golden apples of the Hesperides. Nothing, we admit, is more likely to attract a child than the present of golden apples, yet it seems a little extravagant to send to the farthest confines of the world for a mythical treasure when the same purpose, it seems, could be accomplished with dolls and knuckle-bones. Perhaps then we may allow ourselves to remember that the apples of the Hesperides were symbols of immortality, and that Dionysos was to be born again after his murder, and by his death was to ensure the hope of immortality for the race of human beings which was to follow him.

Archaeological discovery has thrown a most direct and unexpected light on the divine Child and his playthings.[42] We find it in the sanctuary of the Kabiroi at Thebes in Boiotia, excavated by the Germans in the eighteen-nineties. These Kabiroi are gods ✱ of uncertain origin, possibly Phoenician, but possibly also indigenous to Greek soil, whose chief seat in classical times was the island of Samothrace. (The *locus classicus* is Herodotus 2. 51.) They were kindly gods, givers of the fruits of the earth and protectors of seamen, and were worshipped on the island by the celebration of mysteries, into which Herodotus shows himself to have been initiated. There is little literary evidence for their cult on the mainland of Greece, though Herodotus hints that it may have reached Samothrace from Athens, being originally a cult of the Attic Pelasgoi. Beyond this we had a bare mention of the fact that they were worshipped at Thebes, and that the worship there had been founded by one who was an Athenian by birth (Paus. 4. 1. 7). About this cult the excavations have furnished a

wealth of information of that fascinating first-hand kind which
is the peculiar gift of archaeology. They show the Kabiros
(singular) worshipped by the side of a Child, and the votive
offerings suggest that in the minds of the peasant population of
Boiotia the Child was the more important. Seven hundred little
terracotta figures of boys were found as compared with fifty
statuettes of the reclining Kabiros. On a vase-painting of the
fourth century B.C. we are shown the Kabiros reclining on a couch
with the Child standing before him (fig. 12). Both have titles
written over them, *Kábiros* over the reclining, bearded figure, and
over the head of the boy simply *Pais*—The Child. Now the
remarkable thing about the Kabiros is that he exactly resembles
Dionysos as he is depicted on vases of Attic style. He is a bearded
man in a reclining position, his head crowned with ivy and in his

FIG. 12—FRAGMENT OF VASE FROM THE THEBAN KABIRION.

hand a wine-jar. Were there no name written over him, no one
would have hesitated a moment to make the identification.
Everyone knows of course that Thebes, the scene of the *Bacchae*
of Euripides, honoured Dionysos as its chief god, and it looks as
if the Kabiros, in being transplanted to that city, had become
identified with its god. In the light of this discovery, a possible
significance begins to appear in a remark of one of the much
maligned tribe of scholiasts, hitherto dismissed as merely due to
the confusion of a semi-learned mind. The scholiast to Apollonios
Rhodios says (on I. 917) : ' Others say that there were once two
Kabiroi, the elder Zeus, the younger Dionysos '. Confusion there
is in this statement, which nevertheless probably owes its origin to
the existence of this cult in which the worship of Kabiros, Child
and Dionysos had become mingled. With this passage goes the
one in Cicero, *de nat. deor.*, which we have already had occasion

to quote (above, p. 110). In the list of 'multi Dionysi' there given, the third is 'Cabiro patre'.

The most interesting part of the discoveries comes now. Among the heaps of votive offerings found in the shrine were a number of objects, some in bronze and some in clay, which are unmistakably spinning-tops (fig. 13), and yet others in the form of knuckle-bones. Although these are the most striking examples, there are others too whose identification as playthings is scarcely more doubtful, tiny cups and jugs, and glass beads. A list of dedicated objects has also come to light, and includes four knuckle-bones, a top, and a whip.

We find, then, that the literary evidence of the Orphic theogony for the belief in a divine child is illustrated in the most striking way by the existence of an actual cult which takes the Child for the centre of its worship and causes his adorers to bring to him as offerings the sort of gifts which may most naturally be supposed to please him, namely children's playthings. We can scarcely suppose that the two are unconnected, but it is important to see whether we have any evidence which may explain what their connexion is likely to have been. Almost all that we know of the Theban cult of the Kabiroi, independently of the archaeological discoveries, is contained in the passage of Pausanias which has already been mentioned

FIG. 13.—CLAY SPINNING-TOP FOUND IN THE THEBAN KA-BIRION.

(4. 1. 7). This passage in full is as follows : 'Methapos was an Athenian by race, and the founder of mysteries and orgiastic cults of all sorts. (He was besides the present instance the founder of the mysteries of the Kabiroi for the Thebans.) Now he put up also an image in the chapel of the Lykomidai with an inscription which says . . .' Pausanias' point is to prove something by means of this inscription, and the reference to the Theban cult is simply an aside to illustrate the character of Methapos. The information which it gives for our purpose is therefore scanty, but it does tell us that the cult was founded by an Athenian. There is also significance in the fact that he was familiar with the cult practised by the Lykomidai, and indeed, considering that he was thought a suitable person to put

up an image and inscription in their shrine, was probably a Lykomid himself. The Lykomidai were an ancient Attic family who traced their descent from King Pandion, and Pausanias says of them elsewhere (9. 30. 12 = *O.F.* 304) that they knew the hymns of Orpheus and sang them at their religious ceremonies. This literary evidence for an Attic origin of the Theban cult is supported by the character of the finds, which in point of artistic style conform closely to the Attic type. Archaeological considerations also point to the sixth century as the probable date of the introduction of the cult, since the foundations of the earliest temple on the site are of sixth or fifth century date. It does not therefore seem to be one of the cults indigenous to Thebes, or even one introduced at some time in the dark ages as the cult of Dionysos may have been, but one artificially planted there in historic times. (We are reduced to relying on inferences of this sort since unfortunately nothing is known of the date of Methapos himself.) This being so, I draw the following conclusion. The myth of the child Dionysos and his playthings was first expounded at Athens in the sixth century, as we have already seen reason to suppose from the reference of Pausanias to the part played by Onomakritos in its construction. It was an Orphic myth in the fullest sense of having been composed in the name of Orpheus by men who were preaching in that name a new religious doctrine. This myth and the Orphic mysteries were familiar, together with a great deal more mystical lore, to an Athenian of the name of Methapos who was the first to introduce the cult of the Kabiroi in Boiotia. A man of whom Pausanias could say that he was a ' founder of mysteries and orgiastic cults of all sorts ' is likely to have held the belief, easy enough for all devotees of that type of religion, that the gods worshipped under different names and in different places, but in the same way, were in reality only different manifestations of one god. He would not hesitate to identify two of these gods or to transfer the myths of one to the cult of the other. The identification of the Kabiros and Dionysos at Thebes was made particularly easy by the fact that Dionysos and his mysteries were already established there. Thus it comes about that, introduced from Attica and at or after the time when the Orphic reformers were at work, the cult of the Kabiroi adopts an Orphic colouring. I have said before that the element of certainty is less present in this work than in most, but here at least we have a reasonable account which fits the few facts available, and at least we have avoided saying of a cult, as has been said of many, that it ' shows Orphic influence ' without making sure what we ourselves mean by the phrase.

We have been through an account of the Orphic theogony, told plainly and without comment. We have commented on different points of detail within the theogony, separately and in turn. We have not yet paused to consider the theogony as a whole, its nature, how much religious or philosophical thought it contains, and of what sort. It will be best not to attempt a full discussion of these questions at this point, since they will be more in place when we come to consider the relation of Orphic to other Greek religious and philosophic thought, a subject which must clearly be postponed until we have completed the description of Orphism itself by the addition of chapters on its eschatology and its religious practices.

There are, however, certain preliminary problems to which this chapter ought to have given a peculiar contribution. They may be briefly indicated before we close it, since they are of the sort towards which we must adopt a definite attitude before we start upon the business of making a comparison between Orphic and other Greek ideas. I have just spoken of considering how much religious or philosophical thought the theogony contains and of what sort. It is the first of these two questions which I mean by a preliminary problem, and it is a part of the business of this chapter at least to set out, *more Aristotelico*, the problem and its conditions.

It may sound like giving a glimpse of the obvious to say that in an attempt to compare Orphism with the rest of Greek religion we are hampered unless we know beforehand what elements in Greek religion are Orphic and what are not. Yet even a little reading in the literature of the subject will bring one into contact with comparisons made under the limitations of that very disability, and if we are frank we must confess that it is not an easy one to be rid of. The difficulty may be illustrated by an extreme case, the religion of Graeco-Roman times. It is generally agreed that the Neoplatonists read into the Orphic poems ideas which were their own, and had in reality nothing to do with Orphism. Even that, though it can scarcely be called a rash thing to say, needs to be supported by a more exact description of the sense in which the term Orphism is being used. There was still an Orphic religion (a Christian writer says of the *sacra Dionysi, etiam nunc Orphica nominantur*, and a mythographer of the Christian era speaks of the beliefs of the *discipuli Orphei*, Kern, *test.* 99, and *O.F.* 213), and if we are not going to give the name Orphism to the beliefs of one who in a certain age called himself a follower of Orpheus, it is difficult to see what sense we are to attach to the term. But the belief ascribed to the *discipuli Orphei* is that the dismembered Bakchos was the soul of the world. Iamblichos too (*de anima*, Kern, *O.F.* pp. 96 f.) labels as Orphic the belief in a single world-soul pluralizing itself in animals. It was the Orphism of their age, and must be taken into account when the Orphism of that age is the subject of discussion. To the eyes of a student it may seem a very different thing from the Orphic religion of eight or nine hundred years before, but, after all, the differences will certainly be no greater than the differences between the Christianity of to-day and that of the early Christians would appear to be, if only we could bring to bear on the living religion the same objective gaze which we direct at the dead. It may be that when the mythographer spoke of the *discipuli Orphei* he was thinking of the Neoplatonists, whose frequent appeals to the authority of the Orphic poems might well lead a contemporary to think that they deserved the name. I have no doubt that they themselves would not have resented it, and but little doubt that some of them were actually initiated into the Orphic mysteries.

That, however, as I said, is an extreme case, and raises extra difficulties of its own, which will find their separate place in the investigation. The main problem that confronts us is the relation of Orphism to the thought of the classical age, and for that the necessary preparation is to ask what Orphism was in its original form. On this point the investigations of the present chapter have taught one lesson which we must not allow ourselves to forget. Any argument which implies that Orphism was a primitive form of religion is condemned to falsity from the outset. The Orphic showed a genius for transforming the significance of his mythological or ritual material (he would not have been a Greek if he had not), and sometimes saw an opportunity of preaching his religion through the medium of symbols which were in their origin of the crudest and most primitive. When they became Orphic they changed, and if we are interested in Orphic thought we cannot be too careful in distinguishing between the pre-Orphic character of a myth or rite, which may be wholly alien to Orphism, and its character as a part of the Orphic religion. Few would deny this description of Orphism, or the necessity which it lays upon us, but nevertheless the pre-existence of much of its material invites confusion, and the invitation has been by no means always resisted. It has meant, for instance, that a scholar who was as keenly alive as any to the spirituality and the transforming genius of the Orphics did not avoid using the term 'primitive Orphism', a term which cannot help bringing loose thinking in its train.

The artificial character of Orphism has been betrayed to us by indications both internal and external to the theogony. I choose the epithet because it expresses better than any other the contrast between the careful thought which has obviously been bestowed by the Orphic writer upon his mythical material and the natural, spontaneous way in which the myths themselves of a people seem to arise, but I wish it to be understood without the derogatory sense which nowadays is commonly attached to it. Internally, it has shown itself in the ingenious combination of myths calculated to bring out a meaning which the elements of the story in their primitive form were never designed to convey. We have had this strikingly brought to our notice in the tales of the swallowing of Phanes and of the sufferings of Dionysos, the one illuminating for us the notion of a creative god, the other that of the admixture of divinity in the natures of human beings. Externally, the same fact is pointed to by the tendency of the evidence to concentrate on the sixth century as the most likely period to which to assign the beginnings of this religion, and on Athens as the most probable centre of its early development. Sixth century Athens was not a primitive community, it was a hive of intellectual activity, the place in fact to which, even without external evidence, one would most naturally assign the origins of a complicated system of the nature of that which the Orphic theogony presents. Thus do external and internal indications interlock, admittedly with the weightiest part of the testimony centred in the internal, at least as far as our investigations have carried us up to now. Externally, we have had little to guide us so far but the traditions concerning Onomakritos and the Athenian foundation of the cult of the Kabiroi at Thebes. Other evidence will come up for consideration in due course. Such will be the reappearance of Orpheus in Attic traditions (p. 217 below) and perhaps the mutually inextricable natures of Orphism and Pythagoreanism, believed by the ancients to be two sides of the same philosophico-religious system.

In the mass of modern writing which exists on this subject, one returns again and again to the expressions of Otto Gruppe, relieved and enlightened by the clear thinking and consistent argument which are there displayed. It is he who brings before us the picture of the Orphic writer as having a philosophical idea to express, but hindered in his expression of it by the already existing myths to which he has linked it. There lies the answer to some of the most troublesome questions with which the student of Orphism, and still more the student of kindred subjects who wants to know ' what Orphism is ' but cannot devote a period of

specialized study to it, has always found himself beset. What is
' an Orphic myth ' ? Can we suppose that myths as crude as
those which we find in the Orphic writings were intended by
their authors to convey a spiritual meaning ? Of course not, if
we suppose the Orphic writers to have been the inventors of the
myths. Yes, if we suppose them to have caught up the material
handed down from a more primitive age and remoulded it to suit
their own conceptions, as we have now seen them doing. Why
did they trouble to remould it instead of breaking loose from its
trammels ? On that point also we have said something already
(p. 106 above), and in this summing up I prefer simply to counter
the question with another : why is the story of Jonah and the
whale still read aloud in churches in the enlightened twentieth
century ?

When Gruppe argues that the Orphic theogony was intended
by its authors to express a philosophic idea, he was prepared also
to say what in his opinion that philosophic idea was. In this we
shall try to follow him, as I have said, at a later stage in the book.
But we are not closing this chapter without having obtained some
light on a question which has its importance, considered as an
approach to that later stage, the question, namely, what grounds
we have for believing, *a priori*, that the Orphic theogony contained
any philosophic thought at all.

APPENDICES TO CHAPTER IV

1. *The Rending of Dionysos.* (On p. 164.)

I have made the outline in the text as short and simple as possible
for the sake of clearness. On the subject of the rending of the infant
Dionysos there is more evidence to be considered. Let me describe the
evidence first.

(i) In the British Museum is a red-figured Attic vase dating probably
from the early fourth century B.C. on which the scene is depicted. (*B.M.
Cat. Vases*, 3. 188, no. E 246 ; *JHS* 11, 1890, 343 f. ; A. B. Cook, *Zeus*, 1, 654 f.
See fig. 14.) In the middle stands a bearded figure in Thracian dress holding
in his left arm the limp and naked body of a child. With his right hand
he conveys to his mouth a limb of the child which he has torn from the
body. On the left stands Dionysos, recognizable by long, wavy hair
wreathed with vine or ivy, and the *thyrsos* in his right hand. His left
hand he holds out towards the central figure. On the right a tall, bearded
Thracian carrying a staff is running away with a backward glance over his
shoulder. The interpretation of gestures and facial expressions on Greek
vases is very much at the mercy of subjective impressions, but I cannot
feel any doubt that Dionysos by his look and gesture expresses dismay and
protest, and the Thracian on the right both alarm and disgust. (I write
from a view of the vase itself.)

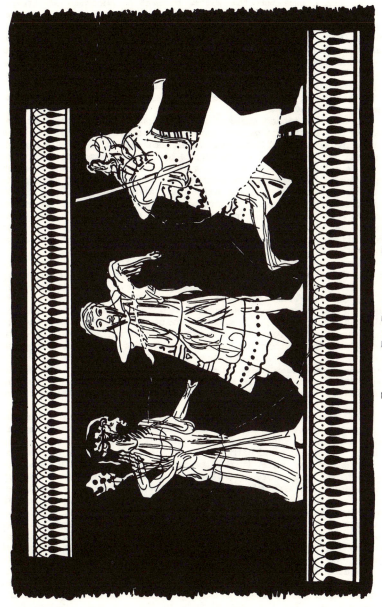

Fig. 14.—The Rending of Dionysos

✱ (ii) The Lenaia was the winter festival of Dionysos at Athens, so called from λῆναι = Maenads. (Hesych. λῆναι· βάκχαι, and see other evidence in Cook, *op. cit.* 1, 667, n. 4.) The scholiast on Aristophanes (Schol. Rav. Ar. *ran.* 479) says that the ceremony included a cry of summons to the god, made by the people at the bidding of a priest, and no doubt this was followed by his epiphany. Clement of Alexandria (*Protr.* 1. 2. 1 f. p. 3, 26 ff. Stählin) calls the tragic poets ' Lenaean ' (ληναΐζοντας), and his scholiast makes this comment on the word : ' A rustic song, sung over the wine-press, which itself included the rending of Dionysos '.

To take the second piece of evidence first, if this song was accompanied by ' a mimetic performance, a passion play ', then it may well ✱ represent the origin of Attic tragedy, as Cook (*op. cit.* 1, 678) has argued. Tragedy was performed in the service of Dionysos, and the number of plays which dealt with the tearing in pieces of heroes, some of them closely akin to Dionysos, is surprising. Cook notes that besides the *Bacchae* of Euripides, there were plays about Pentheus and Pelias by Thespis (Pelias was cut up and boiled in a cauldron by his daughters in the belief that it would restore his youth), two plays on the Pentheus theme by Aeschylus, and more by Iophon and others. We may add the *Bassarids* of Aeschylus which told of the dismemberment of Orpheus (p. 32 above).

More relevant for our present purpose is the song, ' which itself included the rending of Dionysos ', and for which this clear testimony is of the greatest value. It must certainly have contained the germ of the Orphic *hieros logos* on the subject, and who knows but that by the fifth century the *logos* of Onomakritos may itself have been the one adopted, and sung at the *Lenaia* by a rhapsodist ? This is not to assert that those taking part in the festival were in the full sense *Orphici*. None knew better than the Orphic himself that there were many who took part in similar rites but few who were in their full communion (πολλοὶ μὲν ναρθηκοφόροι, παῦροι δέ τε βάκχοι. Below, p. 194.) Those who deserved the Orphic title of pure had undertaken a more exacting and self-denying course, but the dogmas contained in Orphic literature were known to a wider circle than these.

The interpretation of the vase is a more difficult matter. In the first place, I am sure that we confuse the issue unnecessarily if we suppose that any of the figures must represent the Titans of the Orphic story. The slaying and eating of the god in the form of an infant were memorials of the fierce ritual of an earlier, darker age, which had not faded from the memory of a people to whom the thought of actually performing such a sacrifice would have been abhorrent. (For further evidence of survivals from a period of human sacrifice, see *e.g.* the section in *Zeus* on human omophagy (1. 651 ff.), and compare the cult of Zeus Lykaios (*ib.* 654) and the sacrifice of infants at Tenedos, *ib.* 675. Human sacrifice to Dionysos Omestes before the battle of Salamis, considered a terrifying notion but carried out, Plutarch, *Themistokles* 13, quoted *Zeus* 1. 657, n. 1.) Even in the Thracian religion, an animal was early substituted for the human victim, and the Athenians became content to sing a song describing the deed which the ritual was supposed to commemorate, and perhaps to accompany the song with a pantomimic performance. Yet the original form of the rite was not forgotten, indeed it probably exercised, for all its horror, a kind of superstitious fascination as being after all the real thing, and there was not the same objection to depicting it in that form on a vase as there would have been to committing the act oneself. It is a rite that is being represented, not a myth. It scarcely needs remark that there is no inconsistency in the presence of the god at the orgies of his own worshippers. The devout performer of them firmly believed him to be there. There is, however, a suggestion of a mask about the slightly grotesque head of Dionysos which may mean that the figure represents a worshipper taking the part of the god in a sacred drama. If the Athenians had lost their taste for human sacrifice, it was even more revolting to the true Orphic, as I hope to show later. If, then, we are to look for any traces of Orphic influence in this painting (and nothing is more likely in a Dionysiac scene painted at Athens in the fourth century), I would see it in the protesting attitude of the god and the horrified retreat of the second Thracian. Orpheus taught his people that they were worshipping the right gods in the wrong way. Dionysos seems to be saying, like Jehovah through the mouth of Amos, ' Though ye offer me burnt offerings and your meat offerings, I will not accept them '. To point this moral, a man of Orphic persuasion would very naturally depict the rite in the crude and horrible form which had long been abandoned, but which the Dionysiac worshipper was logically forced to confess he regarded as the authentic one. The Orphic did not teach disbelief in the dismemberment of the infant god, but he drove home the lesson that it was nothing more nor less than a loathsome crime.

2. Kore.

There were two Orphic myths of Kore, the story of her violation by her father Zeus and that of her abduction to the lower world by Pluto. Only the former fits in as a part of the theogony and anthropogony, and the account of the latter has therefore been left out until now. The former is an essential link in the chief and characteristic Orphic creation-myth, and its presence needs no justification. The motive for an Orphic version of the familiar rape of Kore by Pluto is not so clear. It may well have been competition with Eleusis, in the form either of trying to gain a footing in the shrine or of enabling the rival system to compete with the established Attic mysteries on their own ground. It is, moreover, a surprising fact, in view of its obvious Cretan and Anatolian affinities, that in the Orphic religion so far as we can see no important place is given to the Mother or the Virgin goddess, to any figure corresponding in nature to the Ephesian ' Artemis ' or Kybele. The adoption of the story of Demeter and Kore may be due in part to a realization of this deficiency in the mythical cycle on which the main body of doctrine was founded. We shall see in a moment that the modifications introduced by the Orphics into the Homeric story consist mainly of importations from Anatolian cult.

Kore, whose name means simply the Maiden, is identified in all traditions known to us with Persephone, the daughter of Demeter and Zeus. Being the daughter of the fruitful earth, or of the corn-goddess, she probably had a double function in popular imagination, as both Queen of the Dead and herself a goddess of fertility. This would make it easier for the double set of legends to arise of which we shall have to speak. According to the ordinary story, on which the rites at Eleusis were founded, she was carried off by Hades to be his consort among the dead. In the Orphic theogony she is violated by her own father

Zeus, by whom she becomes the mother of Dionysos. This union con-
tradicts the usual Greek tradition, and seems therefore to be the
characteristic Orphic version, since it hangs together with the whole
curious story of the Titans' crime, and the birth and consequent dual
nature of mankind. The Orphic version of the rape of Kore by Pluto,
which differed from the Eleusinian in certain significant details, seems
at the same time to form a quite separate myth, within the Orphic
cycle, from that of her union with Zeus and its consequences. Tradition bears us out in supposing that it was not a part of the theogony,
but told in a separate poem. The two need not have been connected
by any rigid intellectual bonds, since even in their original forms we
need not suppose them to have been the work of the same author
or even written for the same community. The Orphic tendency to
a mystical syncretism made their coexistence easier. Hades and
Dionysos were the same, and was Zeus after all very different ? An
Orphic Hymn (admittedly from a later age) describes the Eumenides
as 'the pure daughters of Chthonian Zeus and the lovely maiden
Persephone' (*O.H.* 70. 2 f.). Was their father Zeus or Pluto ?

All this was puzzling to the Neoplatonists, who hated to leave
anything unexplained and expended some of the best of their jargon
on it. Thus Proklos says (*Theol. Plat.* 6. 11, p. 370 = *O.F.* 198) : ' The
order of Kore is twofold, the first made manifest in the supramundane
sphere, where as we hear she is linked with Zeus, and together with him
brings forth the one creator of the divided world (*i.e.* Dionysos), the
second within the world, and this is the Kore who is said to be carried
off by Pluto '. Again (*O.F.* 195) : ' Therefore the *theologos* says that
the two extreme gods (*i.e.* Zeus, god of the upper world, and Pluto of
the lower) create with Kore the first things and the last, but the middle
god (*i.e.* Poseidon, god of the sea) even without her. . . . For this
reason they say that Kore is now violated by Zeus, now carried off by
Pluto '. At another time it is the contrast between Eleusinian and
Orphic that seems to him most curious (*O.F.* 195) : ' For indeed the word
of the *theologoi* who have handed down to us the holy mysteries at Eleusis
says that Kore lives in the first place above, where she stays in her
mother's house, which her mother prepared for her in a remote place
removed from the world, and in the second place below, where she
rules with Pluto over those of the underworld '. So far we have simply
the Eleusinian myth, according to which Kore stayed half the year
above ground with her mother, and the other half below with Pluto.
' From this one would wonder how Kore can be consort of both Zeus
and Pluto, of whom according to the myths the one violated the goddess
and the other carried her off.'

The proof that the Orphic story of the rape is in origin an Attic
work of the sixth century B.C. has been worked out by L. Malten, together with an analysis of the remains to see in what points they show
differences from the Homeric version. His article (*Altorphische Demetersage, Arch. Rel. Wiss.* 1909, 417 ff.) is convincing, and has found general
agreement. The evidence need not therefore be retailed here, but one
or two points of especial interest may be mentioned. A long papyrus
discovered some thirty years ago (*O.F.* 49) is sufficiently well preserved
to show that it is a version or paraphrase of the rape of Kore which the
writer attributes to Orpheus, and to give some idea of its contents.
These correspond to the Orphic version told by Clement of Alexandria
(*O.F.* 50, 52), and take the story back to the first century B.C. Using

the evidence of the papyrus, Malten shows the chorus in Euripides' *Helena* (1301 ff.) to have the Orphic version as its source. The same version is pictorially represented on the altar of Hyakinthos at Amyklai, which is dated by archaeologists at the end of the sixth century. Those are the key positions, but they are supported by a wealth of minor corroborations and by the general evidence for the activity of Orphic writers at Athens in the sixth century, most of which has found its place in this book.

The important differences between the Orphic tale and that in the Homeric Hymn to Demeter are these. In the Homeric version, Persephone was carried off in Sicily. Demeter in her wanderings was told ✱ the truth of the rape by the Sun. When she came to Eleusis, it was Keleos, the king of the place, and his wife Metaneira, who entertained her, and their daughter Iambe who by her jesting persuaded the goddess so far to overcome her grief as to refresh herself with the *kykeon*. The son of the king and queen, whom Demeter nursed, was Demophoon. In the Orphic version the scene of the rape was Eleusis itself. Demeter in her search was entertained by a poor man Dysaules ('ill-housed') and his wife Baubo in their humble cottage, and their sons Triptolemos and Eubuleus informed her of the rape, which they had seen themselves while tending their herds. Clement adds to these Eumolpos, the founder of the Eleusinian mysteries, who therefore at some time which we cannot determine was absorbed in this way into the Orphic tale. The feat of making the goddess smile and drink the *kykeon* was Baubo's, and the form of amusement which she devised for the purpose was obscene. It is probable that Eubuleus is a later addition to the story, but Triptolemos may well belong to the original sixth century version. (Malten, pp. 440 ff. For Eubuleus cp. pp. 179 f. below.) Malten notes as characteristic the difference in religious tone between Keleos the king and Dysaules the poor man.

Baubo is an interesting figure. She has all the characteristics of a creature of primitive popular imagination, a kind of bogey, and in later times became quite naturally an associate of the dread Hekate (*Hymn. Mag.*, Abel, *Orphica*, p. 289, cp. *O.F.* 53). Dieterich has shown beyond doubt that her name meant originally 'that which she showed to Demeter', the female counterpart of a phallic emblem. An inscription from Paros shows that she had a cult there together with Demeter, Kore and Zeus Eubuleus, and Malten supposes that the Orphics borrowed her from there. Gruppe says more reasonably that it was the other way round. (The Orphic version of the rape seems to have had wider influence than other Orphic writings, no doubt owing to its attempt to capture Eleusis, which was at least partly successful, in so far as its mythology had some effect on the Eleusinian. Cp. Malten, p. 441.) Granted this, another piece of evidence assumes importance which has been almost universally ignored by investigators of Baubo. Kern actually begins his article *Baubo* in Pauly-Wissowa with the words 'Der Kult der B. begegnet uns allein auf der Insel Paros'. She is mentioned in an inscription of Galatia (CIG 4142), in the form Βαβό. (Βαβοῖ, dat., is the form used on the Parian inscription.) We are not dependent on this evidence alone. There is also the inscription mentioned below (II. iii), and Asklepiades of Tragilos (fourth century B.C.) said that Baubo and Dysaules were the parents of Mise, who is known to be a figure of Anatolian cult as well as of Orphic tradition. See *e.g.* Dieterich in Philologus, 52, 1 ff., Kern in *Genethl. für Robert*, Halle,

1910, *nachtr.*, and especially Gruppe, *Gr. Myth. u. Rel.* 1437, n. 2. The last-named thinks it probable that Baubo, Mise and Dysaules all have their origin in Phrygian religion, but no one else seems to have taken any notice of the suggestion, nor of CIG 4142, which is just mentioned by Gruppe in the course of a long footnote at 1542, n. 1. There is also the gold plate from Thurii (*O.F.* 47), used by Malten as part of the evidence for his reconstruction of the Orphic version of the rape, which brings Demeter and Kore directly and uncompromisingly into the circle of Kybele. In the examination of the theogony we found ourselves more than once compelled to look to Anatolia for the origin of Orphic myths. The rightness of doing so is surely further borne out by the evidence here presented.

Note.—The ancient evidence for Baubo may be roughly tabulated as follows :—

I. *Literary.*
    (i) Michael Psellos, *O.F.* 53.
    (ii) Magic Hymn to Hekate, Abel, *Orphica*, p. 289, *v.* 2.
    (iii) Hesychios, *s.v. Baubo.*
    (iv) Clement of Alexandria, *O.F.* 50, 52.
    (v) *Pap. Berol.* 44 = *O.F.* 49, *v.* 81.
    (vi) Asklepiades of Tragilos *ap.* Harpokration, *s.v. Dysaules.*
For the etymology :—
    (vii) Herondas, 6. 19.
    (viii) Empedokles *ap.* Hesych. *s.v. Baubo.* See also Dieterich in *Philol.* 52, 3 f. = *Kl. Schr.* 127.

II. *Epigraphical.*
    (i) Inscr. from Paros, first century B.C. IG 12. 5. 227 = Bechtel, *Gr. Dial. Inschr.* 3. 2. 590 f. no. 5441, text also in Cook, *Zeus,* 1, 669, n. 2.
    (ii) Inscr. from Galatia, Roman Imperial date. CIG 4142, mentioned by Gruppe, *Gr. Myth. u. Rel.* 1542, n. 1.
    (iii) Kern, *Inschr. v. Magnesia,* 215*b*, W. Quandt, *de Baccho in Asia Min. culto,* Halle, 1913, 162 f. An image of Dionysos having been miraculously discovered at Magnesia on the Maeander, the city sent to Delphi and was told to found a cult. Three Maenads were imported from Thebes, of whom one was given the name Baubo. The date of the oracle is put in the third or second century B.C. Since there can be no doubt that the Maenad was called after the goddess or daemon of that name, this shows us Baubo on Anatolian ground at an earlier date than that of the inscription on Paros.

III. *Art.*
    (i) A statuette from Priene (Wiegand and Schrader, *Priene,* p. 161) was referred to B. by Diels, *Poet. philos. fragg.* on Empedokles, fr. 153.
    (ii) A terracotta from Italy is illustrated by Cook as B. (*Zeus,* 2, 131 f., fig. 79), though Kern in Pauly-Wiss. contests the attribution.

★   References for modern opinions are given by Cook in *Zeus,* 2, 131, n. 5. To his comprehensive list I would only add Rohde's *Psyche,* Eng. tr. 591, and Kern in *Hermes,* 1890, p. 8, where K. compares the features of Baubo with some of the paintings on the vases from the Theban Kabirion (pp. 123 ff. above), pointing out that caricature is an element in Orphic literature and monuments. R. M. Dawkins in *Journ. Hell. Stud.* 26 (1906) notes that her name has persisted to this day. In a Carnival mummery or ritual play of modern Thrace, Babo ('a word in general local use meaning an old woman') is the name of the old woman who carries about a child in a basket-shaped cradle still called *likno*.

3. I append a version of the actual metrical fragments assigned by Kern to the Rhapsodic Theogony, numbered as in *Orphicorum Fragmenta*. Following the number in each case is the name of the authority in whose writings the quotation is found.

61. Aristokritos the Manichee. (The poet speaks to Musaios.) These things keep in thy mind, dear son, and in thy heart, well knowing all the things of long ago, even from Phanes.

62. Malalas. Lord, son of Leto, far shooter, mighty Phoibos, all-seeing, ruler over mortals and immortals, Helios, borne aloft on golden wings, this is now the twelfth voice of those I heard from thee. 'Twas thou that said it, and thee thyself, far shooter, would I make my witness.

63. *Etymologicum Magnum.* These they call Giants by name among the blessed gods, for that they were born from Earth (Ge) and from the blood of Heaven (Ouranos).

(These fragments are placed at the beginning by Kern because either they or their context tell the number of the *hieros logos* from which they are taken, 'ne quis me reliquias ordine genuino disponere ausum esse opinetur'.)

66. Proklos. Of this Chronos, the ageless one, whose counsels never perish, was born Aither and a great yawning gulf on this side and on that : and there was no limit to it, no bottom nor foundation.

67. Proklos. (All things were in confusion) Throughout the misty darkness.

70. Damaskios. Then great Chronos fashioned in the divine *Aither* a silvery egg.

71. Proklos. (a) And it moved without slackening in a vast circle.
(b) And it began to move in a wondrous circle.

72. Proklos. And at the birth of Phanes the misty gulf below and the windless Aither were rent.

73 and 74. Lactantius. First-born, Phaethon, son of lofty Aither. Proklos quotes the latter half with the variant 'beauteous' for 'lofty'.

75. *Etym. Magn.* Whom they call Phanes . . . because he first appeared in the *Aither*.

76. Hermias. (Of Phanes.) With four eyes looking this way and that.

78. Hermias. (Of Phanes.) With golden wings moving this way and that.

79. Proklos. (Of Phanes.) Uttering the voice of a bull and of a glaring lion.

81. Proklos. Female and Father the mighty god Erikepaios.

82 (a) Proklos, Olympiodoros. Cherishing in his heart swift and sightless Eros.
(b) Proklos. (Of Phanes.) The key of Mind.

83. Proklos. (Of Eros-Metis.) A great daemon ever treading on their tracks.

85. Proklos. An awful daemon, Metis, bearing the honoured seed of the gods, whom the blessed on tall Olympos were wont to call Phanes, the Firstborn.

9

86. Hermias and others.   The Firstborn none saw with his eyes, unless it were holy Night alone.   But all the others marvelled when there burst upon their gaze the unlooked-for light in the *Aither ;* so gleamed the body of immortal Phanes.

89. Lactantius.   (Of Phanes.)   He built for the Immortals an imperishable house.

91. Proklos.   And he devised another world, immense, which the Immortals call Selene and the inhabitants of Earth Mene (both words mean Moon), a world which has many mountains, many cities, many mansions.

92. Proklos.   (Of the moon.)   That it may turn in a month as much as the sun in a year.

94. Proklos.   He appointed for mortals a seat to inhabit apart from the Immortals, where the path of the sun in the middle turns back upon itself, neither too cold above the head nor fiery hot, but betwixt the two.

(With this fr. compare Virgil, *Georg.* 1. 237-9.)

95. Proklos.   And the honourable works of nature are steadfast and boundless eternity.

96. Proklos.   (Of Phanes.)   And he made him (the sun) guardian and bade him have lordship over all.

97. Proklos.   These things the Father made in the misty darkness of the cave.

98. Proklos.   (Of Phanes.)   Himself he robbed his daughter of the flower of her maidenhood.

101. Proklos.   (Of Phanes.)   His splendid sceptre he placed in the hands of the goddess Night, that she might have the honour of royal sway.

102. Alexander of Aphrodisias.   (Of Night.)   Holding in her hands the noble sceptre of Erikepaios.

103. Hermias.   He granted to her (Night) to have the gift of prophecy wholly true.

105. Hermias.   (*a*) Fair Ide and her sister Adrasteia.

(*b*) He (She ?) gave to Adrasteia brazen cymbals in her hands.

106. Proklos.   Nurse of the gods is ambrosial Night.

108. Syrianus.   He took and divided between gods and mortals the universe then existing, over which first ruled famous Erikepaios.

109. Hermias.   (Of Night, though line 2 is quoted elsewhere as if it referred to Phanes.)   She in her turn bore Gaia and broad Ouranos ; and brought to light those that were invisible, and of what race they were.

111. Alexander of Aphrodisias.   (Of Ouranos.)   Who first held sway over the gods after his mother Night.

114. Proklos.   (Earth bore) seven fair daughters . . . and seven kingly sons . . . daughters . . . Themis and kindly Tethys and deep-haired Mnemosyne and happy Theia, and Dione she bore of exceeding beauty and Phoibe and Rheia, the mother of Zeus the king. (Her sons were of the same number), Koios and Krios and mighty Phorkys and Kronos and Okeanos and Hyperion ⌐ ⌐ Iapetos.

115. Eustathios.   And the circle of unwearied, fair-flowing Okeanos, who winds about and enfolds the earth with his swirling streams.

119. Proklos.   Titans of evil counsel, with overweening hearts.

120. Proklos.   (The Titans were defeated by the Olympians.)   For powerful though they were they had set themselves against a mightier foe, out of their fatal insolence and reckless pride.

121. Proklos. (Of Ouranos.) With their inexorable hearts and lawless spirit . . . he cast them into Tartaros, deep in the earth.

127. Proklos. The genitals (of Ouranos) fell down into the sea, and round about them as they floated swirled the white foam. Then in the circling seasons the Year brought forth (so Kern, ' In the circling seasons of the year he brought forth ', Platt. Cp. fr. 183) a tender maiden, and the spirits of Rivalry and Beguilement together took her up in their arms, so soon as she was born.

129. Proklos. But above all others it was Kronos whom Night reared and cherished.

135. Proklos. At this time Okeanos kept within his halls, debating with himself to which side his intent should lean, whether he should maim his father's might and do him wanton injury, conspiring with Kronos and his other brethren who had hearkened to their mother's behests, or whether he should leave them and remain within at peace. Long did he ponder, then remained he sitting in his halls, for he was wroth with his mother, and yet more with his brethren.

142. Proklos. Under Zeus son of Kronos (by Zeus son of K. Lobeck) to have immortal life, with clear cheek . . . wet fragrant locks, nor to be touched with the white growth of weak . . . but thick, luxuriant beard. (For various restorations see Kern. Whatever the meaning of the first words, the passage with which Proklos introduces the lines shows that they refer to the happy lot of men in the past under the rule of Kronos.)

144. Proklos. Until Rhea should bear a child to Kronos in love.

145. Proklos. Aforetime was she Rhea, but when she came to be called mother of Zeus she became Demeter.

148. Proklos. Then Kronos afterwards, when he had eaten the food given him in deceit, lay and snored mightily.

149. Clem. Alex. He lay with his stout neck lolling sideways, and all-conquering sleep overtook him.

152. Proklos. (Of Adrasteia.) Taking the brazen cymbals and tympanon of goat-hide (?).

154. Porphyrios. (Night speaks to Zeus.) Whenever thou shalt see him under the oaks with lofty foliage, drunk with the works of loud-murmuring bees, then bind him (Kronos).

155. Proklos. (Zeus to Kronos.) Set up our race, illustrious daemon.

157. Proklos. (The length of the sceptre of Zeus.) Of four and twenty measures.

158. Proklos. And Justice, bringer of retribution, attended him (Zeus), bringing succour to all.

164. Proklos. (Zeus speaks.) Mother, highest of the gods, immortal Night, how am I to establish my proud rule among the immortals ?

165. Proklos and others. (Zeus speaks to Night.) How may I have all things one and each one separate ?
Surround all things with the ineffable *Aither*, and in the midst of that set the heaven, and in the midst the boundless earth, in the midst the sea, and in the midst all the constellations with which the heaven is crowned.

166. Proklos. (Night to Zeus.) But when thou shalt stretch a strong bond about all things, fitting a golden chain from the *Aither*.

167. Proklos.   Thus then engulfing the might of Erikepaios, the Firstborn, he held the body of all things in the hollow of his own belly; and he mingled with his own limbs the power and strength of the god.   Therefore together with him all things in Zeus were created anew, the shining height of the broad *Aither* and the sky, the seat of the unharvested sea and the noble earth, great Ocean and the lowest depths beneath the earth, and rivers and the boundless sea and all else, all immortal and blessed gods and goddesses, all that was then in being and all that was to come to pass, all was there, and mingled like streams in the belly of Zeus.

168. Porphyrios   and   others.   Hymn to Zeus, which begins : Zeus became first, Zeus of the bright lightning last.   Zeus is head, Zeus middle, and from Zeus all things have their being.   Zeus became male, Zeus was an immortal maiden.   Zeus is foundation of earth and starry heaven.   Zeus is king and Zeus himself first Father of all.

I omit here the rest (there are 32 lines in all), which may be called an elaboration into detail of the pantheistic notion of fr. 167.

170. Proklos.   (On Phanes were from the beginning) Great Bromios and all-seeing Zeus.

174. Proklos.   (Athena.)   Gleaming with arms, a brazen glory to behold.

175. Proklos.   (Athena.)   She is called by the noble name of Arete.

176. Proklos.   (Athena.)   That she might be for him (Zeus) the accomplisher of great deeds.

177. Proklos.   (Athena.)   For she was made the dread accomplisher of the will of Kronos' son.

178. Proklos.   (Athena.)   For she is best of all the immortal goddesses at plying the loom and devising the works of spinning.

179. Proklos.   (The Kyklopes.)   Who made for Zeus the thunder, and fashioned the thunderbolt, the first craftsmen, and taught Hephaistos and Athena all cunning works that the heaven contains.

183. Proklos.   (Described by P. as the birth of the *second* Aphrodite. Cp. fr. 127 above.) . . . and the sea received the seed of great Zeus.   So as the year completed its circling course, in the season of fair springing plants he bore the waker of laughter, Aphrodite, the foam-born.

187. Proklos.   (Of Artemis.)   Unmarried and all untried in childbirth she resolves its issues.

188. Proklos.   (O. calls Artemis Hekate.)   She then, divine Hekate, daughter of fair-tressed Leto, leaving there the body of the child departed to Olympos.

189. Proklos.   (Of Demeter.)   She devised servants, and attendants, and followers ; she devised ambrosia and the fragrance (? ἀρδμόν in Kern ; ὀδμήν *conieci*), of red nectar ; she devised the splendid works of the loud-murmuring bees.

193. Tzetzes.   Plying the loom, an unfinished toil, flowery.

194. Proklos.   (Demeter speaks to Kore.)   But going up to the fruitful bed of Apollo, thou shalt bear splendid children, with countenances of flaming fire.

197. Proklos.   (Kore bears) nine daughters, grey-eyed, makers of flowers.

199. Proklos.   (Of Dionysos.)   And he was called sweet child of Zeus.

200. Proklos.   (Names of the Moon.)   Plutone and Euphrosyne and mighty Bendis.

207. Proklos.   (Zeus makes Dionysos king) for all he was young and but a greedy infant.

208. Proklos.   (Zeus speaks.)   Give ear ye gods ; this one have I made your king.

210. Proklos.   (a) Only the heart, the seat of thought, did they leave.

(b) Seven parts of the child in all did they divide between them.

215. Proklos.   But Atlas holds the broad heaven under the weight of stern necessity, at the bounds of the earth.

216. Proklos.   (Dionysos is often called Wine by the *theologoi* from his gifts.)

(a) Instead of one stock of Wine they put in its place three.

(b) Take up all the limbs of Wine in order, and bring them to me.

(c) Jealous as she was of Wine, the son of Zeus.

218. Proklos.   Zeus then, the father, ruled all things, but Bakchos ruled after him.

219. Clement of Alexandria.   (The Phrygians are said to call water *bedü*.)   And *bedü* of the Nymphs drips down, sparkling water.   (I do not know why Kern assigns this to the Rhapsodies.)

222. Proklos.   All who live purely beneath the rays of the sun, so soon as they die have a smoother path in a fair meadow beside deep-flowing Acheron, but those who have done evil beneath the rays of the sun, the insolent, are brought down below Kokytos to the chilly horrors of Tartaros.

223. Proklos.   (The fate of the souls of animals is different from that of our own.)   The souls of beasts and winged birds when they flit away, and sacred life forsakes the creature, not one of them is brought to the house of Hades, but each flutters aimlessly where it is, until some other creature snatch it up as it mingles with the gusts of the wind. But when it is a man who leaves the light of the sun, then the immortal souls are brought down by Kyllenian Hermes to the vast hidden part of the earth.

224. Proklos and (lines 1, 2) Olympiodoros.   (Souls enter different bodies in turn.)   (a) Fathers and sons in the halls are the same, and neat housewives and mothers and daughters—all come out of each other in the succeeding generations.

(b) . . . since the soul of men in the circles of time goes in turn among animals, now this one and now that.   At one time a horse, then it becomes . . . again a sheep, then a bird, a sight of fear, again the form of a dog with deep-toned bark, and the race of cold snakes that creeps upon the bright earth.

225. Plutarch.   A creature as long-lived as the young palm with feathered top.

226. Clement of Alexandria.   (The first l ne is corrupt, but the sense must have been as follows.   See conjectures in Kern.)

Water is death to soul, and soul to water.   From water comes earth, and from earth water again, and from that, soul, quitting the vastness of *aither*.

(Versus Orphicos ad Heracliti exemplum fictos esse apparet.   Kern.)

227. Clem. Alex.   (Corruption in first line at least.)   Of all the springing herbs with which mortals have to do on the earth, none has an unchanging destiny laid upon it, but all must go full circle, and it is not lawful to stop in any part, but each bough holds to a just share of the course, even as it began it.   (The reference is to the use of young

branches held by worshippers of the gods. They are said by Clement to signify birth and death and in fact the wheel of existence, according to Orpheus. He quotes as parallel the use of wheels in worship by the Egyptians. Cp. p. 208 below.)

228. Vettius Valens. (*a*) The soul of man has its origin from *aither*.

(*b*) As we draw in the air we gather to ourselves divine soul.

(*c*) The soul is immortal and ageless, and comes from Zeus.

(*d*) The soul of all is immortal, but the bodies are mortal.

229, 230. Proklos and Simplicius. To cease from the circle and have respite from evil.

232. Olympiodoros. Men will despatch full hecatombs in all the seasons of the year, and will perform the mystic rites, yearning to be set free from their lawless ancestry. Then thou, for thou hast power in these things, shalt set free whom thou wilt from grievous pain and the endless sting of passion.

(Line 3 should surely be translated so, and not as Farnell and others do, ' to set free their ancestors who have sinned ', with reference to the doctrines of purgatory and prayers for the dead. Kern agrees with the translation above, *Orpheus*, 1920, p. 46.)

233. Malalas and Kedrenos. Beasts and birds and sinful tribes of mortals, burdens to the earth, counterfeit images, knowing no single thing, without wit to perceive the approach of evil, nor to avert disaster from afar, nor skilled when good is at hand to repent and make it yours, but vain and foolish and improvident.

234. Clem. Alex. For there is no worse, no more terrible thing than a woman.

235. Olympiodoros. Many are the wand-bearers, but few the Bakchoi.

NOTES TO CHAPTER IV

[1] To speak of *Theogony* as a formal title for the whole collection is a modern innovation. The separate discourses had their own titles, of which *Theogonia* was one. Others were, *e.g.*, *The disappearance of Dionysos, Concerning Zeus and Hera* (*O.F.* 206 and p. 141). The number of lays is that of the books of the *Iliad* and *Odyssey*. It is chosen, for convenience of reference, because there are twenty-four letters in the Greek alphabet, and some at least of the divisions are therefore arbitrary.

[2] Gruppe, (a) *Orphische Theogonien* in *Griech. Culte und Mythen*, Leipzig, 1887, pp. 612-75, (b) *die rhapsodische Theogonie usw.* in *Jahrb. für Class. Philol.*, 17er *Suppl.*, 1890, pp. 687-747. Kern, *de Orphei, Pherec., Epimen. Theogoniis quaestt. crit.*, Berlin, 1888. Compare also Kern, *Orpheus*, Berlin, 1920, pp. 38-50, and Rohde, *Psyche* (Eng. tr. 1925), Appendix 9, *The great Orphic Theogony*.

[3] Kern, *de theogoniis*, pp. 28 and 34, Gomperz, *Greek Thinkers*, London, 1920, I, p. 539, Rohde, *Psyche*, App. 9.

[4] That is, in *de theogoniis*. More recently he seems to have modified this opinion, for he says in his edition of the Orphic fragments (1922), p. 141 : ' Quo tempore hoc magnum carmen varios Orphicorum λόγους comprehendens compositum sit, obscurum est. Quod quamvis multo ante Neoplatonicorum aetatem factum esse negem, tamen veterum carminum vestigia in eo conservata esse mihi extra omnem dubitationem positum est.'

[5] ὕδωρ . . . καὶ ὕλη, ἐξ ἧς ἐπάγη ἡ γῆ (Damaskios).
ὕδωρ . . . ἀπὸ δὲ τοῦ ὕδατος ἰλύς (Athenagoras).
See Kern, *de theogoniis*, 28.

⁶ Gruppe, as part of his argument that Plato read a different Orphic theogony from the Rhapsodic, says that ' in the sixth generation cease the order of
your song' means ' do not go beyond the fifth '. With this I cannot agree.
Neither does A. E. Taylor, who is solely concerned with the understanding
of the *Philebos* passage. See his note *ad loc.* in *Plato* (1926), p. 433, n. 2.
As far as I understand Gruppe's complicated argument, it even leads him
into contradiction. In *C. und M.* 623, he enumerates his five generations as
Ouranos, Okeanos, Kronos, Zeus, the children of Zeus. Describing the
same theogony in *Suppl.* 703, he says that we must understand Night to have
preceded Ouranos and to count as a generation. This makes six. On the
question of Plato's use of the Rhapsodies I am not here making any pronouncement.

⁷ That Time should come into being after Earth, and indeed be born of
Earth and Water, is to say the least of it curious, and makes it certain that
this account was compiled by an untrustworthy recorder (Eisler, *Weltenmantel
und Himmelszelt*, p. 393, n. 1). This observation, even if it argues late date
of compilation, cannot of course in any way prejudge the question of the date
of origin of any single element, *e.g.* the figure of Chronos, in the theogony.

⁸ Eisler's sole mention of the question of date is in these words (*Welt.
u. Himm.* 424) : ' To-day, when scholars like Diels and Gomperz defend
Lobeck's and Kern's theory of the high antiquity of the Orphic cosmogonies
. . .' I shall quote the words of Gomperz and Kern. Gomperz, *Gr. Thinkers*
(1920), 1, p. 91 : ' Nor need the third version (*sc* of the Orphic theogony)
detain us long. It is expressly stated by its authorities to be opposed to the
current Orphic doctrine, and its distinctive features, which rest on the authority of Hieronymos and Hellanikos, witnesses of doubtful date and personality,
are by no means such as to warrant a respectable antiquity.' Kern, *de
theogoniis* 34 : ' Inter omnes viros doctos constat eam (*sc.* Hieronymi theogoniam) aetatis Alexandrinae signa prae se ferre.' One hardly knows how to
comment.

It is perhaps worth while forestalling a doubt in the mind of the reader by
stating here that in Damaskios the Rhapsodic theogony is described immediately before the Hieronymian. Were their positions reversed, it might be
suspected that D. had cut out the description of Chronos in the Rhapsodies
because it was the same as that in Hieronymos—although as a matter of fact
D. is not our only authority for Chronos in the Rhapsodies.

⁹ Anyone interested may find conjectures regarding the identity of both
in Eisler, *Welt. u. Himm.* 393, n. 1, Gruppe, *C. und M.* 656 f.

¹⁰ See Gruppe in *C. und M.*, and Eisler, *W. u. H.*, vol. 2. Similarly, I
did not think it worth while in the nature of this book to diverge into a discussion of Herakles, who in the Hieronymian version is equated with Chronos
(p. 79). Some interesting evidence has recently been collected by G. R. Levy,
The Oriental Origin of Herakles, Journ. Hell. Stud. 1934, pp. 40-53. She speaks
of the Orphic texts on pp. 44 f.

¹¹ Julius Langbehn, *Flügelgestalten in der ältesten griechischen Kunst*,
Munich, 1881, p. 40.

> Wenn man sich den Kopf zerbricht
> Übers orphische Gedicht,
> Kommt ein Satz, der Trost verspricht—
> ' Diese fliegen, jene nicht.'
>
> Es ist, als scheint' ein neues Licht
> Dem müden Leser ins Gesicht,
> Wenn so knapp ein Deutscher spricht—
> ' Diese fliegen, jene nicht.'
>
> Macht nicht viel das Sinnengewicht.
> Genügt der Ausdruck, wunderschlicht—
> Zeigt Gelehrten ihre Pflicht—
> ' Diese fliegen, jene nicht.'

[12] When I speak of the age of the Rhapsodies, it should be clear by now that I wish the statement to be extended only to the Rhapsodic version of the myth or myths under immediate discussion. I am not speaking of the Rhapsodic Theogony as a whole, because I think it most likely that ' the Rhapsodic Theogony as a whole ' is a phrase of no significance. There is no reason to suppose that a collection going by the name of ' sacred stories in twenty-four rhapsodies ' is the production of a single age, either in its form or in its content. On the date of Phanes himself, it must not be supposed that with the conjecture here tentatively thrown out the last word has been said.

[13] It would be bold indeed to deny the acquaintance of Pindar and Plato with the monstrous Chronos and Phanes after Eisler's further observations in *Orpheus* (Teubner, 1925), 72 ff. The resemblance of the πολυκέφαλον θήριον of *Rep*. 588c to the figure of Phanes is one of those striking facts which seem obvious so soon as scholarly acumen has pointed them out. I do not think it conflicts with the remarks in the text at this point. When all is said, the best commentary on the tragedian's description of time as a god is found in the following quotations, which I have taken from Professor Murray's *Five Stages of Greek Religion* (Oxford, 1925), p. 27 :—

> τὸ δ' εὐτυχεῖν τόδ' ἐν βροτοῖς θεός, Aesch. *Cho.*, 60.
> θεὸς γὰρ καὶ τὸ γιγνώσκειν φίλους, Eur. *Hel.*, 560.
> ἡ φρόνησις ἀγαθὴ θεὸς μέγας, Soph. Fr. 836. 2 (Nauck).

It is not hard to find other similar passages. See also Wilamowitz, *der Glaube der Hellenen*, 1. 18 f.

[14] M. P. Nilsson is strangely unsatisfactory in *Hist. Gr. Rel.* 1925, p. 216. Speaking of the Orphic cosmogony he says : ' The only original feature is that time is made the first principle '. The other elements he calls the common stuff of folk-tales, though he does not specify these folk-tales, either here or elsewhere in the book. He then goes on to express himself incompetent to judge the question whether or not time was taken over by the Orphics from Persian religion. It becomes difficult to see what sense we are here meant to give to the word original, since it clearly does not mean ' independently evolved by the Orphics '.

[15] Those who are interested in following up parallel instances in the mythology of different lands may find the following references useful as a beginning. Gomperz, *Gr. Th.* 1920, 1, pp. 93 ff., Gruppe, *C. und M.* p. 658, n. 54, Budge, *The Gods of the Egyptians* (London, 1904), 2, p. 95. The suggestion of the possible independence of the cosmic eggs of different nationalities was early and well expressed by G. Zoëga, whom Kern quotes, *de theogoniis*, 10 ff. Kern (*ib.* 11) suggests that it would be more useful to look at parallels within the mythology of Greece itself, but those which he cites are not very helpful. I would rather have a cosmogonic egg, even if it is Egyptian, than be reminded of the story of Leda and the swan, just because it is Greek (in spite of Harrison, *Proleg.*³ 648).

[16] Compare on this point Kern's interpretation of the passage in Damaskios, *de theogoniis*, 68.

[17] Besides the references in the text to Orphic and Pythagorean theories, the following may be compared. Anaximenes *ap.* Aet. *Plac.* 1. 3. 4 (RP 24), Diogenes of Apollonia *ap.* Simpl. in Ar. *Phys.* 152. 11 (RP 210), Herakleitos *ap.* Sext. Math. 7. 129 (RP 41). Diog. Laert. in his account of Pythagoras says (8. 30) τοὺς δὲ λόγους ψυχῆς ἀνέμους εἶναι, and in speaking of the Pythagoreans we are reminded of the reason alleged for their ban on eating beans, διὰ τὸ πνευματώδεις ὄντας μάλιστα μετέχειν τοῦ ψυχικοῦ (*id.* 8. 24). Interesting too is the manner of birth of the moon-dwellers in Lucian's *Vera historia* (1. 22). They are born lifeless, ' and they bring them to life by laying them out with their mouths open towards the winds '.

For impregnation by the winds we have Homer, *Il.* 16. 149 ff., Virgil, *Georg.* 3. 271 ff., Pliny, *N.H.* 8. 67, Plutarch, *Quaest. Conv.* 8. 1. 3. The subject is discussed by P. Saintyves, *Les Vierges Mères* (Paris, 1908). To return to Orphic literature itself at a later stage, cp. the address to the Zephyrs in Orph. Hymn 81 as αὖραι παντογενεῖς.

In the translation of the *de anima* passage in the text, the rendering ' space ' for τὸ ὅλον is Rohde's.

[18] Kern (*de theogoniis*, 21 f.), arguing against an Egyptian or oriental origin for E., adopts Diels' suggestion that the name is Greek, meaning ' early swallowed ' (ἠρί, κάπτω). Gruppe rejects this in *Suppl.* 740. In *C. und M.* 658, n. 53, he gives suggested etymologies from Oriental languages, and mentions also the ancient (Malalas and Suidas) interpretation as ' life-giver ' or ' life '. According to Eisler in *Welt. u. Himm.* 475, the name is Aramaic and means ' long-face '.

[19] It ought not to be forgotten that we owe the restoration of these names in the text of Malalas in the first place to the ever-fruitful genius of Richard Bentley. The emendation, which to-day leaps to the eye, was by no means so obvious in the seventeenth century. His remarks should be read, *Epist. ad Mill. ab initio.* (Migne, *Patrol. Gr.* vol. 97, 717 ff.)

[20] Anyone who has seen the remains of the Phrygian tongue as they appear on Anatolian tombstones of the Christian era, during the period of the pagan revival, will be familiar with this mixture. ' *Kakon* ' and ' *eitou* ' (for ἔστω) occur in the same sentence with words like *knoumanei, titetikmenos, addaket.* There is a Phrygian word in a line of Orpheus quoted by Clement of Alexandria (*O.F.* 219. Cp. Chr. Petersen, *der geheime Gottesdienst bei den Griechen*, Hamburg, 1848, n. 117). A passage of Plato (*Cratylus* 410a) illustrates both the acquaintance of the educated Greek with Phrygian, and the similarity of some Phrygian and Greek words.

[21] Keil-Premerstein, *Bericht über eine Reise in Lydien, Denkschr. der wiener Akad.* 1908, 54, no. 12, Wilh. Quandt, *de Baccho in Asia Minore culto*, Halle, 1913, p. 181, Kern, *O.F.* p. 103, and *Genethliakon für K. Robert*, Halle, 1910, p. 93. The last-named article is particularly to be recommended for its illustrations of the way in which archaeological research in Asia Minor is contributing to the elucidation of Orphic problems.

[22] An amusing parallel is to be found in the schoolboys' exercises published by E. Ziebarth, *Aus der antiken Schule*, Bonn, 1913 (*Kleine Texte*), p. 13. Lines of Homer are taken and their heroic words set down in parallel columns with the equivalents in vulgar Greek.

[23] Compare pp. 156, 161 and ch. v, n. 4 below.

[24] The Persian counterpart of Phanes, Zrvān, was bisexual, Eisler, *W. und H.* 414. For the Greek cult of Hermaphroditos and related figures (*e.g.* the masculine Aphrodite in Cyprus ; the cult of H. himself seems to have made its first appearance at Athens in the late fifth century), see Preller-Robert, *Gr. Myth.*⁴ (1894), 1. 2. 509 f. Bisexual beings introduced to point an argument, Plato, *Symp.* 81c (Aphrodite Pandemos), *ib.* 90b (the moon).

[25] Cp. *O.F.* 80, αἰδοῖον ἔχοντα ὀπίσω περὶ τὴν πυγήν. He was in fact, in so far as he was anthropomorphic, a creature just like those described by Aristophanes in Plato's *Symposium.*

[26] It is worth while quoting the words of the standard history of Greek literature about this man, who lived at the beginning of the third century A.D. : ' Alexander is the best expounder, because his only ambition was the scholarly one of completely understanding his author without any admixture of personal views, and without allowing any room for the influence of the mystical tendencies of his age ' (Schmidt-Stählin, *Gesch. Gr. Lit.*⁶ (1920), 2. 833).

[27] I feel justified in using the word original of an idea which was foreign to any beliefs of which the Orphics are likely to have had knowledge. It is nevertheless interesting to note, that according to the most recent anthropological investigation it was probably the oldest of all religious conceptions. It now seems that the worship of the most primitive peoples of all was, and is, directed neither to a vague *anima* inhabiting every stick and stone, nor to a totem, nor to anything else which the last century supposed it to be, but to a truly monotheistic deity explicitly possessed of creative power. See chapter 16 of Father W. Schmidt's interesting book, *The Origin and Growth of Religion* (Methuen, 1931), especially pp. 272 f.

[28] A similar idea will be found in Harrison, *Proleg.*[3] 649 f. The genesis of the passage in the text is that I had originally made a note ' Zeus *creator* an Orphic idea ? ' among a list of suggestions awaiting confirmation and amplification—or the reverse. Later I read the passage in Miss Harrison, and saw there what seemed the most probable lines along which to expand the original jotting.

[29] No doubt the swallowing episode was originally an old folk-tale, and perhaps this is an example of what Nilsson means (see n. 14 above) by saying that all the principles of the Orphic theogony except time are the common stuff of folk-tales. By paying more attention to the form of the myth than to the meaning which the Orphics extracted from it, one might miss the most striking and original part of the whole theogony.

[30] Diodoros himself mentions his sources for this part of his work. He used a compilation of older writings which included some of the *theologos* Epimenides.

[31] The tenses are not to be relied on, either in this version or the original. The present tense is used to describe the actions of the Cretans in their rites, but as it also occurs in the preceding narrative interspersed with perfect and imperfect, we cannot draw conclusions from it. Even after a present tense, Firmicus usually puts into secondary sequence any subjunctive which may be dependent on it.

[32] Verse translations of this important passage are available, by Gilbert Murray in Harrison, *Proleg.*[3] 479, and by A. B. Cook in *Zeus*, 1, 648. I have chosen to make translations throughout in which a close rendering of the Greek should be the foremost consideration. Undoubtedly it is possible to suffer thus a grave loss in the exalted strain of the original, and I hope that readers will remedy the defect by an acquaintance with the other translations. For further discussion of the fragment, see below, pp. 199 f.

[33] The form in Euripides is Ζανός. ' The cult of Zan can be most clearly traced to Crete,' Cook, *Zeus*, 2, 344, where see the evidence.

[34] I translate βούτης or βούτας, which Kern prints in *O.F.* p. 230, following Diels and Wilamowitz. The MSS. of Porphyrios have βροντάς, which Cook and Murray retain. There is other evidence for people calling themselves Herdsmen in the service of Dionysos (see below, p. 260), which gives support to the reading, but there is no need to base arguments on the possible use of the word here. I have accepted it chiefly through mistrust of the zeugma in βροντὰς τὰς δ' ὠμοφάγους δαῖτας τελέσας (which Murray in his version evades). It also allows the καὶ's and τε's of the sentence to run more naturally. Whichever way the sentence does run, I cannot follow Murray in taking the genitive Κουρήτων as dependent on βάκχος.

[35] The god of Crete as a bull. Cp. p. 115, and the remarkable variation on the epitaph which Pythagoras was said to have engraved on the tomb of Idaean Zeus when he visited the island (Porphyrios, *Vit. Pyth.* 17). In Porph. the first line of this epitaph runs ὧδε θανὼν κεῖται Ζάν, ὃν Δία κικλήσκουσιν, ' Here lies dead Zan, whom men call Zeus ', and in the Palatine Anthology (7. 746), ὧδε μέγας κεῖται Ζάν, ὃν Δία κικλήσκουσιν, ' Here lies great Zan,' etc. But in the margin of one MS. of *Anth. Pal.* is written the following variation, ὧδε μέγας κεῖται βοῦς, ὃν Δία κικλήσκουσιν, ' Here lies the great bull, whom men call Zeus'. A. B. Cook (*Zeus*, 2, 345) compares the famous lines of Aeschylus, βοῦς ἐπὶ γλώσσῃ μέγας βέβηκεν, which now appear to embody a Cretan mystic's formula. The epithet μέγας seems to have been a standing one; cp. Aristoph., *Birds*, 570, βροντάτω νῦν ὁ μέγας Ζάν, and the *Cretans* fragment.

[36] These passages are all fragmentary. As far as they go they give no hint that the name Zagreus was especially connected with the Orphic myth. That which is usually considered the oldest is ascribed to the *Alkmaionis*, an epic probably written in the sixth century (Wilamowitz, *Hom. Unters.* = *Philol. Unters. Bd.* 7, p. 73, n. 2, and p. 214). But the ascription rests on a single reference in one of the medieval lexicographical compilations. It is admittedly one of the earlier and better of these (the *Etym. Gudianum*), but was nevertheless not put together before the twelfth century, and the experiment of reading the line aloud has made me at least hope that it was not composed until after the classical age. The line is πότνια Γῆ Ζαγρεῦ τε θεῶν πανυπέρτατε πάντων. πανυπέρτατος itself is a Homeric word, but the whole jingle with which the line ends does not otherwise occur in extant epic.

[37] For authorities see Rohde's notes.

[38] For sacrifices of bulls at Athens cp. also A. B. Cook. *Zeus*, I, 715, n. 6.

[39] Initiate of Idaean Zeus called νεὸς Κούρης, Strabo 468 (Rohde, *Psyche*, ch. 9, n. 114). Zeus is addressed as μέγιστε Κοῦρε in the hymn found inscribed on stone at Palaikastro in Crete. (Roman Imperial date. Published *Ann. Brit. Sch. Ath.* 9, 1908-9, 339 ff. with pl. 20.)   On the Cretan Zeus in general, Nilsson's *Minoan-Mycenean Religion*, ch. 16, and Wilamowitz, *Der Glaube der Hellenen*, I, 132 ff., should be consulted.

[40] Kuretes and Korybantes identified since the sixth century. Cp. the ✱ *Phoronis*, fr. 3, Kinkel.   The first chorus of the *Bacchae* is full of names recalling the Asiatic cult of Dionysos, and lines 119-125 speak of the Kuretes and Korybantes as united in Cretan cult and bring both into close relation with the satyrs, who were and always remained the attendants of Dionysos alone.   Strabo says that to the Greeks the Korybantes are a species of the genus Kuretes, who are divided into two classes, the Cretan and the Phrygian : ' the latter are also called Korybantes ' (Strabo 10. 469).   Strabo also says (468) that the cult of Zeus in Crete was μετ' ὀργιασμοῦ.

In art, compare the relief in the theatre at Athens which shows the infant Dionysos with an armed figure on either side of him, Gruppe, *Gr. Myth. u. Rel.* 820, n. 5. (Best illustrated in *Zeus*, vol. I, pocket at end.) ' Dass ist aus der Zeussage übertragen ', says Gruppe.   The scene on Anatolian coins of Roman Imperial date, Quandt, *de Baccho in A.M. culto*, pp. 234, 165.   The type from Seleukeia in Cilicia might be taken to be Zeus (Gruppe, *ib.*), but on the coins from Magnesia in Ionia (fig. 11, p. 118), the identification is made certain by the presence of the Bacchic *cista*.   (Both types are illustrated in *Zeus*, I, 152 f., figs. 126-128.)

[41] For a detailed account of the meanings of *rhombos* see A. S. F. Gow, *IYΓΞ, POMBOΣ, RHOMBUS, TURBO*, in *Journ. Hell. Stud.* 54 (1934), pp. 5 ff.   He discusses our Orphic lines on p. 8, n. 19.

[42] What follows is dependent on the reports of the excavations in *Ath. Mitt.* 12 and 13, and in particular on O. Kern's important article in *Hermes*, 25 (1890), pp. 1 ff.   In the evidence for the playing child-god, we must not omit to note the inscription Διονύσω παραπαίζοντ[ι] found at Eleusis, on which see Kern, *Orpheus*, 1920, pp. 53 f. (Roman Imperial date.)

CHAPTER V

THE FUTURE LIFE AS SEEN BY ORPHEUS

' Eine orphische Seelenlehre soll erst einer nachweisen.'—Wilamowitz.
' We must ever maintain a real belief in the ancient and sacred stories,
those which proclaim that our soul is immortal, and has judges, and pays
full requital for its deeds, as soon as a man has left the body behind.'—
PLATO, *the seventh letter.*

IT is not every one who believes that this life is a vale of tears, and
death a welcome deliverance from it. With this statement we
may determine at once the genus of the Orphic, although his
species may give a little more trouble in the finding. He belonged
to those who did so believe. The history of Greek civilization
provides examples of both kinds of people. Those of whom
Homer sang belonged to the other. They were at the opposite
pole from the Orphic. They show a belief in gods who were like
a superior ruling class, and whose relations with men must be
purely external, coupling that belief with a lively interest in this
life and an almost complete indifference to anything that may
happen after it—except for the conviction that, whatever it may
be, the deprivation of the good things of this life cannot but be a
horrible calamity. It is obvious that the views which a society
holds on this matter of a life to come must be at least in part a
result of the sort of existence which it is granted them to lead in
the present. The beliefs which I have mentioned are the marks
of an aristocratic and materially wealthy class, whose material
circumstances have induced a predilection for good living and
a matter-of-fact outlook on life and its problems. This society
was based on serfdom, and it is natural to conjecture that the
views of the serfs on the same subject were very different from
those of their masters. Their local underworld deities were
probably with them all the time, and much closer to them than
any Olympian could be to anyone. We are reduced to conjecture
because a feature of the ruling character, of which and for which
Homer sang, is a complete lack of interest in the thoughts and
doings of the lower classes ; but we may put it in this way, that

when Achilles professed himself more ready to be a poor man's servant on earth than the supreme ruler among the dead, it is safe to assume that the statement was based on very little knowledge of what the existence of a poor man's servant was like.

We can see a reflection of a similar society in the poets of the rich and prosperous Ionian colonies which dotted the Asiatic coast and the Islands in the seventh century B.C. These poets came on the crest of a wave of commercial expansion and prosperity and belonged to the society which it produced, a society of luxury and indifference, whose motto was eat and drink, for to-morrow we die, and there is nothing for the dead. There is beauty and pathos in their poetry, and that is the kernel of it.

'What life is there, what pleasure, without golden Aphrodite? May I die straightway, when her charms no longer hold me. Stolen meetings, lovers' gifts and lovers' union—these are the only flowers worth plucking for men and women in their prime. . . . Like are we to the leaves that flowery springtime bears, when swiftly they wax strong beneath the rays of the sun. Like to them we enjoy for a span the flowers of youth, knowing neither good nor evil at the hands of heaven. But the black-robed Fates stand by, and one holds in her hand the goal of hard old age, the other that of death. Brief is the fruit of youth, no longer than the spread of the sunlight over the earth ; but when that spring-time of life is passed, then verily to die is better than life, for many are the ills that invade the heart. . . .

'To Tithonos Zeus gave the doom of everlasting old age, a doom more terrible even than grievous death itself. . . .

'Indulge thine own heart. . . .'

The same view of life is reflected in a very different event, the rise of rationalist philosophy in these same Ionian cities at the same time. The philosopher who empties the word *theos* of all its religious content, as the thinkers of the Milesian school tried to do, is a product of the same circumstances and outlook as the poet Mimnermos, with his eulogies of love and drink and his horror of old age.

In Homer the generally accepted notion is that death is the negation of all the attributes that make life worth living. The dead exist indeed, but they are strengthless, witless wraiths, uttering thin bodiless shrieks as they flit to and fro in the shadowy house of Hades. Truly a poor existence to the robust and warlike mind of the Achaean warrior. The same ideas seem to have dominated the minds of writers in the period of colonization, and it is not until the sixth century, so far as we can see, that a different spirit begins to come to the surface and make itself articulate.

The other was too firmly planted, and too congenial to the matter-of-fact temperament of the average Hellene, to be overcome, but henceforth it is not without a rival.   To use the terminology of a contemporary essayist, which makes up in terseness for what it lacks in elegance, we must henceforth be prepared to meet two types of religion, both the squeak-and-gibber and the harp-and-scream.*   The latter is represented by the mystery-religions, which promise a life of bliss in the next world to those who have been initiated.   One form of these, the mysteries of Eleusis, came to be recognized alongside the worship of the Olympians as one of the state cults at Athens.   It is this emergence of mystery-religions into the stream of history that is meant by those who refer to the great religious revival of the sixth century.   Henceforth the two currents flowed side by side, the choice of belief being a matter of individual temperament, until the final world-wide triumph of a single religion made the belief in rewards and punishments compulsory, as one might almost say, in the name of Christ.   Until then there was no popular feeling about the matter, to make a man avow any belief because it was the proper thing to do, and even that period of spiritual unrest, the Graeco-Roman age, when men flooded the Greek-speaking world with mystery-cults native and imported in the struggle to satisfy the yearnings of their souls, even that age saw a kind of revival of the old Ionian spirit in some of the epigrams of the Anthology and, more striking testimony still, the reflections of them which men carved upon their tombs.   ' Enjoy thy youth, dear heart of mine.   In due time other men will be born, and as for me, I shall be dead and changed to dark earth.'   ' I was not—I was born.   I was—now I am not.   That is the sum.   If any man say otherwise, he lies. I shall not be.'   This too I have seen carved on the tomb of an Asiatic Greek of the Roman Empire : ' I was not—I was born. I am not.   It is nought to me.   Traveller, fare you well.'

Needless to say, it did not need the promulgation of a complex system of dogma like the Orphic to bring into being another state of mind than this.   Among the ruling classes of the Mycenean or Ionian civilizations, the aspiration of mankind towards an im-mortality which should in some measure compensate for the imperfections of this life may have been pushed below the level of our perceptions.   Yet it is an aspiration which rises naturally and spontaneously to the surface, since in most men's hearts it is a native growth, not implanted, although it may be fostered, by any definite religious training.   The Attic orator Hypereides was

---

* Aldous Huxley, *Music at Night*, pp. 99 ff.

uttering words which would find an instinctive response in the hearts of his, or any, populace, when he said : ' But if there is a conscious life in the realm of Hades, and divine care, then it is reasonable to expect that those who died defending the honour of their country's gods should meet with the lovingkindness of the divine power after death '.*   When Socrates says near the beginning of the *Phaedo*, ' I am of good hope that there is something for the dead, and, as has been said from of old, something much better for the good than for the wicked ', he is, as long as he puts it in that general form, simply reflecting a popular hope.   Only, being a philosopher, he has not allowed himself to hold it until his own reason could persuade him of its truth.

We may glance here very briefly at some Greek ideas of a future life which seem more akin to the Orphic than to the views of the Homeric aristocracy, and some of which, we may be sure, the Orphic zealot adopted and turned to his own use in his own peculiar way.   It will then be easier to say what elements of belief were the contribution of the Orphic system, and our answers will have, to put it no higher, a greater semblance of probability.

The conception of Elysium appears once in the *Odyssey* (book 4, 561 ff.).   Menelaos there relates to Telemachos how the sea-god Proteus prophesied to him in the following words : ' But as for thee Menelaos, nursling of the gods, it is not ordained that thou shalt die in horse-rearing Argos, nor meet thy fate there ; but to the Elysian plain and to the farthest borders of the earth shall the immortals send thee, where dwells fair-haired Rhadamanthys, where life is easiest for men.   No snow is there, nor heavy storm, nor rain ever, but always Okeanos sends forth the clear-breathing breezes of the Zephyr.   Thither shall they send thee because thou hast Helen to wife and art in their eyes son-in-law of Zeus.'

This picture departs as little as possible from the usual Homeric notion of the after-life.   Bearing in mind that it represents something which is to be granted to Menelaos as a special privilege, because the gods have accepted him as a kinsman by marriage, we may, if we like, say that there is no inconsistency in it at all. The ordinary man died, and his soul, severed from the body, lived on as a kind of pale image of his bodily form, without blood or strength.   For such as Menelaos is reserved, not a different fate after death, but the privilege of escaping death altogether. This Proteus tells him plainly.   He is not to go to Hades, like the many mighty souls which the wrath of Achilles despatched, but

* Trans. L. R. Farnell, *Hero Cults*, Oxford, 1921, p. 392.

will be transported by the gods to a blessed spot on the confines of the earth.   Let us anticipate for a moment, and remark what a different meaning may be attached to very similar phrases according to the beliefs of the community which uses them.   Elysium remained the name for the abode of the blessed, and entry into it remained reserved for a privileged class.   More, those who considered themselves entitled to it continued to base their claim on the fact of kinship with the gods.   Yet what was kinship with the gods, and how was it attained ?   No longer, certainly, by contracting a marriage with a beautiful woman whose birth had been the result of the visit to earth of an amorous deity with human passions.   We may put it briefly thus, that if a Homeric hero could claim divine kinship, that was due to the humanity of the gods.   Later ages learned to base it on the divinity of man.

From the language of Aristophanes we may judge that in the fifth century it was usual to refer to the dead as ' the blessed,' a phrase which implies a different belief about them than that which Homer speaks of (cp. esp. Kock, *Com. Att. Fr.* (1880), I. p. 517).   L. R. Farnell in his *Hero Cults* remarks too that at the beginning of Plato's *Republic* the old man Kephalos ' speaks as if the ordinary person in full health despised the talk about posthumous retribution and the terrors of the lower world, but when he was approaching his end began to take them seriously '.   That there was talk of posthumous retribution who can doubt ?   The belief in it had never died out entirely.   The myths of the great sinners—Tityos, Sisyphos, Ixion—and their punishments had found their place in Homer and continued to be told.   In Homer it was implied that no such fate awaited the ordinary man, but (to take a single instance of a way in which a different notion may have crept in) what nurse, with stories like that ready to her hand, was going to resist telling a naughty child these examples of the fate which overtook the unrepentant ?   The robust would shake them off.   The more timid might be uneasily haunted, especially as old age brought nearer the shadow of death.   After all, ' it was reasonable to expect. . . .'   Rhadamanthys with his un-Greek name, the ancient king and lawgiver of Crete who was believed to be the son of Zeus by Europa, seems to appear in the passage of the *Odyssey* which I have quoted simply as an example of one who had already won the blessedness which Menelaos was to share ; but in the fifth century myths were certainly current which made him continue for the dead the offices of lawgiver and judge, which had made him famous during his ordinary life.   Enthroned with his brother Minos, he dealt torture or blessedness, and every soul, said the myths, must be prepared to appear before him. The definite phrases of Kephalos, about 'myths of those in Hades, that the man who has done wrong here must pay the penalty there', sound as if the thought of Rhadamanthys made the approach of death uncomfortable for some at least. Perhaps the belief in a judgment seat was an 'Orphic myth'. If that is so, I have no doubt that it was not the invention of the Orphics, but something taken over by them from vague popular belief. Another possible explanation of the words of Kephalos is that an acquaintance with the Orphic myths was not confined to the circle of initiates, and that a man who in his prime would have scorned to take Orpheus as his lord was yet assailed by doubts as he neared his end. Kephalos himself certainly does not speak as an Orphic.

We are coming near to a conception of what Orphism meant and what it contributed. Without Orphism there was no dogma in these matters. The Orphic had his *dogmata* set and hardened in the mould of a mass of religious poetry. Certain men had taken a definite path through the shifting sands of popular belief, and where they went they laid down a causeway so that others of like mind could follow in the same track. For these others their belief was fixed and bestowed by authority. They could not doubt as the rest of the world did, now scoffing, now hoping, now fearing. The Orphic writers had taken what suited them from popular mythology. They had added something to its matter and much to its significance. It was a crystallization around a new centre, and the centre was the story of the dismemberment of Dionysos, the revenge of Zeus on the Titans, and the birth of mankind from their ashes.

Even the briefest summary of classical Greek beliefs in the life after death, exclusive of Orphism itself, can scarcely stand without a mention of the mysteries of Eleusis. I must, however, ✱ ask pardon of the learned for doing little more than mention them. There exist many good accounts of the evidence for them and the conclusions which may be drawn about the nature of the festival, and to add to their number would in the first place be otiose for one who has nothing new to add, and in the second place would not, in my opinion, be relevant. The legends of Kore and the mythology of Eleusis were not foreign to the Orphic writings. It is even likely, since the representatives of Orpheus taught at Athens and it was open to every Athenian (indeed to every Greek) to become an Eleusinian initiate, that many a man was initiated at Eleusis who was also an Orphic. There was no question of intolerance, and where that is absent the cautious man may be well advised to take out an extra insurance policy. (The effect of participation in the Eleusinian mysteries was very much like being insured against accident in the next world.) Consequently contamination was at least possible, and it will be necessary to make further mention of Eleusis at different points in the exposition of Orphic belief. Yet the religion of Eleusis remained fundamentally different from that of Orpheus. First and foremost, Orphism, as we shall see in the next chapter, was a way of life, imposing an ascetic regime which had to be carried into one's daily actions. No such claim was made for Eleusis. It had no moral content and imposed no rules of life. Its root idea is more akin to magic. Perform the correct ritual, see the correct sights and say the correct words, and you are assured of the protection of the great goddesses, carrying with it the certainty of a blessed life after death. This assurance seems to have held good whatever might be the conduct of the initiate in private life. Sophocles wrote : ' Thrice happy are those mortals who see these rites before they depart for Hades ; for to them alone is it granted to have true life on the other side. To the rest all there is evil ' ; to which Diogenes the Cynic is said to have retorted, ' What ! Is Pataikion the thief to have a better lot after death than Epaminondas, just because he has been initiated ? ' (Plutarch, *de aud. poet.* 21 F). The comic counterpart to the lines of Sophocles is in Aristophanes' *Peace.* In consternation Hermes tells the hero, Trygaios, that he is planning a deed which Zeus himself has declared punishable by death. ' Must I really die ? ' says Trygaios (l. 372). ' Assuredly.' ' Well, do lend me three drachmas to buy a pig. I must get initiated before I die.' (The pig was the sacrifice made to Demeter.) Again, the Orphic doctrine of the degradation of the body and all that pertains to it seems to have found no place at Eleusis. One can scarcely speak of doctrine at all in connexion with Eleusis. The Eleusinian hierophant was, literally, a ' showman ', not a teacher. The effect of Eleusis was to convince the initiate of the presence of the deities and of his part in salvation by the immediate evidence of his own senses. The goddess and her child appeared before his eyes, ἐπιφανεῖς. He was awed by sounds and dazzled by sights. Lights and colour and music combined in their effect upon him in the climax of the ἐπόπτεια. How could he doubt that he was a changed and a saved man ? He had looked upon the godhead. The Orphic teacher worked differently. He had his initiations certainly. Indeed so important were they that Orpheus was to an Athenian ' the revealer of *teletai* ', above all others. This is a point where we feel acutely the insufficiency of the surviving evidence, and we must walk warily. Yet we can stand firm on this, that the most striking and distinctive feature of his religion was to the ancient mind ' a mass of books '. The central myth of Dionysos and the Titans held material as appropriate for presentation in the form of a sacred drama as were the myths of Demeter and Kore which in some form or other were set before the initiate at Eleusis. But more was necessary if the Orphic was to become a *bakchos* in the fullest and highest sense. He must be taught the deep significance that lay behind it all, and that significance was revealed in the sacred writings.

At a first mention of the Eleusinian mysteries, it seemed prudent to utter a warning against the possible confusion of them with Orphism. But this has led us momentarily astray from our present purpose, which is simply to enumerate some of the current Greek ideas of immortality in order to avoid unjustifiable confusion with them when we go on to speak of the Orphic beliefs themselves. In this enumeration the Eleusinian mysteries must have an important place, and we must make a brief attempt to say what kind of immortality they stood for.[1] As I see it, it is a development, not a complete contradiction, of the beliefs depicted in Homer. There the soul has nothing which may properly be called life, since it is deprived of all the goodness of life, and of strength and wit. Nevertheless it continues to exist, and the souls which Odysseus sees coming up out of Hades are eager for, and capable of absorbing, the physical nourishment of the blood which has been poured into the trench. Having drunk of the blood, they are able to recognize him. Similar notions, with slightly more definite content perhaps, must have been behind the funeral practices and tending of graves which went on in classical times. This is hardly surprising, considering the extent of Homer's influence. Yet even to Homer the idea of an Elysium for a certain few privileged spirits was not unknown. Now there was going on all over Greece, obscured for a time by the enormous influence of Homer but reappearing as early as the sixth century, the worship of the chthonian gods. In some way (though it may well be that we have not yet got at the right reason for it), men linked with this worship their own hopes for a fuller life after death. The worship at Eleusis was originally of this sort. Demeter, the Earth Mother, and her daughter Persephone, the consort of the King of the Dead, were the chief deities worshipped. It was adopted by the highly civilised city of Athens, which was saturated with the Homeric tradition, and a fusion of ideas took place. The Homeric, barely-conscious, shadowy existence remained the lot of the ordinary man after death. Now, however, the ordinary man was the uninitiated, and the privilege of Elysium, now transferred from the surface of the earth and made into a part of the realm of the dead, was reserved, not for the sons or sons-in-law of Zeus, but for the initiated. The picture of Elysium itself, and of the occupations there pursued by the blessed, was enlarged and made more varied and concrete by the imagination of poets. It is likely that in depicting the kind of paradise which was to be their immediate goal, the Orphics had much in common with the notions held by the rest of the Athenians, though they gave more definition to the unhappy state of the impure. The fundamental difference lies in their theories of the nature of mankind and, dependent on these, of the means whereby salvation was to be secured.

The eschatology of the Orphic must be closely linked both with the Orphic dogmas which have been expounded in the last chapter and the Orphic practices which are to be spoken of in the next. The beginnings of salvation lie within every one of us, since they are identical with the germ of divinity which it is our nature as human beings to possess. Yet it does not follow that everyone is assured of a blessed future simply by reason of his origin. By a life of *adikia*, of sinfulness, the divine element may be stifled and the ' Titanic nature ' in us brought to the surface (Plato, *Laws*, 701c. Plutarch calls it ' the unreasonable and disorderly and violent part of us ', *esu carn.* 996c). The state of those who have let this happen is far worse than if they had merely been ' finished and finite clods, untroubled by a spark '. To mis-use the divine is to use it to our own damnation. Hence the believer will try to lead the Orphic life, to which we shall come later, and which aims at the exaltation and purification of our Dionysiac nature in order that we may in the end shake off the last trammels of our earthly selves and become actually, what we are now potentially, gods instead of mortals.

The Orphic was an ascetic, that is to say, he believed that the source of evil lay in the body with its appetites and passions, which must therefore be subdued if we are to rise to the heights which it is in us to attain. This is precept, but like all Orphic precept it is based on dogma. The belief behind it is that this present life is for the soul a punishment for previous sin, and the punishment consists precisely in this, that it is fettered to a body. This is for it a calamity, and is compared sometimes to being shut up in a prison, sometimes to being buried in a tomb. This doctrine is mentioned by Plato, and we may be eternally grateful that for once the whim took him to ascribe it, not vaguely and mysteriously to ' the wise ', or ' the old and sacred writings ', but expressly to the Orphics. In the *Cratylus* (400c) he is discussing the etymology of the word *soma*, body, and its possible connexion with *sema*, which meant (*a*) a sign or token, (*b*) a tomb (which was built 'to mark the spot'). He says: 'Now some say that the body (*soma*) is the *sema* of the soul, as if it were buried in its pre- ✱ sent existence; and also because through it the soul makes signs of whatever it has to express, for in this way also they claim that it is rightly named from *sema*. In my opinion it is the followers of Orpheus who are chiefly responsible for giving it the name, holding that the soul is undergoing punishment for some reason or other, and has this husk around it, like a prison, to keep it from running away.' This central doctrine of the Orphics had a tremendous, and one is sometimes tempted to say unfortunate fascination for Plato. Some of the finest parts of the dialogues give the impression not that he despised the body, but that, although the soul was the higher principle and must maintain the lead, soul and body could work in harmony together. Yet this unnatural dualism of the Orphics, which divides the two so sharply and makes the body nothing but an encumbrance, the source of evil, from which the soul must long to be purified, permeates the *Phaedo*, together with a great deal of language borrowed from 'the initiators'. I would go so far as to name the Orphics as at least one of the influences which went to form the most characteristic part of Platonism, the sharp separation of the lower world of *sensa* from the heavenly world of the Ideas. It is often puzzling to see how this doctrine, which in itself leads naturally to a lack of interest in the sensible world and a concentration on the higher, seems to be at war with Plato's inborn longing to interfere effectively in practical matters. I believe in fact that it was the teaching of the *hieroi logoi* that set the feet of the philosopher on the upward path from the Cave into the Sunlight, whereas it was the voice of Plato's own heart that sternly bade him return and help his fellow-prisoners still fettered in the darkness of the Cave. The same Orphic idea appealed to Aristotle in his Platonic youth. In the *Protreptikos* he ascribed it to 'the relaters of *teletai*', and illustrated it further by the vivid simile of the torture inflicted by the Etruscan pirates, who bound their victims face to face with corpses (Arist. fr. 60, Rose). This simile has found its way, no doubt by conscious allusion, into our own literature, though it was for a different purpose that Milton used it when in the Divorce Tracts he spoke of an unhappy marriage as being 'as if a living soul were bound to a dead body'.

To return, life on earth was itself a punishment. It was also a period of trial. Together with the punishments suffered by the impure in Hades, it formed the circle of trial and purgatory by which the soul might finally be purified. According to a man's actions on earth, so was his fate in Hades one of punishment or happiness. To illustrate this I choose first of all a passage which is perhaps not a very detailed or circumstantial account of judgment and punishment after death, but which, besides making it quite clear that there were such things, combines again the inestimable advantages of being as early as Plato and fathering the doctrine expressly on the writings of Orpheus and Musaios. It brings to our notice another point too. The language which I have so far used about Orphism in this chapter has tended to represent it as a religion of a uniformly high spiritual tone. Clearly, however, a religion which teaches that there are rites and gods capable of delivering us from punishment after death must make a special appeal to the wicked. They could not have embraced the whole of Orphism, certainly, since it taught besides the performance of purificatory rites the lifelong subjugation of the body, based on the belief that it was nothing but the gloomy prison of the soul. Yet it taught of ritual purity and of 'Gods of Deliverance' (λύσιοι θεοί) too, and to the more carnally minded the short cut to salvation seemed open. Christianity, which shares both characteristics with Orphism, has suffered similar abuses. The sale of indulgences will at once occur to the mind of anyone who reads the passage here quoted.

The passage is *Republic*, 363 ff. Adeimantos is speaking of the crude ways in which right and wrong are popularly regarded, and the unworthy motives from which they are pursued. He has just quoted the temptingly material rewards which Homer and Hesiod (very much in the manner of some of the Psalms) assign to the righteous, and continues : ' But Musaios and his son [2] grant to the just more exciting blessings from heaven than these. Having brought them, in their writings, to the house of Hades, they make them recline at a drinking-party of the righteous which they have furnished, and describe them as passing all their time drinking, with garlands on their heads, since in their opinion the fairest reward of virtue is everlasting drunkenness. There are others who hold out even more extensive rewards than these as bestowed by the gods ; for they say that the just man and the keeper of his oath leaves children's children and a race to follow him. This is the sort of way in which they hold up justice for praise. But the unrighteous and unjust they plunge into a kind of mud in Hades and make them carry water in a sieve . . . (364*b*). And there are charlatans and soothsayers who frequent the doors of the rich and persuade them that they have at their command a grace vouchsafed from the gods, which works by means of sacrifices and incantations, if a man himself or one of his ancestors has committed any sin, to mend the matter in an atmosphere of pleasure

and feasting ; and if a man wish to do some enemy a hurt, for a
trifling fee he can harm him, be the man just or wicked, by means
of charms and binding spells, for it is their claim that they can
persuade the gods to do their will. For all these claims they
bring forward the poets as witnesses.' There follow quotations
from Hesiod and Homer, and then : ' And they produce a mass
of books of Musaios and Orpheus, sons, so they say, of the Moon
and the Muses, according to whose recipes they make their
sacrifices. In this way they persuade not only individuals but ✱
cities that there are means of redemption and purification from
sin through sacrifices and pleasant amusements, valid both for the
living and for those who are already dead. They call them *teletai*,
these ceremonies which free us from the troubles of the other
world, and if we do not perform their sacrifices an awful fate
awaits us.'

Here we see Orphism at its worst, and are reminded that
Orpheus was the teacher not only of a real religion but also of
magic and spells. The lazy, cowardly satyr of Euripides' *Cyclops*
wanted to recite a charm of Orpheus in order to make the brand
leap of its own accord into the Cyclops' eye, and the sale of spells
of Orpheus was shocking the Christians some 800 years later
(above p. 19). The use of ' binding spells ' (κατάδεσμοι) is a
primitive and purely magical practice of which archaeology has
brought many examples to light both in Greece and Italy. The
usual method was to write the name of the man whom it was
wished to harm on a tablet, together with an appropriate formula,
and transfix the tablet with a nail. Many of those which were
inscribed on lead have been preserved and discovered.[3] The
Orphic Bible, like our own, was not a unity but a collection of
books, which evidently varied greatly in their spiritual content.
Suidas mentions one called *Teletai* and another called *Sacrificial
ceremony* (Θυηπολικόν). Whether identical with the extant corpus
of hymns or not, this book must have been a similar collection.
The hymns in our corpus are intended to be sung at sacrifice, and
at the head of each is indicated the appropriate offering.

The jibe about the privilege of the righteous in Hades being
eternal drunkenness is quoted by Plutarch (*comp. Cimon. et
Lucull.* 1, p. 521), who says that Plato directs it at the Orphics
(τοὺς περὶ τὸν Ὀρφέα) simply. A band of people who adopted the
religion of Dionysos, even if they reformed it, could hardly hope to
escape this. Dionysos was the god of wine, and in the Thracian
cult, before the influence of the gentle Orpheus touched it,
drunkenness was certainly one of the means used to attain that
feeling of ecstacy which was interpreted as possession by and

union with the god. It was the idea of union with the god, capable
as it was of a high degree of spiritualization, which appealed
to the Orphic reformer, and which he put in the forefront of his
doctrine. But to suppose that he encouraged drunkenness in the
pursuit of it is inconsistent with what we know of the Orphic
writings. There would nevertheless be those who continued to
take the coarser interpretation. Once more a tempting parallel
offers itself. The drinking of wine is an essential part of the
Christian sacrament of communion, and Paul had need to repri-
mand his Corinthian congregations for turning the holy service
into a drunken orgy. No doubt there were pagan philosophers in
Corinth who made remarks about the Christians similar to those
of Plato about the Orphics.

The unrighteous, says Adeimantos, still with Orphic ideas in
his mind, they plunge into a kind of sticky mud (εἰς πηλόν τινα)
in Hades. This we know to have been a particularly Orphic form
of punishment. In the *Phaedo* (69c), Socrates says : ' It looks as
if those also who established rites of initiation for us were no fools,
but that there is a hidden meaning to their teaching when it says
that whoever arrives uninitiated (ἀμύητος καὶ ἀτέλεστος) in Hades
will lie in mud, but the purified and initiated (κεκαθαρμένος τε
καὶ τετελεσμένος) when he arrives there will dwell with gods '
(pp. 70 f. above). On this passage of Plato the Neoplatonic commentator Olympiodoros supplies the information (*O.F.* 235) :
' He is adapting the Orphic saying, that whoever of us is uninitiated shall lie in Hades as if in mud '. There would be no reason
in any case to doubt the attribution by Olympiodoros to the
Orphics, and a comparison with the passage in the Republic
makes it certain. It is interesting to notice that in quoting the
opinions of the Orphics Adeimantos makes their punishments
apply not primarily to the uninitiated as such (which would not
have suited his argument), but to the morally unrighteous.
ἀνόσιος can be a technical term meaning ' uninitiate,' as ὅσιος
meant ' initiate ' (*e.g.* in the *Cretans* fr., p. 111 above), but its
ordinary meaning was ' unrighteous', and the conjunction of it
here with ἄδικος, ' unjust ', as well as the requirements of the
argument, show that it is in its ordinary sense that it is being
used by Adeimantos. This puts beyond doubt what is often
found difficult to prove, that Orphic teaching had a definitely
ethical side. In the *Frogs* of Aristophanes the travellers to the
infernal regions are told that they will come to ' a mass of mud
and ever-flowing filth,' where lie all the offenders against traditional
Greek morality—those who have wronged a stranger, robbed a
child, struck mother or father, or committed perjury. There is

no mention of their having neglected to take the precaution of initiation. Aristophanes of course is not the ideal man to have in our witness-box, since he is laughing at us all the time, and has no thought of compelling his comic muse to take all her material from the same set of beliefs. (At the end of his list of sinners he adds the light-hearted afterthought : ' Or anyone who has made a copy of a speech from one of the tragedies of Morsimos '— Morsimos being an uninspired and boring writer.) Still, he took the mud from the Orphic Hades, and it does so happen that the sort of people whom he consigns to it are the sort which one would expect to find there from the words of Adeimantos. Even the Eleusinia (and indeed all state ceremonies at Athens) were barred to murderers, not from any moral consideration, but simply because an ineradicable ritual impurity was supposed to cling to them. Yet there is a moral side to murder, for those who like to see it. Also, the inappropriateness of granting a better future to thieves, simply because they had been initiated, must have struck others besides Diogenes. It was not a long or unnatural step to connect initiation with moral righteousness, making the one dependent on the other, and the Orphics took it. (On this point, cp. pp. 200 f. below.)

The same people, says Plato, compel the unrighteous to carry water in a sieve. He refers to this punishment again in the *Gorgias*, in a context which we now know to be Orphic. Kallikles, the upholder against Socrates of the morality of immorality, has been arguing that the best life is enjoyed by the man who lets his desires and passions grow as ravening and insatiable as they can, and takes care that he has always present the means of gratifying them. The life of a man who has no unsatisfied desires is like the existence of a corpse. Socrates replies that Kallikles' own conception of happiness is like the life of the dead, at least according to some accounts which he has heard. ' For I have heard myself (493*a*) some wise man say that in this life we are dead, and that our body is a tomb, and the part of our soul in which the desires are seated is of such a nature as to be easily seduced and turned upside down. This idea was seized upon by some ingenious mythmaker—from Sicily or Italy perhaps—who made a play on the word and because it was both persuadable (πιθανόν) and persuasive called it a jar (πίθος). The foolish he called uninitiated, which also means unsealed, and that part of the foolish man's soul where the desires are seated, the uncontrolled and unretentive part of him, was, he said, like a leaky jar, the point of the comparison being the impossibility of being filled or satisfied. This allegorizer, Kallikles, demonstrates just the opposite from you,

namely that of those in Hades (which he interpreted as meaning
" the unseen ") the most unhappy are these uninitiated, and, said
he, it is their fate to carry water to the leaky jar in a no less leaky
sieve. By the sieve he meant (so my informant told me) to signify
the soul, and he compared the soul of the foolish to a sieve because
it·was so to speak leaky, since it could not hold anything owing
to its lack of faith and forgetfulness. Now I admit that this all
sounds rather absurd, but it brings out the point that I want to
make clear to you, in order if I can to make you change your mind,
and instead of the insatiate and intemperate life choose the life
of moderation and satisfaction with what one has.' [4]

We do not owe our knowledge of this form of punishment to
Plato alone. There is a most interesting illustration of it in the
description by Pausanias of a famous fifth-century painting at
Delphi. This was the scene, or rather series of scenes, painted by
Polygnotos on the walls of the hall of the Knidians. It represented the descent of Odysseus to Hades, and gave a full picture
of the lower world and the characters with which popular and
literary imagination had peopled it. The painting has of course
perished, but the account of Pausanias is exceedingly painstaking
and detailed. The relevant passages are these (Paus. 10. 31. 9,
11) : ' The women above Penthesilea are engaged in carrying
water in broken sherds, and one of them is depicted as beautiful,
the other as advanced in years. There is no separate inscription
over each of the women, but a common inscription over both which
says that they are of those who have not been initiated. . . .
There is also a jar in the picture, and an old man, another who is
still a boy, and women, a young one on the rock, and beside the
old man one of like age to him. All but the old woman are in the
act of carrying water, but she, you may guess, has broken her
pitcher. As much of the water as is left in the broken part, she
is emptying into the jar. We inferred that these people also
were of those who had had no thought for the performances at
Eleusis ; for the Hellenes of those old days held Eleusinian initiation to be as much above all other devout practices as gods are
above heroes.'

Pausanias took the inscription ' Uninitiated ' to refer to
Eleusinian initiation, and doubtless he was right. The punish-
✱ ment of endless water-carrying in leaky vessels (fastened at some
uncertain but probably post-classical date on the Danaids) was an
old and popular superstition, and though adopted by the Orphics
was obviously not confined to them [5] (cp. fig. 15, and Appendix,
p. 190 below). They added it to the torment of burial in filth, which
was more particularly their own and quite possibly an Orphic

invention. Notice, however (to return to a point already made), that whenever the punishment of water-carrying is mentioned in an *Orphic* connexion, we find that allegory is being introduced and the idea of initiation being coupled with that of moral goodness. It was not Socrates himself, but the 'ingenious myth-maker— some Sicilian or Italian perhaps', who taught the equation: 'uninitiated = foolish, lustful and intemperate'.

After what we have seen in the last chapter, we are not likely to be shy of crediting the Orphics with an allegorical habit of mind. When Socrates expresses the probability that the alle-

FIG. 15.—UNDERWORLD SCENE. SOULS EMPTYING PITCHERS INTO A LARGE, HALF-BURIED JAR. SISYPHOS.

gorical interpretation of the myth of the water-carriers in Hades was due to some Sicilian or Italian writer he is no doubt sincere (those places were centres of Orphism and a source of Orphic writings, p. 217 below). The torment of being buried in filth must have had an allegorical meaning for the Orphic too. No classical writer offers to explain it, but the interpretation of Plotinus (1. 6. 6, Rohde, *Psyche*, Eng. tr. ch. 7, n. 15) is reasonable and likely. The good state was for the Orphic represented by *purity*. This could not be attained without initiation coupled with the leading of an Orphic life, which as we have seen included moral goodness. These were the means, the end was to become pure or clean (*katharos*, cp. the language in the *Phaedo*, above p. 160). The uninitiated and immoral were thus unclean. They had not been purified and were therefore fittingly consigned to the filth to which they belonged.

Orphism was a religion with a belief in immortality and in posthumous rewards and punishments. So far so good. But it had a more individual doctrine than that. Hades, with its prospect of torment or feasting, was not the end. There was also the doctrine of the circle of birth, or cycle of births, and the possibility of ultimate escape from reincarnation to the state of perfected divinity. Plato makes use of the circle of birth at the beginning of the arguments for immortality in the *Phaedo*, and we may start from the statement of it there. Some, I hope, who read this book will be of the same sceptical turn of mind as myself, and will ask at first what reason there is for calling this passage of Plato Orphic. That should become clear as we proceed.

Phaedo, 70c (Socrates speaks) : ' Let us put the question in this way : when men have died, are their souls existing in Hades or are they not ? There is an ancient story ' (the familiar vagueness again) ' which recurs to our memory, that they go from here and exist there, and that they come back again here and are born from the dead.' The ' sacred story ' is now tested by arguments of a more properly philosophical kind, and decided to be satisfactory. Closely linked with this belief in Plato's dialogues is the theory that what men call learning in this life is nothing more than a process of recollection, since the soul in its age-long path through different earthly existences, and in the other world as well (where it has actually caught a glimpse of the true reality which is immaterial, as he says in the *Phaedrus*), has seen and learned everything. Reincarnation in a mortal body, with its imperfections and its passions, has dulled its sensibilities and made it forget much of what it knows, but it needs simply to be reminded, not to learn anything that it has never known before. This belief is obviously dependent on the other, as Kebes immediately reminds Socrates in the *Phaedo*, and the two are stated together in the *Meno*, where also the theory of recollection is thoroughly tested. Let us see how they are introduced.

Meno, 80e : Socrates. ' I know what you mean, Meno. Don't you see that you are introducing a contentious argument, that a man cannot seek for knowledge either of that which he knows or that which he does not know ? He would not seek that which he knows, for he knows it, and knowing it has no need of the search—nor that which he does not know, for then he does not even know what he is to look for.'

Meno. ' Well, don't you think that argument is well put, Socrates ? '

S.   ' I do not.'

M.   ' Can you tell me where your objection lies ? '

S.   ' I can. I have heard something from men and women who were wise in sacred lore.'

M.   ' What was their account ? '

S.   ' A true one, I think, and a fine.'

M.   ' What was it, and who are they who tell it ? '

S.   ' Those who tell it are priestly men and women of the kind who make it their business to be able to give an account of (or reasons for) what they take in hand to do.' (In passing, could one have a better description of what we have seen to be the most distinctive characteristic of the Orphics ?) ' Pindar tells it too, and many another of the poets who are divinely inspired. As for what they say, it is this. See whether you think they are speaking the truth. They say that the soul of man is immortal, and that at one time it comes to its end (which they like the rest of men call dying), and at another is reborn, but is never finally exterminated. For these reasons it is necessary to live a life as sinless as possible. For those " from whom Persephone receives requital for ancient doom, in the ninth year she gives back their souls again to the sun above. From them grow glorious kings, and men swift in strength and greatest in wisdom, and hereafter they are called spotless heroes by men." * The soul then, being immortal and often reborn, and having seen all things, both things here and those in Hades, has learned everything that there is.'

The ' ancient doom ' (or ' primal misfortune '), by reason of which we must give satisfaction to the Queen of the Underworld if we are going to raise our estate, can be nothing but the original sin which, owing to our origin from the Titans, is a part of our nature as mortal men. To say that we make requital for a woe or misfortune (ποινὰν πένθεος), rather than for a misdeed, is a curious phrase, but expresses well the Orphic idea that the need for punishment and purification is a consequence of the fact of our origin, and not ultimately the fault of the individual. It is this phrase which puts finally beyond doubt the attribution of the beliefs which we are discussing to the Orphic system. They are attributed expressly to it by Neoplatonic commentators, but since these are known to be almost as bad as modern scholars at affixing the Orphic label to any floating mystery-doctrine which cannot otherwise be pinned down, it is as well to allay suspicion by relying at first on a more ancient source.

* The quotation is from Pindar.

Proklos in his commentary on the *Timaeus* (ed. Diehl, vol. 3, p. 296, *O.F.* 229) says : ' The one way of salvation offered by the Creator to the soul (*sc.* in the *Timaeus*) is this which frees it from the circle of birth and from all its wandering and from fruitless living', and on the next page speaks of the soul being brought ' to the life of blessedness from its wanderings in the region of becoming, that life which is prayed for by those who with Orpheus as their patron are initiated to Dionysos and Kore, " Release from the circle and rest from evil " '.

Compare Simplicius on Aristotle, *de caelo* (ed. Heibig, p. 377, *O.F.* 230) : ' And that by the creating god who assigns to all things their due lot it is bound in the wheel of fate and birth, which it is impossible to be rid of according to Orpheus except by propitiating those gods " on whom Zeus has laid it as a charge to give release from the circle and relief from evil " '.

These passages have given us the doctrine in general terms. If we press for further detail, we shall probably not find our authorities perfectly consistent. It would be surprising if we did, considering the nature of the writers who must serve as our sources. The Orphic books to which I am attributing something like a systematic exposition of these matters are lost to us, save for one or two sorry fragments whose authenticity is dubious, since they are handed down only in the works of religious philosophers of the Christian era. For any account of the doctrine in classical times, we are dependent on authors of strongly marked individuality, whose philosophy, though it might take many of its elements from previous belief and thought, was yet, considered as a whole, their own creation. Most of our information comes from Plato and Empedokles. Of the originality of Plato's mind it would be impossible and unnecessary to speak here ; and Empedokles, although on the religious side saturated with Orphic and Pythagorean notions, was yet the originator of a natural philosophy designed to escape the dilemma into which Greek thought had recently been thrown by the rigidly abstract reasoning of Parmenides. On both these men the potential greatness of the Orphic conceptions made an ineradicable impression. I say potential advisedly, since to both men these conceptions only appeared in their true greatness when they had been caught up into, and made a part of, their own philosophical schemes. This is a necessary introduction, and must not be forgotten when we are trying to extract the Orphic lore from their writings. It is a natural question, how far these doctrines which we find in the philosophers were a matter of general belief. If we had to depend solely on such highly literary sources it would be almost impossible to tell, but fortunately it is given us to see the same beliefs also from an entirely different angle. This must wait until the end of the chapter. I turn to Plato.

The doctrine of reincarnation and the escape from it is given in greatest detail by Plato in the *Phaedrus*, and this is, in summary, the relevant matter. Soul is of one nature, whether it belong to men or gods, and exists at first in the highest region of heaven. But not all souls are perfect, and some cannot stay at that height. These fall, until they come into contact with what is solid (corporeal), and are then forced to take to themselves material bodies to inhabit. The whole, formed of soul and body, is what we call an animal, and the familiar distinction between mortal and immortal is really the distinction between these souls which have become attached to bodies and those which have remained in heaven uncontaminated by matter. The latter are the gods, and we can only imagine what they are like. Hence it is that we picture them as themselves 'animals', souls with bodies, only everlasting. At the first incarnation, it is 'law' that a soul enter the body of a man and not a beast; but they become different types of men, lower or higher, according to the time they have previously managed to keep themselves up in the heavenly regions, and the amount they have seen of the truths which are only to be seen there. Once fallen, the soul cannot return to its true home, the highest heaven, until after ten thousand years, divided into ten periods of a thousand years each, each period representing one incarnation and the period of punishment or blessedness which must follow it. According to Plato, there is one exception to this rule, the soul of the philosopher, who in his life has loved wisdom and beauty. He is set free at the end of the third period of a thousand years, if he has chosen the same life three times in succession.

In the ordinary course of events, the souls after their first life are judged, and some go to prisons under the earth, others to heaven, 'to a life suited to the life which they lived while they were in the form of man'. We have already seen something of the punishments and rewards which are their lot during this period.

When the thousand years are coming to an end, it is given them to choose a second life, and lots are cast to determine the order in which they shall choose. At this point it is possible for the soul of a man to become that of a beast, and the soul of a beast may become that of a man, with the reservation already mentioned that it must have been that of a man first of all. The reason for this is quite Platonic, and probably the reservation too.

The *Republic* adds more details concerning the procedure of choosing lives. It is made quite clear to the souls that the choice is their own. Even he who has to choose last will find it possible to choose a good life which may well content him, and even the first comer must use great discretion if he is not to be misled. The same dialogue mentions a separate class of people, those whose sins are considered incurable. These are not given the chance of reincarnation, but are condemned to stay for ever in the place of torment, in order to serve as an awful example to the others who have to pass through it. These, the only souls to be condemned to *eternal* punishment, are mentioned again in the *Gorgias*, where also the names of the judges are given, Minos, Rhadamanthys and Aiakos, sons of Zeus. This exceptional condemnation of a small number of arch-sinners is due to an unwillingness on the part of Orphic writers to deny the authority of Homer, who is actually mentioned by name in the *Gorgias* as the authority for allotting this fate to Tantalos, Sisyphos and Tityos.

The place where judgment takes place is described in the *Gorgias* as being ' in a meadow, where is the fork from which lead the two roads, the one to the Islands of the Blest, the other to Tartaros '. It is the same in the *Republic*, where the road which the just take after judgment is described as leading ' to the right and upwards through the heaven ', and the other road ' to the left and downwards '. In the *Phaedo*, the lands of the dead are made part of a description of what Socrates supposes the whole earth to be like, and the picture is given a scientific colouring. No one but Plato has made it into the wonderful imaginative whole which we find it to be, but he has absorbed into it the notions of the Orphics, as we are prepared to find when we see that it is preceded by a reference to the judgment of souls and their reincarnation. Here too is another hint that the road to Hades contains ' many branchings and forks ', an idea which we shall find turning up from a very different direction. The earth in this myth of Socrates is spherical, and Tartaros, the bottomless pit, is represented in his mythical geography by a chasm which pierces the sphere right through from side to side. This conception of it is Plato's, but the idea of Tartaros which he is choosing to explain in this way is Orphic, and surely Plato shows this by using Orphic language to describe it. It is a ' great gulf ' (μέγα χάσμα), and has ' neither bottom nor foundation '. Cp. the Orphic hexameters quoted by Proklos, *O.F.* 66 (translated above, p. 137).

μέγα χάσμα πελώριον ἔνθα καὶ ἔνθα.
οὐδέ τι πεῖραρ ὑπῆν, οὐ πυθμήν, οὐδέ τις ἕδρα.

(The words in Plato are πυθμένα . . . οὐδὲ βάσιν.) Plato remarks that Tartaros has been spoken of by Homer and many other poets. I think we can say what school of poets he had chiefly in mind in his own description of it.

The *Katharmoi* of Empedokles was a religious poem of which about 450 lines have survived. As its name implies, it dealt with the fall of the soul and the ways by which it may attain the purity which is necessary if it is to return to its primitive state of blessedness. The soul is a *daemon*, a divine being, who has sinned, and in consequence is condemned for ' thrice ten thousand seasons ' (*i.e.* perhaps ten thousand years, as in Plato. See Frutiger, *Les Mythes de Platon*, p. 255, n. 1) to wander far from the blessed. In the meantime it must go through all kinds of mortal shapes, including those not only of men and animals, but also of plants, which are also thought of as animate. Empedokles speaks much in the first person, bemoaning the hard fate which has sent him to wander in these unfamiliar regions, when his true home is above. ' From what honour, and from what a height of bliss come I, having left to wander here among mortals.' Again, ' I wept and wailed when I saw the unfamiliar country, where dwell Murder and Wrath and hosts of other misfortunes, and parching diseases and decay and floods '.[6] At other times he stresses the other side, the divinity that is his real self, as when he cries, ' I tell you I am a god immortal, no longer a mortal ',[7] and he finishes his account of the fall of the soul and its transformations with the words, ' Of them I also am now one, an exile from the gods and a wanderer, for I put my trust in the madness of strife '.

For the last incarnation before their return, souls are born into the highest types of men, of which Empedokles mentions prophets, priests, physicians and rulers : ' after that they spring forth as gods, highest in honour, with the other immortals sharing hearth and table, free from the woes of men, in which they have no part, untroubled by fatigue '. This sounds like the same belief as that expressed in the lines of Pindar which Socrates quoted in the *Meno*. There seems to be nothing to correspond to the ninth year of that quotation if it is to be taken literally. On the other hand, the number nine is certainly in point, since this last period begins with the end of the ninth incarnation, or cycle of a thousand years.

It will be convenient to mention here what else Pindar has to say when he introduces these notions into his poems. We find him speaking in the second Olympian ode of ' someone ' who gives judgment beneath the earth and allots to the good and the evil a fate according to their deserts. He refers also to reincarnation

11

in the words : ' But as many as have endured for three times in
either state to keep their souls altogether away from injustice,
these travel the road of Zeus to the tower of Kronos.   There the
breezes of Ocean are wafted about the Islands of the Blest ', and
he goes on to describe in more detail the delights of this place.
This sounds as if it were drawn from the same source as Plato's
promise to those who have three times in succession chosen the
life of the lover of beauty and wisdom.   But for Plato the Islands
of the Blest are the place of temporary bliss where all go when
they have lived one good life.   They are different from the final
home of the soul that has reached the term of all its wanderings
and escaped from the wheel of birth.   That is for Plato the outer-
most heaven and the region beyond, ' a place which no poet here
has ever sung, nor shall sing worthily ever '.   The description of
this place as the home of the Ideas is of course Plato's own, but
there must have been something to correspond to it in the doctrine
of the Wheel, which is as manifestly not Plato's own.   If Pindar
seems to confuse it with an exalted form of the Homeric idea of
the Islands of the Blest as the final home of heroes (he mentions
Peleus, Kadmos and Achilles as dwelling there), this is probably
because his knowledge of the Orphic beliefs was very much at
second hand, and brought in only to heighten poetic effect.   His
poetry in general does not suggest the type of mind which would
plunge deep into a mystery-religion.*   In a fragment of one of the
Threnoi we have again a beautiful and poetic description of the
life of those who have reached the Islands of the Blest, or Elysium,
or whatever he may have called it.   The name is not given.

Finally I may quote here the reference to the doctrine of
reincarnation in Herodotus (2. 123), who declares that it was
borrowed by the Greeks from Egypt : ' The Egyptians were the
first to introduce also the doctrine that the soul of man is immortal, but that at the death of the body it enters into one animal
after another, as they are born.   Then when it has gone the round
of all creatures of land or sea or air it enters again into the body of
a new-born man.   This cycle is accomplished in three thousand
years.   Now there are certain of the Greeks who have made use
of this doctrine, some earlier and some later, as if it were their
own.   I know their names but do not write them.'   (It sometimes
seems as if the Greeks consciously conspired to make the task of
the researcher more difficult.)   We can only guess whether the

---

* I hope it is clear that these authors are only being considered here as sources
of information for the doctrine of reincarnation, which I have seen reason to regard
as a part of the Orphic system of beliefs.   The question of their own thought and
their attitude towards Orphism belongs to a later part of the book (chapter vii).

doctrine of which Herodotus knew included as its climax the return of the soul to a divine state after a final re-entry into human form, but at least nothing that he says is inconsistent with that conclusion. There is no mention of the choice of lives, and the definite statement that the soul, human at first, must for three thousand years be reincarnated in the bodies of animals before regaining human shape, is an addition which we have not found elsewhere. It is not inconsistent with anything in Empedokles. It is not necessarily inconsistent with the words of Pindar about those who have endured for three times in either state to shun injustice, since the poet does not say that these three times must be in succession. It will not fit with the fate of those in Plato who have chosen the philosophic life three times in succession, which one would suppose to be a reference to the same doctrine as that in the words of Pindar. In both Pindar and Plato the words refer to an exception from the ordinary lot granted to extraordinary persons, whereas Herodotus might be taken as referring to the usual course of events. It is likely, I think, from what we know of the nature of Orphic writers, that this special dispensation was a refinement invented by them and superimposed on an already existing belief in reincarnation which they had taken over. Pindar reproduced it in poetic form, and Plato seized upon it in order to have an exceptional privilege to bestow on his own ideal man, the true philosopher. This must remain a guess, for, I repeat, we cannot expect to reconstruct in all detail a religious creed when the writings in which it was expounded are lost and we are only looking at it as it was transmuted by the original genius of men like Plato and Pindar.

I said that we have an invaluable counterpart to these literary sources for the doctrines in question. It comes from the side of epigraphy, since the information is contained in the writing found on some thin plates of gold which have been taken at different times from ancient graves, some in Italy and some in Crete. These inscriptions have long been famous, and a whole literature has sprung up around them.[8] The plates were found lying beside the skeleton, some near its hand, others folded up beside the skull. One (that at Petelia) had been rolled up and enclosed in a cylinder attached to a delicate gold chain, clearly in order that it might be worn as an amulet. (This plate is now in the British Museum. See plates 8 and 9.)

The verses which are scribbled on the plates show by their form that they are extracts from a longer poem or book of poems, and the date of some of them makes it certain that the poem from which they are taken must have been at least as early as the fifth century B.C. It may well be earlier than that. The provenance of the oldest of the plates is South Italy, which was known to be a source of Orphic writings. It should be noted that those from Crete are later. They are not earlier than the second century B.C., and Dieterich (*Nekyia*, p. 107) referred them to the second century A.D. They cannot therefore, at least without extreme caution, be used as evidence by those who wish to discover the original home of Orphism.

The purpose of the plates is clear from their contents. The dead man is given those portions of his sacred literature which will instruct him how to behave when he finds himself on the road to the lower world. They tell him the way he is to go and the words he is to say. They also quote the favourable answer which he may expect from the powers of that world when he has duly reminded them of his claims on their benevolence. Where this last is put in, it may be partly because the friends of the dead man thought it no bad thing to remind the deities themselves of what was expected of them. Magic was not alien to Orphism, and that relic of it which consists in believing that a god is more likely to do what you want if you yourself write down for him the way in which he is to act, may have lingered in the minds of these devout persons. The general level of the language suggests, however, that the main purpose of the addition is more likely to have been the encouragement and solace of the soul itself on its journey.

The following is a translation of the writing on the plates.[9] Some details remain, and must probably always remain, uncertain, since the difficulties facing the interpreters have been many. The letters are scratched, sometimes rudely and incorrectly, on the thin shiny gold surface, which has then been folded and creased. It is also clear that abbreviations of phrasing have been used, a word or two being sometimes made to stand for a whole sentence where the sentence was a well-known formula. In general, the writing is in hexameter verse, but one or two short formulas ('Thou art become god from man', and the sentence about the kid and the milk) are inserted in prose.

1. Plate from Petelia, South Italy, fourth-third century B.C., now in the British Museum (pl. 8) :

'Thou shalt find to the left of the House of Hades a spring,
And by the side thereof standing a white cypress.
To this spring approach not near.
But thou shalt find another, from the Lake of Memory

Cold water flowing forth, and there are guardians before it.
Say, " I am a child of Earth and starry Heaven ;
But my race is of Heaven (alone).   This ye know yourselves.
But I am parched with thirst and I perish.   Give me quickly
The cold water flowing forth from the Lake of Memory."
And of themselves they will give thee to drink of the holy spring,
And thereafter among the other heroes thou shalt have lordship.'

2. From Eleuthernai in Crete, second century B.C., now in the National Museum, Athens.   The same formulas were found on three different plates :

' I am parched with thirst and I perish.—Nay, drink of me
(or, But give me to drink of)
The ever-flowing spring on the right, where the cypress is.
Who art thou ? . . .
Whence art thou ?—I am the son of Earth and starry Heaven.'

3. Plate from Thurii, South Italy, fourth-third century B.C., now in the National Museum at Naples :

' But so soon as the spirit hath left the light of the sun,
Go to the right as far as one should go,[10] being right wary in all
things.
Hail, thou who hast suffered the suffering.   This thou hadst never
suffered before.
Thou art become god from man.
A kid thou art fallen into milk.
Hail, hail to thee journeying the right hand road
By holy meadows and groves of Persephone.'

4. Three more tablets from Thurii, of roughly the same date as the previous one, also preserved at Naples.   Some are more fully expressed than others, and the following reconstruction of the formulas represented by all three is based on that of Professor Murray :

' I come from the pure, pure Queen of those below,
And Eukles and Eubuleus, and other Gods and Daemons :
For I also avow that I am of your blessed race.
And I have paid the penalty for deeds unrighteous,
Whether it be that Fate laid me low or the gods immortal
Or . . . with star-flung thunderbolt.
I have flown out of the sorrowful, weary circle.
I have passed with swift feet to the diadem desired.
I have sunk beneath the bosom of the Mistress, the Queen of the
underworld.
And now I come a suppliant to holy Persephoneia,
That of her grace she send me to the seats of the Hallowed.—
Happy and blessed one, thou shalt be god instead of mortal.
A kid I have fallen into milk.'

5. The long persistence of the beliefs and customs represented by these tablets is shown by yet another which belongs to the second or third century A.D. It is believed to have been found at Rome, and is now in the British Museum (pl. 10) :

' She comes from the pure, pure Queen of those below,
And Eukles and Eubuleus, the child of Zeus.[11] Receive here the armour
Of memory,[12] a gift celebrated in song among men.
Caecilia Secundina, come, by law grown to be divine.'

It will be far better for the understanding of these inscriptions if they are read over two or three times for themselves before any attention is given to separate comments on isolated parts. Read in the position which they occupy in the present chapter, the central doctrines should stand out clearly without further interpretation. In turning to comment, I pick out first of all those passages which show most clearly their identity with the doctrines whose Orphic nature I have already been trying to prove.

In plate no. 1, the soul is instructed to say, ' I am a child of Earth and starry Heaven ; but my race is of Heaven '. In no. 2, it says, ' I am the son of Earth and starry Heaven ', and in no. 4, ' For I also avow that I am of your blessed race '. Its claims are based on its divine origin and kinship with the gods. The words ' child of Earth and Heaven ' remind us that for the Orphic these claims were more specific, since they went back to the story of the birth of mankind from the Titans, who were known to Hesiod, and universally, as the sons of Earth and Heaven. The Orphic knows, however, that although the Titans had Ouranos for their father, they were a wicked and rebellious race, and that it is only owing to their crime, which secured that he should have something of the Dionysiac nature in him too, that he can base any claims to divinity on his relationship with them. Consequently it is on that Dionysiac nature that he insists—' But my real lineage is of heaven '. This he could boast if he had lived the Orphic life and so quelled the Titanic and cherished the Dionysiac side of his nature. The two halves of this confession do not fit very well together, and may have been taken from different poems ; but it is easy to see that there can have been a clear purpose in the minds of those who wrote them down together for the use of the dead man.

The soul that has claimed kinship with the gods adds the words : ' And I have paid the penalty for deeds unrighteous '. This must refer to the same tale. The unrighteous deeds are not only its own—though it had those to atone for as well—but the original taint of evil, or bias towards sin, which it inherited from its 'lawless forefathers' the Titans. (Perhaps it is not even fanciful to see in the use of the rare compound ἀνταπέτεισα the meaning 'I have paid the *vicarious* penalty'.) The soul that is still in the bonds of the body prays to Dionysos for 'release from its lawless forefathers' (p. 83 above). On plate 3, if Professor Murray's rendering is correct, the words 'thou who hast suffered the suffering' will refer to the same thing; but it is possible that the line means 'Hail, thou who hast suffered something which thou hadst never suffered before', and refers as a whole to the apotheosis of the next line.

Having made his claim and been approved by the authorities of the Underworld, the dead man is welcomed in the words: 'Thou hast become god from man!' 'Happy and blessed one, thou shalt be god instead of mortal!' It is the same exultant confidence which Empedokles expresses—'I tell you I am a god immortal, no longer a mortal!'—and means that he is in no need of further purification by a course of reincarnation followed by purgatory. He is one of the saints, he comes 'from the pure,' and hence is ready to enter on the final stage of bliss. 'I have flown out of the sorrowful, weary circle', he can say. This is because he has lived a life of purity according to Orphic precepts. These people must have believed that they had reached the last of the incarnations necessary, a fact which no doubt they argued, complacently perhaps, from their personal qualities of purity and piety. Empedokles and Pindar record the belief that the last incarnation is in the form of the highest types of humanity, and who, in Orphic eyes, had a better claim to that description than he who 'came from the pure', that is, had lived as an Orphic himself? It is quite possible that this was considered sufficient evidence, since where a personal hope of eternal and divine blessedness is concerned, men are not likely to have insisted too nicely on that part of their sacred writings which stated that ten, or in exceptionally deserving cases three reincarnations were necessary before this supreme end could be accomplished. Yet it is also quite possible that they were convinced of the fact of their previous incarnations and would have been ready in life to justify their claims on that score also. Men who believe in reincarnation are not shy of speculation on the subject, and in the case of Pythagoras, a believer in the same creed as the Orphics, four of his previous lives are still on record (Diog. Laert. 8. 4, 5). Empedokles, too, in the course of the *Purifications* states: 'For I have already been a youth and a maid, a bush, a bird, and a dumb fish of the sea'.

On plate no. 1, the soul is told to avoid the spring on the left. On no. 2, he is instructed more positively that the one which he is to drink of is the one on the right ; and on no. 3 it is definitely said that if he is one of the saved he will be taking the right-hand road. This reminds us that, as Socrates said in the *Phaedo*, ' the road to Hades has many branchings and forks '. In the *Gorgias* it was put a little more definitely, that the meadow where judgment takes place is ' at the fork from which lead the two roads, the one to the Islands of the Blest, the other to Tartaros ', and in the *Republic* as definitely as it is here on our gold plates, namely that the road taken after judgment by the just leads to the right and the road for the unjust to the left.

This is perhaps the most striking and interesting of the many proofs that Plato and the buried plates were drawing on the same eschatological literature. It is tempting to press the parallel still further. The context of the *Phaedo* passage is this (108a) : ' And so the way there is not as it is described by Telephos in the play of Aeschylus. He says, " Straight is the road that leads to Hades ", but I do not believe that it is either simple or one. Otherwise there would be no need of guides, for there would scarcely be anywhere for a man to go wrong if there were only one road. But now it appears that it has many branchings and forks—as I infer from the sacrifices and practices in use on earth.' (So Burnet. ' Rites holy and customary' has some ms. authority, and is chosen by Harrison, *Proleg.*[3] p. 599.) By practices of those on earth does Socrates mean to refer specifically to the burial with the body of a dead man of tablets containing information to guide him on his way ? This is suggested by Jane Harrison, and it is certainly probable that Plato had heard of the practice which our discoveries illustrate. On the other hand, νόμιμα—*customary, established*, does not seem an appropriate word for the practices of the Orphics, which were far from being established or universal.[13] It would be interesting too if we could find in the plates anything corresponding to Socrates' mention of guides. The myth with which he had led up to the description of the diverse roads to Hades spoke of the soul at death being conducted ' by his own daemon, who had been appointed to him in life ', and added that after judgment he was handed over to ' another guide '. Many of the words on the plates are addressed to the dead man by people unknown to us, but whom the writers of the plates would know as they would be mentioned in the books from which they were quoting. Ignorant as we are, it is most natural for us to put them all into the mouths of the gods of the underworld to whose realm the soul has arrived, but it is possible that some of them might be the words of its own particular daemon or guide. Unfortunately it is not worth wasting words over this, since we can never find out from the evidence which we possess.

Keeping, then, to the right, the soul comes to a spring, and addresses to the guardians that are before it a prayer that it may be allowed to drink of the water, of which it is in dire need: 'I am parched with thirst and I perish'. We may presume that it has passed by the way that is described in the *Republic* as leading to the plain of Lethe,. 'through terrible and suffocating heat ; for it is bare of trees and of all the fruits of the earth'. At the end of that journey too the souls are given water to drink. For the general belief that the dead are thirsty and in urgent need of water we have references which though not frequent are sufficient to indicate that it must have been widely held and not a peculiar tenet of the Orphics. The same prayer occurs in the Egyptian Book of the Dead, and had been adopted from it into the Hellenic religion of this same part of the world, as is shown by several sepulchral inscriptions, found, like the gold plates themselves, in Italy, with the formula : 'May Osiris give thee the cold water'. No doubt the name of Osiris was taken by the Greeks because they found in the Egyptian religion an idea similar to that which they already held themselves.[14]

The word ψυχρόν means of course not simply 'cold' but 'refreshing'. (The two are the same in Mediterranean countries.) It is of the same root as *psyche*, soul, and Dieterich (*Nekyia*, p. 95) compares the word ἀναψῦξαι in the Orphic line (p. 166 above), which literally means 'to be refreshed from evil'. The water is not ordinary water, it is water from the lake of Memory, and it is only the soul whose purity is vouched for which is to be allowed to drink from it. This is the soul which has escaped from the circle of birth, or evil, or woe, and is about to enter on the state of perfect divinity. Consequently it is not, like the souls in the *Republic* which are being prepared for a new incarnation, made to drink a certain measure of the water of Forgetfulness (*Rep.* 620a). That, without doubt, is the fountain on the left which it is told above all things to avoid. For it is reserved the water of life, which will enable it to retain full consciousness.

In Plato we have mention of the water of Forgetfulness, and here of the water of Memory. The water of Forgetfulness, although obviously present in the shape of the 'spring on the left', is not mentioned by its name. To find them both together we have to go to the curious and detailed description of a local cult which is preserved by Pausanias (9. 39). This is the cult of the Boeotian earth-deity Trophonios, who foretold the future to any who performed the proper preparatory ritual and descended into the depths of his cave. The description makes it clear that to enter the cave of this divine dweller beneath the earth was considered equivalent to making a descent into the lower regions. His cave was, in fact, just one of the entrances to the underworld which were localized in various parts of Greece (*e.g.* at Tainaron, in the extreme South of the Peloponnese). The process of preparation took a number of days and involved sacrifice to various deities, but more important than all this was the action which immediately preceded the descent. If this produced unfavourable omens, then the descent must be postponed, whatever the result of the previous sacrifices had been ; and this final act was the sacrifice of a ram ' into a trench ', the same victim and the same manner of sacrifice which were used by Odysseus when, himself at the mouth of Hades, he wished to call up the shade of the seer Tiresias and have speech with him (*Od.* 11. 35 f.).

This sacrifice duly performed, if the entrails have given no unfavourable sign, the candidate is washed by night in the river Herkyna and anointed, and after that is led by the priests, ' not straight to the seat of the oracle, but to springs of water. These springs are quite close to one another. There he must drink both of water called Lethe, that he may get forgetfulness of all that he has had in his mind hitherto, and after that of other water, the water of Mnemosyne, and by this he shall remember afterwards what he saw when he went down.'

A few minor points on the tablets call for mention. They do not affect questions of faith, and if, like Jane Harrison, we suppose them to refer to ritual acts performed while still on earth, we must admit, as she does herself, that we cannot know what these ritual acts were. The same happy lot of the soul which is expressed by the clear statement that he is no longer a mortal but has become a god, is also put into the metaphorical or symbolic formula that he is a kid who has fallen into milk. Ancient sources provide no parallels which will throw a direct light on this, and the opinions of scholars make rather amusing reading. Two will serve to illustrate this. Jane Harrison wrote (*Prol.*[3] 594) : ' This quaint little formulary is simple almost to fatuity ', and L. R. Farnell (*Hero Cults*, 376) called it ' a mystic formula that no one has satisfactorily explained '. One thing it certainly seems relevant to mention. There is evidence (see Harrison, *l.c.*) that among the many forms in which Dionysos was worshipped was that of a kid, with the title *Eriphos* or *Eriphios*, and it is the central point of the mystic's hope that he is to become assimilated to the nature of his god. As for the milk, one can do no better than say that milk and honey, as well as wine, are the good gifts that mark the coming of Dionysos (Eur. *Bacch.* 142, 708 ff., Harrison, *o.c.* 595). This will not mean that there is anything peculiarly Dionysiac about them, but simply that the god is the giver to his worshippers of all good things, among which milk and honey were to a pastoral people the chief, as not only the Greeks knew but also the Israelites when they bent their steps towards Canaan. Professor Conway's interpretation, that to say 'I am like the kid that fell into the milk pail' was just 'a shepherd's proverb for a misfortune unexpectedly turning to great good' (*Bull. John Rylands Library*, 1933, p. 76), errs, no doubt, on the side of simplicity, but perhaps points the way to the truth, namely that to fall into milk meant little more than to attain in abundance that which one had always desired. The comparison with our own sacred literature is not altogether otiose, although it does no more than show how the formula 'flowing with milk and honey' has become proverbially characteristic of the better land, the land of promise. More than this we cannot affirm. (But cp. ch. vi, App. 1 below.)

In the invocation on plates 4 and 5, three deities are called on, the Queen of those below (Persephone), Eukles and Eubuleus. ✱ Eukles, 'the fair-famed', is Hades or Pluto, as Hesychius says, probably so called by a characteristic euphemism. Eubuleus was often used as an epithet of Zeus (Frazer on Paus. 8. 9. 2), but inscriptions show that he was known in Eleusis as an independent god standing beside Demeter and Persephone (Ditt. *Syll.*[3] 83, line 39) and as such he was also worshipped in the Islands. (Inscriptions from Paros, Amorgos, Delos, Mykonos ; see L. Malten in *Arch. Rel. Wiss.* 1909, p. 440 with nn.) This god was at least in later times identified with Dionysos. He resembles Dionysos on a relief of the second century A.D. (Preller-Robert, *Gr. Myth.* 1. 784, n. 1 and reff. there), and Dionysos is called Eubuleus more than once in the Orphic hymns (30. 6, 52. 4). This being so, it is probably better not to agree with Harrison, who says (*Prol.*[3] 587) : 'The two (Eukles and Eubuleus) are manifestly titles of the same divinity', but rather with Olivieri, who sees in the three deities invoked the Trinity of mother, father and son. Father and son were of course often thought of as one, especially in the syncretistic Orphic literature. (Cp. p. 100 above.) 'Dionysos and Hades are the same', said Herakleitos, and Pluto, no less than Dionysos, is addressed as Eubuleus in his Orphic hymn (18. 12), where he is also called Zeus Chthonios. Malten (*l.c.* n. 5) notes that as a *youth* Eubuleus cannot be traced back in the Kore legend before the fourth century, but that is all the more reason to believe, as we suspect already, that he was sometimes imagined as the young Dionysos and not only as the older Zeus Chthonios his father.

I have mentioned this point not simply for its own sake, but also in order to suggest a different interpretation of plate no. 5 from that which is usually given. It is usually supposed that the words 'child of Zeus' refer to Caecilia, and Harrison (o.c. 586) says : ' Caecilia claims descent not from the Orphic Zagreus but from Zeus, who . . . took on, in popular monotheism, something of the nature and functions of Zagreus '. (Incidentally, one could scarcely help supposing from these words that the name Zagreus was mentioned on the other plates. I have said elsewhere what I think of the indiscriminate use of this name wherever Orphic beliefs are in question.) My suggestion is that the translation should run : ' She comes from the pure, pure queen of those below, and Eukles, and Eubuleus son of Zeus ', and Professor Murray's rendering be adopted for the following clause.

After avowing its purity, its kinship with the gods, and the joyful fact of its escape from the circle, the soul adds the words ' I have passed to, or entered upon (literally and most naturally, ★ " set foot upon ") the desired *stephanos* with swift feet '. That the meaning of this is ' I have attained my reward ', there is of course no doubt ; but more than one opinion has been expressed about the detailed interpretation of the words. *Stephanos* means ordinarily a crown or garland, the main uses of which were two, to reward victors in the games and to put on the heads of guests at a banquet. There is much therefore to be said for the view of Comparetti, who understands it in a sense similar to the metaphor of St. Paul, ' So run, that ye may obtain '. The pure soul has run a good race (' with swift feet ') and obtained the prize. Similarly, it seems to me at least possible that it might refer to the banquet of the dead, which aroused such sarcastic criticism against Orphic teaching about the after-life. ' They describe them as garlanded, and spending all their time in drunkenness ', said Plato in the *Republic* (363c), and Aristophanes too, commenting on the good time which it is possible to have in the next world, remarked that the dead are represented as crowned, ' in token of the fact that as soon as you arrive you are set down to drink ' (Kock, *Com. Att. Fr.* 1, p. 517, cp. n. 14 below). These interpretations would involve a less usual, but quite possible use of the verb ἐπιβαίνω.

The other interpretation which has been suggested keeps nearer to the literal sense of the verb, but adopts a more unusual meaning of *stephanos*. From the fact that a crown encircles, it is

occasionally used in poetry in a transferred sense. Thus Pindar
(*Ol.* 8. 33) uses it for the walls that were to encircle Troy, and
Euripides (*Herc. Fur.* 839) speaks of the ' garland of fair children '
which encircles Herakles, and which in a short time he is destined
to destroy in his madness. Hence Dieterich (*de Hymn. Orph.* 35)
took the word here to refer to the boundaries of the seats of the
blessed, Rohde to the kingdom of Persephone. Now the only
parallel use of the word which Dieterich thinks worth quoting is
from the Orphic Argonautica : ' Straightway there appeared to
him the *stephanos* and grim walls and groves of (the city of)
Aietes ' (*O.A.* 761 f.). In my opinion this is the only complete
parallel which he could have quoted, and yet these lines were
written five hundred years or more later than our gold plates.
The few classical references (to which Dieterich refers in a footnote)
show, it seems to me, that the word had not become so generalized
as to mean an encircling wall and nothing more. They are used in
each case with a particular purpose just because they recall to a
reader's mind the primary meaning of *crown*. The sentence in
Pindar refers to the fact that the walls of Troy were built by
gods, and runs : ' Him the son of Leto and wide-ruling Poseidon
called to be their fellow-worker on the wall, when they were
minded to make a *stephanos* for Ilion '. The translation is surely
not ' minded to make a wall encircling Ilion ' but ' minded to give
Ilion a crowning glory '. (Would one infer from the lines ' Where
Cortona lifts to Heaven her diadem of towers ' that the word
diadem ' had come to mean in English *a thing that encloses*', so
that the words ' I have passed with swift feet to the diadem
desired ' might naturally be taken to mean ' to the enclosure, or
city ' ? [15]) Similarly, in Euripides a ' garland of fair children ' is
not the same thing as a ring of children. It is the crown and
glory of the hero's life, and the word is used to intensify the un-
speakable horror of the murder which is to follow.

I should prefer, therefore, one of the interpretations based on
the proper sense of *stephanos*. If the matter must be left in
doubt, we surely need not be dissatisfied with the amount of
certainty which is still left us, since we know that the line means
' I have reached my goal ', and we have just been told in the
previous line what the aim of the soul had been, namely escape
from the circle of reincarnation. The line is repeated after the
next one with the variant *from* for *to*. I have no hesitation in
believing what Professor Murray regards as probable, that this
is simply a mistake. A glance at an epigraphical copy of the
plate, revealing how full of mistakes it really is, removes all
scruples on the score of high-handed or unfair treatment.

✳   There remains the line : ' I have sunk beneath the bosom of the Mistress, the Queen of the Underworld '. It is tempting to agree with Dr. Farnell, who sees in this no more than ' a poetic-religious expression of the fact of interment ' (*Hero Cults*, p. 378). This explanation seems simple and natural. It is nevertheless true that it finds a close parallel in a certain form of adoption-ritual, practised both on secular occasions and in mystery-religions, where the significance was the adoption of the initiate by the deity, or his rebirth into the family of the gods. The point of parallelism lies in the mimetic representation of the act of birth. (Information and passages in Dieterich, *Hymn. Orph.* 38 f. For a conspectus of opinions, *Olivieri*, p. 7.) On this interpretation, the line would form yet another claim of the soul to be well received, based on an act of ritual duly performed while it was still alive. Considering its place in the whole, I think this is only possible if we take the two previous lines in a similar sense, and to me it seems more natural to take all three as the exultant expression by the soul of the happiness to which it knows itself to be entitled on account of being pure and having paid its penalty. It then makes its simple request to Persephone, and has the promise of immortality confirmed.

Concerning the white cypress I do not see that it helps to-wards an explanation to say that by white cypress the writer meant a white poplar (so Comparetti in *Laminetti Orfiche*, Florence, 1910), an admittedly common, as well as extremely beautiful tree, and one, moreover, which had associations with the dead. It is a striking feature of the poem, and I hope that some day our knowledge of infernal natural history may be widened sufficiently to include it.[16]

The foregoing discussion has opened up the main sources of evidence for the Orphic beliefs regarding the fate of the soul after death. It will be convenient to close the chapter by at-tempting a summary of these beliefs, so far as it may be done without seeking to impose a consistency which probably never was perfect (all analogies tend to this conclusion), and which, even if it existed, the second-hand and fragmentary nature of our evidence would make it impossible to recapture.

The belief in life after death is primarily a personal hope. This means that the most reasonable part of any complex of eschatological ideas is likely to be that part which deals with the happiness of the elect, since it is to that class that the framers of dogma suppose themselves to belong. To describe plausibly the fate either of the ordinary outsider or of the positively and outstandingly wicked does not so vitally concern them, in spite of the temptation to let the imagination run riot in inventing picturesque forms of torment for the damned. Consequently if we are going to find a tale which we can follow out at all, it will be the one which describes the fate of the good rather than that of the bad. Let us make the experiment.

The nature of all men is composite. This is the result of a sin, not each man's own sin, but a great, original and ancient sin to which the whole human race is heir. The fact means, however, that each individual man has a part which is prone to sin, the Titanic nature, and a part which, being in origin divine, strives with the Titanic nature to throw it off and be purified from it. It lies with each of us to choose which part shall win in the struggle, and according as we let the divine or the Titanic nature have the upper hand, so are our lives good or bad.

At death we go to Hades and are led before judges, who examine our lives and consign us to an existence which shall be according to our deserts, punishment for the wicked and happiness for the good. In this state we pass so much of our time as together with our previous earthly life shall complete a period of a thousand years. When this period is up, we are brought back from paradise or purgatory and prepared for another life on earth. How far the details of the choice of lives belonged to Orphic dogma, and ✱ are not due to Plato's imagination, it would be hard to say, but the fact of choice was probably there. Free will and personal responsibility are certainly essential and important parts of the Orphic code. When the new lives have been allotted, the souls destined for reincarnation are made to drink a certain amount of the water of Lethe. Thus they may have only a dim and troubled recollection of the truths which their experiences have taught them, lest, presumably, their continuance in the way of salvation be made too easy for them in their coming life. We need not, however, suppose it to be more than a suggested explanation (and some explanation was necessary) of the obvious fact that we do not on earth have more than a vague and troubled feeling of these truths. (Plato also accounts for this fact by contact with the impurities of the body—itself a naturally Orphic idea— but makes great use of the noun *lethe* to describe it.) Here too there is an interesting hint that the element of personal responsibility is not absent. Some people, says Plato in the *Republic*, drink too much, and forget everything. To drink as little as possible is the wisest course, and we know that it was the best thing of all, and granted to the fully purified soul on the threshold of full divinity, not to drink of Lethe at all.

All these things performed, the soul enters again into a mortal body and is born, and the circle has been completed once. How many times it had to be accomplished before release was possible, we cannot say for certain. If we combine the statement of Herodotus with those of Empedokles and Pindar, and as much of Plato as is not inconsistent with it, we may guess that in one form of the belief, the soul was reincarnated every third time as man, and that after three incarnations as man, that is, nine altogether, might hope for its release. If this was an Orphic belief, we may be sure that it depended on the soul's own striving, that is to say, it was what might be attained, not what every soul by virtue of its essence naturally and inevitably did attain. In more general terms we may vouch for the existence of the belief that it was ten thousand years before the ordinary man could hope for salvation, with the reservation that it may have been thought possible to commute this by living three pure and holy lives in succession, the dispensation which Plato in the *Phaedrus* thought fit to bestow on philosophers.

Now it is likely, as I have said, that an initiated and practising Orphic believed himself to be living his last life before the final release from the body. The sacred writings taught that the last incarnation is in the form of the highest types of man, of whom the liver of the Orphic life would certainly be one. No doubt, then, the Orphic believed that he was coming to the end of his periods in purgatory or in that Elysium which was no more than a brief resting-ground. He at death would be rapt to higher places still, in comparison with which the joys of Elysium were gross. This distinction between Elysium and a yet higher sphere is not always easy to maintain, but must certainly have been there. It is the consequence of a distinction which quite obviously was made, that between the fate of the good man who is yet destined for rebirth because his allotted cycles are not completed (his term in Elysium may even be regarded, according to Plato, as a time of trial and testing, since it might make him careless in choosing his next life), and the fate of him who has obtained final release and become a god. Yet we do not find this distinction so clearly drawn when it is a question of the actual places to which each goes. We must remember that Elysium (or the Islands of the Blest ; the two are often used indifferently) was the name for the one and only abode of the blessed, long before the elaborate and in some ways highly spiritual Orphic dogmas were evolved. These things die hard, especially as Orphic eschatology would be familiar to many writers, and half familiar to many more, who were attracted by it and yet

did not see why it should be made more inconsistent than they
could help with old and popular beliefs. Pindar will be an
example, if this supposition is true.

If, then, we draw the distinction between Elysium and the
final home of the good and now deified soul, where are we to place
the latter ?   That question remains for this chapter to answer.
The tendency to use the name Elysium indiscriminately makes the
evidence sound confusing, but all the same there is not much
doubt where the freed soul goes, and it is an idea which we may
easily understand, owing to our having inherited it ourselves.
It goes to Heaven. Elysium may have been ' on the farthest
borders of the earth ', it may even, as we shall see, have been
transported by theologists as far as the moon, but it belonged
properly to the sublunary order of things as much as Tartaros.
Yet that the soul should go to Heaven seems to have been a familiar
idea in the fifth century.   The word used is not usually Heaven,
but *aither*. *Aither* was the substance which filled the pure outer
reaches of Heaven, beyond the impure atmosphere (*aer*) which
surrounds the earth and extends as far as the moon.   It was in
this pure region that divinity dwelt, and the *aither* itself was supposed to be divine.   In Euripides it appears now as the home of
Zeus, now as Zeus himself (Eur., frr. 487, 877, Nauck).   Those,
then, who believed the soul to be immortal and divine, were naturally inclined to suppose it made of an imprisoned spark of *aither*,
which when set free would fly off to rejoin its like.   So Euripides
speaks of the mind of the dead as ' an immortal thing, plunging ✱
into the immortal *aither* ' (*Hel.* 1016).   More specifically, it is
said to fly to the stars, or become a star, for the *aither* is the substance of which the stars, existing as they do in these pure outer
regions, are made.   (Cp. Aristotle, *de caelo*, book 1.)   So in the
Peace of Aristophanes (832 f.), when Trygaios on his return from
the abode of the gods is being questioned about his journey,
his slave asks him : ' Isn't it true then what they say, that we
become stars in the sky, whenever one of us dies ? ' [17]   There
is also evidence (though it is mostly of Graeco-Roman date)
for the belief that the Milky Way was the abode of souls, a belief,
apparently, which is common to many peoples.[18]   We have too
this statement from the *Placita*, to suggest to our minds that the
Orphics themselves believed the stars to be habitable worlds
(*O.F.* 22) : ' Herakleides (*i.e.* Herakleides of Pontus, the contemporary of Plato) and the Pythagoreans say that each of the stars
is a world, earth and surrounding air, all in the infinite *aither*.
These dogmas are current in the Orphic writings, for they make
each of the stars into a world.'

12

The distinction between Elysium, as being itself a place of purification, and the final home of the purified soul is illustrated by a passage in the eschatology of Virgil, *Aeneid* vi (743-751). So far as this distinction goes, Virgil is following the same tradition as Plato.[19]   The lines are :

*   Quisque suos patimur manes, exinde per amplum
Mittimur Elysium, et pauci laeta arva tenemus
Donec longa dies perfecto temporis orbe
Concretam exemit labem, purumque relinquit
Aetherium sensum atque aurai simplicis ignem.
Has omnes, ubi mille rotam volvere per annos,
Lethaeum ad fluvium deus evocat agmine magno,
Scilicet immemores supera ut cònvexa revisant
Rursus et incipiant in corpora velle reverti.

In Elysium are the souls both of those who have suffered their final incarnation and of those who are destined for rebirth. The former obtain there full purification, and though Virgil does not expressly say that they fly up to a yet higher sphere, no other place could well be suitable for that which is *purum . . . aetherium sensum atque aurai simplicis ignem*. They go then to the stars, *aither* to *aither*, leaving the regions of Elysium, which are the highest attainable by souls who have still to suffer rebirth and are described by Virgil as *aeris campi* (887). *Aer* was the less pure atmosphere which fills the space between the earth and the moon, and there is no doubt reference to the widespread belief that the moon itself was a resting-place for souls after death.[20] Since the souls destined for rebirth occupy the levels of air, it is not surprising that according to the same system of belief living beings at birth draw in their new life with the air ; and we have Aristotle for witness that this was an Orphic belief, namely that soul ' comes into us from space as we breathe, borne by the winds '. (See above, p. 94.) [21]

In the *Timaeus* of Plato, certain threads are drawn together to form a general picture, and the following passage forms a fitting close to this chapter (*Tim.* 41d ff.) :

When the Creator first made the individual souls, he made them ' equal in number to the stars, and assigned each one to a star ', and while they were still on the stars he taught them the nature of the Universe, and what was to be their own fate, namely to be implanted in bodies. ' When they had been implanted in bodies by the workings of necessity, . . . first of all the faculty of sensation, one and the same for all, would be naturally aroused in them as a result of violent impressions, and secondly love, mingled with pleasure and pain, and in addition to these fear and anger and all the passions which either result from these or are their contraries. If they conquered these passions, they would live with righteousness, but if they were conquered by them, with unrighteousness ; and the one who lived his appointed time well, would travel again to dwell in his proper star, and live a blessed life according to his true nature.' [22]

APPENDIX TO CHAPTER V

The Underworld Vases

There is a well-known series of South Italian vases of the fourth to third centuries B.C., of which two are reproduced on figs. 16 and 17. They are huge things painted in a repellent style, and the idea which has taken the painter's fancy, and which he has caused to be repeated with variations on a number of vases, is that of a fairly comprehensive representation of the Underworld as it was depicted in Homer and in popular belief. It seems to be a hotch-potch of all that he knew about Hades, and it is not surprising, especially considering the provenance of the vases, that this included some features of the Orphic tradition. A number of the stock dwellers or visitors in Hades appear, Sisyphos with his stone, Tantalos warding off the rock, the Danaids with their pitchers, Herakles with Kerberos, Theseus and Pirithoos and others. Orpheus is there, as he was in the painting of Polygnotos and as he was bound to be in any representation of the House of Hades. The vases show Pluto and Persephone enthroned in the middle in a palace, the most noteworthy feature of which is the wheels which are suspended from the ceiling (p. 208 below). There are also the infernal Judges, named on one of the vases Tri(o)ptolemos, Aiakos and [Rhada]manthys, and Hermes the Conductor of souls. Near Orpheus on one of the vases (fig. 16) is a group of father, mother and child. They have not been identified with any mythological figures, and some have wished to interpret them as a family of human initiates come to enter the blessedness which is their due. Jane Harrison found this difficult to accept, ' in face of the fact that all the other figures present are mythological ', though if she could have accepted it it would no doubt have further confirmed her in her view that the vases ' were obviously designed under Orphic influence '. I am not sure that this latter remark has much significance, yet I think that the suggested interpretation of the doubtful figures is much the most likely. It would find a parallel in the painting of Polygnotos, where the fact that all the other figures were mythological did not deter the painter from inserting a group which he labelled simply ' the Uninitiated ', i.e. a group of human beings (p. 162 above). Whether the figures on the vase are Orphic initiates is another matter ; they are more likely to have been Eleusinian, and a reminiscence of the painting at Delphi.

Much has been written about these vases. I have not thought it worth while to repeat a detailed description here, not so much because I think it certain that they have nothing to do with Orphism as because, whether or not they show Orphic influence, they have little or nothing to add to our knowledge of the Orphic religion. Yet they contain one

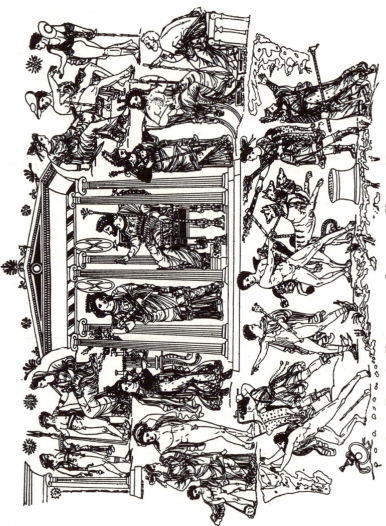

Fig. 16.—Underworld Scene on a Vase in Munich

FIG. 17.—UNDERWORLD SCENE FROM A VASE IN THE NAPLES MUSEUM

or two features which are interesting as illustrations of the literary evidence which has been considered in the text. (The presence of Orpheus himself is of course beside the question.) The Judges themselves are a noteworthy addition when the paintings are compared with the fifth-century work of Polygnotos, and indicate an eschatology more akin to the Orphic in that more stress is laid on rewards and punishments. On one appears a figure with a sword identifiable with the goddess Dike (fig. 16, top r., beside Theseus and Pirithoos), and on another a figure carrying a whip whose inscription has been plausibly restored as Ananke (fig. 17, above Sisyphos). Both these persons have strong Orphic affinities. At the bottom of both the vases reproduced flow the infernal rivers, and on one of them these are shown in a curiously precise and map-like way. An acquaintance with these rivers was not of course particularly Orphic, but it may be guessed from Plato, as well as from our general knowledge of the character of the Orphic writings, that the Orphic poem in which these things were described took especial trouble to give a detailed and circumstantial account of the geography of Hades. There remain two features of particular interest, if we bear in mind the descriptions of the gold plates from Italian graves, as well as some of the words of Plato. The vase of fig. 16 shows in the top left-hand corner, that is, on the left of the palace of Pluto as you approach it, a fountain. We miss the mysterious cypress of the Petelia tablet, but nevertheless this can scarcely be anything else but the fountain of Lethe, which in the Orphic poem the purified soul must avoid. On the same vase, to the right of Herakles, is an object resembling a pepper-pot. It is in the same part of the design that, on the second vase here reproduced, the Danaids appear. In a third vase of the same series, not reproduced here, the Danaids are seen at their work of emptying their pitchers into a large jar sunk in the earth (like the little souls of fig. 15, p. 163 above). It looks as if the object on fig. 16 is intended to suggest the Danaids, who are themselves absent because there was no room left for them. When we have got as far as this, we cannot help being reminded of Plato's words in the *Gorgias* about the fate of the uninitiated, which is to carry water to 'a jar with holes pierced in it' (εἰς τὸν τετρημένον πίθον). The punishment is discussed above, pp. 161 ff. This then is
✱ a picture of the τετρημένος πίθος. No doubt it should have its open mouth upward, and the holes in the bottom which is buried in the earth ; but if the painter had been such a stickler for accuracy, how could he ever have shown the holes at all ?

These points, interesting in themselves, may have their value as further evidence for the spread of Orphic ideas, if they seem sufficient to argue influence ; but perhaps the best reason for not lingering over the vases in the present inquiry is provided by the words of L. R. Farnell, which in any case should be written over the desk of every archaeologist who takes up religious history : ' Art is a difficult medium for the expression of advanced eschatology '.

The vases are published in *Wiener Vorlegeblätter*, Serie E, plates 1-7. See also Winkler, *Darstellungen der Unterwelt auf unteritalischen Vasen, Breslauer phil. Abh. Bd. 3, Heft 5*, 1888. An exaggeratedly mystical interpretation of them was put forward by E. Kuhnert in *Jahrb. des Öst. Arch. Inst.* 1893, pp. 104 ff., and *Philologus* 54 (1895), pp. 193 ff. He was attacked by Milchhöfer in *Philol.* 53 (1894), pp. 385 ff., but has been followed *e.g.* by Dieterich (*Nekyia*, p. 128). Rohde again strikes the sceptical note in *Psyche*, Eng. tr. ch. 7, n. 27. For Harrison's account see *Proleg.*³ pp. 599 ff.

NOTES TO CHAPTER V

[1] It will be obvious from what follows that I have received much light from the chapter on Eleusis in Rohde's *Psyche*, to which the reader may be referred for more definite information. But I cannot follow him entirely. In particular, I cannot understand his refusal in this chapter to admit a connexion in the mind of the Greek between the activity of the chthonian deities as gods of the soil and their activity as gods of the kingdom of souls. The two were always connected with the same deity, and even if the current modern explanation of their connexion (analogy between corn and human soul) is faulty, the fact of it can scarcely be denied. The assertion seems inconsistent with other parts of the book.

[2] By the son of Musaios Plato may mean Eumolpos (traditional founder of the Eleusinian mysteries), who is said by Suidas to be his son (Kern, *test.* 166). Musaios himself always appears in connexion with Orpheus, sometimes as son, sometimes as disciple. Suidas alone says that in spite of tradition he must be older. He seems to have been little more than an indistinct double of Orpheus, to whom some of the writings in the Orphic corpus were attributed. Like Orpheus he was referred to as a *theologos.* Many of the writings attributed to Orpheus himself were addressed to Musaios. For authorities concerning him, see Kern, *testt.* 166-172. Plutarch, who was well informed on the subject of mysteries, says simply that Plato's jibe here is directed against the Orphics (p. 159 above).

[3] For examples, see R. Wünsch, *Antike Fluchtafeln*, Bonn, 1912 (*Kleine Texte*).

[4] We have seen enough now to say that what may be called allegorical philology was a feature of Orphic speculation. To σῶμα = σῆμα we have now to add Ἀΐδης ✱ =*unseen* (perhaps a good shot for once), and, I am much afraid, ἀμύητος=ἀνόητος. Here is further reason for seeing both attempts at etymology and Orphic origin in the passages of Malalas and Apion (*O.F.* 65, 56) quoted in the previous chapter, pp. 98 ff.

[5] Theories of its origin are not relevant to Orphism. They may be found in Frazer's notes on the passage in Pausanias, and in Harrison, *Proleg.*³ 613-23.

[6] E. Maass (*Orpheus*, p. 95) refers these words to the underworld.

[7] χαίρετ᾿, ἐγὼ δ᾿ ὑμῖν θεὸς ἄμβροτος, οὐκέτι θνητός.
Identical is the close of the Pythagorean *Golden Verses* (70 f.) :

ἢν δ᾿ ἀπολείψας σῶμα ἐς αἰθέρ᾿ ἐλευθερὸν ἐλθῇς,
ἔσσεαι ἀθάνατος θεὸς ἄμβροτος, οὐκέτι θνητός.

Dieterich, *Nekyia*, p. 88, n. 2.

[8] The handiest critical text to consult is Professor Murray's, printed as an appendix to Harrison, *Prolegomena.* See also Olivieri, *Lamellae Aureae Orphicae*, Bonn, 1915 (*Kleine Texte*), who gives (p. 3) a conspectus of previous writings on the subject. This is supplemented by Kern, *O.F.* p. 104, where texts are also to be found (= fr. 32).

[9] The translation of plates 1-3 is that printed by Professor Cornford in *Greek Religious Thought* (Dent, 1923), pp. 60 f., with one or two slight verbal alterations. Professor Cornford says : ' I have made use of Professor Murray's translation, making a few changes to suit the text as printed by Diels in his *Fragmente der Vorsokratiker* (1912), ii. 175 '.

[10] Reading and meaning extremely doubtful. The rendering in the text is Diels'. See preferably Kern's note, *O.F.* p. 108. It is fortunate that we do not have to rely on these words for the mention of the ' right-hand road ' on this plate.

[11] See p. 179.

[12] The meaning here is very doubtful. Diels τέκος ἀγλά᾿ (' child of Zeus, glorious '—fem.). Since the tablets have been several times examined and read by experts, I did not think it worth while for me, a complete beginner in this sort

of epigraphy, to try to redo their work.   I have, however, seen this plate in the British Museum, and for what it is worth record a note which I made to the effect that only Prof. Murray's reading (ὅπλα δ' ἔχ' ὧδε) seems to account for an extra letter on the plate here.   This difficulty was apparently noticed by others, and Olivieri prints ἀγλά[a].   See his apparatus *ad loc.*, and compare the remarks of R. S. Conway in *Bull. John Rylands Lib.* 1933, 87 f.

[13] Miss Harrison did not suggest that it was.   Reading ὁσίων καὶ νομίμων, she draws a distinction between ὅσια, sacrosanct rites for the initiated, and νόμιμα, rites for each and all.   On the other hand, even though ὁσίων and not θυσίων be the true reading, I cannot help feeling that if two contrasting kinds of rites were meant, and not simply a pair of adjectives describing the same rites, Plato would have repeated the article with the second epithet.

✱   [14] For the thirsty dead in general, cp. *Etym. Magn. s.v.* δανάκης (the name of a coin which was put into the mouths of the dead to pay their passage across the Acherusian lake.   Gruppe has printed the next lemma, δάνειον, by mistake) : δαναοὶ γὰρ οἱ νεκροί, τουτέστι ξηροί ; also other reff. in Gruppe, *Gr. Myth.* 831, notes 1-3.   T. L. Shear in *Amer. Journ. Arch.* vol. 35 (1931), p. 430, comments on the presence of a well in a tomb at Corinth.   He compares our Orphic plates and refers to the discovery of jars pressed to a dead man's lips, but his quotation from Aristophanes (Kock, *Com. Att. Fr.* i, p. 517) is quite inapt, since it is not the quenching of thirst, but feasting and good living, something like the μέθη αἰώνιος of Plato, that is there referred to.   A vast complex of ideas and rites is bound up with the conception of the thirsty dead.   See further *e.g.* O. Janeiwitsch, *Dürstige Seelen* in *Arch. Rel. Wiss.* 13 (1910), pp. 627 ff., and reff. in P.-M. Schuhl, *La Formation de la Pensée Grecque*, Paris, 1934, p. 119, n. 2, and p. 210, n. 2.

The examples of the prayer to Osiris found in Italy are in *I.G. It. et Sic.*, nos. 1488, 1705, 1782.   See esp. A. Dieterich, *Nekyia*, 95, and Rohde, *Psyche*, Eng. tr. ch. 14, ii, n. 152.   Interesting is Dieterich's comparison of the Christian use of *refrigerium*, as in the sepulchral formulas *in refrigerio anima tua, Deus te refrigeret*, and the even more striking parallel in the burial service of the modern Orthodox Church : Κύριε, ἀνάπαυσον τὴν ψυχὴν τοῦ κεκοιμημένου δούλου σου τοῦδε . . . ἐν τόπῳ ἀναψύξεως, ἔνθα ἀπέδρα ὀδύνη, λύπη καὶ στεναγμός.

[15] Cp. with the English lines Eur. *Hecuba* 910, ἀπὸ στεφάναν κέκαρσαι πύργων. A glance at Liddell and Scott suggests, as a matter of fact, that στεφάνη is more easily generalized in meaning than στέφανος.

[16] I have been privileged to see, in proof, Professor Cook's discussion of the white cypress of Hades for the forthcoming 3rd volume of *Zeus*.   I agree wholeheartedly with the conclusion which he reaches, after discussing possible parallels, that ' on the whole it seems most likely that the tree of the tablets was a miraculous cypress, its peculiarity consisting in its assimilation to that other Borderland tree, the white poplar '.   (For the chthonian associations of the latter, see *Zeus*, 2. 467 ff.)

[17] Cp. further the line of the epitaph on the Athenians who fell at Potidaia in 432 B.C. (now in the British Museum) : αἰθὴρ μὲμ φσυχὰς ὑπεδέχσατο, σώ[ματα δὲ χθών ?] (*I.G.* i, 442).   The idea was even more commonly expressed in the Graeco-Roman age : cp. Rohde, *Psyche*, Eng. tr. p. 541 with n. 135, and esp. the interesting juxtaposition of Elysium and Heaven, *ib.* n. 134.

[18] See reff. in Dieterich, *de hymn. Orph.* 37, n. 3, and Gruppe, *Gr. Myth.* 1037. Dieterich is no doubt wrong in connecting this belief with the ' kid into milk ' formula, as Prof. A. B. Cook thinks (*Zeus*, 2. 119).   Prof. Cook himself would take the *stephanos* of plate no. 4 to refer to the Milky Way.   Although, as I have said, the evidence for the belief is mostly of Graeco-Roman date, it was attributed among the Neoplatonists to Herakleides of Pontus (*Stob.* i. p. 378, 12 Wachsmuth).

[19] He differs from him in positing a preliminary period of purgation by the elements for all souls alike, to free them from the grosser defilements to which all have been subject through the fact of incarnation (735-742).   The discrepancy is a minor one which may well have existed within the same tradition, and the preliminary purification by the elements is reflected in other sources, notably Empedokles.   Cp. E. Norden, *Aeneis* VI, Teubner, 1926, pp. 19, 28.

It may interest readers to know that the account of Orphic eschatology in this chapter up to this point was written without reference to *Aen.* vi. If that book be now read, and especially the speech of Anchises (724-752), the meaning of the oft-repeated phrase that the eschatology of V. ' shows Orphic influence ' may be clearer than before. In the second line of the quotation, the punctuation used is one which I have not seen elsewhere, but it only serves to make clearer an interpretation which is *e.g.* Norden's.

[20] Cp. Norden, *o.c.* p. 23. The material is-abundant, and referred to by N. The most striking extant example of an elaborate eschatology worked out on the basis that the moon represents an intermediate stage in the upward progress of the soul is the myth of Plutarch's *de facie in orbe lunae.* I quote from a summary in a recent article by Mr. W. Hamilton (*C.Q.* vol. 28, 1934, p. 26 ; the distinction between soul and mind is of course not expressed in Virgil) : ' The death which we die on earth liberates mind and soul together from the body, and the two fly up to the space between the earth and the moon, where they are punished and purified. The moon receives after purification the souls of the just ; there they enjoy the delights of paradise, . . . and there finally, if they do not by sin incur the punishment of reincarnation, the second death takes place. Mind returns to the sun which was its source.' The mingling of mythological and philosophical expression, as seen for example in the fitting of the ancient Elysium into a cosmological scheme by placing it in the moon, is rightly stressed by Norden, and has, I think, been shown in this book to be a particularly Orphic trait. Common enough in the philosophical schools of the third and following centuries, it may even have been in the first place peculiarly Orphic.

[21] Here again is a tenet of the Orphic system that is by no means an Orphic invention. Among early philosophers, Anaximenes, Herakleitos and Diogenes of Apollonia at least believed the soul to be air, and though it is quite possible that they were all acquainted with Orphic *logoi*, they are more likely to have been rationalizing a common and popular notion than drawing on specifically Orphic sources. That the breath is the life is a natural and age-old belief. The achievement of constructing the Orphic system seems to me by no means lessened by admissions such as this.

[22] A contrasting view may be mentioned, if only in criticism of a petty type of argument which it is to be hoped may now be regarded as out-of-date. C. C. van Essen (*Did Orphic Influence on Etruscan Tomb-paintings Exist?*, Amsterdam, 1927), speaking of the poem called *Descent into Hades* (Kern, *O.F.* 293-296), says (p. 44) : ' We may gather at once one important fact from the title of this book (*Catabasis*), that Orphic doctrine placed the abode of the wicked as well as of the good in the nether world, and not both, or one of them, in the sky '. This conclusion serves him as an instrument to deny the Orphic character of an eschatological passage of the *Phaedo* (114*b*, *c*) on p. 47 : ' All this sounds very religious, but he had no Orphic doctrine in his mind here as appears clearly from the word ἄνω. Orphic eschatology placed the hereafter beneath or in the world, not in the heavens.' van Essen's treatise as a whole is a curious mixture of sound ideas marred by captious arguments of this type. This particular one is unfortunately being perpetuated, as I see from P.-M. Schuhl, *La Formation de la Pensée Grecque*, Paris, 1934, p. 265, n. 1.

CHAPTER VI

LIFE AND PRACTICES OF THE FOLLOWER OF ORPHEUS

Πολλοὶ μὲν ναρθηκοφόροι, παῦροι δέ τε Βάκχοι, '*Many bear the wand, but few become Bakchoi* '.

THAT is to say, there are many who join in a Dionysiac orgy, but few who carry out all that an Orphic thought necessary for the attainment of union with the god. That the verse is Orphic we may say with confidence, but let us, mainly with a view to establishing its pedigree beyond reasonable doubt, take a look at the context in which it has been handed down. In the *Phaedo* (69c, cp. p. 160 above) Plato says : ' It looks as if those also who established rites of initiation for us were no fools, but that there is a hidden meaning in their teaching when it says that whoever arrives uninitiated in Hades will lie in mud, but the purified and initiated when he arrives there will dwell with gods. For there are in truth, as those who understand the mysteries say, " Many who bear the wand, but few who become *Bakchoi* " '. He then draws his own peculiar moral, and turns the religious verse to his own purposes by adding, ' Now these latter are in my own opinion no others than those who have given their lives to true philosophy '. It comes as no surprise to us, after what we know already, that the Neoplatonist Olympiodoros comments on this passage : ' He is adapting an Orphic verse ', and goes on to compare that part of us which is fettered in the bonds of matter to Titans, and that part by which we rise above it to Dionysos (Olymp. *in Phaed.* p. 48, Norvin = *O.F.* 235).

We know little enough about the sort of life which an Orphic led, and what we do read sometimes sounds so contradictory as to be puzzling in the extreme. The key to the contradictions lies in this verse, in which the Orphic himself reminds us that his religion made no clean sweep, did not build itself up in a void, but was in fact a reform. The religion of Dionysos existed before Orphism, just as Judaism existed before the birth of Jesus, and neither reformer wished to be regarded as a rebel.   The Orphic, like Jesus himself, preferred to say, ' I came not to destroy, but to fulfil '. After the teaching of Jesus, there were in Judaea both those who continued to be bound by the old Mosaic law and those who had accepted the new freedom which, as its author was careful to make clear, was no more than the fulfilment of all the hopes of the Jew's own prophets.   No doubt the former class included some of those who nominally counted themselves as among the followers of Christ, just as to-day there are some who call themselves Christians and yet believe that a purely empty and formal keeping of the Sabbath is in itself a virtue.   Similarly, among those who called themselves followers of Orpheus there would be some who knew little more of him than that he was a priest of Dionysos, whom therefore they continued to worship in the old way, caring little for the advent of the best of the Orphic writings whose new message professed to reveal the true spiritual meaning of that worship.   Do not mistake the point of the parallel.   There is little resemblance between the religion of Judah without its Messiah and the unreformed license of pre-Orphic Dionysiac religion.   Judaism indeed, with its cleansing of vessels and washing of hands, had probably far more in common with the purity which was the aim of the Orphic himself.   All that the simile illustrates is the fact that no religion is born into a void, and that most are more strictly called religious reforms.   The spirit of the reform may be utterly opposed to that of the unreformed state of things, but one may rest assured nevertheless that many of the old ways will be continued under the name of the new.   (Some remarks made in chapter iv, appendix 1 above, are in point here.)

The object of these reflections is to suggest that when we find one scholar (Professor Cornford) saying of the Orphic religion that it ' made possible the alliance of Platonism with the religion of Christ and Saint Paul '—which is high praise indeed—and another (Dieterich) speaking of the ' licentious cult-practices of the Orphics ' * (*lascive Kultgebräuche* and *obscoene Dinge, Philologus* 52, pp. 5, 8), there is nothing here to cause despair.   If we look at the Orphic religion in its historical setting, it is only natural that both should be true.

So much by way of necessary preface.   If we try to examine the surviving evidence for Orphic practices and ceremonies, we find, as we might have expected, that it is more scanty than that which testifies to their beliefs.   What independent statements there are, show that practice was brought into close connexion with dogma, and so encourage the hope that in some matters,

* Referring to the story of Baubo, see p. 135 above.

where no independent evidence exists, we may be able to infer from the nature of a known belief some conclusion regarding an unknown custom or rite. Whoever wishes to do this must of course beware of pressing logic too far in a field where it is by no means an infallible guide, expecting the rational methods of philosophy from what was primarily an ecstatic form of religion. The method in any case is one more suited to the pages of a learned periodical than to the purposes of this book. The three doctrines which are naturally of greatest influence in the sphere of conduct, themselves inextricably interwoven, are the composite origin of mankind, the hope of final apotheosis, and the doctrine of transmigration. The last-named perhaps best illustrates the intimate relation between belief and practice, and its effect may not be obvious on the surface. The reasoning was this. If the soul of a man may be reborn in a beast, and rise again from beast to man, it follows that soul is one, and all life akin. Hence the most important Orphic commandment, the commandment to abstain from meat, since all meat-eating is virtually cannibalism.

In order that salvation might be attained, two things had properly to be regarded as necessary, though there is no doubt at all that there existed a lower form of Orphism in which the two were separated. These were, first initiation, and second the living of a life according to the Orphic canons of purity. To take the Orphic life first, as being the better attested, we are again set on our way by Plato, though here as in other matters pertaining to this religion his reference is isolated, brief, and introduced not for its own sake, but only by way of a simile to illustrate his argument. In the *Laws* (782c = Kern, *test.* 212) we read : ' We see in fact that the practice of human sacrifice persists to this day among many races ; whereas elsewhere we hear of the opposite state of things, when we could not bring ourselves to taste even of the ox, when the sacrifices made to the gods were not of animals, but of cakes, and the fruits of the earth soaked in honey, and other similarly pure and bloodless offerings. Men abstained from flesh on the ground that it was impious to eat it or to stain the altars of the gods with blood. It was a kind of Orphic life, as it is called, that was led by those of our kind who were alive at that time, taking freely of all things that had no life, but abstaining from all that had life.' According to the words which Aristophanes puts into the mouth of Aeschylus in the *Frogs*, Orpheus was famous for two things—he revealed the ways of initiation, and he taught men to abstain from killing. This, then, must certainly have been to contemporaries the most striking feature of the Orphic life. From the words of Aristophanes, it

almost looks as if instead of saying at the beginning of this
paragraph that the two things necessary for salvation were
initiation and an Orphic life, we might have said simply initiation
and a meatless diet. Again in the *Hippolytos* of Euripides the
taunt of Theseus at his son, now turned Orphic and bookworm, ✱
concerns itself with the ' meatless fodder ' in which he glories since
he ' has Orpheus for his lord '. Empedokles, whose eschatology
we have already seen reason to regard as identical with the Orphic,
shows himself again thoroughly Orphic when he cries, ' Will ye not
cease from killing ? See ye not that ye are devouring one another
in your heedlessness ? ' Like Plato's speaker he looks back to a
golden age in the past before such crimes were thought of, when
men worshipped the gods ' with painted likenesses of beasts, with
many-scented unguents and offerings of unmixed myrrh and
fragrant frankincense, casting down also on the ground libations
of yellow honey ; but with the unholy [1] slaughter of bulls was no
altar wet. Nay, this was held the height of pollution among men,
to take away life and devour noble limbs.' Empedokles makes
much of the connexion between this prohibition and the doctrine
of transmigration, with which the poetry of the *Purifications* is
saturated. It appears in the first of the passages just quoted,
and in another fragment he says : ' The father takes up his own
son in his hands, his son changed in form, and slaughters him with
prayer to the gods over his body, so great is his folly. The victims
look up and beseech their murderer, but deaf to their cries he
carries out the slaughter and makes ready the meal of sin in his
house. Even so the son seizes his father, children their mother,
rob them of life and feed on their kindred flesh.' [2]

Both Plato and Empedokles refer to the age of innocence,
before the sin of meat-eating was known among men, as having
actually existed in past times. This too they would find in the
Orphic writings. The idea of the *Saturnia regna*, the Golden Age
when before the coming of Zeus to power a race of men lived on
earth in happiness and plenty and goodness under the kindly rule
of Kronos, was a familiar one to the Greeks, and made immortal
for them by the poetry of Hesiod. There is a tradition that the
Orphics adopted the succession of ages and adapted and altered
it to fit their own scheme. In Hesiod there came first the golden
age of Kronos, then the silver age, the age of bronze men, the age
of heroes, and fifth and finally our own. In the Orphic scheme,
owing to the supremacy of Phanes, Kronos had to be dispossessed
of the golden age, as Proklos reports (*in Remp*. 2. p. 74, Kroll =
O.F. 140) : ' The religious poet (*theologos*) Orpheus gives us three
races of men : first the golden, which he says was founded by

Phanes, second the silver, which he says was ruled by the mighty Kronos, third the Titanic, which he says was compounded by Zeus out of the limbs of the Titans '. We may be sure that when Plato speaks of the tradition of a past age in which men thought it impious to eat flesh or to offer it to the gods, and compares this custom to the Orphic life, then it was a characteristic attributed in some Orphic writings themselves to a pre-Titanic age. These Orphic verses, themselves lost to us, have found their reflection in the philosophers of the classical age, and a more distant echo of them persists in the poetry of Virgil :

> *Ante etiam sceptrum Dictaei regis et ante*
> *impia quam caesis gens est epulata iuvencis,*
> *aureus hanc vitam in terris Saturnus agebat.*

The attempt of Phanes to usurp the kingdom of the Golden Age was not very successful. Almost certainly a newcomer to the company of Greek gods (as the discussions of our fourth chapter showed, he was probably an addition of the sixth-century reformers), he remained of esoteric interest only, and in this later age we find the sceptre restored to old Saturn, for all the Orphic colouring of the previous line. Not so easily suppressed was the association of the Golden Age with the abstinence from flesh.[3]

A second Orphic prohibition is handed down from the classical age in a well-known sentence of Herodotus (2. 81). The Egyptians, he says, do not take articles of wool into their temples, nor will they be buried in them. ' In this they agree with the so-called *Orphica* or *Bakchica*, which are really Egyptian and Pythagorean. For in these rites too if a man have a share, it is not lawful for him to be buried in woollen garments.' Mythological literature is the authority for this prohibition, for Herodotus adds, ' There is a sacred discourse which is told about it '. Probably this prohibition was closely connected with the former, the use of animal products being forbidden in general. To be sure, it was possible to obtain wool without committing the crime of murdering a kinsman, which was involved in eating mutton, but perhaps to rob him was also considered unworthy of the pure. To look for reasons behind these customs sounds a little absurd, but is not so in view of the Orphic's dependence on his *hieroi logoi*. The Orphic leaders were of those who ' make it their business to be able to give an account of whatever they take in hand to do '. This does not alter the fact that, whatever the *hieros logos* may have said, the initiate would observe the laws simply out of a feeling that otherwise he would offend the powers that be and it would be the worse for him. In other words, he sought for no reason beyond the belief in the magical efficacy of the act itself, and the belief in the magic was there before the reformers set themselves to rationalise it.

The fragment of Euripides' *Cretans* which we owe to Porphyrios, that compact treasury of information on the mystic cults of Bakchos, ends with a reference to Orphic prohibitions. We have already made use of the first part of the fragment (above, p. 111), and the last four lines are as follows :

'Clothed in raiment all white, I shun the birth of men nor touch the coffins of the dead, and keep myself from the eating of food which has had life.'

The colour of the clothing was important, as symbolizing purity, but may have had reference to the material (linen) also. To be in the presence of birth or death was a common cause of pollution, said to have been held as such by the Pythagoreans.

The fragment as a whole contains many reminiscences of Orphism, and this is perhaps the best place to consider whether it may be regarded as a perfect document of the Orphic religion. It is usually taken as such, owing to the references to the attainment of 'holiness', synonymous with becoming identified with the god, the stress laid on purity, and the means by which this purity is to be attained, as well as the reference to becoming a *mystes* of Zagreus. All these are undoubtedly elements in the Orphic religion, but I should not for that reason be surprised to find them mingled with others which were not strictly Orphic, since for me Euripides belongs to that class of writers whom I have already mentioned, those who, themselves not strictly Orphics, are familiar with some of the Orphic writings and attracted by them, yet interpret them so as to be no more inconsistent than they can help with popular beliefs. Euripides in particular we know to have been peculiarly fascinated by the religion of Dionysos in its wild and unreformed shape. In the question how far this fragment draws on purely Orphic sources, no conclusion can be more than probable, but I believe that Euripides has introduced one feature at least from the cult of the Cretan Dionysos in its pre-Orphic state. That is the *omophagia*. This represents just the side of Dionysiac religion which the Orphic reformers tried to purge away. The ban on killing extended not only to daily life, but also, and in particular, to sacrifices offered to the gods. I am inclined to think that the prominence given to it, and the deep impression which it made on others as being the peculiar contribution of Orpheus to religion, are due just to this, that the Orphic writings tried to teach men to worship Dionysos without the *omophagia*. The crude idea of the physical absorption of the god must give place to the more spiritual teaching of union with him attained by purity of life. We have seen enough evidence already, in this chapter and elsewhere, to make it impossible to believe that in Orphic eyes a part of the process of becoming *bakchos* was the killing and eating raw of a bull.[4]

We see then that the Orphic ideal of purity was to a great extent at least purely formal. In the language of to-day, their prohibitions were superstitions, and not concerned with morality at all. We naturally ask nowadays, was there not a moral side to their teaching as well? But before we try to answer that, we should remind ourselves that if we had the opportunity of putting the question to an Orphic initiate, we should be hard put to it to translate our inquiry into Greek in such a way that he would see its point. We are brought up in an atmosphere of Christianity, and whether we like it or not, Christian notions of behaviour have sunk into the very marrow of our thought and expression. To us there is a clear distinction between formal or ritual purity and moral goodness, but this distinction would not be nearly so obvious to the Greek. The word *adikon*, which we usually translate ' unjust ', had certainly a moral significance, yet for the Orphic a murder committed from motives of greed, and the eating of flesh against the tenets of his religion, would both alike be *adika*. It is not that he had no moral sense, in our meaning of the word, but that he was not actively conscious of it, that is to say, he did not realize the distinction which our use of the word involves. As I have remarked before, a murderer was considered by all the laws of religion at Athens to be incurably impure and accursed. He had no right to associate with his fellows as an ordinary human being. We too hold him to be impure and remove him from the society of his fellows. We say that the action of the ancient Greek was purely ritual, and that we are moved by motives of morality. Yet the result is the same in either case, and however real may be the distinction of motive which we nowadays perceive, we cannot deny that the same action which inspires us with horror as morally bad inspired an equal horror in the breast of the Greek. Put therefore in the form of asking whether the Orphic religion had ' a moral side ', the question is not likely to lead to fruitful results.

More likely to provide an answer is the question, had it a *positive* side to its ethical teaching? A religion whose sole motive is ritual purity may condemn moral offences as sternly as any. As we saw in the last chapter, there are indications that the Orphics did so, for instance, the introduction of Orphic notions in a Platonic argument where it is questions of morality that are

being discussed, and the allotting of an Orphic punishment to
moral offenders by Aristophanes. But it is not so likely that it
will say ' do this ' as well as ' do not do that '. The most distinctive thing about the ethical teaching of Jesus is that it added
the two commandments ' Thou shalt . . .·' to the ten commandments whose burden is ' Thou shalt not . . .' That is the real
criterion by which to judge between a religion which, in our loose
jargon, preaches an empty formalism and one which has a genuine
moral content, that is to say, one which has the good of others at
heart and not simply the saving of one's own soul. Judged
by this standard, was the Orphic on the side of the angels? I
see no evidence that he was, and feel fairly certain that he was
not. His object was the saving of his own soul. To accomplish
this he had to *abstain* from certain actions, some of which
we too should account as sins and some of which we should
not. He did not distinguish between the two, and the question
whether his prohibitions had a moral side to them would have had
no meaning for him. But that he had to *perform* certain moral
actions, to do good in the Christian sense of the words, we cannot
believe. His religion was the height of individualism. Any
religion which involves the doctrine of transmigration, with its
absorption in ' soul-history ', is almost bound to be, a truth which
is amply borne out in Hindu countries to-day. It is this, incidentally, which may largely account for its obscure position
when Athens was at the height of her power. Everything then
was for the state, and to the glories of the state the state religion
ministered. With the decay of the city-state and the growth of
individualism from the fourth century onwards, the religions of
this type had much freer play.

When we speak of Orphic initiations, the Greek word which
we have in mind is *telete*. This was a word of wide meaning,
as the *Etymologicum Magnum* rightly points out : ' *Telete*, a ✱
sacrifice of a mystic nature. . . . But Chrysippos says that it is
proper to give the name *teletai* to writings about divine matters
. . . for it is a great reward to hear the truth about the gods and
be capable of keeping it to oneself.' A *telete* meant both a religious act and a religious writing. Let the warning be heeded
by those who like to draw hard and fast distinctions between
literary and practising religion. It is born out by the *locus
classicus* on the subject of Orphic *teletai*, where Plato gives a
working, if unflattering, definition of the term (*Rep.* 2, 364*e*,
translated above, p. 159). He says there of the mystery-mongers
whom he is censuring that they ' produce a mass of books of

13

Musaios and Orpheus, according to whose recipes they make their sacrifices '. The *teletai* which they say they have for sale are ' means of redemption and purification from sin through sacrifices and pleasant amusements ', ' ceremonies which free us from the troubles of the other world '. The Orphic did nothing unless there was a warrant for it in his books. No wonder it was natural for Pausanias to say (p. 10 above), ' whoever has *seen an initiation (telete)* at Eleusis or *read the writings* called Orphic '. To know something about an Orphic *telete* it was not necessary to see one performed.

These professional initiators, or begging priests, who found it profitable to ignore the demands of the Orphic life and pretend that *teletai* alone were sufficient to secure salvation, had a special name from their calling, *Orpheotelestai.* Plato is not alone in his condemnation of them as men who made profit out of the purely superstitious side of human nature. Theophrastos (who was about twenty-five when Plato died) writes as part of his character-sketch of the superstitious man that he ' goes every month to the *Orpheotelestai* for initiation ' (Kern, *test.* 207).* Plutarch too knew what they were, and tells a story of a Lacedaemonian king of the beginning of the fifth century who had an interview with one. The *Orpheotelestes* told him that those who had been ' initiated ' by him would secure happiness after death. The king looked at the man's ragged condition and replied, ' Why then do you not die with all speed, you fool, and have rest from bewailing your misery and poverty ? ' If the wandering priest were a true Orphic, he must have found the answer easy, but his character as sketched by Plato and Theophrastos suggests that he was not so familiar with the rest of his Orphic Bible, in which the answer lay, as he was with his recipes for sacrifice.

We cannot know in detail what the Orphic *teletai* were, except in so far as we feel entitled to use the extant corpus of hymns as evidence. It has been doubted whether a poem with the actual title *Teletai* ever existed (*e.g.* by Gruppe, *Gr. Cult. u. Myth.* 1. 639 f., Kern, *O.F.* pp. 315 f.), although it is mentioned by Suidas (Kern, *ib.*). The reason for thinking that our hymns may be relevant is that in some manuscripts they are provided with the title *To Musaios, Teletai,* and that they do consist of a series of

---

* This sentence shows up well how wrong it is t~~ ~~anslate τελετή, τελῶ by the English words ' initiation ', ' initiate ', which imply acts that can only be submitted to once in a life-time. There is probably humorous exaggeration in the words ' every month,' but not to that extent. May one without offence suggest ' to take the sacrament ' ? The parallel is probably close, and the comparison with Christianity only shows how rash it would be to condemn the Orphic religion as a whole by the activities of the dealers in indulgences.

short prayers to the gods with, at the head of each, a statement of
the sacrifice (not, of course, of flesh) which is appropriate to be
made with it. Against this is to be set their late date, making it
uncertain how far they represent the Orphic literature of the
classical age. In so far as they are prayers to the gods for favour,
accompanied by sacrifice, they answer exactly to the description
of some at least of the *teletai* mentioned by Plato.[5] Since Plato's
description is in general terms only, and we possess no *teletai* of his
time or before, we cannot say how closely they correspond in
content. The Lykomidai of Phlya in Attica chanted hymns of
Orpheus over their sacred performances (Paus. 9. 30. 12 = *O.F.*
304), and religious verse which could be put to this use would
surely come under the heading of *teletai*. Hymns, then, *i.e.*
metrical prayers recalling the nature and myths of a god and
asking for his favour, and sung at scenes of sacrifice or possibly
religious drama, were some of the *teletai* revealed by Orpheus. Of
these the hymns which we possess may be a late, and probably
faint, reproduction (cp. ch. viii below). Doubtless that is only
one example out of many. For one thing, the term included
things done as well as the writings which either were recited at the
dromena or provided the warrant for performing them. What the
Orphic did, apart from performing sacrifice with prayer, we must
confess we do not know for certain. There must have been more.
There was the procedure contemptuously referred to by Plato
as playing or amusement, as well as the sacrifices ; but we can only
guess at its nature. One guess is so tempting that I cannot bring
myself to leave it out. At a later date the Christian opponents
of Orphic mysteries made much of the combination of horror and
childishness which they professed to see in the tale of the infant
Dionysos, murdered by the Titans while his attention was distracted by pretty playthings. The toys, as we saw (above, p. 121),
are said by Clement, no doubt truly, to have been used as some of
the symbols in the mystery. The infant god, says Clement, was
distracted with childish playthings (παιδαριώδεσιν ἀθύρμασιν), and
the phrase of Arnobius, another Christian writer, in describing
the same myth, is *puerilibus ludicris* (*O.F.* 34). Now to return to
Plato, the phrase he uses (παιδιᾶς ἡδονῶν) is a curious one. It
arrests the attention, and is difficult to translate. Its literal
meaning is ' the pleasures of childish play ', and is very close to
puerilibus ludicris. The *teletai*, then, are ' means of redemption and
purification from sin through sacrifices and the pleasures of
childish play '. A reference to a representation of the rending of
Dionysos is at least likely.

I think it probable, considering the universal agreement in

ancient authors that the most characteristic feature of the Orphic religion was its dependence on writings, that the phrase ' hymns (or perhaps sometimes *hieroi logoi*) sung at the *dromena* ' covers pretty well all that there was to an Orphic rite ; and moreover, that the recital and the sacrifice were the main thing and the *dromena* of the simplest nature, probably a certain amount of pantomime to illustrate the theme of the recital. One *dromenon* would accompany the rending of Dionysos (cp. above, p. 132), and another, no doubt, the rape of Kore. All this is conjecture, as any statement on Orphic ritual must be. Orpheus as a religious teacher was famous for three things : he was the revealer of mysteries (*teletai*), the *theologos* or singer of the gods, and the preacher of a way of life. Only about his two latter activities can we speak in anything but the most general terms. Fortunately, they are much the most important in any religion of the prophetic type to which Orphism belonged. (But see Appendix 1, pp. 207 ff. below.)

The question is frequently asked whether the Orphics may properly be called a sect. It is usually asked before any thorough examination of the nature of their religion has been completed. Here it appears towards the end of our investigation, and what we have found out already makes its importance less and even its existence as an independent question dwindle. We know that Orphism involved belief in definite and complicated dogma set forth in writings which had to be studied to be understood. We know that, if properly followed, it involved conversion to a new way of life. The dogma included a doctrine of personal salvation dependent on the conversion. These are elements quite alien to the traditional religion of the Greek city-state. It was obviously inevitable that those who followed this way and believed in it should consider themselves as a select band and the rest of mankind as outsiders. That is one of the characteristics of a sect, and to that extent they were sectarian. It is likely enough therefore that it is Orphic exclusiveness which is reflected in the inscription from Cumae which says ' No one may be buried here who has not been made *Bakchos* ',[6] since the ordinary Dionysiac religion had not this sectarian feeling so strongly, and there is, of course, other evidence for the presence of Orphism in Italy. We must not be misled by the fact that the name of Orpheus was a household word among the Greeks and that to a certain extent his character as a religious teacher and even his writings seem to have been familiar to some of the greatest of Greek poets. It should be clear by now that this does not affect the issue. ' Many are the wand-bearers . . .'

One part of the question still remains, however. When we speak of a sect we usually mean not only a collection of people who hold the same beliefs and live the same sort of life, but imply also that they are banded together in some sort of corporate organism. There is little evidence for the existence of organized Orphic communities, but it would be wrong to say that there is none, and its scantiness is only what we should expect from the obscure existence which they led. Before we look further, is there anything significant in what we have already said ? I find it difficult to believe that even to ' live the same sort of life ' could have been possible without some organized priesthood to keep the faithful from backsliding, when it was the particular sort of life which was demanded of an Orphic, with all its peculiar and arbitrary prohibitions. To cite Judaism as an analogy may sound misleading, for that was a national religion, and it is natural for people of the same tribe to hold meetings and to organize themselves under leaders. But apart from that, it is difficult to believe in the possibility of keeping the law if the only inducement to do so were the existence of the books of Moses, without priests or synagogue to enforce it. Unfortunately we cannot bring forward the *Orpheotelestai* in support of this assertion, since they, it is clear, were not the priesthood of any organized sect, but simply free-lances who, with an eye to the main chance, had perceived the possibilities for private gain in pricking the vulnerable spot of the essentially irreligious rich.

The probability (already noted by Kern, *Orpheus*, p. 5 ; one might almost call it more than that) that the inscription telling of a special burying-ground for the initiated of Bakchos refers to *Orphic* initiates inclines us further to believe in the existence of Orphic communities. Better evidence still is the existence of a class of priests called *bukoloi*, who were certainly the officials of an organized society of *mystai*, and whom there is good reason for connecting with the Orphics. The documents which mention them, of which the chief are the Orphic Hymns and a number of inscriptions, are probably all of Roman Imperial date, and must therefore be used with caution, but the connexion, if it existed, may not have been a new one. Owing to its date, it will be more convenient to discuss this evidence in the last chapter.

With this chapter we make an end of our survey of the Orphic religion in isolation. From now on we shall be using the results attained in an attempt to bring it into connexion with other systems and later ages. Let us pause first and take stock with a brief summary, without reference to the evidence, of its nature as the investigations have shown it to be.

We have seen the religion of Orpheus to be dependent on a sacred literature containing both dogma and precept. Its dogmas include an involved mythology whose chief features are a god who is also creator, a succession of divine dynasties, and a story of the origin of mankind which carries with it a doctrine of original sin. The precepts are directed towards eradicating the sin (the Orphic would not have called it sin but impurity), and striving towards perfect union with the god who is in us all the time but stifled by the elements of impurity. They include therefore rites (*teletai*) both of purification and communion, of which the latter almost certainly involved being present at a recital and representation of the sufferings of Dionysos, our divine ancestor and our saviour. Purification was also to be attained by a certain habit of life, the essence of which was the observance of a set of prohibitions. Asceticism appears as an important feature, the result of a mental attitude of contempt for the body, which in Orphic eyes was a mere hindrance to the soul in its search for God. Turning back to dogma, we find there the belief that purity of life and due observance of the rites were ultimately rewarded by the gift of that to which they strove, namely an immortality consisting in the shedding of everything but the divine element and the emergence of the righteous as gods in heaven. Before this perfection of bliss could be reached, we remember that a cycle of births and deaths was necessary as a period of trial and purgation, although this may have been shortened for the consistently righteous liver. Punishment awaited the uninitiated and impure, and in some exceptional cases was eternal, so that the incurably wicked might serve a useful purpose as examples.

This was a religion of an entirely different kind from the civil worship to which the ordinary Greek professed his allegiance. He said that he believed in the city's gods, but he did not have to subscribe to any creed that had been fixed and crystallized in writings which were thought to be inspired. He did not believe, even if he had been initiated at Eleusis, that his daily conduct could have much effect on his life after death. The experience of conversion to a new life was one to which the general Hellenic mind was not prone, any more than the submission to an absolute external authority in matters of belief. For these reasons the Orphics remained few, in spite of the effect of certain portions of their thought on some of the greatest minds of Greece, and they must, one would have thought, have been almost driven to band themselves together in communities if they were not going to lose heart and give up.

Looking back like this, we are struck not only by contrasts with the prevailing religious type of fifth-century Greece, but no less by resemblances with Christianity. Features which it seems at first sight to have in common are these, the idea of conversion, and of religion as a way of life, original sin, communion, and parts of its eschatology. In so far as it helped to make the Greek world familiar with the call to conversion, it helped to prepare it for Christianity. It is, of course, in no sense the origin of Christian conversion, since the call to repentance and change of heart was preached with far more ardour by the Jews' own prophets, and with a positive moral purpose in their preaching which was almost wholly lacking to the Orphic. In speaking of original sin as an Orphic belief, we remind ourselves again that to use the word sin is to show ourselves misled. The Orphic belief was in original impurity, which was largely physical, and in so far as it admitted moral elements admitted them without consciousness of the distinction and as it were accidentally. The root idea of communion is to be met with in primitive peoples and in the crudest physical forms. It may be said for the Orphics that they took an unmistakable and a very long step towards developing communion as a purely spiritual idea. Closely connected with this is their eschatology, since the final reward of the pure was the eternal enjoyment of that union with God to which they had consistently set their faces through their periods of incarnation and temporary happiness in Elysium. (I call it union with God, for it is likely that Orphism, even though not deliberately, became felt as a powerful influence for monotheism.) If Orpheus ever approaches near to Christ, it is in this conception of communion on earth as not only a preparation for, but also a foretaste of the eternal life which is to be at one with God. We shall return to this subject in the last chapter.

APPENDICES TO CHAPTER VI

1. *Some theories of Orphic ritual.*

In the preceding chapter I tried, as far as the nature of the subject allows, to confine myself to facts. Consequently no mention was made of the many conjectures which have been put forward concerning the nature of the Orphic mysteries. This does far less than justice to some of them, which are highly probable although the fragmentary state of the evidence does not allow them certain proof. I have therefore reserved a discussion of them for an appendix.

The discussion of the gold plates in chapter v suggested the possibility that some of the sentences on them might refer to ritual acts performed during earthly life, on which the soul was basing its claim to the favour of the gods of the underworld. Thus the phrase ' I have passed beneath the bosom ' is reminiscent of a form of ritual undertaken to signify adoption. It might be that the Orphic initiate underwent this process in token of his acceptance into the family of the gods (above, p. 182). Again, from the words ' I have flown out of the sorrowful weary wheel,' which are quite naturally explained by the Orphic belief in the wheel of birth (κύκλος γενέσεως), Jane Harrison supposed it ' almost certain ' that there was an Orphic ritual of the wheel. She is able to quote instances of the existence of wheels kept in temples for ritual use, and to point to the presence of wheels hung up in the temple of Persephone and Pluto in the representation of the underworld on the Italian vases, on which Orpheus also appears. (*Proleg.*[3] pp. 590 f. Cp. p. 187 above.) From the line ' I have passed with eager feet to (or from) the *stephanos* desired ', of which several non-ritual explanations were given above in chapter v, the same authority thinks it possible that the neophyte had to step into (or even first into and then out of) a ring or circle. He enters and perhaps passes out of some sort of sacred enclosure. A. B. Cook takes a different view of the line. His conclusion is : ' It is permissible to conjecture that the Orphic initiate actually mounted a ladder in order to ensure his entrance on the Elysian soul-path' (*Zeus*, 2. 124). This suggested piece of Orphic ritual forms part of a long discussion on the belief in pillars of light and in ladders which serve as means of communication between Heaven and Earth. It would be useless to attempt to reproduce that discussion here, but the nature of the arguments may be indicated, although with the free admission that so to reduce it and pick and choose from the learning which it displays, cannot be perfectly fair treatment. From examples of the pillar of light as marking the appearance of a god (examples which include the Thracian religion of Dionysos), Professor Cook passes to the allied belief in a path (not at this stage a ladder) of ascent and descent between Heaven and Earth. (Lucian, *Demosth.* 50, Quintus Smyrnaeus, of the ghost of Achilles : ' So speaking he leaped up like a swift breeze, and straightway came to the Elysian plain, where is made a way of descent from highest Heaven and ascent for the blessed Immortals '. Professor Cook notes that the passage in Lucian is ' complicated by a reference to the *Phaedrus* '. And the Quintus Smyrnaeus by a faint echo of the *Republic* ?) It is next noted that the Thracian women on a vase showing the death of Orpheus are tattooed with the devices of a kid and a ladder, and there is also adduced as evidence a vase usually interpreted as a scene of incense-gathering from trees. The gatherer stands on a ladder, and ' not improbably the gatherer mounted the ladder to symbolize the celestial nature of the harvesting '. One is tempted to remark that no one could paint an ordinary scene of apple harvest without introducing the same motif, since a ladder happens to be a convenient way of getting into trees. Still, there is no doubt that the scene on the vase is of religious import. It is at this point that the conclusion about the Orphic line is introduced, and it is followed up by examples of the belief in a ladder as the soul's means of reaching Heaven. These include Egyptian beliefs, little ladder-amulets found in Roman tombs, a Greek example of the second century A.D., Jacob's ladder, Saint Augustin's remark that we may make a ladder of our faults if we overcome them, and even modern Italian watermarks and the hymns of J. M. Neale. What Professor Cook has proved up to the hilt, in a

fascinating series of illustrations, is the universality of the belief, showing how impossible it is that the Orphics should have been unfamiliar
with it. But of the use of a material ladder as part of the initiation-
ritual of any mystic community, there remains very little evidence ;
and even the belief in the heavenly ladder shows but dimly in the actual
line which we are trying to interpret : ' I have passed with swift feet
to the crown desired '.

Finally we have the formula, ' A kid I have fallen into milk '. Having ✱
given an explanation of this very much on the lines of that in our
fifth chapter, Miss Harrison goes on, ' The question remains—what
was the exact ritual of falling into milk ? ' The question which might
be put first—was there a ritual of falling into milk ?—is not here asked.
Similarly, Professor Cook believes that ' such formulae presuppose a
definite ritual ' (Zeus, 2. 120). Her conclusion, however, is negative :
' The question unhappily cannot with certainty be decided '. On this
subject Professor Cook has more to say. In Zeus (1. 676 ff.) he notes
that among certain tribes flesh boiled in milk, though a delicacy, is
abstained from on ordinary occasions, from the belief that the process
would injure the cow from which the milk had been obtained, but that
they ' will not hesitate to boil milk on certain solemn and specified
occasions '. He thinks it therefore possible that the original Thraco-
Phrygian (Dionysiac) ceremony involved a ritual boiling of milk. A
rite of the Phrygian mother-goddess furnishes a parallel, and the
allegorist Sallustius actually speaks in this connexion of ' the feeding
on milk, as though we were being born again '. Professor Cook continues :
' Let us suppose, then, that the early Thraco-Phrygian " kings ", the
Titanes of the myth, after killing Dionysos as a kid, pitched him into
a caldron and boiled him in milk with a view to his being born again.
The mystic who aspired to be one with the god underwent, or claimed
to have undergone, a like ordeal. He had fallen as a slain kid into the
milky caldron : henceforward he was " a god instead of a mortal ".'
' The Orphic votary,' says Professor Cook elsewhere, ' . . . in all
probability stepped into an actual caldron for a make-believe seething'
(Zeus, 2. 217). To judge of these conclusions it is necessary to read
them in the context of Professor Cook's own learning (e.g. on the
subject of the caldron of apotheosis in general, and in Dionysiac
religion in particular, Zeus, 2. 210 ff.). One remark it is permissible
to make here. The rôle ascribed to the Titans in the sentence quoted
above is, as Professor Cook makes clear, conjectural. The thought
which naturally arises is that, although the Titans' crime did in fact
result in the rebirth of Dionysos, owing to the efforts of his relatives
Zeus and Athena, there is no version of the myth which suggests that
the wicked giants had this kindly purpose in mind, or pretended to
have it, when they carried out their universally reprehended design.
We have to decide whether the myth as we have it is likely to have
been a distorted relic of a vanished version, based on an old tribal ritual
which in some modified form survived in the practices of the Orphics.
Certainly the distortion is quite in the Orphic manner. There is
also the further point that Clement of Alexandria, in describing the
myth, says that the Titans, after tearing the god in pieces, ' put a certain
caldron on a tripod, and throwing into it the limbs of Dionysos, boiled
them first ' (Clem. Alex. Protr. 2. 18, 1. 2 ; 1. 14. 16 Stählin = O.F.
35). It was only after this that they put them on spits and roasted
them. The original purpose of the boiling, if it was what Professor

Cook supposes, had been forgotten, and the myth so transformed as to be no longer consistent with it.

There is another possibility to be considered, the theory that a certain scene in the *Clouds* of Aristophanes is a parody of Orphic initiation, for which it may therefore be used as a legitimate source of information. The suggestion was first of all put forward by Chr. Petersen in 1848 in a note to *Der geheime Gottesdienst bei den Griechen* (Hamburg), p. 41 (not by Dieterich as J. E. Harrison, *Proleg.*³, p. 511, n. 2, says). It has been fully argued by A. Dieterich in *Rhein. Mus.* 48 (1893), pp. 275 ff. = *Kleine Schriften*, 117 ff., and by Harrison, *l.c.* It will be best first of all to give an account of the relevant passages, and then to discuss first the case for their having reference to mystic initiation at all, and secondly the case for the mysteries referred to being Orphic.

Going through the passages in the order in which they come in the play, we notice that a mystic atmosphere is spread about the ' wisdom-shop ' of Socrates from the very first. The old man Strepsiades knocks at the door, and is rebuked by the disciple who opens it for destroying an idea which he has just had. ' What was it ? ' asks Strepsiades (*v.* 139), and is met with the impressive answer, ' Nay, it is not lawful to tell it save to the disciples '. Streps. : ' Don't be afraid ; you can tell me. I myself have come to the wisdom-shop to be a disciple.' Disciple : ' I will speak ; but these things must be held to be mysteries.' (νομίσαι δὲ ταῦτα χρὴ μυστήρια.) (These words, which are surely a cue to the audience as well as Strepsiades, have been curiously overlooked by Dieterich and Harrison, though the aim of both is to prove that the things are mysteries.) When the old man has been introduced to Socrates, the following dialogue takes place (*vv.* 250 ff.) :

Socr. : ' Do you wish to understand divine matters clearly, the solemn truth about them ? '

Streps. : ' By Zeus yes, if that is possible.'

Socr. : ' And to hold converse with the Clouds, who are our Deities here ? '

Streps. : ' I certainly do.'

Socr. : ' Seat yourself then on the sacred stool.'

Streps. : ' I've done that.'

Socr. : ' Now take this garland.'

Streps. : ' A garland ? What for ? Oh Socrates, you're not going to sacrifice me like Athamas ? '

Socr. : ' No ; all this is what we do to those who are being initiated.'

Streps. : ' And what shall I get out of it ? '

Socr. : ' You will become a flowery speaker, a loud chatterer, a slippery one. Just keep still.'

Streps. : ' By Zeus I can well believe you ! I shall become floury by the way you're dusting me.'

Socr. : ' Keep holy silence, old man, and hearken to my prayer. O lord and master, measureless Air, who keepest the Earth in the midst of space, and shining Aither, and ye reverend goddesses the Clouds, harbingers of thunder and lightning, arise, appear in space before the eyes of the thinker.'

Streps. : ' Not yet, not yet ! Give me time to fold this over me in case I get a wetting. How unlucky I am ! To think that I came away from home without even a cap ! '

Socrates, taking no notice of the interruption, continues his prayer, and the Clouds appear. Later touches also remind us of the atmosphere of mysteries. When the Clouds have spoken to Strepsiades and promised him both his immediate request and a life of happiness for all time in their company (v. 463) if he prove a good learner, he is led into the sanctum for instruction. Before he goes in, he is made to lay aside his clothes, and as he enters he takes fright and says, 'Give me a honey-cake first, for I am as frightened at going in as if I were going down into the cave of Trophonios'. (v. 506. The honey-cake was the recognized offering carried by those who went to consult the awful underground oracle of Trophonios in Boiotia, Paus. 9. 39. 11; other reff. in Rogers' Aristophanes *ad loc.* Some information about the descent into the cave of Trophonios above, pp. 177 f.).

We need not spend much time over proving that it is a scene of initiation which is being represented, since Socrates says so plainly enough. It is brought home by reflection on the curious scene which the stage must have presented at the moment of the Clouds' epiphany. Socrates stands as priest (he is actually called *hiereus* by the Clouds at *v.* 359), and in an attitude of prayer, before Strepsiades who sits garlanded on a 'sacred stool' with his head covered up. It also emerges from the dialogue that Socrates has sprinkled him with something. Except for the garland, the scene is exactly paralleled by the relief on a cinerary urn from Rome which shows three scenes from Eleusinian ritual (pl. 11). One of the scenes shows Demeter seated, with Kore standing beside her on one side, and a man with a club on the other. He is caressing Demeter's snake, and is usually taken to be the initiated mystic. The other two scenes show stages in the preparation for this vision of the goddesses, in other words, in initiation. One is the washing of a pig for sacrifice (the regular victim at Eleusis). The other is the scene which is in point here, and shows a man seated on a stool with his whole head heavily veiled. The stool is covered with a ram's skin, and Dieterich argues convincingly that the stool of Strepsiades in the *Clouds* was also so covered. Behind the man stands a priestess, who holds over his head a *liknon.* Dieterich's affirmation that the position of her left hand makes it clear that she is shaking it over him, is open to some doubt, since she might equally well be steadying it. If she is not, yet Socrates may well, during his sprinkling, have imitated her attitude. On the action of Socrates, however, there is more to say.

There is certainly no further confirmation needed for the thesis that in the scene between Socrates and Strepsiades Aristophanes is parodying a known ritual of initiation. Now seeing that the closest parallel to it is provided by a scene of obviously Eleusinian initiation, why do we not simply say that it is a parody of the rites of Eleusis and have done? Having laid stress on the resemblance between the Eleusinian relief and the scene in the *Clouds*, in order to prove (what Socrates had already expressly said) that the latter represents an initiation, the interpreters ignore it entirely when it comes to deciding what sort of initiation is meant. Both give the same reason, the antecedent improbability of Eleusinian rites being publicly made fun of at Athens. It would 'scarcely have been tolerated by orthodox Athens'. (I wonder how much of Athens was orthodox in 423 B.C., and indeed what orthodoxy meant to an Athenian.) Miss Harrison admits that Aristophanes elsewhere parodies the Eleusinian mystics, but maintains that a direct parody of the actual ceremony of initiation would appear quite a different matter.   I do not see that we have the evidence to judge.   I certainly think it is a hit at those who go to Eleusis for initiation when Strepsiades' first reaction to the information that he is being initiated shows itself in the question, ' What shall I get out of it ? '   The argument of improbability is in itself not unlikely, but it is purely conjectural, and has to stand up against the visible resemblance between the scene under discussion and a representation of rites which beyond reasonable doubt are those of Eleusis.

Where then are the traces of Orphism which might make us change our minds ?   The garland which Strepsiades is made to put on is absent in the Eleusinian picture, but (apart from the fact that Strepsiades put it on before he covered up his head, and the Eleusinian initiate might have done the same) there is no evidence for connecting it specifically with Orphism.   Garlands were often put on for religious occasions.   Many cults had priests called *stephanephoroi*, and a vase-painting representing two *mystai* (so labelled by an inscription) confronted by a priest shows the *mystai* wearing chaplets.   It is impossible to say which mysteries the vase depicts.   (It is reproduced in Harrison, *Proleg.*[3] 157.)   The putting on of garlands was the final stage of initiation or ordination for hierophants and other priests (Theo Smyrn. *Mathem.* p. 15, Hiller, quoted *Proleg.*[3] 593).

The central argument for the rites being Orphic is the action of Socrates which calls forth from Strepsiades the protest that he is being ' dusted '.   The scholiast on the passage says, ' With these words Socrates rubs and knocks against each other pieces of *poros* stone, and collecting the fragments, pelts the old man with them '.   Strepsiades is sprinkled with the white dust got by rubbing and knocking two pieces of stone together.   In illustration of this, Dieterich cites first of all the passage of Demosthenes (*de corona* 259) from which we learn that in the rites of Sabazios the initiate was ' purified with clay '. With this he compares a part of the article in Harpocration on ἀπομάττων (literally ' wiping clean ', the same word as that used by Demosthenes which I have translated ' purifying ') :   ' Some give a more elaborate explanation, *viz.* putting a coat of clay or pitch around those who are being initiated, as we speak of coating a statue with clay (to take a cast).   For they used to smear the initiates with clay or pitch in imitation of the myth which is recounted by some, how the Titans made an attack on Dionysos all plastered with gypsum in order to disguise themselves.   This custom fell into disuse, but later they were plastered with clay by way of convention.'

The myth ' recounted by some ' is certainly the Orphic myth. Dieterich suggests that the worship of the Phrygian god Sabazios, which had reached Athens by the fifth century, influenced the rites of the Orphics.   They borrowed from it the smearing with plaster as part of the purification necessary for initiation, and later, in order to provide a reason for what was now their own practice, added to the story of Dionysos and the Titans the detail of the Titans' disguise. It is a disadvantage of this argument that part of the proof that the rites in question were Orphic consists in making the admission that they were borrowed by the Orphics from another religion which was simultaneously in vogue at Athens.   How, therefore, we are to tell which of the two was being parodied by Aristophanes, I cannot say.

It is certainly impressive to compare Socrates' hymn of invocation to the Clouds with some of those in the extant corpus of Orphic hymns.

There are striking resemblances in form (pointed out by Dieterich). One cannot help thinking, in particular, that the line containing the words ' Arise, appear to the thinker ' is taken from the concluding line of an actual hymn, with ' thinker ' substituted for *mystes*. Chaos and Aither, too, are invoked along with the Clouds, and these are principles at the beginning of the Orphic cosmogony.

The process of ceremonially seating the candidate for purification and initiation (*thronismos*) is common to various mysteries. We hear of it particularly in the orgies of the Korybantes and the Great Mother of Phrygia. (See Rohde, *Psyche*, Eng. tr. ch. 9, n. 19.) It was customary at Eleusis, and no doubt among the Orphics too. Suidas, incidentally, mentions *Thronismoi Metrooi* as the title of an Orphic poem (Kern, *test.* 223*d*).

We have seen, then, that the supposedly Orphic elements in this scene are not exclusively Orphic, although taking it as a whole, the theory that it parodies the Orphics is likely enough. Most likely of all is it that Aristophanes has heightened the farcical effect of his scene by mixing up different rites, as he mixed different cosmogonies in the parody of the *Birds*.

These comments have erred, no doubt, on the side of caution. My apologia would be, first that most investigations of the Orphics hitherto have erred, some of them badly, on the other side, and secondly that I have tried to state the evidence fairly before making any comment at all. I close with a general observation, in explanation and criticism of the attitude of Harrison and A. B. Cook towards the gold plates. I refer to the attitude of antecedent certainty that ' such formulae presuppose a definite ritual '. In so far as it rests on definite evidence, this feeling is based on a comparison with the formulas repeated by the Eleusinian initiate, which show striking parallelism in form to those on our gold plates and undoubtedly do constitute a recital of ritual acts duly performed. Here they are, as preserved by Clement (*Protr.* 2. 18) : ' I have fasted, I have drunk the *kykeon*, I have taken from the chest, I have put back into the basket and from the basket into the chest '. Now whatever the significance of these actions, no one could suggest that they were anything but part of a ritual. Phrases like ' I have passed out of the sorrowful wheel ' or ' I have passed with swift feet to the desired crown ' on the other hand do not at first sight suggest ritual, especially when we know that Orphic belief included the notion of life as a sorrowful wheel. But the question now before us is the general one of antecedent probability. Miss Harrison says (*Proleg.*[3] 156), ' It is significant of the whole attitude of Greek religion that the confession (*sc.* of the Eleusinian initiate) is not a confession of dogma or even faith, but an avowal of ritual acts performed. This is the measure of the gulf between ancient and modern. The Greeks in their greater wisdom saw that uniformity in ritual was desirable and possible ; they left a man practically free in the only sphere where freedom is of real importance, *i.e.* in the matter of thought.' These remarks are just and wise, in so far as they refer to the typical Hellenic religion. But Miss Harrison would have been the first to admit that the Orphic was far removed from the temper of the ordinary Hellene. In the eyes of the Greeks he was ' a dissenter and a prig ' (*Proleg.*[3] 516). Is it not in this that the difference chiefly consisted, that whereas to the ordinary Greek his creed was not a matter of great importance, to the Orphic it was the life and soul of his religion ?

2. Prayers for the dead as a feature of the Orphic religion.

It is commonly taken as proved that the Orphics believed it to be possible for those still living to secure, by prayer or the performance of initiatory or other ritual, an easier lot in the next world for their kinsmen who were already dead.* This if true is obviously highly important and interesting, both because the conception is unparalleled in ancient religion prior to Gnosticism and also for the striking parallel which it offers to the usage of the Christian Church. (See in particular 1 Cor. 15. 29.) It is therefore worth while pointing out what I believe to be true, namely that the evidence on the point, when examined, dwindles to something very small indeed, in fact to a single word of Plato which itself is open to more than one interpretation.

The evidence usually adduced consists of a fragment of Orphic poetry quoted by the Neoplatonist Olympiodoros, to which two sentences of Plato are supposed to give confirmation, proving that the belief goes back to the Orphism of the classical age. (Rohde, Psyche, Eng. tr. ch. 10, n. 66.) The words quoted by Olympiodoros are (O.F. 232) : ὄργιά τ' ἐκτελέσουσι, λύσιν προγόνων ἀθεμίστων μαιόμενοι. This is taken by e.g. Rohde and L. R. Farnell (Hero Cults, p. 381) to mean 'They shall perform mystic rites, seeking redemption for those of their forbears who have sinned'. I have already (pp. 83, 142 above) translated it in what I regard as the most natural way, namely 'yearning to be set free from their lawless ancestry', that is, from the pollution which is the result of their being born from the overweening Titans. (The Titans, incidentally, are addressed in Orph. Hymn 37 as ἡμετέρων πρόγονοι πατέρων.)

The words of Plato are from the passage describing the activities of the Orpheotelestai (Rep. 364b-365a). First comes the sentence : 'There are charlatans and soothsayers who frequent the doors of the rich and persuade them that they have at their command a grace vouchsafed from the gods, which works by means of sacrifices and incantations, if a man himself or one of his ancestors has committed any sin, to mend the matter in an atmosphere of pleasure and feasting. . . .' I see no reference here to rites carried out for the sake of the dead ancestor. It is his own lot which the rich man is persuaded he may better, whether it be his own sin or that of some ancestor that has brought trouble upon him. The Greeks were no strangers to the belief that the sins of the fathers might be visited on the children. Orestes might well pray that the sin of Pelops should be blotted out without thereby expressing any kindly interest in the present fortunes of his great-grandfather.

A little lower down we have this, the last bit of evidence for the practice : 'In this way they persuade not only individuals but cities that there are means of redemption and purification from sin through sacrifices and pleasant amusements, valid both for the living and for those who are already dead'. (εἰσι μὲν ἔτι ζῶσιν, εἰσι δὲ καὶ τελευτήσασιν.) This may mean that their clients by performing the proper ceremonies would secure redemption not only for themselves but also for any dead friends whom they would like to help, and may therefore be the only extant reference to an Orphic practice of prayers for the dead. On the other hand it may equally well mean that the instruction which they received now would stand them in good stead not only in this life

* See for instance A. Dieterich, der Untergang der antiken Religion, Kl. Schr. 478 f., and E. Norden, Aeneis VI, p. 7, n. 3.

but also when they died and arrived in the next world. We know from the gold plates that instructions on procedure were necessary to the soul on his arrival there. On this assumption the words might be translated ' means of redemption and purification from sin . . . which could be used both now in life and after death as well '. If this rendering, which I believe to be the more likely, is correct, the last shred of evidence for an Orphic belief in prayers for the dead has vanished.

NOTES TO CHAPTER VI

[1] The suggestion of R. Eisler (*Orpheus*, Leipzig, 1925, p. 131, n. 5) to read ἀρρήτοισι φόνοισι for the MSS. ἀκρήτοισι, is attractive, especially in view of σμύρνης τ' ἀκρήτου two lines above. Diels translates the MSS. reading *lauteres Stierblut*, which is pointless. Another suggestion is ' unmixed and so untempered, violent ' (F. M. Cornford in *Greek Religious Thought*, Dent, 1923, p. 70).

[2] Cp. the Orphic lines quoted by the Neoplatonists, *O.F.* 224 (translated above, chapter iv, app. 2). The doctrine which there reappears is thus clearly as old as the sixth or fifth centuries, even if the verbal form of the lines, by the time Proklos knew them, may owe something to the influence of Empedokles. If a doctrine is common to Plato, Empedokles and popular belief (as shown by the gold plates), and attributed to Pythagoras, it was obviously not the invention of either Plato or Empedokles, but a part of their common background. The argument that the ' Orpheus ' of the Neoplatonists is simply a copy of Empedokles or some other sixth- or fifth-century philosopher has little weight and is indeed practically meaningless.

[3] This notion of a past age in which sacrifices were bloodless is perhaps historically correct, a dim recollection of a state of things that once existed. Cp. the development of the Latin word *immolare* (commented on by C. Bailey, *Anc. Rom. Rel.*, Oxford, 1933, p. 83 ; cp. pp. 77 f.).

[4] The interpretation of the *sparagmos* vase which I have suggested above (chap. iv, app. 1) tends to the same conclusion, but I would emphasize once again that in using these pictorial sources of evidence for religious custom we are on very slippery ground.

[5] For hymns as a form of *telete* cp. also Proklos, Hymn 4, *v.* 4, Abel, *Orphica*, p. 280 (of the souls of men) : ὑμνῶν ἀρρήτοισι καθηραμένας τελετῇσι.

[6] For reff. to publications of this inscription, see Kern, *Orpheus*, p. 5, n. 2. It is described as archaic.

CHAPTER VII

ORPHEUS AND OTHER GREEK RELIGIOUS THINKERS

WITH the close of the previous chapter, the main task of this book has been completed. It is its primary aim, in view of the inclination of researchers to see Orphic influence in one religious or philosophical doctrine, and a source of Orphic teaching in another, simply to present a picture of what, so far as we know, the main features of the Orphic religion were, in the hope that those who interest themselves in ancient religion may find here a securer *a priori* basis for their inferences than has hitherto been available. The matter of the following sections will be treated much more briefly. They will consist largely of co-ordination and expansion of matter already present or implicit in the previous part of the work, and their intention is to serve as no more than an introduction, often only a tentative one, to those whose interest is primarily in interactions and influences.

The first thing that demands consideration is naturally the relation which existed between Orphics and Pythagoreans. A reference, say, to transmigration, to abstinence from flesh or other forms of *katharsis*, will frequently be found to be attributed by ancient authorities to both indifferently, and in modern times the epithet Orphico-Pythagorean is often found convenient as a description of these practices or beliefs. In the foregoing attempt to reconstruct an Orphic system, the fact that any given feature is also described as Pythagorean has not usually been noted, provided that it was independently attributable to Orpheus or his followers as well. It has certainly not been thought necessary to follow Wilamowitz in his latest phase and treat the mention of Orphics as irrelevant and the whole system as purely Pythagorean. (See *Der Glaube der Hellenen*, vol. 2, 1932, p. 199.)

Pythagoras lived and taught in the second half of the sixth century at Kroton, in that part of Italy which had already been Greek for nearly two centuries. To these parts tradition ascribed a number of the writers of Orphic poems, Orpheus of Kroton (who probably was older than Pythagoras ; cp. Kern, *Orpheus*, p. 3), Orpheus of Kamarina, Zopyros of Herakleia in Lucania, Brontinos of Metaponton, Kerkops and others. (See Kern, *testt.* 173 ff., 223.) Of these the last two at least were Pythagoreans, and Ion of Chios (fifth century) wrote that Pythagoras himself had composed writings under the name of Orpheus (Kern, *testt.* 222, 248). This gives some idea of the impossibility of disentangling the two systems from external evidence, which is equally unhelpful when we come to consider the related question of whether S. Italy and Sicily can claim to have been the original home of Orphism or whether it arose first at Athens.   The names of the Italians concerned point to the sixth century as the date of their activity, a date beyond which the existence of Orphism cannot be traced. But it is to the very same date that Orphic activity at Athens is also traceable, and indeed the leader of it, Onomakritos, is said according to the only evidence which we possess on the point to have been personally associated with the Orphics of the West. He was one of the committee appointed by Peisistratos to edit the text of Homer, and among his colleagues were Orpheus of Kroton and Zopyros of Herakleia (*test.* 189 ; the statement is from Tzetzes, but can be traced back on good grounds through Proklos to Asklepiades of Myrlea, a grammarian of the second century B.C.   See Kern, *Orph.* p. 3, n. 1).   Further colour is given to the idea that Athens is the home of Orphic writings by some lines in the *Rhesos* of Euripides.   The Muse who is mother of the slain Rhesos (and aunt, of course, of Orpheus) blames Athena for the death of her son, and adds to her reproaches by pointing out that she and her sisters have always been particular friends and benefactors of Athena's own city (941 ff.) : ' And yet thy city have we sister Muses honoured especially, and have used thy land as our own ; and the solemnities of the secret mysteries were revealed to thy people by Orpheus, own cousin to this man whom thou hast killed.'   (See also p. 126 above.)

Clearly the best hope of discovering something about the relations between the Orphics and the Pythagoreans lies in an examination of the two systems themselves.   First of all, what features had they in common ?   Both enjoined a certain way of living, instead of being simply an academic system of ideas or dogma.   If Plato in the *Laws* could describe the Orphic life, in the tenth book of the *Republic* he could mention the ' Pythagorean way of life ' (600*b*).   These ways of life were similar, *e.g.* the abstention from meat was the foremost requirement of both, and both proclaimed the same end, *katharsis* or the purification of the soul.   The notion of *katharsis* is dependent for the Orphics on the

14

belief in transmigration, the circle of birth, and the sharply dualistic conception of body and soul, according to which the former is no more than the tomb or prison of the latter. This doctrinal basis for their practice was accepted also by Pythagoras or his immediate followers.[1]

That is a large amount of common ground, and fully supports the suggestion of close relationship and interaction which is given by the external evidence. But there are differences too. First of all, where the Pythagoreans are in question, we hear little or nothing of Dionysos or Bakchos. The god of Pythagoras was Apollo. By the sixth century of course these gods were not enemies. They were living reconciled at Delphi, the centre of Apollo's worship, and the Orphic story itself told how, after the outrage of the Titans against Dionysos, it was Apollo who, at the command of Zeus, gathered up the remains of the divine child and took them to his own shrine. According to the legend of Aeschylus' play, Orpheus himself, in an earlier age when the two gods were still at enmity, incurred the wrath of Dionysos by deserting him for Apollo. In general, he appears in story as a more Apolline figure, and the Orphics must have liked to make out that the reconciliation of the two gods had been due in part to the influence of Orpheus in modifying the religion of Dionysos in that direction and so rendering it more suitable for acceptance by his brother-god. The difference then is not a contradiction, and would not prevent the Pythagoreans from accepting, or even (as it seems they did) originating, much of the Orphic dogma. It is, however, sufficient to keep the two distinct, fraternal but not identical. One might compare the position, in a country where the cult of saints is very strongly developed, of two cities which both accept the body of Christian dogma but have a different patron saint.

More important is the fact that Pythagoreanism was a philosophy as well as a religion. In its theory of the human soul, and its precepts for right living, it may have been identical with Orphism, but the same cannot be said of its cosmogony. The Orphic cosmogony is mythical, expressed in terms of personal agents, of marriage and procreation. The world of Pythagoras is of divine origin, but he sought for a rational, and in particular a mathematical explanation of it. Pythagoras was the discoverer of mathematics, and, like many pioneers in a new world of thought, believed that in his own discovery lay the clue to all reality alike. Consequently his cosmogony was expressed in terms of numerical ratios, of the Tetraktys and the generation of numbers from the primal Monad. The Orphics did not talk like this. That the two systems are in many ways parallel is a striking and important fact. Although the parallelism cannot be worked out exactly, since the translation into mathematical and philosophical terms naturally involved some alteration in the ideas also, yet in many respects the one is the mythical counterpart of the other. The inference would be unmistakable, even if it were otherwise unsupported, that Pythagoras was working on a mythical background. This has been said of the Milesian school too, but we can be sure that Pythagoras was not, like them, only unconsciously influenced by a mythological background which in his own mind he had rejected as false, but was deliberately trying to account rationally for beliefs which he believed to be true in essence, although their expression might be dismissed as purely mythical. It is not only that single principles in the Pythagorean universe can be identified with their counterparts in the Orphic system (*e.g.* the primal Monad with the World-egg), but more important still, the Pythagorean cosmogony is permeated with the idea of a moral dualism which forms the basis of the Orphic religion. The world is a mixture of the principles of form, limit, light, etc., with those of the formless, the unlimited, darkness ; and of these the former series are all good, the latter evil. In so far as the universe is good, it is because it exhibits harmony and order, and the study of ' physics ' has a moral end in view, since the contemplation of the harmony and order of the universe leads to the implanting of a similar harmony and order in the individual soul. It needs no explanation that the holders of theories like these believed the Orphic stories of the birth of the world from chaos, and of the mingled good and bad in human nature, to contain lessons that were both true and edifying. We need not wonder any longer that they were active missionaries in the Orphic cause, nor on the other hand lose sight of the fact that they had their own, distinctively Pythagorean theories as well. Pythagoras then had both an intellectual and a mystical side to his teaching, but it was natural that among those who were attracted to his school there would be some whose interest was mainly mathematical and others to whom the religious side made the strongest appeal, and room would be found for both. These were different types, and it is not surprising to hear that according to tradition a split occurred within the school between the *Mathematikoi*, or intellectual party, whose interest was centred in the number-doctrine, and the *Akusmatikoi*, so-called from the *akusmata* or secret religious lore of Pythagoras, who clung rather to the mystical religious side of the movement.

There was indeed good reason for Pythagoras and his followers to revere the greatest musician of legend, who by the tunefulness of his lyre had tamed all nature and brought the wildest beasts to gentleness, and to consider him the author of their faith. It was experiments in music which had led Pythagoras to the understanding of numerical ratios and hence to the foundation of mathematical science, and, partly at least for that reason, music always held a dominating and mysterious position in Pythagorean beliefs. The universe was described not simply as an order, an observance of due proportions, but as a *harmonia*, a ' being in tune '. This was no metaphor, as the theory of the ' music of the spheres ' bears witness. Since the human soul must strive to imitate the orderliness of the universe, its aim too is described as *harmonia*, and it was only natural therefore that, as we learn, music was considered to have virtue in the healing of sick souls. Small wonder that Pythagoras numbered Orpheus among the chief of his patrons.[2] One might have expected his followers to let themselves be known as Orphics simply and solely, but there were two good reasons why they should not. First, there were undoubtedly Orphics who were not Pythagoreans, and though some no doubt would have brought nothing but credit on the brotherhood, there were others who put the name of Orpheus to less respectable uses. Secondly, the fact that their real founder was one of the most original geniuses of all time did not make for the obscuring of his name by that of a figure of earlier legend, however potent. Instead, he became a figure of legend himself. Men said that he was the son of Apollo, or Apollo in human form, that he had a golden thigh, that he had descended into Hades. Pythagoras himself may have liked to be known as a follower of Orpheus ; his disciples wanted nothing better than to be called followers of Pythagoras.

After what has been said, the difficulty of deciding whether Orphism or Pythagoreanism came first needs no further emphasis. It nevertheless seems most likely from the character of the two systems, and in particular from the fact that Pythagoreanism takes up Orphism into itself but has as well an intellectual system to reinforce it, that Orphic dogma was already formulated, at least in its main outlines, when Pythagoras founded his brotherhood. Those who formulated it were themselves no thoughtless primitive minds. They were consciously trying to solve the same problem as Pythagoras—the generation of the many out of the One. But to the present writer at least the most natural assumption seems to be that Pythagoras had the mythological solution before him, and, realizing its religious value but impressed by the claims of the intellect as well, evolved as a complementary scheme his mathematical conception of reality. The two are nearer together than they seem at first sight, and although the one may be a little in advance of the other, they belong undoubtedly to the same mental age—the age of the first stirrings of intellectual curiosity about the origins and nature of the universe.

Contemporary with the beginnings of Pythagoreanism, the same curiosity was being reflected in a different way by the Milesian or Ionian school. Now in trying to satisfy this curiosity, every Greek, were he Orphic *theologos*, Pythagorean mathematician or Ionian physicist, made the same fundamental assumption, the assumption that there must be a unity somewhere behind or beneath the manifold phenomena of the world. Thus the problem of the origin of the world presented itself to them all in the same form, namely, what was the nature of this primal or underlying unity and by what sort of process did it multiply itself in order to produce the multiplicity of gods, men and nature? ' How can all things be one and yet each one separate?' It was the question of the Orphic Zeus and it was the question of the age. The Orphics wanted an answer chiefly that they might have a religious faith to live by, and were content with an explanation which, though elaborate and sophisticated, remained mythological. The Pythagoreans, who themselves demanded of philosophy that it should be a rule of life, revered this explanation but added that it was the divine revelation of something which could be made intelligible to human minds as an abstract, mathematical conception. Their peculiar answer was in terms of the primal Monad, not itself a number but above and behind all number. It generated the odd and the even and the whole series of numbers, and from them came the physical world. Even when we allow for their geometrical conception of arithmetic, making easy the transition in thought from abstract number to solid body,* this yet seems to us, with its absence of all attempt at mechanical explanation, the answer of a mystic rather than of a physical philosopher.

Thirdly, there are the Ionians. Putting the question in the same form, they steadfastly rejected the answers both of mythology and of purely abstract reasoning, and were the first to seek an explanation from the nature of the physical world itself. Everyone knows their conclusion, that the seeming variety of the physical world is no more than a series of different states or manifestations of one single, primary, underlying physical substance. Their attention therefore was directed solely towards

* 1 = point, 2 = line, 3 = first plane figure (triangle), 4 = first solid (triangular pyramid), and so on.

discovering what this underlying substance was, and by what process it had come to manifest itself in the diversity of forms in which we now behold it. (It was left for the next century to question whether our senses might not be deceived.) Thales said that it was water, and anything else which he may have had to say on the subject is lost to us. Of Anaximander we know more, and though this is not the time to go into his system in detail a few points must be mentioned. He said, reasonably enough, that the underlying substance could not be any of the four ' simple bodies ' of the developed world (earth, air, fire or water), but must be something different, from which they had all evolved. This other something he called The Unlimited, and supposed it to be an undifferentiated mass, in which the qualities of sensible bodies existed as it were potentially, or in a state of complete fusion and hence neutrality. In this state were all things at first, and with this all space was filled. When it came to explaining how the manifold world began, Anaximander supposed the existence somewhere in the primeval Unlimited of a nucleus or seed (*gonimon, i.e.* generative), which contained the ' opposites ' (the hot and the cold, the wet and the dry) in a state of incomplete fusion and becoming more and more completely separated. From this beginning come in the end earth and sea, sky and heavenly bodies. Finally, by a continuation of the same process of the ' separation of opposites ' (in this case it is the effect of the hot sun on moist slime), living creatures are evolved. What it was that first started the separating motion in the Unlimited the fragments do not make clear, and it is unlikely that Anaximander himself had thought of inquiring after a first cause of motion. The distinction between inanimate matter and life was not yet formulated, and the first physicists thought of their primary substance as alive, in the sense chiefly of being able to initiate its own motion. (It was probably conscious too, and the Ionians called it God. More than motion and consciousness the name can scarcely have implied.)

The intention in thus stating the chief points of Anaximander's cosmogony has been to lead up to the view (notably represented by Professor Cornford) that in spite of their efforts to put forward a purely scientific scheme, the speculations of the Ionians were unconsciously conditioned and moulded by the pre-existing mythological solutions of the same problem. We are first set on this track by a fragment of Anaximander in which he (*a*) shows himself familiar with the belief that the process of birth and decay is a circular one, and (*b*) lapses into mythological expression in his formulation of it : ' Things of necessity are resolved at death into the same elements out of which they had their birth ; for they do justice and make recompense to one another according to the ordinances of time '. (Diels-Kranz,[5] fr. 1, p. 89, printed by Kern, *O.F.* 23, *ad fin.*) However much or little significance one may attach to the introduction of justice as a cosmic principle, and the at least semi-personification of time (Justice was a great goddess according to Orpheus, and shared the throne of Zeus ; this is taken by *O.F.* 23 back to the fourth century ; see p. 233 below), it must be conceded that both the thought and the phraseology of this passage are striking enough to start a certain train of thought.

We come next to the parallelism exhibited between the physical scheme of Anaximander and the mythological cosmogony of the Orphics. It is difficult to work this out exactly, owing to the doubtful nature of our information about the earliest form of the latter, but what we have had to say about it has made it likely that the earlier form of the cosmogony was that which more closely resembled Anaximander's. If we may take it that according to the earliest version Night came first and laid the egg from which sprang Eros-Phanes, as in the cosmogony of Aristophanes' *Birds* (a conclusion which has been shown to be probable, above, pp. 102 ff.), then a parallelism can be found between the scheme of the *theologos* and that of the natural philosopher as exact as the following table represents it :

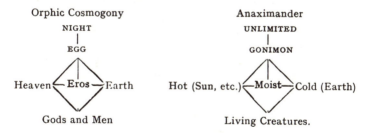

Orphic Cosmogony		Anaximander
NIGHT		UNLIMITED
EGG		GONIMON
Heaven ← Eros → Earth		Hot (Sun, etc.) ← Moist → Cold (Earth)
Gods and Men		Living Creatures.

This assumes a version of the Orphic theogony like that preserved by Athenagoras (above, p. 79), according to which the two halves of the egg from which Eros sprang went to make Heaven and Earth. The parallel is in other ways so striking that it is perhaps permissible to bring the argument full circle and infer from Anaximander that this sentence in Athenagoras does preserve a fragment of the oldest stratum of the theogony. In the mythical story Love was necessary to serve as the principle of union and bring about the marriage of Heaven and Earth and the rest and render possible the birth of the younger gods and of men. In

Anaximander the power of generation is supposed to lie in the moist, which is midway between the hot and the cold, and the moist thus serves for the philosopher the same purpose of mediation as Love for the *theologos*.

These examples are, I think, sufficient to show what an indelible impression was made, even on the most original and open-minded thinkers, by the mythical cosmogonies which were constructed in the name of Orpheus probably at the beginning of the sixth century. These cosmogonies doubtless represented the first conscious attack upon the problem of the One and the Many. This problem obsessed every Greek philosopher, and the earliest mythical solution of it died harder than the Greeks themselves realized. But it is not on that note that even this brief and partial discussion of Ionian philosophy should end. Resemblances have shown that its thought was unconsciously moulded by its predecessors, but what excites our admiration is nevertheless the truly remarkable extent to which, in a myth-ridden world, these early thinkers succeeded in casting off mythical expression and speaking in the language of science. It was in reaction against the mythologists that they put forward their own systems, and in spite of what has been said, the reaction was astonishingly successful. To understand the achievement of Anaximander, we must not dwell on what his Unlimited or his *Gonimon* may owe to the Orphic Night or Chaos or cosmic egg, but rather remember certain points of detail, as for example this about the generation of animals: ' Living creatures arose from the moist element as it was evaporated by the sun. Man was like another animal, namely, a fish, in the beginning. . . . The first animals were produced in the moisture, each enclosed in a prickly bark. . . . Further, he says that originally man was born from animals of another species. His reason is that while other animals quickly find food for themselves, man alone requires a lengthy period of suckling. Hence, had he originally been as he is now, he would never have survived ' (trans. J. Burnet).

When we turn to the next in the succession of Greek thinkers,
✱ Herakleitos of Ephesos, known even to his ancient commentators as The Dark Philosopher, we find that in recent years one determined attempt has been made to interpret his beliefs as built entirely on an Orphic foundation. It is that of V. Macchioro.[3] Since our knowledge of the Dark One is very fragmentary, it is difficult to give a coherent picture of him at all. I shall, however, try, first of all, to present very briefly the more usual view of the philosopher and a few of his most characteristic doctrines, and then to place Macchioro's version beside it, inserting in parenthesis

the fragments on which each statement is chiefly based. It should
then be possible to add a few general probabilities.

Herakleitos is usually pictured as a haughty and solitary
genius, who despised the work of all previous thinkers as well as
the understanding of the common man. ('Though this Word is
true evermore, yet men are as unable to understand it when they
hear it for the first time as before they have heard it at all. . . .
Other men know not what they are doing when they are awake,
even as they forget what they do in sleep', fr. 2, Bywater. In
trying to reproduce the more orthodox view of H., I give Burnet's
translation of the fragments. Cp. 'I searched myself', or 'I
have sought for myself', fr. 80, and 'The learning of many things
teacheth not understanding, else would it have taught Hesiod
and Pythagoras, and again Xenophanes and Hekataios', 'fr. 16.)
In particular he set himself against Pythagoras. ('Pythagoras
practised inquiry beyond all other men, and choosing out these
writings, claimed for his own wisdom what was but a knowledge
of many things and an art of mischief', fr. 17.) This opposition
is borne out by his own positive beliefs, the essence of which is
expressed in the sentences : 'Men do not know that what is at
variance agrees with itself. It is an attunement of opposite tensions, like that of the bow and the lyre' (fr. 45) ; 'Strife is justice,
and all things come into being and pass away through strife'
(fr. 62) ; 'War is the father of all and the king of all' (fr. 45) ;
'It is sickness that makes health pleasant, evil good, hunger
plenty, weariness rest' (fr. 104). The gist of these fragments is
that the Pythagorean ideal of a 'harmonious' world is wrong,
since it means a world all goodness, all health, all plenty. To
desire this is to desire a static and therefore a deathlike state
(cp. fr. 43). Things are not only appreciated, but thrive and exist,
simply in so far as their opposites also exist. The true harmony
is a balance or tension of opposites. The encroachment of the
elements on each other, fire swallowing up water and water
quenching fire, is not, as Anaximander said, an injustice. It is
right and just, being in fact what keeps the world alive ; for, to
pass to another cardinal doctrine, all things are flowing, and
nothing remains the same for two instants together. It is because
the world is ever-changing that it can live. 'Fire lives the death
of air, and air lives the death of fire ; water lives the death of
earth, earth that of water' (fr. 25). This everlasting process is
called the 'way up and down' (fr. 69). Herakleitos also says that
the world 'was ever, is now, and ever shall be an ever-living fire'
(fr. 20). The commonest interpretation of this is that he chose
fire, not so much as primary substance in the Ionian sense (there

could not be such a basic substance, since everything was constantly changing), but as a symbol of the ever-changing universe. A flame may look steady and be regarded as a constant thing, but in reality it is ever-moving and ever-changing.

On the human soul we have only one or two obscure fragments. Like everything else it is subject to the ' way up and down ', and so is liable to be encroached on by each of the elements in turn : but we may take it that its real nature is akin to fire (the warm and dry), and that death is due to the encroachment of the cold and wet ('It is death to souls to become water ', fr. 68 ; ' The dry soul is the wisest and best ', fr. 74). But since there is no such thing as actual extinction, because the condition of all things must continue to alternate on the upward and downward path, therefore ' it is the same thing in us that is quick and dead, awake and asleep, young and old ; the former are shifted and become the latter, and the latter in turn are shifted and become the former ' (fr. 78).

Finally it is said that, as might be expected from his contemptuous and exclusive character, he particularly despised mystery-religions and the orgiastic worship of Dionysos. By those who believe this, the relevant fragments are translated thus : ' Night-walkers, magians, priests of Bakchos and priestesses of the wine-vat, mystery-mongers ' (124) ; ' The mysteries practised among men are unholy mysteries ' (125) ; ' For if it were not to Dionysos that they made a procession and sang the shameful phallic hymn, they would be acting most shamefully.[4] But Hades is the same as Dionysos, in whose honour they go mad and keep the feast of the wine-vat ' (127).

There seems little here to support the theory that Herakleitos was an Orphic. He censured Pythagoras, and despised mystery-religions. His own central doctrine is highly individual, and if he seems to hint at a cycle of life, saying that dead souls come to life again just as surely as live souls die, and even that ' all the things we see when awake are death ' (fr. 64), that is simply a logical consequence of the central doctrine and need not be explained in any other way. Let us see what Macchioro says on the other side.

First comes an appraisal of the evidence. Our richest source of information on the content of Herakleitos' writing is the work of the Christian apologist Hippolytos called *A Refutation of All Heresies*. The method of refutation which he employs is to demonstrate that these heretical teachers, who call themselves followers of Christ, are in reality only reproducing the doctrines of the pagan philosophers. Following this method, when he comes to the teaching of Noetos (bk. 9, chh. 7 ff.) he compares it with the philosophy of Herakleitos, to demonstrate that the two are the same : ' that they (the Noetians) may be clearly shown that they are not as they think disciples of Christ, but of the Dark One '. Macchioro argues that Hippolytos had no mere Stoic or other compilation of extracts before him, but the actual work of Herakleitos, and moreover that all his quotations are taken from a single chapter or section of that work, which may therefore be to a certain extent reconstructed, and into which, as Hippolytos says himself, Herakleitos put ' all his real meaning '.   M.'s arguments on this point are clear and persuasive, and leave no room for reasonable doubt.   We must then take the comments of Hippolytos on his quotations as seriously as that fact warrants, and it is at least reasonable to suppose that there did in fact exist a resemblance between the heresy of Noetos and the philosophy of Herakleitos.   As M. points out, had it really been the Stoic philosophy, with its own adaptations of Herakleitos, which the heresy resembled, there would have been no temptation for the apologist to ascribe the resemblance to Herakleitos, since either would have served his purpose equally well by demonstrating the pagan origin of the heresy.   What then was the central doctrine of Noetos, to which the orthodox took exception ?   It was the identity of the Father and the Son, with as its logical consequence the attribution to the Father of the passion of the Son.   We look then in the words of Herakleitos for something which either was, or could be made to seem, identical with this doctrine.

This M. finds, as Hippolytos found it, in the identification of opposites.   It is in fact in this doctrine and its consequences that the case for an Orphic background to Herakleitos is primarily rooted.   Among the opposites identified by Herakleitos are mortal and immortal, created and eternal, and, according to Hippolytos, father and son.   On this last he says confidently, ' Everyone knows that he said the Father and the Son are the same '.   It was necessary for Hippolytos' argument that Herakleitos should have said that the Father and the Son were the same, and that this Son should have been of such a nature that he could mistakenly have been identified with Christ.   Now, says M., it is easy to give him a name, since there is only one myth in all Greek mythology and theology which complies with these two requirements, the myth of the Orphic Dionysos (M. calls him Zagreus), born of Zeus and Kore, torn by the Titans, and brought to life again by Zeus.   This he supports by reference to another fragment, a strange sentence which had certainly not been satisfactorily explained by others: [5] ' Aion (Age or Eternity) is a child playing draughts ; the kingdom is the child's '. In Christian and Neo-platonic writers can be found the identification of Aion with Dionysos, and in the mention of draughts M. sees a reference to the playing of Dionysos when he was surprised by the Titans. (He would actually identify draughts, *pessoi*, with dice, *astragaloi*, which is certainly wrong.) The meaning of the last clause then follows naturally, since in the Orphic story the kingdom was given to the child Dionysos by his father Zeus. The weakness of this is that the identification of Dionysos with Aion is not only un-attested before the Christian era but savours strongly of the peculiar allegorical syncretism of that age ; yet it is likely that Orphism from an early date owed much to the Persian worship of Zrvān (Aion to the Greeks), in the form of an assimilation to him either of their own Chronos or of Phanes-Dionysos. See pp. 86 ff. above, and 254 below.

The identity of opposites, in this case of life and death, is also made by M. a proof of the presence in Herakleitos of the Orphic doctrine of palingenesis. In using Hippolytos here we must be careful to distinguish between the actual words quoted from Herakleitos and the apologist's commentary on them. Hippolytos introduces a fragment with the words : ' He speaks also of the resurrection of this visible flesh in which we are born, and recognizes God as the author of this resurrection, in the words. . . .' This may well be a subjective interpretation of the apologist, but even if it were correct it would argue a real 'anti-cipation of Christian rather than a reproduction of Orphic doctrine. In any case, the only relevant fragments of the philosopher him-self are brief, and fully support his reputation for obscurity : ' Immortal mortals, mortal immortals, living the death of the one, dying the life of the other ' (fr. 67), and ' for the one who is there (?) they rise up and become wakeful guardians of the quick and the dead ' (fr. 123). The latter seems to me incapable of certain inter-pretation without its context, and the former to be a general state-ment of the cosmic law of change ; cp. ' fire lives the death of air ', etc., above. M., however, takes immortal mortals to be human beings, who are partly divine and may finally become ' gods in-stead of mortals ', and mortal immortals to refer to Dionysos, who though a god was killed by the Titans. That is strained, but a passage of Sextus Empiricus quoted by M. is certainly striking (*Pyrrh. Hyp.* 3. 230, M., p. 103, n. 1) : ' Herakleitos says that both life and death are in both our living and our dying ; for when we live our souls are dead and buried in us, but when we die our souls revive and live.' Following this, M. claims that Herakleitos' whole doctrine of the identity of opposites has its origin in the Orphic doctrine, which, holding that the body was but the tomb of the soul, said that life was death and death life. In the first place, however, it is uncertain whether Herakleitos said all that Sextus attributed to him, or whether the latter half of the statement is an unwarranted interpretation of Sextus himself ; and in the second place, the Orphic doctrine would be in reality an unsound foundation for Herakleitos' theory that opposites were identical, since what it taught was not that death and life are the same, but only that we have got them the wrong way round : what we think is life is in fact death, and vice versa. The two remain as distinct as they ever were. The words of Euripides, ' Who knows if life be death, and death be thought life in the other world ' are nearer to the Orphic conception, and have a very different meaning from Herakleitos' ' The living and the dead are the same ' (fr. 78).

Those passages make the strongest arguments for palingenesis. Herakleitos also said : ' Man kindles for himself a light in the night when he has died ', which without its context might mean anything, including palingenesis as M. holds, and ' when men die there awaits them what they do not expect or think ', which could certainly be explained on the current interpretation of his philosophy.

Interesting are M.'s remarks on the simile of the bow and the lyre, and even if they are not thought to prove his case, they deserve attention as serious arguments for an alternative to previous interpretations. In this simile, he argues, Herakleitos is not illustrating the necessity for the simultaneous existence of opposites, but the *succession* of opposite states in the same thing. The point of the simile has usually been supposed to lie in the fact that at the moment when the bow is being drawn, the two hands must pull in opposite directions at the same time. In accordance with this, the simile has been most commonly interpreted by means of the bow, the lyre being rather hurriedly passed over, because in fact the action of playing the lyre is not the same.[6] In order to give a sense which will apply equally well to both bow and lyre, M. would interpret it of the alternate stretching and letting go of the string. Both are necessary if the arrow is to be dispatched or the musical note sounded, and so in the world there must be an alternation of opposite states. When, however, he considers this evidence for a belief in the Orphic wheel of birth, he is on less secure ground, and even if he has found the correct interpretation of the simile, it remains un-doubted from the other fragments that Herakleitos did believe also in the necessity for the simultaneous existence of opposites if the world was to be kept alive.   The two beliefs were complementary in his system, (a) that everything was constantly changing, so that that which now was hot and dry must in time become cold and wet, and in course of time hot and dry again, and (b) that at any one moment there must exist some things which were hot and dry, and others which were cold and wet.   If M.'s inter-pretation of the simile is to replace the other, it will only mean that the simile was intended as an illustration of (a) instead of, as was previously thought, (b).   The sum of Herakleitos' beliefs remains the same.   Finally, Herakleitos said that good and evil were one, and that can be quite naturally interpreted as the logical consequence, expressed in paradoxical form, of the doctrines (a) and (b) above ; but it would be a very strange thing for an Orphic to have said.

It remains for M. to account for those fragments which have been universally taken as showing that Herakleitos condemned mystery-religions, and the rites of Dionysos in particular.   His view is that the condemnation is only directed against the mechanical conception of purification, insisting simply that true purification must be from within.   Here again he has done good service in showing up the undoubtedly tendentious character of previous translations.   Burnet's ' mystery-mongers ' for the Greek *mystai* may be cited as an extreme example.   M.'s view finds its best support in a passage of Iamblichos (*de myst.* 5. 15, included by Bywater as fr. 128, but omitted by Burnet in *Early Gk. Phil.*[3]) : ' I distinguish two kinds of sacrifice, first those of the completely purified, such as one gets here and there with a single individual, as Herakleitos says, or with a few men easily numbered, and secondly the material . . . such as befit those who are still in the grip of the body '.   In the same sense M. interprets fr. 125 : ' The mysteries practised among men are unholy mysteries '. Herakleitos is not, we must suppose, condemning the mysteries themselves, any more than Paul would be condemning the com-munion rite by rebuking men for eating and drinking the elements to their own damnation.   Fr. 127 yields the same lesson.   The processions and phallic hymns *would be* shameful, were it not for the meaning behind them . . . but Hades and Dionysos are the same, *i.e.* there is a mystic lesson in it all. (The chthonian character of Dionysos was of course a feature of Orphic belief.)   M. has certainly shown us that, were his theories proved on other grounds, these fragments in themselves could give no valid reasons for disbelief.   But although he himself has no doubts, the slightness of his positive evidence must always prove a stumbling-block to

others, and as I have tried to show, the theory that the identity
of opposites is a conclusion based on the Orphic *soma-sema*
doctrine, is illogical and unlikely.   Arguments against it might be,
and have been, multiplied.   How for instance is the Heraclitean
theory of universal flux to be reconciled with the strongly marked
individualism necessary for a belief in transmigration, punishment
after death, final blessedness and so forth ? [7]

The great Parmenides need not detain us long.   All students ✷
of Greek philosophy know that the challenge which his acute logic
threw down necessarily made a turning-point in its history, and in
that achievement he is not likely to have been indebted to anything but his own original genius.   In all probability he started
life as a Pythagorean, but he grew up to put the speculations of
his teachers, as of all his predecessors, out of court for confusing,
as it has . been well expressed recently, ' the starting-point of
becoming with the permanent ground of being '.   Familiar he
would naturally be with Pythagorean and with Orphic beliefs, and
we need not be surprised to find that, as has been argued, his
language contains expressions which had their origin in the
Orphic writings.   This is the more reasonable because, following
the fashion of the day, he put forth his views in a poem, whose
introduction gave them a mythical setting, claiming that the
truths which he was about to set down had been revealed to him
by a goddess.   The parallels are interesting, but are not, of course,
evidence for an influence on his thought. [8]

There is no need to discuss here the position of Empedokles,
since in using him earlier (chapter v) as a source of Orphic
doctrine, it emerged clearly that he himself held firmly to the ✷
beliefs of which he was writing.   Empedokles is a curious, and
yet a complete character, one who could scarcely have been
produced by any age but his own.   There was much in him of the
Orpheotelestes, for instance his belief that the knowledge which he
possessed was the key to a magical control over the forces of
nature.   He was also, tradition says, something of a *poseur* in
externals, and had a lively appreciation of sacerdotal pomp and
impressiveness.   At the same time, the fragments of the *Katharmoi* show that he had both a knowledge of the real Orphic beliefs
and an inward feeling for their truth, and was capable of a high
degree of mystical experience.   Besides all this, he takes his place
in the philosophical succession as one of the moulders of pre-
Socratic Greek thought, and was indeed the first to tackle the
difficulties raised by Parmenides and to construct a system which

should ' save the phenomena ', taking account of Parmenides' propositions but escaping his distasteful conclusion that the evidence of sense-perception was completely out of touch with reality. With that side of his thought we are not concerned here, but may allow ourselves to remark that there is no longer any ground for believing that Empedokles kept his religion and his science in water-tight compartments, preaching Orphism in his religious poem, and in his cosmogony a physical system which excluded the possibility of an immortal soul. This suspicion of a state of affairs more comprehensible in nineteenth-century England than fifth-century Greece has now been effectively dispelled.[9]

There is no trace of Orphic doctrine in Anaxagoras, the next of the great philosophers to set up a physical system in opposition to the abstract logic of Parmenides. He has been classed by Kern as a thinker ' a quo Rhapsodiae respectae esse videntur ' (de theogg. 52 f.), solely on the strength of his having thought the moon to be inhabited. With this belief Kern compares the Orphic fragment quoted by Proklos (O.F. 91, above p. 138). If it is true that Anaxagoras thought the moon to be inhabited, the connexion can nevertheless hardly be said to be proved, and the juxtaposition of the statement with the Orphic lines, as if no further proof were required, is an example of that kind of criticism which fails by neglecting to take into account what we know of the whole mental character of a thinker, and so brings into disrepute the whole case for the early date of the Rhapsodic Theogony by making it seem dependent on arguments of an arbitrary and mechanical nature. Anaxagoras' use of the Rhapsodic Theogony could not be argued from the mere coincidence that he said that the moon was inhabited and the Rhapsodies spoke of it as having ' many cities and many mansions '. It could not, because for anyone who is familiar with Anaxagoras' type of mind, it has to stand up against the fact that he was perhaps the most truly scientific of all the pre-Socratic philosophers, one capable of combining deep thought with experimental methods, and, so far as one can see, quite uninfluenced by religious preconceptions. This would be true, even if he did say that there were men on the moon ; but it is far from certain whether he ever did, since not only is the evidence on the point ambiguous but the statement is hard to reconcile with the rest of what we know about his physical theories.[10]

Turning from the philosophers to the poets, we find Aeschylus [11] keenly interested in the legends of Orpheus himself, and choosing his fate to be the theme of a tragedy, the Bassarids, in which it is

used as a vehicle for portraying the early conflict between Dionysiac and Apolline religion (p. 32 above).   This play was a piece of
religious history, for by the time of Aeschylus the two were
reconciled, and shared in turn the homage of worshippers at
Delphi.   Orpheus appears as the champion of Apollo, which
doubtless he originally was.   The time at which the Orphic
theologians set to work was, I take it, when the two had become,
or were in process of becoming, reconciled.   These writers, wishing
to teach an esoteric form of the Dionysiac religion which was to
have many peculiar features, chose Orpheus as their patron, the
one-time servant of Apollo, who like his master might be considered as reconciled, though not identified, with his former
enemy.   Among themselves, as I have already suggested, they
would possibly like to have the actual reconciliation attributed to
this character of peace and gentleness, but that it was so attributed in general, or that the Orphics had any great share in
bringing the reconciliation about, is unlikely, since the blending
and assimilating of the two cults was a great, widespread and
popular movement, whereas all that we know of the Orphics
suggests that their religion was the work of a few, and made too
high demands on intellect, spirit and body, to spread far beyond
the few in its effects.

To return to Aeschylus, our information about the contents of
the *Bassarids* is plain enough evidence that he took a lively interest
in the legends of Orpheus, and no doubt this was partly because
he himself felt something of the spell which this magic figure has
in all ages been able to cast.   He introduces him again by way of
a simile in the *Agamemnon* (1629 f.), where a disgruntled Aigisthos
tells the chorus that their taunts have just the opposite effect
to the singing of Orpheus, who ' drew all things by the sweetness
of his voice '.   But was Aeschylus interested, not only in the
legends of Orpheus, but in the religion of the Orphics ?   In support
of this have been cited the occasional mentions in his poetry of
the goddesses Ananke (*P.V.* 105, Kern, *de theogg.* 45), Adrasteia
(*P.V.* 936, ·Kern, *ib.*), and Dike daughter of Zeus (*Septem* 662,
Cho. 949 ; cp. *Ag.* 383, *Cho.* 244, *Eum.* 539, etc.   There are also
many other passages where it is hard to say how far Dike is personified).   These powers, two of them simple personifications
(Necessity and Justice), were great figures in the Orphic theogony
used by the Neoplatonists, and Dike in particular seems to have
been raised to a position of supreme importance by the Orphic
theologians.   Compare a passage in the speech against Aristogeiton attributed to Demosthenes (25. 11 = *O.F.* 23) : ' Inexorable
and awful Justice, whom Orpheus the revealer to us of the most

15

holy mysteries spoke of as sitting by the throne of Zeus and beholding all the affairs of mortals '.[12] No doubt Aeschylus knew the Orphic writings, as did Sophocles when he wrote (*O.C.* 1381 f.) of ' ancient Dike, who shares the seat of Zeus '.

There is a strange sentence in Cicero, which is not supported by any information as to its source or the thought which prompted it.* It speaks of Aeschylus as ' non poeta solum, sed etiam Pythagoreus ; sic enim accepimus '. If Aeschylus was a Pythagorean, tradition has, except for this remark of Cicero's, been silent on the point. He certainly had intercourse with those of the West, for he travelled to Sicily and in fact died at Gela. He would not miss the opportunity of meeting and conversing with members of the leading school of Western religious thought, especially since the same fundamental problem occupied his and their minds alike, the problem namely of individual free-will and responsibility for sin. The Pythagorean was a school which trained many a great mind to think for itself, and the epithet need by no means imply a lifelong adherence to its doctrines. One has only to mention the names of Parmenides and Plato. Aeschylus had his own approach to the problem of sin and punishment. Sin is a curse which runs in families. The sins of the fathers are visited on the children, and this is meant in a literal sense. It is not simply that future generations of the human race must pay for what has been done in the past, but that what my grandfather did affected my father's life and conduct, and this in turn has at least to some extent predetermined mine. It is the curse of the House that makes an Aeschylean tragedy, and the shadow of guilt that overhangs it is the guilt of shedding the blood of a kinsman, husband or father or daughter. Klytaimnestra murders Agamemnon that she may enjoy her paramour, but seeks to justify her deed in the eyes of others, and indeed justifies it in her own eyes, by pointing to his sacrifice of his own daughter to Artemis. She in turn must be slain by her own son Orestes. That is Apollo's express command. It is the sacred duty of a son to avenge his father ; hence Orestes cannot disobey. But it is crime and pollution for a son to slay his mother ; hence he is hunted from his home by Furies, an outcast with a curse upon him, until he can find means of purification. That is how ' ancient transgression is wont to breed fresh transgression among mortals who sin ', and that is the problem which the tragedies of Aeschylus present. How far is Orestes responsible for the sin of matricide when the deed was forced upon him by the evil doom of the house, when indeed it would have seemed a sinful want of piety to refrain, and a direct disobedience of the commands of Heaven ?

* *Tusc.* 2. 10. 23.

At first sight there is a striking parallelism between this problem and the problem of the Orphics. How, asked Aeschylus, can Orestes be held responsible for his sin, when it was only the inevitable working out of the doom which had lain upon his house since the primal curse of Pelops ? How, asked the Orphics, can we human beings be held responsible for our sins when we are fore-doomed to them by our very nature, being under the common curse of our forefathers, born of the Titans who ate the infant god even as Thyestes ate his own infant children ? Both were oppressed by the thought of how the individual is shackled at birth by a load of inherited sin, and presented the problem of responsibility in this way, by the picture of natures predestined to evil through the guilt of ancestors. Nevertheless the differences between the two presentations are far more striking than the resemblances, for they reflect two fundamentally different conceptions of society, and hence of social and religious obligations. The society which is reflected by the ethical problems of an Aeschylean tragedy is a society still based on the ties of blood, whose unit is the House, the family or clan. It is wrong done to kindred which brings guilt, and the curse descends from father to son, from Atreid to Atreid or from Labdakid to Labdakid. The end of the *Oresteia* does indeed suggest that the solution, which within this framework has been sought for in vain, is to be found by the dissolving of the old family ties in the new and wider unit of the city-state which was attaining predominance in the poet's own time. But unless it is set forth within the old social framework of the clans, the problem itself, as Aeschylus presented it, loses all meaning. It is a long step, surely, from a statement of the problem in these terms to one which involves the idea of a unity, a kinship in fact, of all mankind alike. It has been said that the rise of mystical cult-societies, or non-social religious groups, seems to coincide with the breaking-up, in the sixth century, of the old social units based on the theory or fact of blood-kinship. We see the morality of these old social units subjected to a searching test in Aeschylus. But of the Orphics it may be said with truth, that they did not simply reflect and keep step with a social change which was taking place in the Greek world in which they lived (as the statement just quoted might seem to imply), but that they far outstripped that social change in promulgating a religious theory, that of the brotherhood of mankind, which did not find even philosophical expression until the advent of the Stoics, and for its popular acceptance had to wait until the days of Christianity.

About Pindar I have already hinted at what I believe to be

the truth (p. 170 above).   Three things may fairly be said about him.   He was in the first place a poet, in the second place a staunch defender of the traditional Olympian religion, and in the third place a mercenary, that is to say, his poems were commissioned by particular people, and certain portions of them were therefore written because they were calculated to please or interest a particular audience.   I mention these points because I think that, owing to the first, his mind was struck by the opportunities for poetic description afforded by the notions of Elysium and the Islands of the Blest ; owing to the third, we must not forget that the second Olympian ode, which is our chief Pindaric source for transmigration and the life of the blessed, was written for recital before a Sicilian audience, who might be supposed to be more interested than others in Orphico-Pythagorean beliefs, and for a king who was nearing the end of his own earthly life ; and owing to the second, he was unlikely to have been a wholehearted subscriber to those beliefs himself.   This second point perhaps requires a little expansion.   Pindar is sometimes thought of as a critic rather than a supporter of the orthodox religion, because he rebelled against some of the cruder and more offensive parts of the current mythology.   But this purification was itself a labour of love.   If he indignantly rejected some of the tales told of the gods, it was because they were dear to him and he would clear their names from slander.   His criticism breathes an entirely different spirit from that of Euripides.   ' If the gods do aught shameful, then are they no gods ! ' cried Euripides ; your gods do shameful things, was his meaning, and are therefore unworthy of worship.   Pindar's attitude is represented by his well-known treatment of the story of Demeter eating the shoulder of Pelops : ' To me 't is impossible to call one of the blessed gods a glutton '. The stories must go, only that the honour of the Olympians may be purged.   Euripides recounts the stories with gusto, since for him it is the honour which is false.

In conformity with this, Pindar's thoughts on religion, and his whole philosophy of life, reflect the prudent, cautious outlook of popular Greek wisdom, to which the fine abandon of the Orphic ' God am I, mortal no longer ! ' offers such a striking contrast. Know thyself, said the wisdom of Greek proverbs, and, For mortals mortal thoughts are best.   The gods are jealous, and it is therefore unwise. to be in any way outstanding, lest thou be thought to vie with them ; therefore nothing too much.   This spirit is Pindar's too.   ' Seek not to become a god ' ; ' Seek not to become Zeus . . . mortal things befit mortals best ' ; ' Take the measure of all things by thyself ' ; ' Mortal minds must seek what is fitting at the hands of the gods, recognizing what is at our feet, and to what lot we are born. Strive not, my soul, for an immortal life, but do the thing which it is within thy power to do ' ; ' It is meet that a man speak fair things of the gods, *for so the blame is less* '.[13] Since in all this Pindar is only putting into poetry some of the most typically Hellenic of thoughts, the quotations bring out yet again how far beyond the grasp of the ordinary Greek the religious views of the Orphics were. They may serve to dispel any lingering feeling of surprise that these views never acquired any general hold on the popular mind until after the break-up of the classical age.

Euripides was one of the most inquiring spirits in an age of inquiry. In his search for truth he tapped all the available sources, and they were many. If his thought shows most plainly the influence of the Sophists, it shows also an interest in the physical speculations of men like Anaxagoras and Diogenes of Apollonia. It shows that he knew the writings of the Orphics, and we may judge that he felt a certain sympathy for the ascetic ideal which they upheld, since in the drama in which Theseus taunts Hippolytos for making them the arbiters of his life, it is Hippolytos who is the hero, and Theseus who is to be proved in the wrong. The famous ' Who knows if life be death, and death be thought life in the other world ? ' also shows a knowledge of their doctrines, though it is something which by Euripides' time need not have been got direct from the Orphic books themselves. But Euripides was a restless spirit, in the truest sense a free thinker. These lines have nothing about them of the dogmatic assertion of the Orphic, the exultant certainty of the Gold Plates or Empedokles. ' Who knows ? ' says Euripides, and in another mood, as in the *Alcestis*, speaks in far more pessimistic language of the vanishing from existence of the dead. Yet again the soul is for him an immortal thing because it is akin to the immortal *aither*, which it rejoins at death, a notion which, as we saw, was shared by the Orphics with a certain section of popular belief. But the references of Euripides to the *aither* suggest that his conception of its nature, and its relation to the stuff of the human soul or consciousness, had a more definitely philosophical foundation, and arose rather from his studies in the Ionian school of thought. Euripides might be called an eclectic, not in the sense that he was a philosopher who constructed a system out of the various elements of earlier thought, but because he studied all earlier thought with avidity, and threw out a hint now of this belief and now of that according as his mood, or his sense of the dramatic, might suggest. The adherent of an elaborate religion like the Orphic, in which dogmatic certainty was of the essence, he could never have been.[14]

The conclusion about the Orphics to which we seem to be tending is that they were a small band of religious devotees with what was to most Greeks, philosophic and religious leaders as well as ordinary laymen, an unusual and original message to deliver. Their language and a few of their ideas occasionally caught the fancy of philosopher or poet, but in general the gospel which they preached with such enthusiasm and confidence was a cry in the wilderness, because it was a gospel for which the age was not yet ready. It had indeed behind it the simple idea of union with the divine, and the immortality consequent on that union, which must have been familiar to the common people since the most primitive times, and which in one of its forms was raised to an enormous popularity by the mysteries of Eleusis in the classical age. But there were many simpler and pleasanter ways than the Orphic of attaining that feeling of ecstatic union and that new-born hope for the future. To ' pay honour to the vapourings of wordy volumes ' is not a characteristic of the ordinary man. The Orphic demanded not only the performance of an inspiring ritual, but the carrying out of certain precepts in daily life, not only the acceptance of a strange and complicated myth, but also an understanding of its significance, all its implications of primal impurity, brotherhood of man and so forth. There was no place for a religion of this sort in an age when the ties of the family-unit were breaking up only to give place to the equally rigid demands, the new enthusiasms, of the growing city-state. In a word, Orphism was too philosophical for the masses, too mythological for the intellectual pride of youthful philosophy. To find a wider response, it had to wait until the distinctive greatness and distinctive limitations of the classical age had broken down.

This conclusion I believe to be in the main true, but before we leave the philosophic and religious thinkers of the sixth to the fourth centuries, we have yet to take into consideration the greatest of them all. Plato was not only the greatest original genius of Greek religious thought, but also the one to whom the Orphic cycle of beliefs made the strongest appeal. The question how far he actually believed in them is a much debated one, but by taking due account of the hints which he gives us himself, it is not impossible to answer. That he felt the greatest possible interest in them is obvious from the pains which he takes to expound them at length, and it may be inferred from this that he did not consider them altogether valueless. But how exactly did they appear to him ? This is only a particular aspect of the

question how Plato intended his own great myths to be taken,
and on this too he gives us clear enough indications.[15] The chief
thing is to avoid mechanical generalizations, as for instance taking
the words of Socrates in the second book of the *Republic*, when he
is speaking of the primary education of children and says ' We
begin with children by telling them stories (*mythoi*) ', to be a
general definition of Plato's conception of the function of myth.
The result of this is to take the description of these tales (' they
are for the most part false, though there are truths to be found
in them ') and apply it to the great myths of the *Phaedo* and
Republic 10. This opinion has been held, although it would be
equally logical to regard the great myths as wholly suitable to be
told to very young children.

In his own work Plato uses myth for two main purposes. In
the first place it is his habit to take a myth, or it may be no more
than a line of Homer or a reference to a popular belief (they are
all in general what we may call with Plato ' probabilities '), and
use it to support or corroborate his own strict deductions, like a
body of peltasts behind the hoplites, as Werner Jaeger has put it.
To make this serve as the sole description of Plato's use of myth,
however, is to leave out of account the finality of the great
eschatological myths of the *Republic*, *Phaedo* and *Gorgias*, which
do not simply support the rest of the dialogue but make their
own points independently. They illustrate the second purpose of
myth in Plato, which is to provide some sort of account of regions
into which the methods of dialectical reasoning cannot follow.
That there are such regions he fully admits. It is a part of his
greatness to have confessed that there are certain ultimate truths
which it is beyond the powers of human reason to demonstrate
scientifically. Yet we know them to be true and have to explain
them as best we can. The value of myth is that it provides a way
of doing this. We take account of myth not because we believe
it to be literally true, but as a means of presenting a possible
account of things which we know to exist but must admit to be
too mysterious for exact scientific demonstration. Examples of
these mysteries are free will and divine justice, and in speaking of
these Plato makes free use of the Orphic myths. His own attitude
towards them he makes clear, for example at the end of the myth
in the *Phaedo* (114*d*) : ' Now to maintain that these things are
just as I have said would ill befit a man of common sense ; but
that either this or something similar is the truth about our souls
and their dwelling-places, that (since the soul has been proved to
be immortal) does seem to me to be fitting, and I think it is a risk
worth taking for the man who thinks as we do '.

This passage brings out well how in certain instances the difference between dialectical argument and myth was a difference in their actual field of inquiry. The immortality of the soul he thought could be proved, and devoted much argument to the proof in the body of the dialogue. It must therefore lead a certain kind of existence in the other world, but in speaking of the life it leads we go beyond the scope of scientific inquiry and ·must fall back on myth. The same difference is to be observed in the *Phaedrus*, where the immortality of the soul is subjected to a brief dialectical proof (245c), and the details of the doctrine of transmigration are then expounded in mythical form.

This is in conformity with Plato's views on the nature of poetic inspiration. Consider first the way in which he introduces the largely mythical account of the creation in the *Timaeus*. There is first a disclaimer of the possibility of accurate scientific knowledge on such a subject (29c) : ' Do not therefore be surprised if in treating at length of many matters, divine powers and the origin of the whole universe, we do not find it possible to submit accounts which are worked out with precision and in every way and in all directions consistent with one another '. When he comes to the generations of the lesser gods, he states his policy thus (40d) : ' Concerning the other divinities, to know and tell of their birth is a task beyond our powers, but we must be persuaded by those who have spoken in the past, who were, so they said, the sons of the gods, and may be supposed to have had a clear knowledge of their own parents. We must not therefore disbelieve the children of the gods, although they spoke without convincing and rigorous demonstrations, but must follow custom and take their word as that of men who claim to be telling of their own kith and kin.' The sons of the gods are of course the old *theologoi*, of whom Hesiod and Orpheus were the chief.

These words have sometimes been taken as ironical, and there is certainly a gleam of humour in the expression that the poets ought to know their own family history. But they are in accordance not only with Plato's procedure, but also with his theory of poetic inspiration, put forward in the *Ion* and the *Phaedrus*, and probably a legacy from Socrates, since it appears in Socrates' mouth in the *Apology* (22c). Poetry is a form of *mania*, it is said in the *Phaedrus*, where the four chief kinds of *mania* are enumerated as that of prophets and seers, that of the authors of rites of purification and initiation, that of poets and that of lovers. The object of the passage is to show that ' the greatest of all good things come to us through *mania* ', and that the word does not mean madness in the ordinary sense, but divine inspiration or possession. It is thus that poetry is described in the *Apology* and *Ion*, where poets are compared to prophets and Korybants, and said to speak by divine power. It is true that in these two latter dialogues the object of the comparison is to point out that poets cannot have knowledge of what they write, in the philosophical sense of being able to explain their own meaning and teach others what they themselves can do. The poet is simply the mouthpiece of the god, like the Delphic priestess, and writes as it were at dictation. This theory of Plato's has been felt as a stumbling-block in the way of believing that he meant his borrowings from the theological poets to be taken seriously, but in fact it makes them ideal instruments for the purpose for which he requires them. So long as he is treating of matters where philosophical knowledge is possible, he does not bring them in, but where the subject transcends that knowledge, then we can have no better witnesses than these men. They have no ' knowledge ' of what they say ; but neither can we, and the general truth of their revelations, in spite of the necessary absence of ' rigorous demonstrations ', is vouched for by the fact of their divine inspiration.

Besides the employment of myth to give a ' likely account ' of subjects which do not lend themselves to dialectical proof, we have also in Plato, as I have said, their introduction in support of a thesis which has already been proved, or is immediately afterwards proved, by dialectic. The effect produced is something like this : we know this is true, because we can prove it to be so ourselves ; but it is satisfactory to know that in believing it we find ourselves in accordance with the divinely inspired words of the poets, or it may be with an article of age-old belief. When using myth in this way he makes use not only of the elaborate mystical doctrines of an Orpheus or Musaios, but also of popular faith or a poet like Homer : in the great and final myths he takes his material only from the former. (Examples of the use of Homer in this connexion, which it is not relevant to quote here, are the discussion of the soul as a harmony in the *Phaedo*, with its conclusion at 95*d, e*, and the discussion of relativity in the *Theaetetus*, 152*d* ff.) As examples of the use of Orphic myths in this way we may quote first the theory of recollection in the *Meno* (cp. pp. 164 f. above). The belief is introduced by a reference to ' priestly men and women ' and described in the mythical words of Pindar ; but before it is accepted as true, we have the elaborate test carried out on Meno's slave by means of the geometrical problem, with all its apparatus of scientific experiment. The use is illustrated again in the *Gorgias*, where the comparison of the foolish soul to a leaky jar, the work of the ' mythologist from Sicily or Italy ', is introduced in order to combat the view that the best life consists in the continual gratification of insatiable desires (p. 161 above). This does not prevent the objectionable doctrine from being subjected to a dialectical refutation as well.

If Plato only used the Orphic myths in the first of these two ways, in order to give an account of separate matters which were not susceptible to dialectical proof at all, then it would be open to anyone, were he perverse enough, to argue that Plato himself only believed the doctrines which he treated dialectically, and used the great myths, which profess to enlarge the field covered, as a mere ornament or literary tail-piece. When, however, the same doctrine is shown now as the subject of an Orphic myth, and now as the object of dialectical proof, it becomes impossible to avoid the conclusion that Plato thought of the Orphic myths as the complementary mythological expression of profound philosophical truths. The theory of recollection is the most striking instance, since it is shown to be inextricably bound up on the one hand with the whole doctrine of transmigration, even down to its details, and on the other with the characteristically Platonic theory of Ideas.

It is obvious, then, that Plato regarded the speculations of the Orphic theologians not only with interest but with a respect that was near akin to reverence. They did much more than simply serve to illustrate his points, and must indeed have powerfully affected the form which his own religion took. (Compare on this point pp. 156 f. above.) Plato is the supreme example of this combination of keen philosophical intellect with a ready acquiescence in the reality of the divine such as made the direct inspiration of prophets seem a credible and natural phenomenon. Nevertheless the presence of the first of these faculties ensured that he did not give up his own independence altogether even in the realms which might be thought to belong most properly to the *theologoi*. He had no hesitation in censuring those elements in their religion which seemed to him unworthy, as we saw from his remarks about the crudely material rewards which they anticipated for the good in Elysium (p. 158 above). The *Politicus* provides another example (272b-d). If all the good things provided for men in the golden age of Kronos were used by the men of that age for the pursuit of philosophy, well and good. They were indeed blessings. But if, as the tales about them say (and Orpheus was one of those who described life in the golden age, p. 197 above), they simply stuffed themselves with food and drink and told each other stories, that is a different matter. The fact is that Plato thought of the Orphic religion and his own philosophy as complementary. The Orphics taught of transmigration, and instilled the great truth that there was a much better fate awaiting the good after death than the bad. Directly following on this comes the famous corollary that the best life consists in ' practice for death '. One of the ways in which the philosophy of Plato supplemented this religion was by giving it a philosophical background, linking it with the theory of Ideas. Another was by accepting the central doctrine that the good and the bad did not have the same fate after death, but going further into the question of who were the good and who the bad, and how in fact ' practice for death ' might best be carried out. A passage of the *Phaedo* which we have had to refer to already is an invaluable testimony to Plato's attitude (69c, cp. pp. 70 f., 160, 194 above) : ' It looks as if those also who established rites of initiation for us were no fools, but that there is a hidden meaning in their teaching when it says that whoever arrives uninitiated in Hades will lie in mud, but the purified and initiated when he arrives there will dwell with gods. For there are in truth, as those who understand the mysteries say, many who bear the wand, but few who become *Bakchoi*. And these latter are in my opinion no others than those who have given their lives to true philosophy.' Undoubtedly there is irony here, but it does not saturate the whole passage, and must not be allowed to overstep its proper limits in our minds. Put dully and straightforwardly, the meaning is this : ' Truly the initiators have a valuable lesson to teach, for they bring it home to men that the fate of all after death is not alike. In this they rise far above the conceptions of the common man, who thinks that he is doing the best for himself by getting all that he can out of this life, in pleasure and material advantage. Let us be warned by their teaching then, that the elect after death will dwell with gods, and the rejected suffer torments. But let us bear in mind at the same time that salvation is not to be attained by mere initiations and perfunctory purifications (it is in the "hidden meaning" that the irony lies), but by the pursuit of true philosophy.'

To sum up, as we saw reason in an earlier chapter to assign many of the myths of Plato in the main to an Orphic origin, in particular the elaborate eschatologies of the *Phaedo, Gorgias* and *Republic*, so now we may affirm that these myths are there because the writer felt them to be true. The conclusion which was reached a little way back about the extent of Orphic influence in the classical age, exclusive of Plato, may have seemed to be one which considerably diminished the interest and importance of the movement, but we can now make amends by emphasizing how much we were leaving out by stopping short at that point. Orphism, we

said, was not of the age because owing to its peculiar character
it had too much of philosophy in it to please the masses who followed the procession in the *Panathenaia* or were dazzled by the
epopteia at Eleusis ; and was too steeped in mysticism and religious fervour to awaken a general response in the prevailingly
rationalist tone of the philosophers. But in Plato it found one
who combined with the intellect of the rationalists a religious
faith as deep as any mystic's. Plato took it up, realized its
value, and wove it into the texture of his philosophy in that
inimitable way which to read is to understand, to analyse, were
that possible, would be to destroy. Philosophy may be the warp,
and religion the weft, of a Platonic dialogue ; but the warp and
the weft together do not make a carpet. They are only the
background on which the artist creates his pattern of brilliant
colours and intricate design. There is a third ingredient to a
Platonic dialogue, the poetry. The influence which these unique
productions have had on later ages, whether in philosophy, religion
or literature, is too well known to need emphasis here. They
alone were sufficient to ensure that, even had all other channels
been closed, the doctrines of the Orphics would have been well
known, and have made an irresistible appeal, to the later religious
thought of Europe.

That is the climax of our chapter, and should perhaps have
been its conclusion ; but it is tempting to consider what must
have been the reactions to Orphism of Aristotle, and to do this
in closing may bring out more vividly, by contrast, the necessary
characteristics of any philosophy which attaches itself to Orphism
as its religious counterpart.[16] In this we are expanding the answer
to the question with which our fourth chapter closed, of what was
the philosophic idea behind Orphism. Under one aspect the
question has been answered already, namely that it was in its own
way an attempt to solve the problem of the one and the many.
But in its solution what philosophical presuppositions did it
make ?

Orphic speculation had two sides, a cosmogonical and a psy-
chological, an account of the creation of the world and one of
the nature of the human soul. Aristotle was in profound disagreement with both. It was not simply that he disliked their
mythological form, although that is true. Nor was it because
his genius had a preference for certainty, whereas Plato was
content to leave the highest matters where they were, in the
realm (philosophically speaking) of probability. Too much
has been made of the contrast between the two in this respect.

Of Plato Frutiger says with justice, ' Nul ne sait mieux dire, quand il le faut, κινδυνεύει '—' it may be '. But the remark is equally applicable to Aristotle, as Sir Thomas Browne knew better than some modern interpreters. In his eyes Aristotle was he who ' in matters of difficulty, and such as were not without abstrusities, conceived it sufficient to deliver conjecturalities. . . . He that was so well acquainted with ἢ ὅτι, and πότερον utrum, and an quia . . . with ἴσως and ἐπὶ τὸ πολύ, fortasse and plerumque, as is observable throughout all his works ' (Pseudodox. 7. 13).

The difference lies deeper than that. To take psychology first, Aristotle's theory of the soul as the form of the body excluded transmigration. He censures all beliefs which speak of soul and body as two separate things. There are not two things, soul and body, there is just one thing, the person. To speak of the body as the tomb or prison of the soul naturally becomes absurd. In his own words (de anima, I. 3. 407b 13) : ' We may note here another absurdity which is involved in this as in most other theories concerning the soul. They attach the soul to, and enclose it in, body, without further determining why this happens or what is the condition of the body. And yet some explanation would seem to be required, as it is owing to their relationship that the one acts, the other is acted upon, that the one is moved, and the other causes it to move ; and between two things taken at random no such mutual relations exist. The supporters of such theories merely undertake to explain the nature of the soul. Of the body which is to receive it they have nothing more to say : just as if it were possible for any soul taken at random to pass into any body, as the Pythagorean stories have it. This is absurd.'

On the cosmogonical side the Orphic and similar systems came into conflict with Aristotle on an equally fundamental point. To his mind the effect of their theogonies was to make the development of the world to a certain extent evolutionary. The most perfect was not in existence at the beginning, but appeared at a later stage. In his own terms, they made the potential prior in time to the actual, and that for Aristotle was the greatest heresy. For him the best must have existed from all time, and the progress of the world is not simply an attempt to raise its own level (that level at any given time being the highest in existence), but an attempt to reach an actually existing perfection which is, as it were, all the time before its eyes. The difference between Aristotle and the theologoi (Orpheus among them) on this point is best brought out by a passage in the

Metaphysics (N. 4. 1091*a* 30 ff. I quote the Oxford translation) :
' A difficulty, and a reproach to anyone who finds it *no* difficulty,
are contained in the question how the elements and the principles
are related to the good and the beautiful ; the difficulty is this,
whether any of the elements is such a thing as we mean by the
good itself and the best, or this is not so, but these are later
in origin than the elements. The mythologists seem to agree with
some thinkers of the present day, who answer the question in the
negative, and say that both the good and the beautiful appear in
the nature of things only when that nature has made some progress. . . . And the old poets agree with this inasmuch as they
say that not those who are first in time, *e.g.* Night and Heaven
or Chaos or Ocean, reign and rule, but Zeus. These poets, however, speak thus only because they think of the rulers of the
world as changing ; for those of them who combine two characters
in that they do not use mythical language throughout, *e.g.*
Pherekydes [17] and some others, make the original generating
agent the Best. . . .'

One of Plutarch's *Problems of the Symposium* deals with the
question whether the egg or the bird came first, a question whose
philosophical importance is considerably greater than might at
first sight appear. In support of the former theory one of the
banqueters refers it to a ' sacred Orphic story ' (Plut. *Quaest.
Conv.* 2. 3. 1), and that is only another way of putting this same
point, that according to the Orphics perfection did not come at
the beginning, or in other words that the potential was prior in
time to the actual. A philosophy which appealed for its authority
to the Orphic *logoi* ought, strictly speaking, to differ from the
Aristotelian on this fundamental point.

NOTES TO CHAPTER VII

[1] In trying to understand Pythagorean beliefs I have been particularly helped
by the two articles of Prof. Cornford, *Mysticism and Science in the Pythagorean
Tradition, Class. Quart.* 1922 and 1923. They form the best and most convenient
brief survey.

[2] Compare on this point the interesting speculations of R. Eisler, *Orpheus*
(Teubner, 1925), pp. 68 ff., especially the quotation from Iamblichos (*vit. Pyth.*
64), *ib.* p. 68, n. 5.

[3] V. Macchioro, *Eraclito : nuovi studi sull' Orfismo*, Bari, 1922. M. has weakened his position in this country by an unfortunate summary of his arguments
in English, in *From Orpheus to Paul* (Constable, 1930), pp. 169 ff. The summary
consists partly of dogmatic assertions, partly of obvious misinterpretations,
e.g. of Aristotle, *Met.* A 987*a*, 29 ff., and Plutarch, *de def. orac.* 415. The latter
passage runs : ' I see the Stoic doctrine of a final conflagration infecting the
writings of Hesiod, just as it has those of Herakleitos and Orpheus '. M.'s remark
is, ' Plutarch attributes the final destruction of the world by fire both to Orpheus

and Heraketos '. It is worth stating that in the Italian work the case is argued more soberly.

In his review of Macchioro's work (*Class. Rev.* vol. 36, 1922, pp. 30 f.), A. W. Pickard-Cambridge expressed the hope that some one ' who has specialized on the early Greek philosophers, and above all in the necessary *Quellenkritik*, will undertake the task ' of giving it full criticism. That cannot be attempted here, but a statement of the problem may give a basis (and possibly even an incentive) to future research.

⁴ So Burnet, but there is grave doubt about the meaning of the Greek. See Wilamowitz, *der Glaube der Hell.* vol. 2 (1932), p. 209, n. 2.

⁵ Burnet, *e.g.*, brings it in incidentally thus : ' The living and the dead are always changing places (fr. 78) like the pieces on a child's draught-board ' (fr. 79), (*Early Gk. Phil.*³ p. 154), and says no more about it.

⁶ That at least is M.'s claim. He goes too far when he says that an explanation like that of Campbell is impossible (Campbell, *Theaetetus*, p. 244 : ' As the arrow leaves the string, the hands are pulling opposite ways to each other, and to the different parts of the bow (cp. Plato, *Rep.* 4. 439), and the sweet note of the lyre is due to a similar tension and retention ') ;. but his own meaning is certainly one which is more *obviously* illustrated by both bow and lyre.

⁷ For fuller discussion of these objections, see the long note in Rohde's *Psyche*, Eng. tr. ch. 11, n. 19. Most important of all, there came into my hand when this book was already in proof, the latest monograph of M. A. Delatte, *Les Conceptions de l'Enthousiasme chez les Philosophes Presocratiques*, Paris, 1934. M. Delatte concludes after long and persuasive argument that not only the language of H., but also his ideas, are inspired by contemporary mystical currents, and shows, moreover, that there is no need for a holder of this view to have recourse to the more improbable of Macchioro's interpretations of the fragments. Pp. 12-21 of this monograph must henceforth be the starting-point for any study of the relations of H.'s thought to the mysticism of his time.

⁸ Parmenides as Pythagorean, *Psyche*, Eng. tr. 373 f. with n. 30, as critic of the Pythagoreans, Cornford in *Class. Quart.* 1933, 106 f.

Language implying knowledge of the Orphic religion : Dike, Dieterich, *Kl. Schr.* (Teubner, 1911), 413 (Kern, *Orph.* 50, *de theogg.* 12, *O.F.* p. 196, Gruppe, *Suppl.* 708) ; Daimon, E. Pfeiffer, *Stud. zum. Ant. Sterngl.* Στοιχεῖα 2, 1916, 126 ; address to mortals paralleled by Orphic frr., Cornford in *Class. Quart.* 1933, p. 100, n. 2.

⁹ By F. M. Cornford, against the earlier opinion of Burnet and others. See the *Cambridge Ancient History*, vol. iv, pp. 563 ff.

¹⁰ It is nowhere testified that Anaxagoras said there were men on the moon. Once, in Diog. Laert., he is reported as having said that there were dwelling-places (οἰκήσεις) there, but the passage must be set down in full and compared with other *testimonia* about the nature of the moon. The relevant passages are these (referred to but not quoted by Kern) :

(i) *Aët. Plac.* 2. 25. 9 (Diels, *Dox.* 356) : ' Anaxagoras and Demokritos say it (the moon) is an incandescent solid, having in it plains, mountains and ravines '.

(ii) *Hippol. Refut.* 1. 8 (*Dox.* 562) : ' The sun, the moon and all the stars are stones on fire. . . . He declared that the moon is of earthy nature and has in it plains and ravines.'

(iii) *Diog. Laert.* 2. 8 : (' He said that) the moon has dwelling-places, and moreover mountain ranges and ravines '.

(iv) *Schol. Apoll. Rhod.* 1. 498 : ' The same Anaxagoras says that the moon is a flat land ; the Nemean lion is believed (δοκεῖ) to have fallen from it '.

Anaxagoras, it would seem, believed the moon to be made of the same stuff as the earth, but fiery hot. We surely know to-day that to say that the moon is like the earth and has mountains and ravines is not the same as to say that it is inhabited. Diogenes or his authority probably took an unwarrantable step of his own in adding dwelling-places to the list of its features, though even that only implies that it was habitable, not necessarily inhabited. In all probability, however, Anaxagoras believed the moon to be too hot to support life, though not quite fiery enough to shine with its own light. (Cp. *Aët.* 2. 30. 2, Diels, *Dox.*

361. A. not only knew that the moon borrowed its light from the sun, but discovered the correct explanation of its eclipses.) He was quite aware of the moderation in temperature required for the former. Cp. *Aët.* 2. 8. 1, *Dox.* 337: (A. held that the universe at its birth tilted towards the South) ' in order that some parts of the universe might become uninhabitable and others habitable, according as some became cold, some burning hot, others temperate '. It is scarcely likely that the man who wrote like this borrowed the idea that the moon was inhabited from the Orphic theogonies.

Passage (iv) is used by Kern to prove by similar means that A. used the theogony of Epimenides, since there are some lines attributed to the latter by Aelian (*de nat. anim.* 12. 7, Kern, *de theogg.* 64, 74 f.) which say that the Nemean lion fell from the moon. But did A. himself say so ? I suggest that all that the learned scholiast is attributing to A. is the view that the moon is a flat land. This finds confirmation in mythology, he adds in effect, for there is a story (δοκεῖ) that the Nemean lion fell from it. The passage runs in Greek : τὴν δὲ σελήνην ὁ αὐτὸς 'A. χώραν πλατεῖαν ἀποφαίνει, ἐξ ἧς δοκεῖ ὁ Νεμεαῖος λέων πεπτωκέναι.

(In the above translations of the opinions of Anaxagoras I have made use of the versions of T. L. Heath, *Greek Astronomy* (Dent, 1932), pp. 26 ff.)

[11] M. Bock, *de Aeschylo poeta Orphico et Orphico-Pythagoreo* (Jena, 1914), has been best summed up by Schmidt-Stählin in the *Geschichte der Griech. Litt.*[6] in one word—*unreif.*

[12] On the date of this speech, which is probably not later than the Alexandrian age and certainly much earlier than the Neoplatonists, see Kern, *de theogg.* 37. On the passage cp. Kern, *ib.* and Harrison, *Proleg.*[3] 506, and for Dike as an Orphic goddess see also Dieterich, *Kl. Schr.* 412 f.

[13] Pindar, *Ol.* 5. 24, *Isth.* 5. 14, *Pyth.* 2. 34 (cp. *Isth.* 8. 13), 3. 59, *Ol.* 1. 35. Cp. Harrison, *Proleg.*[3] 476 f.

[14] See also the discussion of the *Cretans* fragment, pp. 199 f. above. For Euripides' religious outlook the discussion in Rohde's *Psyche*, Eng. tr. 432 ff. is valuable.

[15] For a complete treatment of the nature of the Platonic myths and their relation to his philosophy, the excellent study of P. Frutiger, *Les Mythes de Platon* (Paris, 1930), may be recommended as an antidote to much that has been written earlier on the subject.

[16] That is, if in accepting Orphism it was alive to all its presuppositions, as Aristotle was in criticizing it. This did not always happen, especially in later centuries.

[17] Pherekydes of Syros was a younger contemporary of Anaximander and the reputed teacher of Pythagoras. He placed Zeus with Chronos and Chthonie (Time and Earth) or Chthonie and Eros at the beginning of his cosmogony, and so earned the distinction accorded him here.

CHAPTER VIII

ORPHEUS IN THE HELLENISTIC AND GRAECO-ROMAN WORLD

To come near to an understanding of the development of Orphism in the post-classical world, so far as this is possible, it is necessary to begin by repeating certain general truths about the changed conditions of that world and their consequences for the history of religion.[1] We have seen Orphism to be a system of belief whose message was universal, because it was addressed to every individual as an individual, and we have noticed that this non-social character formed a contrast with the reigning spirit of Hellenic religion, which had its roots in the reigning political conception, that of the city-state. We come now to an age in which, whether or not Orphism was able to take advantage of it, that particular hindrance to its expansion had been removed. ' Man as a political animal ', says our greatest authority on Hellenistic civilization, ' a fraction of the *polis*, or self-governing city-state, had ended with Aristotle ; with Alexander begins man as an individual '. Realizing his individuality, man asks for two things from his philosophy or his religion, guidance for the regulation of his own life and a new definition of his relations to his fellows, whom he thinks of now not as his own blood-relations merely, nor even as his fellow-citizens, but as all the rest of the inhabited world (*oikumene*). Hence it is to this age that we owe the rapid development of the ideas of the brotherhood of man and of the world-city, ideas which the same authority would attribute to Alexander himself.[2] They were enlarged on by the Stoics, and found perhaps their most telling expression in the words of Marcus Aurelius. ' The poet hath said, Dear city of Kekrops, and wilt thou not say, Dear city of Zeus ? '

That is one change which the new order brought about. But the conquests of Alexander, the establishment by his successors of kingdoms all over the Greek world and further East, and later the rise of Rome, had another, and for our purpose a yet more important result. Up to the fourth century, in spite of isolated instances of the importation of foreign cults, usually by foreigners and for their own benefit, the tendency of Greek religion had on the whole been insular. The Greeks were a home-loving people, going abroad only when war or trade demanded it and returning always with thankfulness, and since for the last two centuries at least their culture had been superior to that of their barbarian neighbours, they were well protected by their own robustness against the infiltration of foreign cults and beliefs. Under the successors of Alexander, however, their whole life was changed. They were needed for service of all kinds in Eastern lands, service which demanded that they should spend the rest of their lives away from Greece, and which led frequently to intermarriage and the founding of mixed Greek and Oriental families on Eastern soil. Meanwhile in Greece itself, the rapid growth of trade brought ever-increasing settlements of foreign merchants, who formed organized groups and carried on the worship of their country's gods in the traditional way. The temptations of the curious Greek to become first interested in, and later fascinated by these strange cults, were increased tenfold. In the East, the Greeks were the ruling class, and just as their language super-seded to a large extent the native dialects, even for the purposes of cult, so the Oriental gods were brought, at least superficially, under the dominion of the Greek. To Hellenize the religion to some extent was a matter of policy, but the Greeks were never good bigots, and the Hellenism was more often than not a mere veneer. The old business of identifying Greek gods with a foreign equivalent, which in literature had been already set on foot by the curiosity of Herodotus, became a popular and universal phenomenon. Dionysos-Osiris was followed by Zeus-Helios (Baal), Artemis-Anaitis, Aphrodite-Astarte and so forth, and it would be wrong to suppose that the original nature of the Syrian or Persian deities was wholly suppressed by the imposition of a new Greek title. Thus the interaction of Greek and Oriental religions, the result of the new political expansion, gave immense impetus to syncretism, which begins by identifying the deities of different places who serve something the same needs, and ends by paving the way for monotheism, the belief that the many gods of earlier belief are but one god with many names. The Emperor Alexander Severus is said by his ancient biographer to have worshipped every morning in his *lararium* before the statues of Apollonios of Tyana, Christ, Abraham and Orpheus, as well as his deified predecessors *et huiusmodi ceteros* (Kern, *test.* 147). As for the other side of the picture, the influx of foreign deities into Greece itself, we find that by the fourth century permission has

been given at Athens for resident foreigners from Egypt and
Cyprus to carry on the worship of their native deities, Isis and the
Semitic Aphrodite. A dedication of the third or second century
B.C. records the presence of Isis at Eretria, and Sarapis also is
introduced to Greek lands by the third century. At Delos we can
trace the progress of his cult from its introduction as an entirely
private concern in the middle of the third century to its recognition
as public and official early in the second. The Phrygian Kybele
had of course been known on the Greek mainland long before, and
by the end of the third century had been joined there by Men,
another deity from the same country. The Syrian goddess
Atargatis also rose to prominence in various parts of Greece in
the third and second centuries B.C. Gods, like men, were becoming
cosmopolitan.[3]

Two religious phenomena have been noticed as accompanying
this interaction and confusion, universality and syncretism. Both
were sympathetic to Orphism, the first for reasons already stated,
the second because Orphism itself was already a long way on the
road to monotheism. At heart it worshipped one god, Dionysos.
Thus he became to them a god of many functions and many
names, Phanes, Dionysos, Hades. Also it was particularly easy
for them, as it was always easy for the ancient world, to say to
others, ' You are worshipping the same god really, but without
understanding his nature '. Both this and other mystery-religions,
in fact, taught much the same as St. Paul when he said : ' Whom
therefore ye ignorantly worship, him declare I unto you '. Besides
universality and syncretism, there was a third thing which marked
the spirit of the new age, being in fact just another product of
' the beginning of man as an individual ', and which no less than
them contributed to form an atmosphere sympathetic to Orphism. This was the multiplication of mystery-religions and the
wider response which they aroused. Man's consciousness of his
individual soul was exactly what Orphism had fostered in an age
when competing interests drove it from the minds of all but the
few. Many of these interests had now lapsed through force of
circumstances, and men were thrown back upon themselves.
Under these changed conditions it was natural that longings
hitherto half-suppressed should rise to the surface, and some of
these longings were of the sort that could only be satisfied by
some form of mystery-religion, with its assertion of a higher self
and its promise of a blessed future. Caution is perhaps needed
here. Professor Nock has recently emphasized the point that
adherence to the cult of a deity in whose worship mysteries were
performed did not necessarily mean participation in the mysteries.

Initiation was not a necessary preliminary, but an act of special devotion, and was, moreover, in many instances expensive. Yet without exaggeration we may speak of the ' Hellenistic mystery-religions ' as an outstanding feature of the age, and may conceive that they both filled a new need that was beginning to make itself felt, and by their presence fostered its growth. These new cults, moreover, were of a nature more akin to Orphism than the Eleusinian mysteries of classical Greece, in that they sometimes demanded not only the attendance at a ritual of initiation, but the surrender of the initiate to the service of the deity for life. This service might demand an asceticism as strict as the Orphic.

Our knowledge of the religious features of this age forms a complicated and shifting picture, which is constantly being enlarged or modified by the discovery of fresh material as well as by the ever-increasing mass of modern scholarship. I have chosen to mention, in broadest outline, two or three of those features, which at the same time should be the most indisputably established and should have some bearing on our own search. We have seen at least that many of the most essential ideas of Orphism, which in the classical age were, if not unknown, at any rate rarely met with and contrary to the reigning spirit of the time, had become in the new age a part of the general religious atmosphere with which the ordinary man found himself surrounded. In these circumstances one of two things might happen. Men might turn to the teachings of Orpheus, discovering at last that in them was the medicine which their souls were needing, and Orphism might become for the first time a great popular movement ; or else, considering the enormous variety of cults which were simultaneously made available, it might just as easily be stifled in the competition for favour. It might live to see an age in which at last men were in the proper frame of mind to receive its message, only to find itself crushed by more powerful rivals who had similar privileges to offer, and who were partly satisfying, partly helping to create this same need in men's souls themselves. The evidence on the point is scarcely sufficient to enable us to decide which of these alternatives is the true one. On *a priori* grounds the second appears the more likely, at least if Orphism retained much of its original character, since it rested on a theology too elaborate ever to make a widespread popular appeal. The mysteries of Kybele, Isis or Adonis do not seem to have made the same demands on the intellect of their devotees, or on their capacity for absorbing dogma. But before we try to decide the question on these general grounds, there are certain actual testimonies which demand consideration.

The most striking thing is that the conspiracy of silence is broken. I am not referring to the copious quotations from Orphic writings in the Neoplatonists, to which we shall come later on. References to the Orphic writings, though rare, do occur in the classical age, and lines of Orpheus are quoted by Plato. What I have been tempted to call the conspiracy refers to Orphic rites. With the doubtful exception of the passage in Herodotus (2. 81),[4] the classical age provides no single explicit mention of Orphic rites. Anyone who has read this book will remember with what tantalizing frequency Plato, for example, speaks of 'the initiated', and what a weary detour must sometimes be made before we can feel satisfied that the people referred to are Orphic initiates. But in writers of the Graeco-Roman age we find explicit refer- ✱ ences to Orphic rites and initiations as well as writings. To take some examples, Plutarch in his life of Caesar (ch. 9) says, in describing the rites of the *Bona Dea* : ' The women by themselves are said to perform many things that resemble the *Orphica* '. Lactantius (*Div. Instit.* 1. 22. 15-17 = Kern, *test.* 99) describes Orpheus as having introduced the rites of Dionysos in Greece, and goes on : ' *Ea sacra etiamnunc Orphica nominantur, in quibus ipse postea dilaceratus et carptus est* '. (*Ipse* is presumably Orpheus, not Dionysos. But the Christian writer, knowing the legend of Orpheus' death, may have misinterpreted what he had heard of the rite.) Cicero (*de nat. deor.* 3. 58 = Kern, *test.* 94), going through the different forms of Dionysos, speaks of one *cui sacra Orphica putantur confici*. In beginning a story about Antisthenes, Diogenes Laertios says (6. 4) : ' Once when he was being initiated into the *Orphica*. . . .' (Compare also pp. 10 f., above, and the tablet of Cecilia Secundina, p. 174 and pl. 10).

These expressions are quite unparalleled in the literature of the sixth to the fourth centuries B.C. They make it difficult to understand the view of Cumont when he says (*Religions Orientales*, 1929, p. 303) : ' Or, l'orphisme est un mouvement mystique . . . qui, pour les contemporains d'Auguste, appartenait à un passé lointain'. Even the remark of Professor Nock seems strange, that ' Orphism was not the force it had been in the sixth century B.C. ; its missionary activities were weakened, and, if one may say it, subterranean ' (*Essays on the Trinity, etc.* 63). It looks rather as if Orphic religious activity, as distinct from its literary tradition, is at last coming to the surface after its undoubtedly subterranean existence in classical Greece. We have admittedly still to take account of Cumont's next statement, that ' ce vieux fond de croyances avait été transformé au cours des siècles par bien des apports étrangers à son essence primitive ' ;

but this can scarcely be proved so far as Orphic rites are concerned, seeing that in the extant writings of the classical age Orphic rites are not mentioned at all. In Graeco-Roman times they are at least known to us by name, and we have, if nothing else, at least the statement of a Christian apologist that they included a *sparagmos*, a feature whose attachment to the *Orphica* of classical Greece, however confidently we may believe in it, we must confess to be a matter of inference alone.

To descend from certainties to possibilities, one mark of the new age was the spread and increased importance of private and esoteric cult-societies, many of them Dionysiac (Nock, *Essays, etc.* 65). Now that we have seen Orphic rites to be well known in this age, it is at least possible that some of these societies were 'addicted to the *Orphica*', to translate a phrase which Plutarch uses more than once (*Vit. Alex.* 2, *Quaest. Conv.* 2. 3. 1). The passage of Plutarch last mentioned shows that the Orphic life was still lived, since it introduces the subject of eggs into the conversation by a remark of one of the guests that, having given up eggs for a season, he had been taxed by some one with being addicted to Orphism. The question of the nature of the rites is here, as we saw it to be in the classical age, not worth a long discussion, since so little is known about them. It could scarcely be profitable to ask how much they had changed in the interval, when we have so little certain information on what they were like to begin with. The argument from analogy suggests that they probably remained much as they had been. In spite of the fundamental similarity of the various mystery-religions which competed for favour in the Hellenistic world, they do not seem to have borrowed much from each other as far as actual rites were concerned. The alliance between the worships of Mithra and Kybele is a well-known example, but there were special circumstances in the case, and there are probably not many that could be set beside it.[5] Nevertheless it is proper to mention in this connexion the evidence of two reliefs suggestive of a syncretism between Orphic and Mithraic theology. The first, of the second century A.D., shows a winged youth with a snake coiled around his body, and with the heads of a lion, a ram and a goat at his waist. He has sprung from an egg, whose lower half is below his feet, the upper above his head. Around him runs an elliptical band containing the signs of the Zodiac, and in the corners of the relief are the heads of the four winds. This relief was identified by R. Eisler as Phanes, by A. Boulanger, perhaps more accurately, as the Mithraic Zrvān with the attributes of Phanes. With it is to be compared a relief from Borcovicum (Housesteads in Nor-

thumberland) which shows Mithra being born from an egg.[6]
(See plates 12 and 13.)

Whether or not this is true of the rites and mysteries of the
age, that in spite of their proximity they remained comparatively
uncontaminated by each other, the same can certainly not be
said of sacred literature. Syncretism and the mingling of religious traditions were the order of the day. Sometimes there
was not even an older literary tradition to which the new ac-
cretions might be attached, save by the most obvious pretence.
The Hermetic literature, so called from the Egyptian god Thoth,
whom the writers call Hermes Trismegistos and from whom they
pretend to be translating, presents a truly Hellenistic mélange
of religion and philosophy in which Greek and Egyptian elements
are blended not only with each other but with many other traditions, including the Hebrew and Christian. In this atmosphere
any existing sacred literature was bound to suffer, and the most
outstanding example of a sacred literature was the Orphic. It
was outstanding because it was in peculiar sympathy with the
religious and philosophical ideas of the time. With a certain
amount of distorted interpretation on the one hand, and judicious
interpolation on the other, it could be made to seem totally in
sympathy, whether you were Stoic pantheist, Jewish monotheist,
or a mystic of the revived Pythagorean and, later, Platonist
school. The attempt was worth making, for this was an age in
which the pedigree of a supposedly ancient hero or *theologos*
was not inquired into with critical nicety, and the correspondence,
if proved, was evidence that your beliefs could boast the respectable antiquity of a pre-Homeric origin. It was realized by
the ancients themselves in the Graeco-Roman age that this was
the procedure adopted in some schools of thought. Cicero has
some interesting remarks on the practice of the Stoic Chrysippos,
who, he says (*N.D.* 1. 15. 41), in the first book of his work *On
the Nature of the Gods* expounded the Stoic theology itself ; ' in
secundo autem vult Orphei, Musaei, Hesiodi Homerique fabellas
accommodare ad ea, quae ipse primo libro de diis immortalibus
dixerit : ut etiam veterrimi poetae, qui haec ne suspicati quidem
sint, Stoici fuisse videantur '. (Cp. Eisler, *Orph.* 1925, p. 75 n. 2.)

Thus also the Christian apologists knew of a *Testament* of
Orpheus (a title which, significantly, does not appear in Suidas'
list of his writings), in which the ancient *theologos* wrote a palinode,
denying his former teaching about the many gods of paganism,
and acknowledging the one true God.[7] This poem, or at least
those parts of it which give it its peculiar monotheistic tendency,
was a forgery in Jewish or Christian interests, and proved most

useful. In the *Exhortation to the Gentiles* that goes under the name of Justinus, the poem is introduced thus (*O.F.* p. 255) : ' If any unwillingness, or ancient superstition of your forefathers, still prevents you from reading the prophecies of the holy men, through which it is possible for you to learn that there is one God alone (which is the first token of true religion), yet may you at least believe him who first instructed you in the lore of many gods, but who later thought it good to make a profitable and necessary palinode. You may believe Orpheus, I say. . . .' Cyril *against Julian* (*O.F.* 245) puts it like this : ' Of Orpheus son of Oiagros they say that he was the most superstitious of men, and that he anticipated the poetry of Homer, that is to say that he was older than him in time, and that he made up songs and hymns to the false gods and obtained no mean glory thereby ; that then he condemned his own teaching, realizing that he had wellnigh left the highway and wandered from the true road, and turned to better things and chose truth instead of falsehood and spoke thus about God. . . .'

Of the Neoplatonists enough has already been said to make it clear that they used the Orphic literature extensively. This is not the place to go into the details of their interpretations, which would involve a statement of the Neoplatonic philosophy. The question how far the poems which they used belonged to the older strata of Orphic tradition will probably never be settled, and has already been dealt with (in chapter iv) as far as it seemed necessary for our present purposes. It is on the whole unlikely that the actual poems were altered or forged by the Neoplatonists themselves in order to give support to their own doctrines. There were probably few Neoplatonic interpolations on the lines of the monotheistic passages inserted by Jews or Christians. My ground for saying this is an observation of the extremely free and high-handed, as well as clever methods which they habitually employed in interpreting the meaning of the poems which they quote. When you have the ingenuity to extract a reference to the opposition between the Intelligible and Sensible worlds, or to the ineffable One which is beyond being and thought, from lines which in themselves contain no such reference, then you cannot feel the same necessity for inventing new lines which do reflect your own doctrines. There is also an obvious advantage in sticking to the old, if your object in quoting Orpheus is to borrow the authority of an ancient or supposedly ancient tradition.

It is to this age, almost certainly quite late in the Roman Imperial period, that we must attribute certain poems or collections of poems under the name of Orpheus which have come

down to us complete. These are the *Argonautica*, the *Lithica* (a
treatise on the magical virtues of stones), and the *Hymns*. The
Hymns of Orpheus, which it has already been found necessary to ✳
mention (pp. 159, 202 f., 205 above), deserve that something more
be said about them.[8] The collection contains over eighty short
hymns, each addressed to a different deity, or in a few cases to the
same deity with a different epithet. Almost all mention after the
title the offering to make with it ; this is usually a kind of incense,
myrrh, frankincense, storax, poppy and so forth. An alternative
title in some manuscripts is *To Musaios, Teletai*, and the actual
hymns are preceded by an address to Musaios in which Orpheus
promises to teach him prayer and *thyepolia*, and a prayer to all the
gods to be graciously present at this *thyepolia*. The word used
here recalls the language of Plato when he is describing the
charlatans who make sacrifices (θνηπολοῦσι) according to the
instructions in books of Musaios and Orpheus. In the best manu-
script of the Hymns, the word *Thyepolikon*, in abbreviated form,
is added in the margin at the beginning of the introductory address
and prayer, and when Suidas puts this name in his list of the
writings of Orpheus, it may be to our collection of hymns that he
is referring (cp. *O.F.* pp. 299, 318). The fascination of the collection lies in the probability that it is the actual hymn-book once in
use in a pagan cult-society, and thus a specimen of something
which, common as it must have been in antiquity, is rare indeed
to-day. Lobeck, it is true, held the view that it was a purely
literary effort composed *animi causa* by a scholar in his study,
but this has been generally rejected, largely owing to the researches
of A. Dieterich (cp. his *de hymnis Orphicis*, Marburg, 1891) and
Otto Kern. It is impossible to believe any longer that Lobeck
was right. If then we regard the hymns as written for the use of
a living cult-society, can we say that this was an Orphic society ?
Before we can know this, we must investigate a little more closely
both the nature of the hymns themselves and the meaning which
the phrase ' an Orphic society ' could have had in the age (it cannot
well have been before the birth of Christ) in which they were
written.

The hymns would well repay a detailed study. Only some
introductory observations can be made here. Each has as its
main section a series of epithets or descriptive phrases addressed to
the deity, and closes in the last line or two with a prayer. This is
sometimes for general blessings, plenty, peace and health, sometimes a summons to the deity to present himself before the
mystai in gracious form. There is great variety in these prayers.
One (61 Abel) is for ' a good understanding ; put an end to hateful

unholy thoughts, overweening and fickle ' In another (55) the suppliant states his claim to a hearing : ' For I call to thee with heart devoted and holy words '. The prayer is often appropriate to the god. Thus Hephaistos is appealed to solely that he may ' stop the raging madness of unwearied fire ' (66), Dike for a just fate, the Charites for wealth, the Clouds for rain, and Eileithyia for children.

A classification of the titles of the hymns, with a glance at the contents of each to see what character the deity is given, does not afford much hope of assigning them to any one sect of religion or philosophy. By far the largest number are names from the ordinary pantheon of Greece. Some, being personifications of natural phenomena, suggest a Stoic circle, *e.g.* the hymns to Nature, Aither, Stars, Clouds, Winds. Certain phrases suggest the same thing, *e.g.* of Hephaistos (who in this hymn never loses his earlier character as god of fire) it is said, ' thou dwellest in the bodies of mortals '. The Dionysiac interests of the writers are obvious, since there are seven hymns addressed to Dionysos himself in various forms. (Zeus comes next with three.) A specifically Orphic atmosphere is suggested only by four, those to Nyx, Protogonos (also addressed as Phanes and Erikepaios), the Titans and Eros, but the hymns to Dionysos are of course particularly at home there, and there is no reason why the other Greek gods should not have had their place in Orphic worship too. Orphic tendencies are also quite probably to be seen in some half-dozen personifications, notably Dike, Dikaiosyne, Mnemosyne. The rest of the hymns point to an Asiatic, and in particular Anatolian, origin. All but Adonis are from Thraco-Phrygian religion (*e.g.* Sabazios, Semele, Korybas, Rhea, *Meter Theon*), though Attis does not appear. There is no hymn to an Egyptian god, though the name of Isis once occurs, nor to any Oriental other than the Phrygians and Adonis.

The society is a mystic one. The suppliants speak of themselves as *mystai* and invite the gods to their sacred *teletai*. Other terms used are *mystes neophantes, orgiophantes, mystipolos* and *bukolos*. It was then an Orphic society at least in so far as it was a cult-society, primarily Dionysiac and practising mysteries, which used the name of Orpheus as its patron. It is worth noting that the literature of the period to which it is most likely that the hymns belong, contains a reference to the singing of hymns of Orpheus in the worship of Dionysos. Philostratos, writing at the beginning of the third century A.D., describes how the prophet Apollonios of Tyana rebuked the Athenians (Philostratos was himself an Athenian) for their unseemly behaviour at the festival of Dionysos. It shocked him to see them 'dancing lascivious dances to the flute, and in the midst of the poetry and hymns (*theologia* [9]) of Orpheus play-acting now as Horai, now as Nymphs and now as Bacchants' (*Vit. Apoll.* 4. 21).

It is unlikely that the society which used our hymns was Orphic in the strict sense of accepting the whole body of Orphic dogma. There is certainly no reference anywhere in the hymns to the most characteristic Orphic beliefs. This does not prove that the users of them were un-Orphic in their ideas, since these short hymns are not the best place for an exposition of dogma. Yet the hope of an Orphic immortality might have been expected to find a place in the brief final prayer. Also the collection reflects rather too strongly the general tendency of the age, both in the catholicity with which it provides an address to all the gods of the pantheon, and also perhaps in the syncretism which is discernible in the epithets applied to each. This latter must be admitted, although I would plead against the uncritical way in which these epithets have usually been dismissed as, for instance, 'epiphorematum ampullae nullo discrimine in saccum fusae' (R. Schöll). (See n. 14 below.) The society was Dionysiac, and Orpheus was its saint, but it was a child of the age in that it was familiar with the current philosophical ideas, especially the Stoic, and had a tendency to syncretism. The neglect of the gods of Egypt, however, is one example of several that might be cited to show that it resisted some of the strongest temptations to lose its individuality in a general confusion of the cults which permeated the Graeco-Roman world.

Where did this society exist? In all probability in Asia Minor. Chr. Petersen, writing about the hymns in 1868 (*Philologus*, 27, p. 413), quoted three of them as proof that the writer had access to lost Orphic literature, because the deities to whom they are addressed, Mise, Ipta and Meilinoe, were otherwise unknown. The names of all three have since turned up (the last as an epithet of Hekate) on inscriptions from the soil of Asia Minor. Epigraphical discoveries of this sort, of which Lobeck could never have dreamed, turned the thoughts of investigators in a new direction. Kern first drew attention to them in 1910 (*Genethliakon für Robert*, 89-101), making out a good case which was immediately rewarded by surprising confirmation in the results of the excavation of the Demeter-*temenos* at Pergamon. Kern therefore followed up his arguments with an article in *Hermes*, 46 (1911), 431-6, in which he definitely maintained that the hymns were collected and used at Pergamon. The audacity of the claim to certainty on a point like this naturally aroused the instinct of caution, and in the next report on the finds from Pergamon (*Ath. Mitt.* 37, 1912, p. 293) it was suggested that the connexion might be less direct, but ' auf einer beiden gemeinsamen Sehnsucht nach der *Soteria* überhaupt gegründet '. The fact remains that Kern brought forward definite and striking evidence, whereas vague statements like the one just quoted are no help to anyone. Kern's opinion was supported a little later by W. Quandt, *de Baccho, etc.* 254 f.

The precinct of Demeter at Pergamon (pl. 14) is a large walled terrace levelled out on the side of the huge acropolis-hill and containing temples, statues, altars, rooms and halls, and in one corner a row of seats in tiers which looks as if it were intended for the spectators at a sacred performance. The inscriptions, which range in date from the first Attalids to the Roman Empire, reflect the worship of a remarkable pantheon of gods. Besides the Olympians they mention several of the gods of Eleusis [10] (whereby the presence in the Orphic hymns of Demeter Eleusinia, Eubuleus, Dysaules might be accounted for), including the Orphic Mise (cp. p. 135 above). There is a dedication to Nyx, one to the Winds and another to Helios, and the Orphic collection is also suggested by the large number of abstract ideas personified. The inscriptions also leave no doubt that the cult was mystical, since there are references to hierophants, *daduchoi* and *mystai*.

The mystic cult of Dionysos is not testified to in the Demeter-*temenos* itself, but there is ample evidence for its presence in Pergamon. One Pergamene inscription is dedicated to King Eumenes by "the *Bakchoi* of the god of the wild cry '. This epithet of Dionysos (*euastes*) is a poetic one which it is unusual to find on an inscription, but he is addressed as *euaster* in Orph. hymn 30. In another an official is honoured ' because he re-gulated the mysteries devoutly, and worthily of Dionysos Kathe-gemon '. This brings us to a further point. The official thus honoured was *archibukolos*. These *bukoloi* are mentioned on six inscriptions from Pergamon, and others from Ionia and Pontus, which make it clear that they have some sort of official position or priesthood among the *mystai*. The word means ' ox-herd ', which sounds strange to us, but only by its unfamiliarity, since it is no stranger a term than that of shepherd or pastor by which we call our own priests. (I am not suggesting that the two are used by an identical or similar metaphor.) It is a reminder of the time when Dionysos was worshipped in the form of a bull. There are hints that the term was used in the Dionysos-worship of fifth-century Athens,[11] whither it had no doubt been imported from Thrace or Phrygia, but for the Graeco-Roman age not only does all the epigraphical evidence point to the North and North-West of Asia Minor, but there is a passage in Lucian which leads in the same direction. Speaking of Bacchic dancing (*de salt.* 79), he says that the dancers represent ' Titans and Satyrs and Kory-bants and *bukoloi* ', and adds about it that ' it is pursued mostly in Ionia and Pontus '. Returning to the Orphic hymns, we find that two of them (1 and 31) end with a prayer to the deity to appear in gracious wise to the *bukolos*.[12]

Another fact which the Pergamene inscriptions reveal is that the singing of hymns was an important part of worship there. The officials connected with it have various names, *hymnodoi*, *hymnodidaskaloi*, *hymnestriai*. They are known in other parts of Asia Minor,[13] where they mostly appear as officials of the Emperor-cult. (See J. Keil in *Jahrb. des Öst. Arch. Inst.* 11, pp. 101 ff.) Here, however, they are Dionysiac. The cumulative effect of the evidence is overwhelming, and we may take it that the cult-hymns of Orpheus which we possess were used in Pergamon, or, if we choose to press caution to a point where its significance becomes small indeed, by an identical society in a neighbouring part of Anatolia.[14]

It has seemed worth while dwelling a little on the hymns, because they are probably our best evidence for deciding what ' an Orphic cult-society ' is likely to have been in the Graeco-Roman age. Here we have a group of worshippers of Dionysos, with mysteries as a part of their religion, and, like the Lykomidai in Attica, ' singing the hymns of Orpheus at their ceremonies '. They do not answer the question whether that society believed in the Orphic dogmas, though they make it probable that it did not. No doubt there always had been people who celebrated the mys-teries of Dionysos and sang the hymns of Orpheus without master-ing the teaching of the *hieroi logoi* or living up to their precepts. They show also that the worship of the society was extended to all the chief gods of Greece and Phrygia, and had at least a flavour of the popular Stoicism of the day, though it had enough individual strength to prevent it from becoming a mere hotch-potch of all the mystery-religions, Oriental and Egyptian, which were flooding Greece and the Near East.

It remains to say something on a much-debated question, the relations of Orphism to Christianity. (Cp. also p. 207 above.) We cannot here attempt to deal with the endless speculations which this subject has aroused. A writer may be forgiven if at this stage of a modest volume he shrinks appalled from the immense learning of Dr. Eisler's *Orpheus*, with its four hundred

FIG. 18 (a).

This series of paintings from the Christian Catacombs is chosen to show how easily the representation of Orpheus playing to the beasts faded into that of the Good Shepherd. The intermediate figure is still Orpheus (or did some think of him as David ?), but his audience has been reduced to sheep.

FIG. 18 (b).

FIG. 18 (c).

pages of ' Orphic-Dionysiac mystery-thought in ancient Christianity '. Were the results certain, it might be possible simply to indicate in outline how they affect our conception of our religion and the influence which the pagan mysteries of Dionysos have had upon it. But their nature makes it impossible to discuss them profitably without a thorough examination, which is out of the question. Readers may make up their own minds about them, a process which is richly rewarded by the wealth of interesting and out-of-the-way material to which they will be introduced. It will, moreover, be in conformity with our policy only to touch on this subject, since we have made it our aim to discover what Orphism means and how long it lasted, not to make lengthy comparisons, of which, I hope, this book may be the starting-point.

There is no doubt that the early Christians, like all men from classical Greece down to the present day, were profoundly impressed by the personality and legends of Orpheus. This is attested, for instance, by his presence in the art of the Roman Catacombs. On pl. 15 is illustrated one side of an ivory *pyxis* preserved in Bobbio. The pious legend attached to it is that it was a gift from St. Gregory to St. Columban, the Irish founder of Bobbio, on the occasion of St. Columban's visit to Rome to worship at the tombs of the saints. The scenes carved on it have no specifically Christian associations. On one side is a hunt, on the other this charming picture of Orpheus playing to a bewildering crowd of listeners. These include not only a varied assortment of animals, a sheep, a goat, a monkey (perched on the lyre itself !) and others, but also a selection of mythological figures, a centaur, a winged griffin, and a satyr or Pan. (*Boll. Arch. Crist.* 1897, p. 9, and Eisler, *Orpheus*, 1925, p. 14.) A study of parallel designs in A. B. Cook's *Zeus*, 1. 60 ff., suggests the interesting possibility that the semicircular arch under Orpheus' feet represents the sky, in which case Orpheus would be represented in the exalted position of highest god. But perhaps the carver was more interested in the artistic than the religious significance of his conventions.

The adoption of Orpheus by the Christians was only a continuation of a previous adoption by Jews. It was easy to see in the characteristic picture of Orpheus not only a symbol of the Good Shepherd of the Christians (and we remember the Orphic *bukoloi*), but also parallels to the lore of the Old Testament (fig. 18).[15] It too had, in the person of David, its magical musician playing among the sheep and the wild beasts of the wilderness, and the resemblance did not pass unnoticed. The pictures of Orpheus, in which wild and tame animals were represented as lying down in amity side by side, all alike charmed by the notes of his lyre, suggested also the prophecy of the lion and the lamb lying down together. These things were useful at a time when it was wise to use a symbolism which would excite no comment in the pagan world. Its real meaning would be clear to those whom it concerned. There are many examples of this crypto-Christian symbolism in the first three centuries A.D., especially in the sepulchral art and inscriptions of Asia Minor. A word of Jesus became chosen for illustration by symbol not for its intrinsic virtue alone, but also because it was capable of representation in a way which would not attract notice. The Church in those days did not seek notoriety. It even disapproved strongly of some of those who sought it, as the Montanists did in Phrygia. So we have for example the vine-symbolism growing out of the words ' I am the

FIG. 19.—HAEMATITE SEAL-CYLINDER OR AMULET OF THE THIRD CENTURY A.D., NOW IN BERLIN. (Scale 2 : 1.)

true Vine '. Other sayings seem equally worthy of illustration, but we need not therefore suppose that the choice of the vine-symbol rests on any deep affinity with Dionysiac beliefs. It was a very convenient one to use.

To this part of the inquiry belongs a mention of the curious and much-discussed seal or amulet in Berlin.[16] The design on this seal (fig. 19), which is dated in the third or fourth centuries A.D., shows a crucified man. Above the cross are a crescent moon and seven stars, and across and below it is the legend *OPΦEOC BAKKIKOC*. ✱ This has usually been supposed to be the work of some Gnostic sect exhibiting a syncretism of Orphic and Christian ideas. Just as Christ is to be seen in Christian monuments with the attributes of Orpheus, so here, by a tribute from the other side, Orpheus is represented in the attitude of Christ. Eisler (*Orpheus*, 338 ff.) has with great ingenuity argued a purely pagan origin for the design.

Arguing by analogy from an isolated tradition preserved in Diodoros (3. 65) that Lykurgos, the enemy of Dionysos, was crucified by the god, and from stories that Dionysos himself and other Dionysiac figures were ' bound to the tree ', he suggests that there was also an old tradition of the crucifixion of Orpheus. It is only an accident that in the wreck of Greek literature which has come down to us no memory of it has been preserved. The strongest point in favour of this is that Christian representations of the Crucifixion in art do not go back beyond the fifth or sixth century. It had of course a tremendous prejudice to overcome— the historical founder of a new religion depicted as a common malefactor on the gallows. Yet if we are to believe that our complete ignorance of the crucified Orpheus is an accident, it is surely not too much to believe that our lack of earlier representations of the Christian Crucifixion may be an accident too. It is clear that no story of the crucifixion of Orpheus or Dionysos was known to Justin Martyr. He declared (*Apol.* 1. 54) that the story of Dionysos was invented by ' demons ' to correspond with a certain prophecy in Genesis (49. 10 f.), in order to bring the true Christ into doubt. For this reason they brought into it, and other stories of those whom they called sons of Zeus, the divine paternity, the virgin birth, the passion and so forth. ' But,' he goes on (ch. 55), ' the Crucifixion they never imitated, nor ascribed it to any of the sons of Zeus ; for it was not understood by them, since all the sayings relating to it are told in symbols '. This testimony goes further to weaken a case for which even its learned author did not like to claim *volle Sicherheit*, and we cannot regard the puzzle of the seal as solved ; but the suggestion itself, and the evidence brought forward for it, are of the greatest interest, and, like much of Dr. Eisler's learning, deserve to be more widely known. It remains a mystery who it was who had the temerity to

> score the mythic harper's name
> Beneath the fallen head and outstretched arms.

Whoever it was, to look at his seal and think what his religion and his state of mind may have been, is to deepen and illuminate our idea of the religious possibilities of the age.

The personality of Orpheus, we have said, made an impression on the early Christians and is reflected in their art. But ' le citharède des Catacombes n'est pas le docteur de l'orphisme ', as Boulanger justly remarks and as this book has tried to show. For the influence of Orphic doctrines on Christianity the evidence is mostly internal and therefore at the mercy of subjective impressions, the formation, or at least formulation of which I would rather leave to others. A few points may be briefly mentioned. The Christian apologists on the whole regard Orpheus with anger and contempt, as an impostor. They were certainly not willing pupils. He appears mostly as the champion of polytheism and superstition. Yet the passage of Justin, of which a part was quoted in the previous paragraph, shows that a similarity was noticed in his time between the myth of Dionysos and the story of the Christ sufficiently close to constitute a danger and necessitate a warning against confusion between these two representations of a suffering son of God.

In conclusion a short summary of the resemblances and differences between Christianity and Orphism, with a word of warning that we may be making an initial mistake in regarding either of these as one thing, instead of as a shifting complex of religious ideas which was never the same from one century to another. I take first some points in which they have already been said by one writer or another to show striking resemblances. Both Christ and Dionysos were the sons of God, and both suffered, died and were resurrected. But why choose the Orphic Dionysos for comparison with Jesus on these points ? They are commonplaces of the gods of the decline of paganism. They are true of Osiris and Adonis and many another god who was at least as well known in the Graeco-Roman world as the Orphic Dionysos, if not better. If there is borrowing by Christianity here, it is from the general religious atmosphere of the age, not from the Orphics. And it is true—it was inevitable—that this atmosphere in their surroundings did have an effect on the early Christians at the time when their dogmas were hardening and setting.[17] The process went on in succeeding centuries too, until almost all the paganism of the world into which Jesus was born has crept back into his religion and is to be found in some part or another of the world, and especially of the Mediterranean. The steady influx of these external elements into the presentation of Christ in the Gospels has been remarkable, and to some at least, sad. It is a process which was started by Paul, who was the preacher above all to the Greeks, and whose Hellenism no doubt contributed to his success with them. He did not minimize the individuality of the central Christian message, nor did he seek to gain an easy assent, as some have thought, by borrowing the language of the mysteries ; [18] but he was peculiarly well fitted to put his teaching in the form in which the Greeks might most easily understand it, and his words made it possible for those who came after to read into them a paganism which was not the Apostle's. Even so, the differences in the original story remained over and above the reabsorbed paganism. Foremost of these is the fact that the death of Jesus, unlike the sufferings of Dionysos or any other mystery-god, was a conscious and voluntary self-sacrifice. It must have made a difference too that the death of Jesus was a comparatively recent historical event. The tomb of Dionysos might be shown at Delphi, but even if there were any who on that account believed the story of his sufferings to be a historical fact, it nevertheless was one clouded by the mists of an immeasurable antiquity.

Orphism is said to resemble Christianity, as opposed to the normal Hellenic religion, in that it is a religion with a view of the origin of the world and of man, and a view involving the doctrine of original sin. Put thus generally that is true, with the qualification that the Orphic meant by sin something quite different from the Christian (pp. 200 f. above). But of course all resemblance ceases when we come to details. The dying and resurrected god, Dionysos, may be the means of salvation from our inherited impurity, but his death is also, in the strange Orphic story, a necessary act in the original drama which caused our natures to be thus compounded of good and evil. There is little in this to correspond to the Judaic legend of the Fall, and the appearance of the Christ in historic times to save us from the sin of Adam.[19]

The Christian communion service resembles the pagan communion by eating the god. Others have thought this Orphic, but I have indicated already my belief that it was something which the Orphics gave up. This sacramental turn to the Christian service, making it open to comparison, though at a very far remove, with the revolting rite of the *omophagia*, was probably given by Paul, who thus brought more into line with Greek mystery-religions something which had only been intended as a simple act of commemoration, based on a certain Jewish Passover which had been celebrated in peculiarly tragic circumstances. Even so it is unlikely that he intended it to have all the mystical content which it has been given in later ages. Professor Nock has convincingly depicted the immense difference between the central ceremony of an early Christian community and the ritual of contemporary mystery-religions, although the sacramental meal was certainly a feature of them. (It was prominent for example in the typically Hellenistic cult of Sarapis, whose priests invited men to 'the table of the Lord Sarapis'. See Deissmann, *Light from the Ancient East*, 1927, p. 351, with notes 2 and 3.) 'It might seem to him (an educated pagan) as extempory prayer in public worship does to a man brought up in the tradition of the Roman liturgy. . . . The culminating point was but the distribution of bread and wine with a formula, after a long recital of God's mercies. . . . Even in the fourth century, when the Eucharist acquired a dignity of ceremonial appropriate to the solemn worship of the now dominant church, it is not to me clear that there was any deliberate copying of the ceremonial of the mystery-dramas or that any special appeal was made by the ritual to the new mass of converts.' (*Conversion* 203 f.   The whole chapter should be read.)

It is in the realm of eschatology, and perhaps there alone, that we find Christian writers offering dogmas which have their ultimate origin in the Orphic books.   This does not of course argue knowledge of the actual books.   There were many intermediate sources available, of whom Plato and Virgil are the most famous, and some of the most excruciating torments are no doubt due to the fertile imagination of the Christian zealots themselves. The Apocalypse of Peter (first century : see Boulanger, *Orphée*, 130 ff.) contains a terrifying list, which includes the Orphic lake of filth (p. 160 above).   It looks also as if one of the most striking and influential features of Christian eschatology, the idea of Purgatory, had its origin in the Orphic notion of an intermediate stage between life on earth and the final bliss of the deified soul. Yet the most characteristic part of Orphic eschatology, to which this notion of an intermediate stage was closely linked, namely, reincarnation and the wheel of birth, finds no place in orthodox Christianity.   It in turn is bound up with the conception of the body as wholly evil, a place of punishment and trial for the soul. The soul cannot be fully purified in one earthly life, and therefore has to be born again in another body ; but its final hope is to be rid of the body altogether, since that is the state identified by the Orphics with full purity and full happiness.   Incidentally the Christian talk of the resurrection of the body could not but be repulsive to the holders of such doctrines.

Christianity would be represented to the pagan as a cult whose initiates claimed to be born anew.   This again would put it for him in the category of the mystery-religions, whose initiatory sacraments were usually thought of as sacraments of rebirth. The rebirth of the Christian differed in that it promised to confer a special grace which would enable the initiate to withstand temptation and live a morally better life.   Here is perhaps the most striking difference between Christianity and Orphism or any of the mystery-religions among which it was born, that it taught a positive ethic and made that the kernel of its message.   The Orphic religion was purely selfish.   The Christian insistence that love of God involved the practical expression of a love for all men must have made it seem nearer in spirit to one of the philosophical schools than to one of the religions of the time. When Julian wished to show the world that the gods of paganism were as well worth worshipping as the God of the Christians, one of the things which he had to do was to found hospitals and asylums for the poor in the name of Apollo. Lucian writes of the Christians, as of all devotees of religion or philosophy, in a spirit of mockery, but even he seems impelled to a sort of wondering, unwilling admiration when he describes the spirit of their communities. It is in relation to their treatment of the unscrupulous Peregrinus, who imposed on them and attached himself to them for what he could get. When he was in prison, ' there came some even from the cities of Asia, brought by the Christians at the common expense, to assist and entertain and console him. It is wonderful what celerity they display when some such matter of common interest is afoot. At the shortest notice they will lavish everything. So it was now with Peregrinus. A great deal of money came to him from them on the score of his imprisonment, which he made a rich source of revenue ; for the poor wretches have persuaded themselves that they are wholly immortal, and will live for ever, wherefore they despise even death and for the most part give themselves up to it with willingness. Moreover, their first lawgiver persuaded them that they are all each others' brothers, when once they are converted and deny the gods of Hellas, and they worship this crucified sophist of theirs and live according to his precepts. Thus they look down on everything alike, and think it all dross, having taken over such teachings with no sure test of their truth. If then there comes to them some sham wizard, a man of any ingenuity and knowledge of affairs, he gets rich in a very short time, making game of their simple hearts.' It looks as if some at least of the early Christians were acquiring in the eyes of the world the sort of reputation which their Master himself would have had them acquire.

One final point on the comparison between Christianity and Orphism itself. What would have been the attitude of the Orphic towards the divinity of Christ ? Clearly he would have said that Christ was divine because divinity is the heritage of all men born on earth if they know the true doctrine and have the wisdom to free it from the grosser elements with which it has become contaminated. He would add, moreover, that in so great a prophet the godhead already shone forth with far greater purity, and that therefore he might rightly be called more divine (*theios*) than the rest of mankind. To say that this approaches near to the true Christian doctrine may seem to some a watering-down of that doctrine which robs it of one of its most distinctive tenets. In truth, however, it is a tenet (cult of the founder) which Christianity shares with more than one pagan religion, and there is a disclaimer of it in the Gospels themselves which comes very near to the Orphic point of view. I mean the answer of Jesus to the accusation of blasphemy, 'because thou, being a man, makest thyself God'. 'Jesus answered them, Is it not written in your law, I said, ye are gods? If he called them gods unto whom the word of God came (and the Scriptures cannot be broken), say ye of him whom the Father hath sanctified and sent into the world, Thou blasphemest, because I said I am the Son of God?' (John 10. 34 f.).

A comparison as brief as the foregoing cannot but be inadequate, and on some points is lucky if it avoids being misleading as well. It is only from a feeling that a book on the Orphics which did not contain some comparison with the Christians would probably be thought intolerable, that I have been persuaded to depart even so far from the principle that the study here attempted is not a comparative one. I should like to close my sketch of the Orphics and their religion with a reiteration of that principle. Where it seemed that anything not ostensibly Orphic would, if it turned out to be so in reality, help our reconstruction of the Orphic system, I have tried to furnish proof of its origin in order that it might contribute towards that aim. Farther than this I have not tried to go. The oft-repeated questions, whether the fourth Eclogue of Virgil is Orphic, or the paintings of the Villa Item at Pompeii, or the stuccoes of the underground basilica at the Porta Maggiore in Rome, or the Apocalypse of Peter, or many another monument of the religions of antiquity, these I leave for readers to answer as they please. Is it too much to hope that the answers which suggest themselves may now be a little less arbitrary and capricious than they have been in the past?

NOTES TO CHAPTER VIII

[1] In the attempt to understand something of the vast and difficult field of later Greek religion, I have been greatly helped by the work of Prof. A. D. Nock, especially *Early Gentile Christianity* (in *Essays on the Trinity and the Incarnation*, ed. A. E. J. Rawlinson, 1928), and *Conversion* (Oxford, 1933). For works introductory to the subject, see *E.G.Ch.*, *Essays, etc.*, p. 53, n. 1, and *Conversion*, pp. 272 f. Indispensable are Cumont's *Les Religions Orientales dans le Paganisme Romain*, 4th ed., Paris, 1929, and P. Wendland's *Hellenistisch-Römische Kultur* (Tübingen, 1912). A. Dieterich's *Der Untergang der antiken Religion (Kleine Schriften*, pp. 449 ff.) is full of interesting ideas, not all equally acceptable. He is a notable upholder of the view to which Cumont objects, that the influence of Orphism grew with the centuries, and was at its height in the third and fourth centuries A.D. See *Kl. Schr.* p. 479.

² See W. W. Tarn, *Hellenistic Civilisation* (Oxford, 1927), p. 69, and compare his *Alexander the Great and the Unity of Mankind* (Raleigh Lecture on History to the British Academy, 1933, *Proc. Brit. Acad.* vol. 19).

³ For the evidence on which this paragraph rests, compare Nock, *Conversion*, ch. 3 and 4.

✱ ⁴ In spite of the opinions of modern scholars (Maass, *Orph.* p. 164, n. 63, Rohde, *Psyche*, Eng. tr. ch. 10, n. 8, Wilamowitz, *der Glaube*, 2. 189), Lobeck may after all have been right in regarding the relevant word as masculine. It would suit the construction with ὁμολογέουσι better. πολλὰ τοῖς Ὀρφικοῖς ὁμολογοῦντα (Plutarch, *Caes.* 9) means naturally 'many things conforming to the *Orphica*'. ὁμολογέουσι (οἱ Αἰγύπτιοι) τοῖσι Ὀρφικοῖσι, on the other hand, should mean 'the Egyptians agree with the *Orphici*.'

⁵ For this alliance see especially Cumont, *Religions Orientales*, p. 62, S. Dill, *Roman Society from Nero to Marcus Aurelius* (Macmillan, 1925), pp. 555-557, with notes. Cp. *Bull. Corr. Hell.* 51, p. 127.

✱ ⁶ Phanes relief (now in Modena) : R. Eisler, *Weltenm. u. Himmelsz.* 2. 400, F. M. Cornford, *Gk. Religious Thought*, p. 56, n. 1, A. Boulanger, *Orphée*, p. 62, n. 1. A. B. Cook in *Zeus*, 2. app. 9, accepts the identification with Phanes. For consensus of opinions see Eisler, *Orpheus*, 1925, p. 2, n. 2.
Mithra relief : Eisler, *o.c.* 2. 410 f.

⁷ Kern, *O.F.* 245-248. To Kern's reff. add Eisler, *Orpheus*, 1925, pp. 5. f. E. holds that, although the title has been added, the kernel of the poem is *echtorphisch*, arguing that a complete invention could never have had the influence exerted by a few ingenious alterations and interpolations in an already well-known work. Cp. Rohde, *Psyche*, Eng. tr. ch. 10, n. 24. The beginning at least is from an old poem, for there is verbal allusion to it in Plato, *Symp.* 218b.

⁸ On the Hymns see especially (besides reff. given in the text) Lobeck, *Aglaoph.* 389-410, R. Schöll, *Satura Philologica H. Sauppio oblecta* (Berlin, 1879), 176 ff., O. Gruppe in Roscher's *Lexikon*, 3. 1149 ff., also *Suppl.* 728-736, L. van Liempt, *de vocab. hymn. Orph. atque aetate* (Purmerend, 1930 ; a successful refutation of M. Hauck, *de hymn. Orph. aetate*, Breslau, 1911), Schmidt-Stählin, *Gesch. Gr. Litt.*⁶ 2. 2. 982. They are available in Abel's *Orphica*, but badly need re-editing.

⁹ A *theologia* in this sense was a solemn recital of the praises of the god. The custom was a common one in the later days of paganism, and *theologoi* are coupled with *hymnodoi* in an inscription from Pergamon (*Inschr. von P.* pp. 264 ff.). At Pergamon they performed both in the Emperor-cult and the mysteries, elsewhere in Asia Minor they were usually officials of the Emperor-cult alone. Cp. Dittenberger, *Sylloge*³, 1109, n. 54.

¹⁰ The suggestion in *Ath. Mitt.* 37 (1912), p. 288, that the connexion with Eleusis was not so strong as Kern makes out, does not invalidate this argument.

¹¹ The line of Aristophanes (*Wasps*, 10), τὸν αὐτὸν ἄρ' ἐμοὶ βουκολεῖς Σαβάζιον, though from an Athenian play, is a reference to Phrygian religion. Cp. also Euripides, *Antiope* (fr. 203, Nauck), ἔνδον δὲ θαλάμοις βουκόλον | κομῶντα κίσσῳ στῦλον εὐίου θεοῦ, and the passage in the *Ath. Pol.* of Aristotle which speaks of the *Bukoleion* as the place where a sacred marriage with Dionysos took place. Kratinos wrote a play called *Bukoloi* which seems to have been connected with the Dionysiac religion. These passages are discussed by Dieterich, *Hymn. Orph.* pp. 10 ff. In the late Imperial age, *bukoloi* appear at Rome (Diet. *o.c.* p. 9 f.).

¹² The evidence for the preceding paragraph (Dionysos-cult in Pergamon, *bukoloi*) is most conveniently collected by Quandt, *de Baccho, etc.* 251-255, where reff. to modern literature will also be found.

¹³ There are interesting parallels in inscriptions from Didyma and Tralles, for which see Kern in *Hermes*, 52 (1917), 149 f. Orders are given for a ὑμνικὴ προσαγόρευσις, in the one case of Poseidon, in the other of Apollo, and some lines are quoted to show what the hymns are to be like. They give a string of epithets, and are very similar in style to the Orphic Hymns. The texts in W. Peek, *der Isis-Hymnos von Andros, etc.* (Berlin, 1930), afford interesting material for comparison, though these are nearer akin to *theologiai* (n. 9 above) or *aretalogiai* than to our hymns.

¹⁴ I believe that the case for an Anatolian origin would be further strengthened, and other interesting light be thrown on questions of Graeco-Roman cult,

by a thorough examination of the hitherto despised list of epithets of which the Hymns are largely composed. An experimental survey of the Hymn to Athena along these lines (*Class. Rev.* 1930, pp. 216-221) gave some promise of results.

[15] Cp. Eisler, *Orpheus*, 11 ff., 52 ff.

[16] O. Wulff, *Altchristliche Bildwerke*, I (1909), 234, no. 1146, tab. 56. Reproduced by Eisler *l.c.* and Kern, *test.* 150. Most recently commented on by R. S. Conway in *Bull. John Rylands Lib.* 1933, pp. 89 f. The use of seals by early Christians, as well as some of the symbolism employed, is illustrated by an interesting passage in Clement of Alexandria (*Paedagog.* 3. 2, 1. p. 270, Stählin = Kern, *test.* 152) : ' Let our seals be a dove or a fish or a ship running with a fair wind *or a lyre* . . . or an anchor '. The lyre may be a general reminiscence of Orpheus and the peace and harmony wrought by his music, or may be connected with the comparison of the soul to a lyre. Philo of Alexandria speaks of the Spirit of God as ' musically tuning the soul as it were a lyre '. For Eusebios the *logos* ' takes into its hands a musical instrument, man ' (Kern, *test.* 153). For the ramifications of the idea in Greek, Hellenistic-Jewish and Christian writers see Eisler, *Orpheus*, 65 ff.

[17] See especially in this connexion A. Deissmann's *Light from the Ancient East* (English ed. 1927), the conclusion to Boulanger's *Orphée* (*Orphisme et Christianisme*) and Nock, *Conversion*, ch. 13.

[18] A. D. Nock has maintained that the language of the New Testament gives the impression, not of borrowing, but actually of deliberate avoidance of the terminology of the mysteries. See *The Vocabulary of the N.T.*, *Journal of Biblical Literature*, 1933, pp. 131-139.

[19] This is not to deny the possibility of a combination of the two being attempted by some Gnostic writer. I hope I may be forgiven for the brief generalisations in these last few pages on a subject where such summary treatment is almost bound to be misleading.

SUPPLEMENT

(a) BIBLIOGRAPHY

(Other references will be found in the notes below)

THE following reviews of this book should be noted :

by A. J. Festugière in *Rev. Ét. Gr.* 1936, 306 ff.
by Ch. Picard in *Rev. Arch.* 1936, 224 ff.
by A. Boulanger in *Rev. Ét. Anc.* 1937, 45 ff.
by O. Kern in *Gnomon* 1935, 473 ff.
by H. J. Rose in *J.H.S.* 1935, 260 ff.
O. Kern, *Die Religion der Griechen*, vol. ii (1935), esp. ch. v (Orakel, Wundermänner, Theologen), vol. iii (1938).
M. P. Nilsson, *Geschichte der griechischen Religion*, vol. i (Munich, 1941), esp. IV. iv (Der Orphizismus und verwandte Strömungen), vol. ii (1950).
Pauly-Wissowa, etc., *Realencyclopädie* : articles on *Die orphischen τελεταί* (Kern) (xvi, 1935, 1279 ff.), *Orpheus* (K. Ziegler) (xviii, 35th half-vol. 1939, 1200 ff.), *Orphische Dichtung* (R. Keydell and K. Ziegler) (xviii, 36th half-vol. first third, 1942, 1321 ff.).
M. P. Nilsson, *Early Orphism and Kindred Religious Movements*, *Harv. Th. Rev.* 1935, 181 ff.
A. Krueger, *Quaestiones Orphicae*, Halle 1934, and *Zur orphischen Dodekaeteris*, *Hermes* 1938, 127 ff.
W. Rathmann, *Quaestiones Pythagoreae Orphicae Empedocleae*, Halle 1933.
R. Delbrueck and W. Vollgraff, *An Orphic Bowl*, *J.H.S.* 1934, 129 ff. (On this cf. also M. P. Nilsson, *Gesch. Gr. Rel.* ii, 411.)
A. J. Festugière in *Rev. Biblique* 1935, 192 ff. (*Les Mystères de Dionysos*), 366 ff. (*L'Orphisme et la Legende de Zagreus*).
R. Pettazoni, *La Confessione dei Peccati* pt. ii, vol. iii (Bologna, 1936), ch. xv. 2 *Orfismo* (on confession as an element in Orphism).
K. Kerenyi, *Pythagoras und Orpheus*, Berlin, 1937.
P. Boyancé, *Le Culte des Muses chez les Philosophes grecs* (*Bibl. des Écoles françaises d'Athènes et de Rome, fasc. 144, 1937*), première partie : incantations orphiques et pythagoriciennes.
M. Tierney, *The Mysteries and the Oresteia*, *J.H.S.* 1937, 11 ff.
H. W. Thomas, *'Επέκεινα*, Munich, 1938.
I. M. Linforth, *The Arts of Orpheus*, Univ. of California Press, 1941. (The only recent full-length study of Orphism ; takes up a more sceptical position than the present work.)
I. M. Linforth, *Soul and Sieve in Plato's Gorgias*, Univ. of California Press, 1944.

(b) NOTES

Page

12 As H. J. Rose has pointed out (*J.H.S.* 1935, 260), λέγει δέ που καὶ Ὀρφεύς in Plato *Crat.* 402b probably does not mean ' O. says somewhere ' but ' Isn't it O. who says ? '

15 To imply that the term ἱερὸι λόγοι itself is frequent in Plato is an exaggeration, but if we include παλαιοὶ λόγοι there are a number of references. Cf. *Phaedo* 70c, *Laws* 715e.

Page

21 Add as a possible representation of O. in art the basalt head of a lyre-player in Munich, perhaps the O. dedicated by Micythos, sculptor Dionysios (fifth cent. B.C.). See L. Curtius in *Rev. Arch.* 1936, I, 246, and Ch. Picard in *Rev. Arch.* 1936, II, 224.

21 ' Treasury of the Sicyonians.' ' Pas le Trésor de Sicyone, mais le monoptère sicyonien antérieur ', Picard in *Rev. Arch.* 1936, II, 224.

27 (and pl. 2) Delphic sculpture of O. with the Argo. Sixth century ? See Picard in *Rev. Arch.* 1936, II, 224.

31 On the Eurydice story cf. J. Heurgon, *Orphée et Eurydice avant Virgile, Mél. d'Arch. et d'Hist. de l'École française à Rome*, xlix (1932), 6 ff., Nilsson, *Early Orphism*, etc., *Harv. Th. Rev.* 1935, 189.

35 On the oracle of the severed head, cf. W. Deonna, *Orphée et l'oracle de la tête coupée, Rev. Ét. Gr.* 1924, 44 ff., H. W. Parke, *Hist. of the Delphic Oracle* (Blackwell, 1939); 351.

50 For the custom of tattooing Thracian women cf. also the Διssoì λόγοι (Diels-Kranz, *F. der V.*⁵ ii, 408, line 14) : τοῖς δὲ Θραιξὶ κόσμος τὰς κόρας στίζεσθαι · τοῖς δ'ἄλλοις τιμωρία τὰ στίγματα τῷ ἀδικέοντι.

65 For the kylix mentioned no. ix, Picard (*Rev. Arch.* 1936, II, 224) refers to H. Philippart, *Coupes attiques à fond blanc* (1936), no. 33, but agrees with the text against P. that the weapon is a double axe.

67 n. 19. Eurydice is also of course the name of the wife of Kreon in Sophocles' *Antigone*, and Pauly-Wissowa, *Realenc.* vi, 1325 mentions several other mythical examples of the name.

68 n. 28. Yet one more etymology ! Linforth (*Arts of Orpheus*, p. 23 n.) suggests ' a wild sheep ', on the analogy of ὄναγρος.

87 On the affinities of Zrvān in Greek mythological speculation see A. D. Nock, *A Vision of Mandulis Aion, Harv. Th. Rev.* 1934, 53 ff.

94 ὑπηνέμιον. Cf. the use of ἀνεμιαῖον in Plato, *Theaet.* 151e.

95 Wilamowitz, somewhat arbitrarily, denied that the Tritopatores had been wind-spirits (*Der Glaube*, i. 266 n.). For full discussion and evidence, see Cook, *Zeus*, iii (1940), 112 ff.

99 (Anatolian elements in Orphism.) In view of Orphic beliefs concerning the fate of the soul after death (ch. v), it is perhaps relevant to mention the view of Sir William Ramsay that deification of the dead was an Anatolian custom, illustrated by the close relation between dedicatory and sepulchral formulas or ceremonies. See, *e.g.*, Ramsay, *Studies in the . . . Eastern Roman - Provinces* (Aberdeen, 1906), 237 ff. ' The old Anatolian custom regarded the dead as merged in the deity, and the gravestone as in itself a dedication to the god . . . In Greece, on the contrary, the dedicatory or votive offering was wholly distinct from the gravestone.' Cf. J. G. C. Anderson in *J.H.S.* 1899, 127.

113 Wilamowitz (*Glaube*, i. 250) makes no reference to the theory that Zagreus is connected with Mount Zagron, and accepts the etymology from ἀγρεύς as original. He approves (*ib.*, n. 1) a restoration by Hermann of the Aeschylus line according to which Z. is son of ὁ πολύξενος.

123 On the Kabiroi in general, see now Bengt Hemberg, *Die Kabiren* (Uppsala, 1950). O. Kern collects evidence for their Anatolian (Phrygian) origin in *Rel. d. Gr.* i (1926), 235. E. Lapalus has written on the Cabiric vases in *Rev. Arch.* 1935, 8.

132 On the Lenaia see M. Tierney, *The Parodos in Aristophanes' Frogs, Proc. R. Irish Acad.* 1935, 199 ff. Against Cook's theory of the origin of Attic tragedy see A. W. Pickard-Cambridge, *Dithyramb, Tragedy and Comedy* (Oxford, 1927), 208 ff.

135 It is untrue, and a regrettable slip, to say that the scene of the rape of Persephone is already Sicily in the Homeric Hymn to Demeter. (Cf. E. A. Freeman, *Hist. of Sicily*, vol. i, 1891, 175 f.) On this paragraph cf. M. P. Nilsson, *Die Eleusinischen Gottheiten* (*Arch. f. Religionswiss.* 1935, 79 ff., esp. p. 88).

136 For modern literature on Baubo see also Nilsson, *Gesch. Gr. Rel.* i (1941), 110, n. 4.

Page

144 n. 17. (The soul as air.) Democritus may also be cited as a subscriber to the theory. (Aristotle, *De resp.* 4. 472a7.)

147 n. 40. For the Kuretes see my *Greeks and their Gods* (1950), 42 ff., 49 n. 3.

153 For Eleusis see esp. Nilsson in the work cited above (note to p. 135).

157 For Linforth's objection to the ascription of ' *soma = sema* ' to the Orphics, see his *Arts of Orpheus* (1941), 147, and my *Greeks and their Gods*, 311 n. 3.

159 ' not only individuals but cities '. For whole cities to submit to purification was of course not uncommon. Examples (cited by A. J. Festugière in *Rev. Ét. Gr.* 1938, 197) are : Athens (by Epimenides) Plato *Laws*, i. 642d, Aristotle *Ath. Pol.* i ; Halos in Thessaly Hdt. vii. 197 (by the sacrifice of Athamas) ; Delos Thuc. iii. 104.

162 ' some uncertain . . . date '. The earliest reference in literature to the Danaids carrying water is ps.-Plato *Axiochos* 371e, in art the ' Apulian ' underworld-vases of second half of 4th cent. B.C. (Cook, *Zeus* vol. iii, 1940, 369 ff. On the vases cf. below, appendix to ch. v.)

179 For the individuality of Eubouleus cf. Nilsson, *Arch. f. Religionswiss.* 1935, 84 (the triad θεϑός, θεά and Eubouleus on monuments of Eleusis).

180 On the *stephanos* cf. A. W. Pickard-Cambridge, *The Wheel and the Crown*, *Class. Rev.* 1945, 52 f.

182 On the formula δεσποίνας ὑπὸ κόλπον see A. J. Festugière, *Rev. Biblique* 1935, 371 n. 9 and 381 ff.

183 On the question whether the choice of lives is Plato's invention, see W. Stettner, *Die Seelenwanderung bei Griechen und Römern* (1934), 37 and 40, with references in notes to other opinions.

185 To the passages from Euripides add *Suppl.* 533 f. πνεῦμα μὲν πρὸς αἰθέρα τὸ σῶμα δ'ἐς γῆν.

186 On *manes* at Virg. *Aen.* vi. 743, see Headlam's note to Aesch. *Ag.* 1663 (G. Thomson's *Oresteia*, 1938, vol. ii, 157), where it is said to render ' rather unintelligibly ' the Greek δαίμων.

190 On the τετρημένος πίθος in the vase-painting, see also Cook, *Zeus*, iii (1940), 422.

191 n. 4. Is it perhaps relevant to the Orphic *penchant* for etymologizing to note that Verrall remarks : ' The whole art of interpreting ὀνόματα seems to have been in its origin Sicilian ' ? (Ed. of Aesch. *Agamemnon* 1889, 84. V. refers to *Journal of Philology*, ix, 197.)

192 n. 14. On δανάκης see Cook, *Zeus*, iii, 362 n. 2. Instances of *refrigerium* are collected by G. van der Leeuw in *Mnemosyne*, 1935, 125. See also R. Parrot, *Le ' Refrigerium ' dans l'au-delà* (*Rev. Hist. Rel.* 1936 and 1937), E. R. Goodenough in *Journ. Bibl. Lit.* 1938, 104 ff., C. Marot, *Refrigerium* (*Acta Litt. et Scient. Reg. Univ. Hungariensis*), Szeged, 1937 (in Hungarian and German). In the Canon of the Roman Mass the priest desires daily for the Christian dead *locum refrigerii, lucis et pacis.* (A. D. Nock in *Class. Rev.* 1938, 146.)

197 M. Tierney has an article on the character of Hippolytus as an Orphic in *Proc. R. Irish Acad.* 1937 (*The Hippolytus of Euripides*). D. W. Lucas, *Hippolytus* (*Class. Quart.* 1946, 65 ff.) suggests that Eur. *Hipp.* 952 ff. do not mean that H. has become an Orphic. The point of the taunt is rather : ' You are such a hypocrite that you may as well go the whole way and become one of those arch-impostors the Orphics.' This seems quite probable.

201 On the meaning of τελετή cf. H. Bolkestein, *Theophrasts Charakter des Deisidaimons als religionsgeschichtliche Urkunde*, *Rel. Vers. und Vorarb.* xxi. 2 (1929), 52 ff.

209 S. H. Hooke (*Origins of Early Semitic Ritual*, 1938, 35) connects the formula ' a kid I have fallen into milk ' with the Canaanite rite of seething a kid in milk. This seems dubious.

224 On Herakleitos see H. Leisegang, *Philosophie als Mysterion*, in the *Festschrift for Poland* (1932), 245 ff., P.-M. Schuhl, *La Formation de la Pensée grecque* (1934), 278–284, O. Gigon, *Untersuchungen zu Heraklit* (1935), W. Rathmann, *Quaestt. Pyth. Orph.* (1933), 88 ff. Gigon's work should be read with the remarks of his reviewers, e.g. W. Hamilton in *Class. Rev.* 1935,

Page

133, H. Cherniss in *Am. J. Philol.* 1935, 414 ff., W. Bröcker in *Gnomon*, 1937, 530 ff.

231   J. Dörfler, *Die Eleater und die Orphiker* (Prog. Freistadt, 1911) may be noted, and on Empedocles the views of Wilamowitz (*S.B. der Berliner Akad.* 1929, 626 ff.) should be taken into account. See also W. Kranz in *Hermes*, 1935, 111 ff., for E. and the Orphics. Kranz's recent book *Empedokles* (Zürich, 1950) is of interest.

247 n. 7.   On Delatte's *Conceptions de l'Enthousiasme* as it concerns Herakleitos, see the critical remarks of W. Hamilton in *Class. Rev.* 1935, 17.

248 n. 12.   For the date of the speech against Aristogeiton cf. also A. Dieterich, *Nekyia* (1893), 139, who sees clear traces of Stoicism in it, and Schläfke, *De Demosth. quae dicitur adv. Aristog. orat.* (Diss. Gryphiswald. 1913), who puts it back to the period of Demosthenes himself. (W. Rathmann, *Quaestt. Pyth. Orph. Emped.*, 12 n. 16.)

253   On Orphism in Roman times cf. the remarks of Nilsson in *Gesch. Gr. Rel.* vol. ii (1950), 410.

254   For Orphic and Mithraic syncretism see also the dedication at Rome which appears to identify Mithras and Phanes explicitly (Διὶ 'Ηλίῳ Μίθρᾳ Φάνητι), Cumont in *Rev. Hist. Rel.* 1934, 63 ff., Nilsson *Gesch. Gr. Rel.* ii, 411 n. 1.

257   For the Orphic Hymns cf. the full discussion by R. Keydell in Pauly-Wissowa etc. *Realenc.* 36th half-vol., first third (1942), 1321 ff. They have now been edited by W. Quandt, *Orphei Hymni* 1941.

260   M. Tierney apparently connects the epithet εὐαστήρ with ἀστήρ, ' star ' (*The Parodos in Aristophanes' Frogs*, *Proc. R.I.A.* 1935, 214). This seems improbable.

265   In his review of this book in *Gnomon*, 1935, 476, Kern recants and expresses himself convinced by the expert opinion of J. Reil and R. Zahn ("Άγγελος, *Arch. f. neutest. Zeitgesch. und Kulturkunde*, 1926, 62 ff.) that the ΟΡΦΕΟC BAKKIKOC gem is a forgery.

272 n. 4.   Cf. also A. D. Nock, *Herodotus ii. 81*, in *Studies Presented to F. Ll. Griffith*, London, 1932.

ib. n. 6.   For the Modena relief see now Nilsson, *The Syncretistic Relief at Modena* in *Symbolae Osloenses*, fasc. 24, 1945, *Gesch. Gr. Rel.* ii, 479 n. 5. His references to earlier literature are fuller than mine.

GENERAL INDEX

A Roman figure preceding an Arabic indicates a reference to chapter and note.
For references to modern scholars see also the Bibliographical Index.

ABRAHAM, 250.
Acherusian lake, v. 14.
Achilles, 149, 151, 208.
— Tatius, ii. 7.
Adonis, 98, 252, 258, 267.
Adrasteia, 79, 80, 101, 102, 233.
Aelian, 40, vii. 10.
Aeschylus, 32, 33, 42, 45, 49, 54, 176, 196, **233 ff.**; *Ag.*, 36 f., iv. 35; *ib.* 1629 f., 39, 233; *Bassarides*, iii. 1, 132, 218, 232 f.; *Oresteia*, 234 f.; *fragments*, iii. 18, 113.
Aetiological tales, 50, 51 f.
Agave, 55.
Agriope, 30.
Aiakos, 168, 187.
Aietes, 28, 181.
Aion, 228.
Aither, 80, (in Hesiod) 84, 185 f., 210, 212, 237.
Akusilaos, 71.
Akusmatikoi, 219.
Alexander of Aphrodisias, 74, 103 f., iv. 26.
— the Great, 25, 249 f.
— Severus, 250.
Alexis, 11.
Alkidamas, 40.
Alkmaionis, the, iv. 36.
Amos, 133.
Amphion, 39.
Amyklai, 53, 135.
Anaitis, 250.
Ananke, 80, 190, 233.
Anatolia, 35, 99, 114, 118, 133, 136, iv. 20, iv. 41, 258 ff., viii. 14.
Anaxagoras, **232,** 237, vii. 10.
Anaximander, **222 ff.,** 225.
Anaximenes, iv. 17, v. 21.
Anthology, Palatine (7. 746), iv. 35.
Anthropogony, Orphic, 83, 84, 120, 153, 165, 174, 214, 235.
Antigonos of Karystos, 35.
Aornon, 60.
Aphrodite (masculine), iv. 24.
Apocalypse of Peter, 269, 271.

Apollo, 29, 32, 35 f., 39, 42, 270, viii. 13; and Hyakinthos, 53 ff.; at Delphi, 43; character of prophecy, iii. 17; father of Orpheus, 27, iii. 1; god of the Pythagoreans, 218, 220; Hellenic origin, 44, iii. 2b; relations with Dionysos, 43, 46, 218; takes body of D. to Delphi, 82.
Apollonios Rhodios, 14, 27 ff., 74; bk. 1, v. 23, iii. 1; bk. 1, vv. 492 ff., 28; bk. 4, v. 1547, 29.
— of Tyana, 250, 258.
Argonautika, Orphic, 15, 27; vv. 245 ff., 28; vv. 680 ff., 28; vv. 761 f., 181; vv. 991 ff., 28.
Argonauts, **27 ff.,** iii. 3.
Argos, women of, maddened by Dionysos, 55.
Aristaeus, 31.
Aristophanes, 106, (in the *Symposium*) iv. 25, 152, 180, v. 14, 201; *Birds*, v. 570, iv. 35; vv. 571 ff., 86; vv. 693 ff., 92 ff., 104, 223; *Clouds*, 210 ff., v. 985, 115; *Frogs*, vv. 145 ff., 160 f.; v. 357, 115; v. 1032, 17, ii. 6, 196; *Peace*, vv. 372 ff., 154; vv. 832 f., 185; *Wasps*, v. 10, viii. 11.
Aristotle, 12, **244 ff.,** vii. 16, 249; attitude to myth, 71; denied existence of Orpheus, 57 ff.; *Ath. pol.*, viii. 11; *de an.*, 407b 13, 245; *ib.* 410b 28, 94, 186; *de caelo*, 185; *de phil.*, 12, 57 ff.; *hist. anim.*, 559b 20, 94; *ib.* 560a 6, 95; *met.*, 983b 27, 12; *ib.* 987a 29, vii. 3, *ib.* 995a 27 (quoted), 1; *ib.* 1071b 27, 103; *ib.* 1091a 30, 246; *ib.* 1091b 9, 71; *ib.* 1091b 24, 103; *protr.*, 157; *frag.*, 7, 58 f.
Arnobius, 203.
Arthur, King, 25.
Asceticism, 156.
Asia Minor (and *see* Anatolia), 98 f., 112, iv. 21.

279

BIBLIOGRAPHICAL INDEX

1. Abel, E., *Orphica*, Leipzig, 1885 . . . . 135, vi. 5, viii. 8
2. *Annali del Instituto di Corrispondenza Archaeologica di Roma* . iii. 8
3. *Annual of the British School at Athens* . . . . . iv. 39
4. *Athenische Mitteilungen des Deutschen Archaeologischen Instituts* . .
   ' 260, viii. 10
5. Bailey, C., *Ancient Roman Religion*, Oxford, 1933 . . . vi. 3
6. Bechtel, F., *Sammlung der Griechischen Dialektinschriften*, Göttingen,
   1884 136
7. Berliner *Klassikertexte* (papyri), edited by the *Generalverwaltung d.*
   Königlichen Museen in Berlin, 1904-23 . - 136
8. Bock, M., *De Aeschylo poeta Orphico et Orphico-Pythagoreo*, Jena, 1914 vii. 11
9. *Bollettino di Archaeologia Cristiana* 264
10. Boulanger, A., *Orphée, Rapports de l'Orphisme et du Christianisme*,
    Paris, 1925 . . . . . . 9, 46 f., 269, viii. 6, viii 17'
11. Boulanger, A.; *L'Orphisme dans les Argonautiques d'Orphée, Bulletin*
    Budé, Jan., 1929, pp. 30-46 . . . . . . iii. 3
12. *British Museum Catalogue of Vases*, London, vol. 3 (1896) . . 130
13. *British Museum Catalogue of Jewellery*, London, 1911 . . xvii
14. Budge, E. A. W., *The Gods of the Egyptians*, London, 1904 . iv. 15
15. *Bulletin de Correspondance Hellenique* . . . iii. 16, viii. 5
16. Burnet, J., *Early Greek Philosophy*, Black, 3rd ed. 1920 (4th 1930) .
    224 ff., vii. 5
17. Bywater, I., *The Fragments of Heraclitus*, Oxford, 1877 . . 225, 230
18. Campbell, L., *The Theaetetus of Plato*, Oxford, 1883 . . . vii. 6
19. Casson, S., *The Technique of Early Greek Sculpture*, Oxford, 1933 ii. 8
20. Comparetti, D., *Laminette Orfiche*, Florence, 1910 . . . 180, 182
21. Conway, R. S., *From Orpheus to Cicero*, in *Bulletin of the John Rylands*
    Library, 1933, pp. 67-90 . . . . 179, v. 12, viii. 16
22. Cook, A. B., *Zeus, A Study in Ancient Religion*, Cambridge (vol. 1)
    1914, (vol. 2) 1925, (vol. 3 in preparation) . 89, 99, 113, 130-2,
    136, iv. 32, iv. 33, iv. 35, iv. 38, iv. 40, v. 16, v. 18, 208,
    209 f., 264, viii. 6.
23. Cornford, F. M., *From Religion to Philosophy*, Arnold, 1912 . . 87
24. Cornford, F. M., *Mysticism and Science in the Pythagorean Tradition*, in
    Classical Quarterly, 1922-3 . . . . . . vii. 1
25. Cornford, F. M., *Greek Religious Thought*, Dent, 1923 191, vi. 1, viii. 6'
26. Cornford, F. M., *Mystery-Religions and Pre-Socratic Philosophy*, in
    The Cambridge Ancient History, vol. iv (1926), pp. 522-78 . vii. 9
27. Cornford, F. M., *Parmenides' Two Ways*, in *Class. Quart.*, 1933, pp.
    97-111 . . . . vii. 8
28. *Corpus Inscriptionum Graecarum*, Berlin, 1828- . . . 135 f.
29. Christ, W., *see* Schmidt-Stählin (no. 134)
30. Cumont, F., *Les Religions Orientales dans le Paganisme Romain*,
    Paris, 4th ed. 1929 . . . . 253, viii. 1, viii. 5
31. Dawkins, R. M., *The Modern Carnival in Thrace and the Cult of Dionysus*,
    in *Journal of Hellenic Studies*, 1906, pp. 191-206 . . 136 f.
32. Deissmann, A., *Light from the Ancient East*, English ed. 1927 268, viii. 17
33. Delatte, A., *Les Conceptions de l'Enthousiasme chez les Philosophes*
    Présocratiques, Paris, 1934 . . . . . vii. 7

287

34. Diels, H., *Doxographi Graeci*, Berlin, 1879 . . . . . vii. 10
35. Diels, H., *Poetarum Philosophorum Fragmenta*, Berlin, 1902 . . 136
36. Diels, H., *Die Fragmente der Vorsokratiker*, Berlin, 4th ed. 1922, 5th ed. revised by W. Kranz in progress (1934-) . 215, 223
37. Dieterich, A., *De Hymnis Orphicis capitula quinque*, Marburg, 1891 (also in no. 40) . . . . 181, 182, v. 18, 257, viii. 11
38. Dieterich, A., *Die Göttin Mise*, in *Philologus*, 1893 (also in no. 40) 135, 195
39. Dieterich, A., *Über eine Szene der aristophanischen Wolken*, in *Rheinisches Museum*, 1893 (also in no. 40) . . . . 210 ff.
40. Dieterich, A., *Kleine Schriften*, Leipzig and Berlin, 1911 . . . 136, vii. 8, vii. 12, viii. 1
41. Dieterich, A., *Der Untergang der antiken Religion* (in no. 40) 214, viii. 1
42. Dieterich, A., *Nekyia*, Leipzig and Berlin, 2nd ed. 1913 . . . 172, 177, 191, v. 14
43. Dill, S., *Roman Society from Nero to Marcus Aurelius*, Macmillan, 1925 viii. 5
44. Dittenberger, W., *Sylloge Inscriptionum Graecarum*, Leipzig, 3rd ed. 1915-23 . . . . 179, viii. 9
45. Dottin, G., *Les Argonautiques d'Orphée, texte établi et traduit*, Paris (Budé), 1930 . . . . iii. 3
46. Eisler, R., *Weltenmantel und Himmelszelt*, Munich, 1910 . . . 85, iv. 7, iv. 8, iv. 9, iv. 18, iv. 24, viii. 6
47. Eisler, R., Orpheus, *Orphisch-dionysische Mysteriengedanken in der christlichen Antike*, Leipzig and Berlin, 1925 . . . 21, iii. 14, iv. 13, vi. 1, vii. 2, 255, 263 f., 265 f., viii. 6, viii. 7, viii. 15, viii. 16.
48. Farnell, L. R., *Greek Hero-Cults and Ideas of Immortality*, Oxford, 1921 . 151, 152, 178, 182, 214
49. Fraenkel, M., *see Inschriften* (no. 77)
50. Frazer, J. G., *Pausanias* (text, trans. and comm.), Macmillan, 1898 . iii. 6, iii. 14, 179, v. 5
51. Frutiger, P., *Les Mythes de Platon*, Paris, 1930 . 169, 245, vii. 15
52. Gerhard, E., *Über Orpheus und die Orphiker*, Berlin, 1861 45, 59, iii. 22
53. Gerhard, E., *Trinkschalen u. Gefässe des Königlichen Museums zu Berlin*, 1848 . . . . iii. 8
54. Gerhard, E., *Auserlesene Griechische Vasenbilder*, Berlin, 1847 . iii. 8
55. Gomperz, Th., *Greek Thinkers*, Murray, 1920 . 87, iv. 3, iv. 8, iv. 15
56. Gow, A. S. F., *ΙΥΓΣ ΡΟΜΒΟΣ* RHOMBUS TURBO, in *Journal of Hellenic Studies*, 1934 . . . . . . iv. 41
57. Gruppe, O., Article *Orpheus* in Roscher's *Lexikon* (no. 128) . . 30, 43, iii. 1, iii. 4, iii. 8, iii. 28, viii. 8
58. Gruppe, O., *Die griechischen Culte u. Mythen in ihren Beziehungen zu den orientalischen Religionen*, vol. i (all published), Leipzig, 1887 79, iv. 6, iv. 9, iv. 10, iv. 15, iv. 18, 202
59. Gruppe, O., *Die rhapsodische Theogonie u. ihre Bedeutung innerhalb der orphischen Litteratur, XVII. Supplementband d. Jahrbuchs f. class. Philol.* (1890) . . ii. 5, 77, 99, iv. 18, vii. 8, viii. 8
60. Gruppe, O., *Griechische Mythologie u. Religionsgeschichte*, Munich, 1906 iii. 21, 136, iv. 40, v. 14, v. 18
61. Guthrie, W. K. C., *Epithets in the Orphic Hymns*, in *Class. Review*, 1930, pp. 216-21 . . . . viii. 14
62. Hamilton, W., *The Myth of Plutarch's de facie*, in *Class. Quarterly*, 1934 v. 20
63. Harrison, J. E., *Some Fragments of a Vase presumably by Euphronios*, in *Journal of Hellenic Studies*, 1888, pp. 143-6 . 3. viii.
64. Harrison, J. E., *Introductory Studies in Greek Art*, Unwin, 1885 . . 87
65. Harrison, J. E., note in *Archiv f. Religionswissenschaft*, 1909, p. 411 iii. 19
66. Harrison, J. E., *Prolegomena to the Study of Greek Religion*, Cambridge, 3rd ed. 1922 . 35, 62, iii. 12, iii. 13, 95, 111, iv. 28, iv. 32, 176, 178, 179, 180, 191, v. 5, v. 13, 208 f., 210, 212, 213, vii. 12, vii. 13
67. Hauck, M., *De Hymnorum Orphicorum Aetate*, Breslau. 1911 . viii. 8

68. Hauser, F., *Orpheus und Aigisthos*, in *Jahrb. des deutschen archaeologischen Instituts*, 1914, pp. 26-32 . . . . . . iii. 8
69. Head, B. V., *Historia Numorum*, Oxford, 2nd ed. 1911 . . 99, 112
70. Heath, T. L., *Greek Astronomy*, Dent, 1932 . . . . . vii. 10
71. Helbig, W., *Wandgemälden der verschütteten Städte Campaniens*, Leipzig, 1868 . . . . iii. v
72. Helbig, W., *Untersuchungen über die campanische Wandmalerei*, Leipzig, 1873 . . . . iii. 1
73. Helbig, W., *Führer durch die Sammlungen klassischer Antiquitäten in Rom*, revised by H. Amelung, 1913 . . . . . iii. 14
74. Heydemann, H., *Tod des Orpheus*, in *Archaeologische Zeitung*, 1868 iii. 8
75. Heydemann, H., *Neaplische Vasensammlung d. Museo Nazionale*, 1872 iii. 8
76. *Inschriften von Magnesia*, ed. O. Kern, 1900 136
77. *Inchriften von Pergamon*, ed. M. Fraenkel, Berlin, 1891-5 . viii. 9
78. *Inscriptiones Graecae*, Berlin (in progress) . . 136, v. 14, v. 17
79. Jaeger, W., *Aristotle*, Eng. ed. Oxford, 1934 13
80. Jahn, O., *Beschreibung der Vasensammlung König Ludwigs in der Pinakothek zu München*, 1854 . . . . . . iii. 8
81. Janeiwitsch, O., *Dürstige Seelen*, in *Archiv f. Religionswissenschaft*, 1910 v. 14
82. *Journal of Hellenic Studies* 130
83. Keil, J., *Zur Geschichte der Hymnoden in der Provinz Asien*, in *Jahrbuch des österreichischen archaeologischen Instituts*, vol. xi . . 261
84. Keil, J., and von Premerstein, A., *Bericht über eine Reise in Lydien*, *Denkschriften d. wiener Akademie, phil.-hist. Klasse*, vol. liii (1908) . . . . 99, iv. 21
85. Kern, O. (and see *Inschriften*, no. 76), article *Baubo* in Pauly-Wissowa, *Realenzyklopädie* . . . . 135 f.
86. Kern, O., *De Orphei Epimenidis Pherecydis Theogoniis quaestiones criticae*, Berlin, 1888 ii. 5, iv. 2, iv. 3, iv. 4, iv. 5, iv. 8, iv. 15, iv. 16, iv. 18, 232, 233, vii. 8, vii. 10, vii. 12
87. Kern, O., *Die böotischen Kabiren*, in *Hermes*, 1890 . . 136, iv. 42
88. Kern, O., *Die Herkunft des orphischen Hymnenbuchs*, in *Genethliakon für K. Robert*, Halle, 1910, pp. 89-101 . . . 135, iv. 21, 259
89. Kern, O., *Das Demeterheiligtum von Pergamon*, in *Hermes*, 1911, pp. 431 ff. 259
90. Kern, O., *Hymnologicum*, in *Hermes*, 1917 . . . . . viii. 13
91. Kern, O., *Orpheus, eine religionsgeschichtliche Untersuchung*, Berlin, 1920 43, iii. 2, iii. 6, iii. 12, iii. 25, 142, iv. 42, 205, vi. 6, 217, vii. 8
92. Kern, O., *Orphicorum Fragmenta*, Berlin, 1922 . . . *passim*
93. Kock, T., *Comicorum Atticorum Fragmenta*, 1880-88 . . 152, 180, v. 14
94. Kuhnert, E., *Unteritalische Nekyien*, in *Jahrbuch des deutschen arch. Inst.*, 1893 190
95. Lamb, W., *Greek and Roman Bronzes*, Methuen, 1929 . . . 89
96. Langbehn, J., *Flügelgestalten in d. ältesten griechischen Kunst*, Munich, 1881 . . . . 88, iv. 11
97. Levy, G. R., *The Oriental Origin of Herakles*, in *Journal of Hellenic Studies*, 1934, pp. 40-53 . . . . . . iv. 10
98. Lobeck, C. A., *Aglaophamus, sive de theologiae mysticae Graecorum causis*, Leipzig, 1829 . . . . . 85, 121, viii. 8
99. Maass, E., *Orpheus, Untersuchungen zur griechischen römischen altchristlichen Jenseitsdichtung u. Religion*, Munich, 1895 ii. 1, ii. 5, iii. 1, iii. 2, iii. 5, iii. 6, iii. 11, iii. 19, iii. 28, v. 6, viii. 4
100. Macchioro, V., *Eraclito : nuovi studi sull' Orfismo*, Bari, 1922 224 ff., vii. 3
101. Macchioro, V., *From Orpheus to Paul, A History of Orphism*, Constable, 1930 . . . . iii. 24, vii. 3
102. Malten, L., *Altorphische Demetersage*, in *Archiv f. Religionswissenschaft*, 1909 . . . . 134 ff., 179
103. Milchhöfer, A., " *Orphisch* "-*Unterweltliches*, in *Philologus*, 1894, pp. 385-99 190
104. Murray, G. G. R., *Critical Appendix on the Orphic Tablets* (in no. 66) . 96, v. 8, v. 12

105. Murray, G. G. R., *Five Stages of Greek Religion*, Oxford, 1925 .   iv. 13
106. *Musei Etrusci Gregoriani Monimenta*, Rome, 1842 . . .   iii. 8
107. Nilsson, M. P., *A History of Greek Religion*, Oxford, 1925 . ,   iv. 14
108. Nilsson, M. P., *The Minoan-Mycenean Religion and its Survival in Greek Religion*, Lund, 1927 . . . . ii. 8, iii. 20, iv. 39
109. Nilsson, M. P., *Homer and Mycenae*, Methuen, 1933 . . . iii. 27
110. Nock, A. D., *Early Gentile Christianity*, in *Essays on the Trinity and the Incarnation*, ed. A. E. J. Rawlinson, 1928 . 253, 254, viii. 1
111. Nock, A. D:, *The Vocabulary of the New Testament*, in *Journal of Biblical Literature*, 1933, pp. 131-9 . . . . . viii. 18
112. Nock, A. D., *Conversion*, Oxford, 1933 . 268 f., viii. 1, viii. 3, viii. 17
113. Norden, E., *Vergilius Aeneis Buch VI*, Leipzig and Berlin, 1926 . v. 19, v. 20, 214
114. *Nuovo Bollettino di Archaeologia Cristiana* 264
115. Olivieri, A., *Lamellae Aureae Orphicae*, Bonn, 1915 (*Kleine Texte*) . 179, 182, v. 8, v. 12
116. *Papyri Berolinenses = Berliner Klassikertexte* (no. 7)
117. Peek, W., *Der Isis-Hymnos von Andros u. verwandte Texte*, Berlin, 1930 viii. 13
118. Petersen, Chr., *Der geheime Gottesdienst bei den Griechen*, Hamburg, 1848 . . . . iv. 20, 210
119. Petersen, Chr., *Über den Ursprung der unter Orpheus Namen vorhandenen Hymnen*, in *Philologus*, vol. 27, pp. 385-431 . . . 259
120. Pfeiffer, E., *Studien zum antiken Sternglaube*, in *Stoicheia* 2 (1916) vii. 8
121. Pickard-Cambridge, A. W., review of Macchioro (no. 100), in *Class. Review*, 1922 . . . . vii. 3
122. Pickard-Cambridge, A. W., *Dithyramb, Tragedy and Comedy*, Oxford, 1927 . . . . iii. 17
123. Preller, L., *Griechische Mythologie*, Berlin, 4th ed. revised by K. Robert, 1894 . . . . iv. 24, 179
124. Quandt, W., *De Baccho ab Alexandri aetate in Asia Minore culto*, Halle, 1913 . . . . . 136, iv. 21, iv. 41, 260, viii. 12
125. Robert, K., *Die griechische Heldensage*, Berlin, 1920 . . 26, 33, 62, iii. 1, iii. 2, iii. 7, iii. 8
126. Robinson, E., *Museum of Fine Arts, Boston : Catalogue of Greek, Etruscan and Roman Vases*, Boston and New York, 1893 . . iii. 8
127. Rohde, E., *Psyche, The Cult of Souls and Belief in Immortality among the Greeks*, Eng. ed., Kegan Paul, 1925 . 50, iii. 13, iii. 17, 95, 113, 136, iv. 2, iv. 3, 163, 191, v. 14, v. 17, 213, 214, vii. 7, vii. 8, vii. 14, viii. 4, viii. 7
128. Roscher, W. H., *Ausführliches Lexikon d. Griech. u. Röm. Mythologie*, 1884- 30, 43, 62
129. Rose, H. J., *A Handbook of Greek Mythology*, Methuen, 1930 . iii. 6, iii. 20, 100
130. Rose, V., *Aristotelis qui ferebantur librorum fragmenta*, Teubner, 1886 . 59, 157
131. Saintyves, P., *Les Vierges Mères*, Paris, 1908 . . . . iv. 17
132. Shear, T. L., in *American Journal of Archaeology*, 1931 . . v. 14
133. Schmidt, W., *The Origin and Growth of Religion*, Methuen, 1931 iv. 27
134. Schmidt-Stählin. W. von Christ's *Geschichte der Griechischen Litteratur*, 6e Aufl., *unter Mitwirkung von O. Stählin u. W. Schmidt*, Munich, 1920 . . . . ii. 7, iv. 26, vii. 11, viii. 8
135. Schöll, R., article on the Orphic Hymns in *Satura Philologica H. Sauppio oblecta*, Berlin, 1879, pp. 176 ff. . . . . viii. 8
136. Schuhl, P.-M., *Essai sur la Formation de la Pensée Grecque*, Paris, 1934 v. 14, v. 22
137. Seltman, C. T., *Greek Coins*, Methuen, 1933 99
138. Tarn, W. W., *Hellenistic Civilisation*, Oxford, 1927 (2nd ed. 1930) (quoted) 249, viii. 2
139. Tarn, W. W., *Alexander the Great and the Unity of Mankind*, Proc. Brit. Acad., 19 (1933) . . . . viii. 2

140. Taylor, A. E., *Plato, The Man and his Work*, Methuen, 1926   .   iv. 6
141. van Essen, C. C., *Did Orphic Influence on Etruscan Tomb-paintings Exist?* Amsterdam, 1927 . . . . v. 22
142. van Liempt, L., *De vocabulario hymnorum Orphicorum atque aetate*, Purmerend, 1930 . . . . viii. 8
143. Wendland, P., *Die hellenistisch-römische Kultur in ihren Beziehungen zu Judentum u. Christentum*, Tübingen, 3rd ed. 1912   .   viii. 1
144. Wiegand, Th., and Schrader, H., *Priene*, Berlin, 1904   .   .   . 136
145. *Wiener Vorlegeblätter* (various dates) 190
146. Wilamowitz-Moellendorff, u. von, *Homerische Untersuchungen* = vol. 7 of *Philologische Untersuchungen*, ed. Kiessling and Wilamowitz, Berlin, 1884 . . . . iv. 36
147. Wilamowitz-Moellendorff, u. von, *Der Glaube der Hellenen*, Berlin (vol. i) 1931, (vol. ii) 1932   .   .   . iv. 13, iv. 39, 216, vii. 4, viii. 4
148. Winkler, A., *Die Darstellungen der Unterwelt auf unteritalischen Vasen, Breslauer philol. Abhandl. Bd. 3, Heft 5*, 1888 190
149. Wulff, O., *Altchristliche Bildwerke*, 1 (1909) . . . . viii. 16
150. Wünsch, R., *Antike Fluchtafeln*, Bonn, 1912 (*Kleine Texte*)   .   v. 3
151. Ziebarth, E., *Aus der antiken Schule*, Bonn, 1913 (*Kleine Texte*)   iv. 22

MYTHOS: The Princeton/Bollingen Series in World Mythology

Philip E. Slater / THE GLORY OF HERA
Daisetz T. Suzuki / ZEN AND JAPANESE CULTURE
Jean-Pierre Vernant (Froma I. Zeitlin, ed.) / MORTALS AND
    IMMORTALS
Jessie L. Weston / FROM RITUAL TO ROMANCE
Heinrich Zimmer (Joseph Campbell, ed.) / MYTHS AND SYM-
    BOLS IN INDIAN ART AND CIVILIZATION

PLATES

PLATE 1

ORPHEUS
FROM A WALL-PAINTING AT POMPEII

PLATE 2

ORPHEUS WITH THE ARGONAUTS (INSCR. *OPΦAΣ*)
SIXTH CENTURY RELIEF AT DELPHI

PLATE 3

ORPHEUS, EURYDICE AND HERMES
COPY OF RELIEF OF *c.* 400 B.C.

PLATE 4

THE DEATH OF ORPHEUS
FROM A RED-FIGURED VASE IN BOSTON

PLATE 5

RED-FIGURED *HYDRIA*
OTAGO MUSEUM, DUNEDIN

PLATE 6

ORPHEUS AMONG THE THRACIANS

DESIGN FROM A RED-FIGURED ATTIC VASE OF THE MIDDLE OF THE FIFTH CENTURY, FOUND AT GELA
(PRESERVED IN BERLIN)

PLATE 7

a   *b*

STATUE OF ORPHEUS

FOUND ON THE ESQUILINE HILL AND NOW IN THE CAPITOLINE MUSEUM, ROME

c

MONUMENT OF A GUILD OF *TIBICINES*

FOUND IN THE SAME PLACE AND MADE OF THE SAME COARSE PEPERINO

PLATE 8

GOLD PLATE FROM PETELIA

SCALE 2 : 1

PLATE 9

GOLD CASE AND CHAIN FOR THE PLATE FROM PETELIA
(SEE PLATE 8)

SCALE 1 : 1

PLATE 10

GOLD PLATE OF CECILIA SECUNDINA
SCALE 2 : 1

PLATE 11

RELIEF ON A CINERARY URN IN ROME
Showing a Scene of Eleusinian Initiation

PLATE 12

PHANES IN THE ART OF THE SECOND CENTURY A.D.
RELIEF NOW IN MODENA

PLATE 13

MITHRAIC RELIEF FROM BORCOVICUM

PLATE 14

ENTRANCE TO THE PRECINCT OF DEMETER AT PERGAMON

The Altars Flanking the Staircase are Dedicated to *Arete* and *Sophrosyne*, and *Pistis* and *Homonoia*, respectively

PLATE 15

IVORY *PYXIS* IN BOBBIO
Said to have been the Gift of St. Gregory to St. Columban